Joining

The War

ATE DUE

At Sea

1939-1945

Franklyn E. Dailey Jr.

DAILEY INTERNATIONAL PUBLISHERS
19 BROOKSIDE CIRCLE
WILBRAHAM MA 01095

1998

D1592480

Author's Signature Edition

ISBN 0-9666251-0-2

Second Printing January 1999
by
Van Volumes, Ltd.
1311 Park Street
Palmer, Massachusetts 01069

Cover Design by Claire Keefe

Dedications

This true story is dedicated to the wives, to the parents and grandparents, and to the children and relatives and neighbors who stayed home and provided the support that enabled the soldiers, sailors and airmen of the United States to emerge victorious from World War II, a long, costly war

I'll begin with my wife and lifetime partner of nearly 55 years. Here's to you Peggy. You gave up a Railroad Retirement Act pension from the Norfolk Southern Railway Company in April of 1944 to marry me. You were a secretary in the Traffic Department of that railroad. You raised eight children and lived in 17 apartments and homes.

In every household, someone kept the ship of home on course. Their resolves endured bad news and false news. For those who came home, this country had a place waiting. The rest of us are forever indebted to those who did not come home. Blank pages have been left for appropriate pictures.

I owe my webmaster partner, author Morris Rosenthal, a huge vote of thanks for helping me through word processing challenges, for being a gracious reader, and for giving articulate guidance, chapter by chapter, for my storytelling. In addition to his books published by McGraw-Hill on upgrading PCs and building new PCs, Morris runs a midnight website Q&A feature on PC builds and upgrades. (See URLs in Appendix) These are short-titled, FAQs, for Frequently Asked Questions.

I suggested to my wife that after completion of this story, she and I might work together on a website feature, entitled, "Family Questions: Ask Peg and Frank." She responded directly, "Our children will get right on the Internet and tell people, **don't** ask Peg and Frank." My FQs idea went down in flames. Here is Marguerite Parker Dailey.

Mementos of this family's sacrifices for the United States in armed conflicts of the 20th century can be placed here.

288

Franklyn E. Vaily Jr.

Copy No.   Signature

Contents

List of Illustrations

JOINING THE WAR AT SEA

Prologue

1939-1945 Revisited, Why Now?

A reader might well ask why a person would wait almost 60 years to tell a personal experience story. The first part of the answer is simple. Our wartime marriage was blessed with eight children. It took three careers to get the children launched. There has been a career in the Navy, a second career in industry, and a third as a self-employed technology consultant and writer. The second part of the answer involves convictions that have matured in my life. These convictions form a backdrop for this story.

The Smithsonian Institute mounted an exhibit in commemoration of the 50th anniversary (1945-1995) of the dropping of the atomic bomb on Japan. A section of the Enola Gay, the B-29 aircraft that dropped one of the two atomic bombs on Japan, was re-assembled for display in Washington DC. What the exhibitors undertook to portray around this aircraft artifact was the act of an aggressive nation, the U.S., against a beaten enemy, the Japanese. Indignant U.S. veteran's groups learned from news media of the plans and the Smithsonian then was moved to make some modifications to its version of "history". About this same time, some other elements of society obtained publicity for their view that the Holocaust, memorialized in another museum display in

Washington DC, did not really occur at all. I wanted to believe that a silent majority, at least those in a free press country such as the U.S., would come alive to counter such attempts to rewrite history. The general public's tepid reaction to these news stories saddened me.

A consistent defender of historical fact during the news report period (centered on 1995) of these aberrations in historical recall was the Wall Street Journal. By 1997, however, readers of the Journal began to take note of articles carrying the byline of Thomas E. Ricks. Mr. Ricks wrote frequently about matters that affect the U.S. armed forces. He became recognized for articles on military personnel. On May 30, 1997 under the headline, "Latest Battle for the Military Is How Best to Deal with Consensual Sex", Mr. Ricks included the following paragraph in an otherwise excellent article on this complex subject:

"A key fact about today's U.S. military is that military experts generally agree it's the world's best, arguably for the first time in history. So today's generals aren't just being politically correct when they express support for the gender-integrated military. They would also rather command a force of competent volunteers of both sexes than the main alternative - a force of less-trained and sometimes surly male draftees."

That last sentence, particularly the phrase "sometimes surly male draftees", revealed that Mr. Ricks and the Journal were involved in a bit of history rewriting of their own. Only the Wall Street Journal knows how the paragraph ever got by its editors into a Journal feature article The phrase had no relation to Mr. Ricks' central points. Neither the Journal nor Mr. Ricks responded to a letter I wrote to the Journal about it. It is not objectionable to find "today's generals" proud of their forces. Ricks did not identify any sources in the group, "they also would." The reader was left to guess why the last sentence ever went beyond "a force of competent volunteers of both sexes" to disparage "sometimes surly male draftees". Men are taking hits these days. Denigrating three generations of draftees in World War II, Korea, and Vietnam, by suggesting that they could "sometimes" be surly is a bum rap.

I have never met a surly draftee. In 1968, two wars after the one providing the backdrop for this story, one of my sons "volunteered" for duty in the Vietnam conflict as he was about to be drafted. The line can be very faint between draftee and volunteer. It certainly disappears in the body bag. I have met many young men, spanning three generations, caught in the same circumstance as my son. The soldiers, sailors and airmen of the Korean and the Vietnam conflicts, on the eve of their being called to duty for their country, were not different from the young men "sweating" duty in World War II. When I think of the sacrifices these men have made, and the conditions under which they fought, it occurs to me that most of today's generals, writers and editors are not likely to have had contact with those draftees except by reading about them. So, generals, writers and editors, currently active in your professions, read what I have to relate.

Nothing of such historical significance as the Holocaust or the Atomic Bomb will be covered here. This story will provide brief insights into "ship's company." Some World War II regulars, reservists, and draftees will come briefly alive. Some of these men fought the destroyer USS Edison from 1941-1945 and they fought her well. The story will be told in a series of episodes and will include other warships in the line of fire. It will also include U.S. and foreign merchant ships, amphibious forces, and the troops we supported in five major landings. U.S. destroyers escorted cargo ships, tankers and troopships. I will try to revisit life and death on some of those vessels. These choices reflect my own curiosity. In the rush of war, the Navy escort vessels had very little insight into what was happening aboard the lifelines of democracy that they were assigned to defend.

Some episodes are about triumph in the heat of battle. Some are about mistakes that are made when millions of men and women are taken from peaceful lives and thrown together in battle action preceded by a modicum of often just as dangerous training for that action.

I will try to be an honest storyteller, but will not undertake the role of the historian. Many hours have gone into running down the facts. There remains a potential for error. Where living eyewitnesses have been located, and this tale has been confronted with discrepancies between their recollections and the written word of history-writers, I tend to favor the eyewitness account. Memory does play tricks, but historians rely most often on second hand accounts. World War II covered a lot of territory.

A Ship Revisited

Most of the actions described in this story are covered from my point of observation, the USS Edison, DD 439, a destroyer commissioned early in 1941 and decommissioned in 1946 after the end of World War II. The very early photo that follows shows the ship with no guns and with no "war paint". There is also a prominent superstructure aft above her after deckhouse. Later photos will reveal important changes.

PROLOGUE

Most of the changes were applied to the World War II's "entering class" of foc'sle deck U.S. destroyers during the early stages of active U.S. participation, and many of those changes were influenced by considerations of topside weight. Although Edison's wartime enlisted complement was over 200 men, in the span of her service, 940 served aboard her. Such numbers would be typical of her class.

Illustration 1-Edison Afloat

PROLOGUE

My Granddaughter, Genevieve Kvam, interviewed me in 1997 for her high school history term paper. "How did you feel about going to war?" was her first question. My first answer was that war came to me, rather than my going to war. A 1935 New York State high school graduate who then earned two years of college credits toward a Chemical Engineering degree, ran out of money, went to work, but still wanted to get a college degree. A political Uncle knew the Honorable Caroline O'Day. She was then the Congresswoman-At-Large from New York State, and my Uncle prevailed on her to offer me a Principal Appointment to the U.S. Naval Academy. With no Naval Academy entrance exam required because of my satisfactory college credits, the only remaining obstacle was a physical exam. That was taken June 5-7, 1939 at the U.S. Naval Academy (USNA) at Annapolis, Maryland. An eye condition called farsightedness caused a one day delay but I was sworn in with the Class of 1943, USNA, on June 7, 1939. I was 18 years old. Charles Edison, the Acting Secretary of the Navy, signed my appointment as Midshipman, United States Navy. Just three years later, I was ordered to report to the USS Edison, a destroyer named after inventor Thomas Alva Edison, Charles Edison's father. For those interested in more on coincidence, the Edison's hull number was 439. Those numbers were the last three numbers on the Social Security card issued so I could accept employment at Eastman Kodak in Rochester, NY in 1936. It took a very supportive, fact-aware wife, to later point these coincidences out to me.

In my early teens, I had been an avid reader of current events but I still thought of my goal as getting an education. The going-to-war sequence did not figure prominently in my thoughts. I could not respond to the "fear" implications behind my granddaughter's questions because I was "in the flow" toward active duty from the time I entered the Academy. The new Midshipman uniforms hid a landlubber who could not tell a Chief Petty Officer from a Commissioned Officer. (The appointment available from Congresswoman O'Day was for the Naval Academy. I'm sure that if her available appointment had been to West Point, I would have gone there.) The choices faced later by others, to enlist or be drafted, to get into graduate school or work in a war plant, or to apply for status as a Conscientious Objector, were never before me. I was already in the service when President Roosevelt's thinly disguised "neutrality patrol" began in the Atlantic Ocean. Patriotism was important to me from early childhood but it was not a factor in my joining the war at sea.

Hitler's invasion of Poland in 1939, followed by the invasion of Norway, and the overrunning of Holland, Belgium, Luxembourg, and the defeat of France in 1940 forced a speedup in the USNA academic schedule. The Naval Academy Class of 1943 was rescheduled to be graduated in June of 1942, one year early. The attack by Japan at Pearl Harbor on December 7, 1941 put all midshipmen on armed watch schedules. One classmate used his .45 to commit suicide while on one of those watches.

When I reported aboard Edison as the "junior" Ensign in July 1942, the ship already had acquired some War History and one star on her service ribbon. I would be aboard while she earned five more stars on that ribbon for close fire support for amphibious landings at Casablanca, Sicily, Salerno, Anzio and Southern France. A number of other episodes will also be recounted in this story, some tragic, some zany, and some touching. There were no dull days on the Edison.

PROLOGUE

A Web edition of this story was presented at Universal Resource Locator (URL), www.daileyint.com, in chapter increments, one chapter per month, from May 1997 to May 1998. From Chapter Five on, readers contacted the author by e-mail. Some of the readers were present for one or more of the events described and others were descendants of those who served in the Atlantic/Mediterranean theaters of World War II. Most of these communications added information to supplement or fill in some gaps in the events portrayed in the story. These readers were acknowledged in "Feedback" sections of the Web edition chapter that usually followed the chapter relevant to their comment. A summary of the correspondent acknowledgments also appears at the end of Chapter Twelve of the Web edition. Those acknowledgments are made in Appendix A to this edition. In this edition, the Web reader's feedback has been moved to the relevant chapter and is also acknowledged there.

A few pages in this book are numbered and left blank. The reader may find these pages useful for notes or for mementos of the reader's family.

Chapter One - Unfinished Business

The coin of the realm in World War II was called "materiel", favoring the less ambiguous variant derived from the French of the word "material". It was materiel, authorized in the U.S. Lend/Lease programs of World War II, when it arrived at U.S. seaports and was loaded into and onto freighters, which were then formed, ship behind ship in six, eight or ten columns, in convoys stretched across the sea. Steam locomotives and fighter aircraft were lashed to the main decks of many freighters. On arrival at an overseas port, these large vehicles were just one or two maintenance steps away from service or combat. The U.S. literally drowned its adversaries in materiel. Getting it there was a major effort and will be discussed in important episodes in this story.

Some of the machinery responsible for the U.S. victory in World War II made its way from the heartland of the U.S. on railroad flat cars to the shipbuilding yards of the U.S. At the peak of this shipbuilding frenzy, the Kaiser yards in California were reported to be launching one merchant hull per day. After shaping, assembly and welding, some of the materiel delivered by railroad flat cars to shipyards became a naval warship's hull and machinery. The warship was then built, launched and commissioned. Next for the ship and its machinery came an underway "shake down" cruise. Those reservists, draftees and the relatively small cadre of regulars who were aboard for the launch, who were present at the commissioning (the commissioning "detail"), and the shakedown, could all claim to be called "plank owners."

From the time the keel was laid until addition of the ship's armament after commissioning, the ship's human complement expanded daily toward full war strength. This small flood of nameless men from 'anytown USA' became ship's crew. Before their names became known, their identities emerged first as deck seamen or below decks machinists and water tenders and firemen. Most were strikers, striking to become petty officers. A few were already qualified radiomen, signalmen and quartermasters, or sonar men (correctly, "sonar operator's mates"), or shipfitters, or electricians, or gunner's mates or torpedomen or other members of the ordnance gang who had main deck, above deck and below deck work stations. The construction of a ship from base metal is a remarkable creation. The evolution of a crew, the bringing together of the right ratings in several disciplines, their development into cohesive teams from countless drills, all combine to suffuse a ship with life. The whole is greater than the sum of its parts. For the Edison as with all war duty ships built for World War II, the complex of men and machinery was created before E-mail, cell phones or pagers. It took a blizzard of communications, some letters, some dispatches, and even some phone calls. Still, errors were made and some of these had the wrong man going to the wrong place. Once a man began to carry out the last set of orders he had received, re-directing him was almost impossible.

Air and sea define continuums. These are joined at the water's edge to form the *elements*, otherwise known as nature's condition. The elements extend no a priori favors; they have no friend or foe. A new ship has just one formally defined shakedown cruise. The elements conduct repeated shakedowns of men and machinery.

World War II found the U.S. of the 1930s reluctant to rearm, A nation at peace had "done its part" in World War I.

Thirty minutes of 1990s' U.S. media news briefs might convince the just-arrived alien that conflict is the only human condition. What news there was of conflict about the world of the 1930s remained much more muted in news stories earlier in this century. After World War I, much of the world went to sleep with the League of Nations, convinced (or wanting to believe) that the killing fields, both on land and at sea in World War I, could never happen again. A strong vein of isolationism held sway in the U.S. This nation has been remade periodically from waves of immigrants. The sympathies of those who arrive in the U.S. are at first rooted in the origins of their forbears. The sympathies of those who arrived in the early 1900s did not quickly realign to present a counter force to the strong vein of Middle America's isolationism. On August 12, 1941, 23 years after the Armistice of World War I, by a margin of just one vote, the U.S. House of Representatives extended a hastily revived U.S. draft.

Considering the scope of the conflict that came to be known as World War II, the U.S. was even less prepared than it had been for World War I. Hostilities at sea between Britain and Germany in the North Atlantic began in 1939. The two adversaries first renewed the pattern of U-boats sinking merchant vessels, then being hunted by armed surface craft. The U.S. created the Neutrality Patrol. In other important aspects, matters had changed. Germany had developed new capacities for active prosecution of a land war. Japan had sided with the Allies in World War I but between the wars its military had convinced its industrious, unquestioning citizens that Japan's expansion objectives were valid and that these demanded different alliances. After its foray into China in the 1930s, Japan focused its expansionist efforts against Britain, the U.S. and the Netherlands.

Politically, most of the nations of the world, including the U.S., had learned little from World War I. Militarily, except for Germany and Japan, it was pretty much the same. A small cadre of U.S. Naval Officers, with experience in World War I, who were called upon to serve again in World War II, brought some valuable experience forward. This was especially true in shipping and shipping protection in the Atlantic. Without them, the disastrous early shipping losses of World War II might never have been slowed. Two men who led the war effort in their respective nations deserve special note in this respect. Both came from naval backgrounds. The two were U.S. President Franklin D. Roosevelt and British Prime Minister Winston Churchill. A revived U.S. draft and this residual leadership experience from World War I were critical factors in Germany's eventual defeat. These two national leaders, with World War I experience, were able to find enough advice in their naval establishments to gradually craft a winning response to the second U-boat war. The civil inertia in both England and France, like that in the U.S. was hard to overcome. France was quickly defeated. In the early going, the prospect of defeat faced Britain and the United States. Perseverance, especially necessary in convoy skill development, paid off. It was a very close call.

'Your men and your machinery' against 'their men and their machinery'? Not always. Sometimes it is your men and machinery against the air and sea elements. Meteorologists could provide early warning, but when bad weather arrived, the strength of the elements at the air and sea boundary always presented a new challenge. When a destroyer's inclinometer shows a roll of 58 degrees, a young watch officer can become transfixed by the reading on that instrument. A more experienced skipper keeps a stopwatch in his hand. The key is that the time duration of a roll of the ship is more important than the angle of heel. A roll too slow was the danger signal that she might really go over. If you changed course to bring the sea on the quarter, a destroyer would sometimes pound her bow down so hard that one could imagine the keel snapping. All flat metal up forward would bend or be dimpled by those seas.

One focus here will be on seamen and their machinery. Measured strictly by elapsed time, episodes reminding one of the "presence" of an "enemy" came regularly during the extensive daily photo slide training ritual run by the Recognition Officer. In these daily sessions, a ship or plane pictured in the fraction of a second set by the projector's shutter action, reached your consciousness first as "friend" or "foe" even before a specific national identity flashed into your mind. Except for these recognition sessions and occasional broadcasts from the BBC, acute awareness of an "enemy" came in fast paced battle action episodes. There was no shouting from trench to trench as in land warfare. The Captain might try to get into the enemy's mind but everyone else fought based on the 'situation-at-hand'. Getting performance out of men and machinery was the task. Chance controlled the rest.

In a sequence of episodes, this story will cover U.S. men and their machinery. In my case this microcosm was defined as a U.S. destroyer. The story centers on challenges to its survival. Defined threats came from the armed forces of Germany, Italy, and briefly, the Vichy French. The elements took a heavy toll, but differed from battle encounters in that weather's respites could be accepted with less suspicion. Some events in the War in the Pacific against Japan will be covered very briefly to provide a time context for the Battle of the Atlantic and for the assault landings in the Mediterranean.

Britain and her loosening confederation of Empire nations were in the war two years before the U.S. Tabular views of time and decision (sometimes indecision) leading up to full scale U.S. involvement will be presented in a series of illustrations.

Adolf Hitler began his rise to power in 1933. The failure of British Prime Minister Neville Chamberlain's diplomacy to deal with Hitler's goal for Germany is encapsulated for all time in the word "Munich". Even that word does not begin to express the loss of the opportunity that France and Britain had presented to them for a "Triple Alliance" with Russia before Russia made its deal with Germany in 1939. Winston Churchill, who was not in the British government during Germany's arms buildup, later characterized his country's leadership in one sentence: "Britain's ruling class takes it weekend in the country while Hitler takes his countries in the weekends."

The illustrations in the next few pages summarize events leading up to World War II. One finds support for the position that World War I, whose hostilities ceased with the Armistice of November 11, 1918, followed by the Treaty of Versailles, was never really concluded. The U.S. President, Woodrow Wilson, was ailing in the crucial months that bracketed conflict and peace. The U.S. Congress failed to ratify U.S. membership in the League of Nations. This was a blow to Wilson.

These factors provided an environment for militarists abroad to operate behind a veil of peace. Germany, Italy and Japan fell under the spell of men whom diplomats completely failed to evaluate. Indeed, Adolf Hitler seemed like the Messiah of national rebirth to the German people. Asian co-prosperity sounded good to many Asians.

The next tabulation, Prelude to War, covers the period 1935-1939, and ends with the beginning of armed hostilities, when Germany, led by Adolph Hitler, invaded Poland.

Where specific dates are given, they are U.S. dates.

Illustration 2-Prelude to War

Event-Cycle 1: Europe/Africa	Event-Cycle 2: Americas/Asia	Country Making Decision
Ethiopia Invaded		Italy: 1935
	New Destroyers Authorized	United States: 1935
Militarization of the Rhineland	.	Germany: 1936
	Invasion of China	Japan: 1937
Anschluss with Austria		Germany: 1938
Agreement at Munich		Germany, France, Britain: 1938
Hitler in Prague		Germany: March 1939
Albania Invaded		Italy: April 1939
Conscription		Britain: April 1939
Pact of Steel		Germany/Italy: May 22, 1939
Non-Aggression Pact		Germany/Russia: agreed to on Aug. 26, 1939
Invasion of Poland		Germany: Sept. 1, 1939

After Polish military resistance ended, and Germany and Russia finished dividing the spoils of their non-aggression pact, a period of nervous waiting ensued in Europe during which Hitler prepared his next moves. From his observations of the Prime Minister Neville Chamberlain's government of Britain in earlier diplomatic action, Hitler had concluded, incorrectly, that Britain would not act militarily when Germany invaded Poland.

Hitler, therefore, made some revision of Germany's expansion plans when Britain and France declared war. Britain and France failed to take advantage of the interregnum of nearly eight months that followed Germany's conquest of Poland. This gave Hitler, his generals and his admirals time to make necessary revisions in their war plans.

The next tabulation fills in some key events in the period from the first actual hostilities of World War II in 1939 to the announcement of the Tripartite Pact in September 1940. The United States, whose policies had been largely controlled by isolationists in the Congress during the period between World War I and World War II, was in its "waking up" phase.

Illustration 3-Britain and France Go to War

Event Cycle 1: Europe/Africa	Event Cycle 2: Americas/Asia	Country Making Decision
Declaration of War on Germany		France, and Britain: Sept. 3, 1939
	President Franklin Roosevelt decrees Limited National Emergency under Neutrality Act	United States: Sept. 8, 1939; Neutrality Patrol for 300 miles off its coasts.
	U.S. Navy Department re-commissions 40 old destroyers.	United States: Sept. 14, 1939
On April 9, 1940, Germany moved against Norway. May 10, The Low Countries, France, fall. Ship losses rise with success of wolf pack.		Germany: Spring and Summer, 1940. Hitler consolidates Western Europe. Italy enters war with Germany. Africa next.
Churchill in government; France capitulates		Britain: May 10, 1940 France: June 25, 1940

The Britain of September 1939 was no longer the Empire that emerged victorious in World War I. That Empire embraced Dominions, Crown Colonies, protectorates and Chinese treaty towns. The Statute of Westminster in 1931 decreed that the Mother Country and her dominions (one being our close neighbor Canada) were autonomous communities within the British Empire. By the time of her emergence from World War II, Britain had undergone a drop in territories from one fourth of the world's territory to the United Kingdom and Ireland. The Armistice Day, 1918, figures tell the story. Over 3 million of the King's subjects had fallen in action, nearly 1.2 million of whom had been killed. Britain herself lost just under one million.

Illustration 4-The "Axis" Is Formed

Event Cycle 1: Europe /Africa	Event Cycle 2: Americas/Asia	Country Making Decision
British lease to U.S. rights to bases in Bahamas, Jamaica, Antigua, St. Lucia, Trinidad and British Guiana.	After months of pleas by Churchill, Roosevelt agrees to swap 50 old destroyers for leases to bases.	Britain. United States: Sept. 2, 1940.
Tripartite Pact: If any one gets into war against the U.S., the other two would join.	Tripartite Pact: If any one gets into war against the U.S., the other two would join.	Japan: formally signs pact with Germany and Italy on Sept. 27, 1940

Illustration 5-U.S. Neutrality Redefined

Event Cycle 1: Europe/Africa	Event Cycle 2: Americas/Asia	Country Making Decision
	U.S. protects Greenland.	United States: April 9, 1941.
	North Atlantic Rim extended to Newfoundland, Nova Scotia, Maine and Bermuda.	United States: April, May, June and July 1941. U.S. Navy establishes Caribbean Patrol
	"Belligerent neutrality" now Unlimited National Emergency.	United States: May 27, 1941

After the British and French forces defending Western Europe against the Wehrmacht spring/summer offensive of 1940 had been split, their armies fell back, defeated. France capitulated in short order. Hitler now had control or de facto control of the heart of Europe. This was a complete reversal of the result in 1918. (I will often use the term "Wehrmacht" as a synonym for German Army, German Armies or German land forces.)

In the shadow of this defeat, the armada of "anything that could put to sea" took the defeated British Army off the beaches at Dunkirk and back to England. This polyglot fleet performed a near-miracle. They played the role of the gas pilot light that stays lighted after the main burners have been extinguished. The incredible number of vessels and their improbable lineage defy description. What they accomplished, some barely more than motorized row boats, was the salvage of thousands of important soldiers for Britain in its next two years of dogged resistance Dunkirk turned out to be essential to the final, successful result in 1945.

In addition to the defeat of its land forces at the hands of Germany, Britain suffered an additional sobering and immediate consequence of Dunkirk. The rescue of their Army forces cost them 10 destroyers sunk and another 75 disabled.

Churchill's return to government as Prime Minister and as Minister of Defence on May 10, 1940 meant that the evacuation at Dunkirk and the impending fall of France were unparalleled crises greeting his return to government. Though he had protested most of the decisions of the Chamberlain and Baldwin governments that preceded him, he and Britain were left to deal with the consequences. While Dunkirk was a defeat for Britain, the fight that the British showed in military defeat set the tone for the next two years. The first result was survival and the second was victory. But, a war was still to be fought.

The next illustration shows how the USS Edison looked just after receiving her main battery of 5" 38 cal. guns in March and April 1941 at the Brooklyn Navy Yard. A word is helpful here about gun nomenclature. Usually, guns are 5inch or 14inch or 88mm, without the additional distinction of length of barrel measured in calibers. The Navy had many different 5inch guns. The secondary battery on the older Atlantic Squadron battleships consisted of 5" 51 caliber guns. These were not designed for AA (Anti-Aircraft) use. The gun most referred to in this story was the 5" 38 caliber DP-Dual Purpose gun, the main battery of all U.S. World War II commissioned destroyers. The caliber of the bore was 5 inches in diameter and length of barrel was 38 calibers long. That works out to be 190 inches or just short of 16 feet. The

Dual Purpose means that it was used for both AA fire, and for shore bombardment and ship against ship or submarine.

Pictured off Staten Island, the Edison has her main guns but no 20mm or 40mm guns. This photo was provided to the Edison News by Vern Willmert, Edison's first Yeoman.

Illustration 6-Edison At Anchor; Five Guns

In its "short of war" period, "neutral" U.S. warships could escort shipping, including British ships, in the U.S. neutrality "zone" and would hand them over to British/Canadian escorts at transit from those expedient new markers delineating the "Western Hemisphere". Those who followed the news stories of those months more than superficially knew that the United States was sympathetic to the British cause. Though not publicly stated, and even rarely noted in conversation, a substantial body of the U.S. citizenry felt that the United States would be at war soon. The anticipation was that we would be at war with Germany. Many U.S. citizens went to Canada to sign up with that country, already at war.

Recall that Germany and Russia had signed a non-aggression pact in August of 1939. Then, Germany, Italy and

Japan had agreed in a Tri-Partite pact in September of 1940 to act together if any one became involved in war with the United States. Germany and Japan had each acted to prepare for what each anticipated would happen, although it is not known if they disclosed to each other what their specific anticipations were.

The first U.S. Naval Task Force, TF 19, was organized for Foreign Service. On June 15, 1941, Iceland, just 450 nautical miles from Scotland, was named an outpost of the Western Hemisphere. On June 16, President Roosevelt ordered U.S. troops to relieve the British garrison on Iceland. On July 1, 1941, U.S. Marines left Argentia, Newfoundland, in a force of 25 ships, with destroyer USS Buck heading the outer screen. On July 5, the screen destroyer, USS Charles F. Hughes, was ordered to locate possible survivors of SS Vigrid which had been torpedoed June 23. At dusk, the Hughes found a lifeboat with Vigrid's skipper and four U.S. Red Cross nurses. Another boat with six remaining nurses was never found. The Hughes rejoined TF 19 at Reykjavik, Iceland on July 8, 1941.

At least one of those four Red Cross nurses rescued by the destroyer Hughes in 1941 was still alive in October of 1998. That lady is Margaret Somerville. She was 27 years old when a vigilant destroyer crew found her in a drifting lifeboat after its occupants experienced two agonizing weeks in the cold North Atlantic in July 1941. Robert W. "Bob" Burns, in an e-mail to the author dated 10/04/98, states that his "Aunt Peg" is 85 and could use some medical help, which he is trying to obtain for her. Since Red Cross nurses were not members of the Armed Forces, Bob Burns will discover if a grateful United States can find a way to give Aunt Peg some help with medications and an occasional home health visit. Margaret Somerville had been reluctant to apply for help because the United States was not at war when her ship was torpedoed. United States soldiers, sailors and civilians died for their country during the Neutrality Act period.

Roosevelt asked the U.S. Congress to extend the one-year service period for National Guard and Selective Service "trainees" to 30 months. The U.S. Senate approved Aug. 7, 1941

On August 9, 1941, two "former naval persons", as they became known, arrived on their respective warships at Placentia Bay, Argentia, Newfoundland. Roosevelt came on the USS Augusta, and Churchill arrived on HMS Prince of Wales. At this "Atlantic Conference", Prime Minister Churchill and President Roosevelt set early Allied objectives for the global war to come

The U.S. House of Representatives completed approval of Roosevelt's request to extend involuntary military service by one vote, 203-202, on August 12, 1941.

The coming pages of this story will show how unprepared and vulnerable the U.S. was for its massive role ahead in World War II. The review being made here is intended to demonstrate that the U.S. under President Roosevelt's leadership had taken *some critical steps* to ready itself in the 1939-1941 period. Roosevelt's overall popularity as President helped get some of his unpopular war preparation agenda through the Congress.

Japan attacked the U.S. at Pearl Harbor, Hawaii on the first Sunday in December 1941. This was not the war that most United States citizens anticipated. The "Axis" powers became a full reality just four days after President Roosevelt's "day that will live in infamy", the day of Japan's surprise attack on Pearl Harbor, Dec. 7., 1941. On December 8, the U.S. declared war on Japan and on December 11, Germany and Italy declared war on the U.S. Japan, Germany, and Italy were now at war with Britain, the U.S., the free French and the Polish and Norwegian units which had escaped the Nazi net in Europe. By November 1941, the U.S. Army had 1.5 million men in uniform, but few were adequately armed. The revived U.S. Navy shipbuilding effort was just beginning to show results, particularly in modern destroyers.

The 1940 air Battle of Britain had been over almost two years when I participated in my first action episode on the Edison in August 1942. This is covered in Chapter Four of this story. The Pilotless Bombardment of Britain, as Winston Churchill called it, became intense in the summer of 1944. For the British, it was a very long war.

In the preface to Volume 1 of his History of U.S. Naval Operations in World War II, covering the period September 1939-May 1943, historian Samuel Eliot Morison stated, "Thus the Battle of the Atlantic was second to none in its influence on the outcome of the war. Yet the history of it is exceedingly difficult to relate in an acceptable literary form."

I have tried to show here the interweave of events and the challenges faced by Churchill and Roosevelt in playing two hands of poker as if they were one, against powerful cards in the hands of men who would lead with death, until death.

Our Navy of World War II can be grateful that Hitler was a late convert to the U-boat, favoring investments in air power and his land armies. Entreaties from Germany's then Commodore Doenitz, and Britain's entry into the active war, persuaded Hitler to raise U-boat production in 1939 from just over three per month to 25 per month. The U-boat fleet swelled from 45 boats in 1939 to 300 boats at sea in 1941 with 800 targeted for 1943. 587 Type VIIC U-boats were commissioned from 1940 to 1945

Chapter Two - A Destroyer Is Created

The two world conditions of greatest moment in my pre-teen and teen years were the depression and onset of World War II. Help from others, known and unknown to me, saw me through both. I will cover in later chapters some of the memorable instances of man's regard for man, which sustained me through World War II.

I have stated that this is not an historian's account. There will be no footnotes or endnotes. Where an historian like Samuel Eliot Morison has refreshed or sharpened my memory, I will acknowledge it in the text. Most of the sources beyond my own memory or knowledge will be from still living witnesses of that war. And almost all of their "updates" have occurred as the result of publishing the first edition of this story on the World Wide Web in 1997 and 1998. An important exception is the Edison News.

In January 1970, The Edison News was born in Lafayette, Indiana. Founder, Publisher and Editor Robert Cloyd had been a Motor Machinist 1/c aboard the USS Edison. Cloyd kept his letter size, multi-page, slick paper tabloid going for 32 issues and then turned it over to Jean Whetstine in Linden, Michigan, in the spring of 1976. Jean was the wife of Larry Whetstine, another Edison sailor. As these words are being written in 1998, Jean Whetstine is still publishing the newsletter in Byron, Michigan. She survived husband Larry Whetstine's sickness and death and her own near fatal brush with cancer. The Edison's 27th Reunion took place at the Holiday Inn in Portsmouth, Virginia in October 1997. The 28th has been scheduled for Michigan in the fall of 1998.

Some of the access to the Edison living witnesses was made possible through reunion notices and roster updates printed in the Edison News. Edison ranks high in maintenance of a living history but is by no means unique in this respect. Hundreds of World War II units from all U.S. armed services are active with newsletters and reunions.

Edison's ordnance configuration changed rapidly in her early days. In the Prologue, the photo of the USS Edison underway showed no main battery gun mounts at all. Launched in late November 1940 at Federal Shipbuilding and Drydock Company in Kearny, New Jersey, Edison was commissioned at the Brooklyn Navy Yard on 31 January 1941. Her shakedown consisted of short cruises in February and March 1941 and then she returned to the Brooklyn Navy Yard for a six weeks installation of her main battery of five 5"/38 cal. DP guns.

Like many Atlantic destroyers just before and during World War II, Edison exhibited five war paint jobs during her relatively short life. The first was plain gray. Then came a North Atlantic wavy camouflage paint job followed by one of Mediterranean medium gray over dark blue. Her fourth, and most used, was a Mediterranean/North Atlantic "zigzag" camouflage. Edison finished her duty in the Pacific painted in the dark gray used there.

The number of different Edison silhouettes almost matched the number of her paint jobs. The Edison photos in sequence reveal three different main battery configurations, namely no 5" guns, then five guns and then four guns, in that order. In a letter that appeared in the Edison News' 20th issue in September 1971, her first Commanding Officer, Admiral Albert C. Murdaugh USN (Ret.) provided some 1940 insight not available in official records. The next two paragraphs in quotes came from Al Murdaugh's reflections on being ordered to command the Edison. These were printed in a 1971 letter to the Edison News.

"I was ordered to the Edison from duty at the Naval Gun Factory in Washington, DC. The first thing I did, on getting the word unofficially, was to handpick a main battery. Meanwhile, the Federal Shipbuilding Corporation at Kearny, NJ seeing a war coming on and wishing to establish a good performance reputation for the sake of future contracts, decided to deliver the Edison six weeks ahead of schedule. A classmate who was superintending construction at Kearny tipped me off. I hastened to get the guns shipped and found, to my consternation, that F.D.R. had given them to one of the small British AA cruisers in the Mediterranean, who were then hard-pressed. Next, I went to BuPers (Bureau of Naval Personnel), who simply didn't believe me (that Edison would be ready early). Finally, I persuaded them to look into it, and they ended up by ordering the Edison detail (officers and men who would put the ship into commission), which I had just begun to assemble. Some of the men arrived for commissioning with only three weeks of boot camp. Fortunately, in desperation, I at last reached a sympathetic ear at OpNav (Naval Operations). They, in effect, told us (the ship and its crew) to go and get lost for six weeks. Things couldn't have worked out better. The recruits learned far more aboard ship than they would have at Newport (the Navy's torpedo station). We were able to concentrate on basics and when the guns were finally installed, gunnery technique was quickly mastered, as the record shows."

"On the question about the number (439) on the bridge wings in the old photo (the "old" photo Murdaugh is referring to is Illustration 6 and the profile of the port wing of the bridge on which the number appears runs almost from the mast, forward, to the front of the enclosed pilot house), my recollection is somewhat hazy after so many years. The circumstances were somewhat as follows. Few people, except specialized historians, now know that on 1 September 1941, Admiral King (Ernest J. King, Commander-in-Chief Atlantic, later Chief of Naval Operations) issued an operation plan setting up regular convoy operations in the North Atlantic. Presumably, to delay full realization by the Germans of what was happening, orders were issued to paint out bow numbers and put them on the bridge wing, like the British and Canadians. Many ships were just too busy at the time to get around to it. The order reached us in the Navy Yard, where compliance was easy. After Pearl Harbor, the numbers were put back in the accustomed place."

This next picture shows Edison with early "war paint." Gun 3 of the five 5" 38 cal. guns in the original installation at the Brooklyn Navy Yard has been removed courtesy of the same Navy Yard and the high superstructure aft has disappeared. A 36-inch searchlight now occupies the place of the missing gun.

Illustration 7-Edison Ready for War

Edison's war history was compiled with four 5"/ 38 cal DP guns as her main battery. It could reasonably be assumed that the original high superstructure aft had been intended to give the after conning officer a high visibility platform in situations where the bridge, pilot house and forward conning structure had become inoperable due, for example, to battle damage. But, topside weight considerations eventually dominated all modification decisions. A number of U.S Navy destroyers capsized in storms. Boards of inquiry decided that a key factor was too small a margin of metacentric height (a linear measurement representing the difference between the center of gravity and the center of buoyancy). In a ship's roll, a sufficiently positive measure of metacentric height provides the lever arm in the restoring moment to bring the ship back level. Later additions to Edison and her class were two quad 40-mm Bofors AA gun mounts to complement the 20-mm Oerlikon guns that had been installed earlier. A torpedo director was added on the flying bridge. The cylindrical object, showing in Illustration 6 on the after quintuple torpedo tube mount just forward of the after deckhouse, was removed.

USS Edison DD439; Build, Commissioning and Outfitting Data:

Keel laid 18 March 1940 at Federal Ship Building and Dry Dock Company, Kearny, New Jersey. She was built alongside her sister ship, USS Ericsson DD440. (The USS Ericsson was named for John Ericsson, who was the inventor/builder of the Union's first iron clad ship, the Monitor.) Edison was launched 23 Nov. 1940 and commissioned 31 Jan. 1941 at the Brooklyn Navy Yard. Named for Thomas Alva Edison, famed U.S. inventor. Mrs. Mina Edison Hughes, widow of the inventor served as sponsor. A February 13, 1941 photo in the New York Mirror shows Mrs. Hughes with her son, Governor Charles Edison of New Jersey, as he addressed the crew of the Edison in the Brooklyn Navy Yard. In an e-mail received in March 1998, in response to the Web edition of this story, Captain Bill Steagall, USNR informed me that his grandmother, Ruth Wallgren, was the sponsor of the USS Ericsson when that ship was launched. Ruth Wallgren was inventor Ericsson's closest living relative in 1940 and was herself an active design engineer for Westinghouse, the manufacturer of the steam turbines aboard Edison and Ericsson.

Hull and power plant: 1630 tons displacement, 348 feet at waterline, 36 foot beam, just under 12 foot draft without stores. There were two Westinghouse, 25,000 shaft horse-power, steam turbines, driven by four Babcock & Wilcox triple drum boilers rated 600-psi, 750 degrees Fahrenheit. Edison was of the Benson/Livermore class, two stacks with a foc'sle deck. I use the term "Benson/Livermore" to signify the two stack, foc'sle deck destroyers, hull numbers beginning at 421,which came after the USS Buck (DD420). The Buck was the last of a series of single stack destroyers also built with a foc'sle deck. After the two stack Benson/Livermore foc'sle deck classes came the flush deck, 2100 ton, Fletcher class. The latter would be the mainstay destroyers for the war in the Pacific. These 1630 ton displacement two stackers, with a foc'sle deck a level above the main deck, had hull numbers mainly in the 400s although there were a few in the 500s and some in the 600s.

The Bensons were slightly different from the Livermores. The Benson (DD421) was an outgrowth of a 1500-ton destroyer building program that had grown into 1620 ton ships. By the time of the launch of the Livermore (DD429) the class had become officially categorized as 1630 ton destroyers. In fact, as fought, both of these near identical subclasses came in well over advertised weight. The Bensons had flat-sided stacks and the Livermores had rounded stacks. Specifically, Edison was a Livermore. While nuances of turbine design, displacement and profile differentiated the destroyers we will cover in this story, their fighting armament for all effective purposes was pretty much the same. I am indebted to Orlando Angelini, a Machinist Mate aboard the USS Mayo (DD422) in the period covered by this story, for helping me recall some of these finer distinctions.

Armament: four 5"/38 cal Dual Purpose guns controlled by a General Electric Mk 37 (amplidyne drive) director, a Sperry stable element (gyro), and a Ford Mark 1 (electromechanical, analog) computer; two quad mount 40 mm AA guns; eight single 20 mm AA guns; ten 21-inch torpedoes in two center mounted quintuple mounts; a torpedo director on the flying bridge; two 600 pound depth charge racks, tilted, for roll off on the stern; six K-guns for throwing 300 pound depth charges abeam, three on each side, from midships aft.

Sonar and Radar: high frequency sonar transmitter and echo detector in a faired dome on the hull; long range aircraft detection radar, designated as SC, with its antenna on main mast high; main battery fire control radar, designated FD, with its antenna on top of the MK 37 Gun Director, having its azimuth controlled by training the director, and with its elevation control independent of the director. The FD radar used both A-scope and B-scope Cathode Ray Tube presentations for data. The system also employed an azimuth centering technique called "lobe switching. This technique was never mastered sufficiently to provide a verdict on its effectiveness.

Personnel Complement: Varied from seven officers and about 100 men at commissioning in 1941, to 24 officers and over 200 enlisted men when the U.S. finally got its military manpower at war strength in 1944. When the number of ship's officers exceeded the number of bunks available in the officer's quarters, I was shifted to the Division Commander's stateroom since we had no Division Commander aboard. I slept next to the FD radar magnetron. I was directed to wear a bitewing (dental) x-ray patch pinned to my undershirt. This precaution was based on good intentions, but no one was ever available with equipment to check the x-ray patch to see if radiation was present outside the transmitter. I tossed the

patch away when I left the ship. The spare magnetron (affec-
tionately called the "maggie) for the FD radar transmitter was
stored under the FD radar cabinet in my room and only
Holmes O. Bridges, Edison's Chief Radioman, who had gone
to the Bellevue Laboratories Radar School in Washington
DC, knew it was there. Though I had precious few sleeping
hours during which I used this cabin, I came across this
spare, and very secret, magnetron. I have not told anyone
about my discovery until writing these lines.

A Special Note on Radar. Radar was very secret in early
World War II. In late 1942, after the North African invasion,
Edison returned to the Brooklyn Navy Yard for installation
of the Raytheon SG radar. The SG radar's PPI-Plan Position
Indicator, a large oscilloscope with its main glass face up and
the electron gun underneath and pointing up, was installed in
the pilothouse to the right of the binnacle. (The binnacle is
the non-magnetic stand on which the ship's magnetic compass case is supported. On the Edison and like destroyers that
stand was directly in front of the helm.) The SG radar's horizontally rotating small parabolic antenna was installed on the
main mast under the SC radar antenna. The trace on the oscilloscope mimicked the antenna sweep, a vast improvement
from A-scope and B-scope presentations. (More about the
importance of the SG radar can be found in later chapters.
SG radar was one of a number of very significant U.S. wartime tools that made a crucial difference in World War II.
We had it. The enemy did not.)

Smoke Generators. Not exactly armament, but important in
enemy action situations, were the destroyer smoke generators. These were used on many occasions, most memorably
during a surprisingly close call for Edison along the northern

Mediterranean coast of Italy in 1944. Look for this occasion of the use of smoke in a late chapter.

Service Summary

Edison's main service was in the Atlantic and Mediterranean from 1941-1945. After a brief period in Far Eastern waters in the last half of 1945, Edison returned to Charleston, South Carolina in early 1946. She was decommissioned there on 18 May 1946. Her last years were spent as part of the inactive "mothball" fleet in the Philadelphia Navy Yard. In June 1965, the Edison (DD439) along with the Ericsson (DD440), and Woolsey (DD437) were sold for scrap. Edison was sold to Lipsett of New Jersey for $87,000. She began and ended her life in New Jersey. The Ludlow (DD438), alone of the 437-440 foursome, remained on active duty after the war and was sold to the Greek Navy in 1951 where she served a second career before being scrapped in Greece.

The Shipyard that Built Edison

Let me add a personal note. As the ship's welfare officer for most of 1942 and 1943, I handled large, semi-annual, money contributions to the ship's welfare fund given by the workers at Federal Shipbuilding and Dry Dock Company that had built Edison. These funds were used for ship's parties and other "worthy" uses. I can never forget the unparalleled generosity of the shipyard personnel who built an extraordinarily seaworthy ship. If any of them survive to read this, let them know that their efforts and financial generosity were matched by a dedicated crew, consisting of many reservists and draftees, who fought the Edison brilliantly against an unforgiving sea and a desperate enemy.

The Ship's Armament Usage

Usage summaries are offered here which will help the reader anticipate some of the engagement activity in which the ship participated. This activity will be told in future chapters. With summaries out of the way, the later pages can emphasize the flow of the action. The reader will already have an overall picture of the ship's life cycle.

The torpedo battery: The World War II destroyer evolved from the pre-World War I torpedo boat. In World War I these torpedo boats evolved over a series of class building upgrades into destroyers. In the sea war in the Pacific in World War II, a few division or squadron-strength destroyer torpedo attacks were pressed home against Japanese warships. No mass torpedo attacks were recorded for U.S. destroyers in the Atlantic or Mediterranean theaters. While the Edison fired torpedoes in training, she never fired one in action against an enemy. Interestingly, the Edison was part of the destroyer detachment which screened the battleship USS Iowa with President Franklin D. Roosevelt aboard when he made the famous trip that culminated in the Cairo (Egypt) meetings with Chiang Kai-shek of China and Prime Minister Churchill. Edison was part of the Mediterranean screen from Gibraltar east. A different screen brought Iowa from U.S. waters to Gibraltar. It was during the Atlantic transit part of the trip on 14 November 1943, that the USS William D. Porter (a destroyer later sunk in a Pacific battle) fired a torpedo, mistakenly, at the Iowa. Porter was conducting a training exercise and the crew in training made the mistake of choosing Iowa as the training target. The destroyer then compounded the mistake by actually firing the torpedo. The crew likely did not know what "cargo" the Iowa carried. According to one newspaper story, reprinted in the Edison News, Iowa took evasive action and the torpedo exploded harmlessly in her wake. Training exercises took an enormous human toll in the period of the author's tour aboard Edison. Some situations that ended tragically will be cited later in our story.

The secondary AA batteries, 20mm and 40mm guns: Ring sights were used in early engagements. Later a MK 14 gunsight was added to the 20mm guns and this sight was included in the one man MK 51 director for the 40mm guns. The guns themselves worked fine. Proficiency with the MK 14 gunsights came slowly and in action firing situations, personnel often fell back on the old fixed "ring" sights. One 40mm "premature in the breech" due to a tracer ignition in a lot of Triumph (manufacturer) shells caused eye damage to a young Gunner's Mate, H. George Koerber. The author (by then the Assistant Gunnery Officer) had just received an urgent message warning of this possibility in a given lot of 40mm shells and was consulting Edison's magazine inventory when the ship went to General Quarters against air attack. It was then that the accident occurred. Edison, unfortunately, had that lot of 40mm shells aboard. The failure specifics were precisely as predicted. Edison's first set of two quad 40mm gun mounts had to be replaced because the drives were friction-coupled and salt water quickly decomposed the friction surfaces (sandpaper). Pouring a quart of oil into a hole marked "Oil Here" did not help. The hydraulic drive replacements worked fine. Edison's secondary AA batteries were in action frequently. German planes did not press attacks home like the Japanese so leading the enemy aircraft sufficiently in azimuth was usually the key to local control success with the secondary batteries.

While some formal training was given for torpedoes and for the light AA guns, most of this training was what the ship itself could work in on its own. Priority for training, with full exercises scheduled, was given to ASW, and to AA and shore bombardment for the main battery 5"/38 cal guns. For the Edison, a ship that always seemed to be selected for close-in support of the amphibious forces making assault landings, training priority was given to shore bombardment.

Depth charges: Used frequently against sonar targets that were classified by the sonar operator as probable submarines. Edison trained several times during each watch in setting various "patterns" for depth charge explosions. These drills came without warning to the watch standers. Setting a given pattern in less than 30 seconds was an objective. For the crew, this involved going from a lookout watch station down to the main deck, often in rough weather, and getting enough illumination and "feel" if in darkness to make the setting. Any setting other than "safe" armed the charge, causing it to go off at a given, "set", depth. Edison SOP (standard operating procedure) was to leave charges on "safe" at all times except when attacking a suspected submarine. The reasons for the SOP will become clear in later chapters. When conditions permitted, Edison also trained with other destroyers in "creeping attacks", where one destroyer "ping"ed with its sonar and barely kept steerage way in order to provide minimum sea noise, while the other did not ping but was vectored in by the pinging destroyer in a creeping movement to get over the target for release of depth charges. The British came up with this scheme which provided better sonar performance and kept the sub puzzled about what was going on.

Main battery, 5"/38 cal. Dual-Purpose guns: Edison had to be re-gunned (new barrels) twice while the author was aboard. Very likely the ship was near the top of all U.S. Navy

World War II destroyers in terms of rounds fired per 5" gun barrel. A gun barrel could "wear out" in several hundred rounds, with extensive firing intensively concentrated in relatively short time periods causing accelerated wear. The only other "wearing" components were the "bloomers" which (almost) sealed the aperture in which the gun moved in elevation in the mount against the saltwater elements. The bloomers would simply burn up during concentrated periods of fire. The early leather bloomers were replaced with canvas when the Navy figured out that bloomers had become a "consumable". This battery of guns, director, computer and when needed, stable element (gyro), experienced near flaw-less system performance. Chief Gunner's Mate Kerns and Chief Fire Controlman Jackson and their men deserved much of the credit. These gun mounts had hydraulic drives. Tiny air bubbles in the hydraulic fluid were an occasional cause for a given gun mount to "hunt" in azimuth or elevation. This took some maintenance crew nursing, but could be dealt with. The extremely reliable General Electric MK 37 Direc-tor had an amplidyne drive. The director, on a pedestal above the flying bridge, was clear of most of the sea spray. (Num-ber 1 Gun mount up on the foc'sle would often have its front face bashed in due to heavy seas. One way we learned to minimize this damage was to leave the # 1 gun trained out to the starboard bow so that the sea did not have a flat frontal surface to pound.) The range finder in the main director had both coincidence and stereo range solution options. Chief Fire Controlman Jackson had sharply curved eyeballs and I often thought he did not need the rangefinder's stereo feature at all. Chief Jackson certainly used all available optics with deadly effectiveness. In AA shooting he would open up in range right on the enemy plane and usually with one small azimuth or elevation spot (correction) would be able to call for "rapid fire". The Sperry gyro and the Ford computer allowed the ship to go into "automatic" fire with just small spots needed for correction. After the Raytheon SG radar was put aboard, the Skipper (Captain "Hap" Pearce) would on occasion have the shipfitters make a floating metal target to anchor near a beach whose shallow gradient did not give good SG radar echoes. Then, shore bombardment could proceed in "automatic" with reference to this marker, again with just small spots radioed from shore fire control parties (SFCPs). The computer would simply take into account the ship's movement and grind out the "problem". The 5" battery used "semi-fixed" ammunition, a shell, and a brass cylinder which held the "powder" propellant. These had to be mated in the gun's loading tray and a rammer pushed them "home" and then the breech could be closed. An electric plus impact primer was in the flared end of the brass cartridge.

On the port side about amidships was a 5" gun "loading machine". It was used constantly to train crews. Edison could fire with a Condition ONE gun crew, all guns manned, battle station situation, or with a ready gun crew in the regular "watch in three" Condition THREE situation, or with two guns manned in the watch and watch, Condition TWO situation. These different gun crew personnel situations required a lot of men to know a variety of jobs in firing the guns. On the loading machine, for one, two or three minute periods, the crew objective was 20 rounds per gun per minute! Edison crews achieved those rates in combat. The Germans likened the effective rate of fire of U.S. destroyers to machine guns with large shells. The ship usually carried some star shells for night illumination, some armor piercing shells for special targets, some 'influence" or "proximity" shells essentially for AA, and some white phosphorus shells to help shore party spotters move our fire to the target. We used all of these on appropriate occasions. The proximity shells, with so-called VT fuses, came with so many restrictions to their use (so the enemy would not capture a dud and learn the secrets of construction) that we never used them in action situations on the Edison while I was aboard. The majority of shells aboard were referred to as High Capacity or HC. These could be fired at ground or air targets. There was a nose ring time fuze, set automatically in the fuze setting hoist, which derived its setting remotely and automatically from the computer's solution. This was the primary fuze for AA fire and also for anti-personnel fire on ground targets when seeking an above-ground detonation. There was a nose impact fuze. And there was a base detonating fuze. In other words, fuzing was redundant. After all the work to deliver the shell to a target's vicinity, if the most optimum detonation did not occur, the backup objective was to make "something" occur. I was aboard when two sets of gun barrels were worn out and I do not recall a malfunction of this battery during action. If one held a contest to name the most effective piece of conventional ordnance in World War II, my nomination would be the 5"/38 cal. gun system in the US Navy.

The Edison's Engineering Plant Usage

I was involved directly in ordnance aboard the Edison and the amount of detail on ordnance furnished in this Chapter reflects that. Of necessity, officers specialized in wartime. I rarely got into the engineering spaces. Many below-decks personnel had to actually be ordered topside when we were in port. The sparseness of detail on engineering in this story reflects those wartime realities. Also, deck logs are the officially archived logs of a ship. Little information has been preserved of the record of Edison's power plant for her active years.

I can attest that the Edison power plant was always on line when it was needed. It never failed. The conning officers, and I was one, often called for tremendous acceleration, well beyond the printed acceleration curves defining the limits for increasing speed. Engineering Officers were not daunted that the Captain might be conning the ship, even if we were at General Quarters. I heard one such officer warn the Captain of dire results if we changed speeds so fast. Still, we on the bridge always got the desired result from the engineers below. Sometimes the impact of a shell landing close aboard silenced the protests in the engineering spaces. Yes, we lost "suction" on one or two occasions, but Edison's corrective procedures restored such situations immediately. These lines are written with gratitude, if not with a complete grasp of what these men contributed.

Engine Miles Steamed

Year	Nautical Miles
1941	43,769
1942	78,680
1943	60,875
1944	52,855
1945	51,979
1946	4,973
Total	293,131

The peak year 1942 reflects a period in which Edison repeatedly operated in escort of convoy duty. In 1943 and 1944, the convoy duty was restricted to escorting combat forces to an amphibious landing or returning from one. By this time, the Edison's "steaming" hours were prioritized toward actual landings and shore gunfire support. There were fewer trips back and forth across the Atlantic and Edison was actually home-ported at Mers-el-Kebir, Algeria, near Oran, on the south shore of the Mediterranean.

Fundamental engineering maintenance went to the boilers. Sometimes these had to be "re-bricked" in yard overhauls after extensive steaming or when there had been emergency accelerations or decelerations. Firebrick would break down under those conditions. While in port we always kept at least one boiler "lighted off." Printed schedules were followed for bringing other boilers back on line in carefully timed sequences and propeller shafts were slowly rotated before getting underway to make sure that the turbine-propeller systems were working properly. Edison's "black gang", as the propulsion system personnel had become known from coal-fired days, were very conservative and always let the bridge know when the (getting) underway "special sea details" of personnel in the pilothouse would try to "speed things up". Edison's boilers were fed bunker fuel #6 with a little Diesel laced in to help keep the innards clean. Fueling at sea in bad weather was an often risky, "all-hands evolution." The challenge of fueling at sea occurred frequently and will covered in later chapters. In normal steaming, destroyer protocol in World War II called for "split plant" operation so that an underwater explosion would still leave the ship likely to have thrust on one propeller to keep way on.

Commanding Officer and CPO "Usage"

This might seem an unusual category to include in a materiel-emphasized portion of this ship's story. The point of view is helpful in setting forth an additional toll of war. That toll is on the lives of men who are not killed or even wounded in action, but on whose lives the war took a big toll. It applies to both officer and enlisted personnel, and it relates to the age of persons enduring periods of intense vigilance and conflict. Generally speaking, the young endured physically much better than the middle-aged. This does not mean that any age bracket acquitted their assigned responsibility better than any other but reflects my own observations on what happened to these groups after the war.

The plank-owner detail of the Edison included a high percentage of experienced officers and senior petty officers. The term "high" is used in comparison with ship's company at later periods in the war. In the years following World War II, I subscribed to Shipmate, a magazine for alumni of the U.S. Naval Academy, and also to an Annual Report of the Navy Mutual Aid Society, an insurer of Naval personnel, mostly officers but also of some higher ratings in the enlisted category. Both sources published death notices. My observations were that personnel of "middle age" (in the 1940s, men in their 40s were regarded as on the threshold of middle age) who had been actively engaged in combat roles in the Atlantic or Pacific theatres often died relatively soon after the war's end.

The next table, a list of the Edison's Commanding Officers, illustrates how a rapidly expanding wartime Navy, taking combat casualties, was forced into lowering the age of its combat personnel. As time went on, the younger men were not less experienced. Experience had simply come to them faster.

Edison Skippers

Name	Naval Academy Class	Took Command	At age
LCDR A.C. Murdaugh	1922	31 Jan. 1941	40
LCDR W.R. Headden	1925	1 Mar. 1942	38
LCDR H.A. Pearce	1931	24 Feb. 1943	33
LCDR W.J. Caspari	1940	1 Apr. 1945	26

In her total period of service, 940 officers and men served aboard Edison. Eight enlisted men served the entire period of just over five years, from commissioning to decommissioning. (This statistic on the total number of personnel who served on Edison is not found in official Navy records, but was compiled by Edison sailor Robert Cloyd in 1971.)

Awards

Edison Combat Awards: six battle stars were authorized on the European-African-Middle Eastern Area Service Medal for participating in the following operations:

1 Star/Escort, ASW and special operations, Convoy ON-67; 21-26 Feb. 1942

1 Star/North African Occupation

For actions off Casablanca; 8 November 1942; Algeria-Morocco Landings; 8-11 November 1942

1 Star/Sicilian Occupation, 9-15 July, 28 July-17 August 1943

1 Star/Salerno Landings; 9-21 Sept. 1943

1 Star/West Coast of Italy Operations
For Anzio-Nettuno Advanced Landings; 22-31 Jan. 1944, 2-5 Feb. 1944, and 8-11 Feb. 1944
1 Star/Invasion of Southern France; 15 August to 25 Sept. 1944

The USS Edison also earned the Navy Occupation Service Medal, Asia for the periods from 2-26 Sept. 1945 and 20 Oct. to 4 Nov. 1945.

I was not aboard for the first Star or the last Medal.

It needs to be noted that while the Edison was a "small boy", a term applied to destroyers by Pacific Admirals in command of large carrier task forces, the 940 men who served aboard Edison related to nearly 2,000 parents, hundreds of wives and children, and countless neighbors. This extended family made up the 'home front", putting magnifying glasses over V-mails and devouring public news sources every day to obtain wholly insufficient fragments of information about what "their boys" were doing. A few such "fragments" will be included in later chapters.

JOINING THE WAR AT SEA

Chapter Three - Convoy Indoctrination

The period covered in this chapter extends from early 1941 to July 1942. The Navy's warship building programs were beginning to take effect. The number of new destroyers joining the Atlantic fleet had grown from a trickle to a fresh stream. The learning process ramped up rapidly.

A destroyer can practice gunnery with towed targets or in sham invasions of friendly beaches. A destroyer can practice sub hunting with friendly submarines. Since most friendly U.S. subs were on patrol in the Pacific during this time, there was all too little of this kind of training for a 1941 destroyer about to enter the fray. There were no "practice convoys." It was all on the job training. Readers have seen those magnificent photos of columns of stately cargo ships marching tranquilly off into the rising or setting sun. These made good photos that received wide distribution but they portrayed rare respites in Atlantic convoy passages. It was much harder to take a decent photo in a smashing sea.

Each convoy had a different heartbeat. Each faced some set of conditions that no convoy before or after it faced. With the U-boat wolfpack's rapidly evolving tactics, last month's convoy escort dogma had to be unlearned and more aggressive defenses put in place. There was one constant. A destroyer was rarely on the base course. Its rudder was "over" all the time as it fishtailed around its assigned angular bearing from the convoy.

December 7, 1941, the day of the Japanese attack on Pearl Harbor, came during the Edison's indoctrination period. For refreshing my memory, I had anticipated making use of the

USS Edison's log, most of which in the 1980s was held at the National Archives on Pennsylvania Avenue in Washington D.C. I made two visits there. The Pearl Harbor attack did not merit a mention in Edison's log. Many of the log entries were my own. In National Archives' visits in the 1980s, I was on a search for detail and did not find the detail I expected to find. The lesson in reading many Edison log entries in my visits to the National Archives reeducated me to the reality that a Navy vessel's log was confined to events related directly to that ship. Even those events were covered in terse phrases. The only exceptional event that Edisons's log on December 7, 1941 noted was a line with the information, "two explosions astern." This was followed by brief mention of an effort to determine a source for the explosions, followed by a notation that Edison returned to routine steaming. This reminded me of the most repeated line in a ship's log. The opening phrase for each watch period in which an Officer of the Deck underway relieves another is the phrase, "Steaming as before." In my two visits in the 1980s to the National Archives in Washington DC to look at Edison's logs, I discovered a good many log entries which might be called, "non-sequiturs." For each, a reader might ask, "Well, what happened then?" To the next Watch Officer, the interesting incident of the previous watch (as looked at out of context, 55 years later) seemingly never happened.

One of Pearl Harbor's impacts for naval ships in the Atlantic was that the term "Neutrality Patrol" abruptly disappeared from all conversation just as it did from print and radio broadcasts. A more concrete impact was an intensified effort to bring the personnel complements of new naval vessels recently added to the active fleet up to numerical wartime strength. At commissioning, these ships had a mix of experienced sailors and boot camp graduates aboard. The

40

flood of new construction meant that the small cadre of experienced sailors was made even smaller in order to supply still newer ships being launched almost every day. In every port, then, bluejackets with seabags would be departing. A numerically larger group of inexperienced men would be coming aboard. Ship's quarterdecks were busy places. Warren Blake came aboard Edison at Casco Bay on a bitter January night in 1942. As an enlistee well before Pearl Harbor, Warren had not only been to boot camp but had the benefit of formal skills training after boot camp. Here, in his own words, is an account of Warren's journey from home to an Edison at war.

Warren E. Blake: Boot Camp, and Trade School

"I enlisted in April of 1941 with deferred reporting until I graduated from high school on the 13th of June. On the 24th of June I left New Haven, Connecticut for NTS (Naval Training Station), Newport, RI. After eight weeks of boot camp and a short leave, I was off to Machinist Mates School at Great Lakes, where classroom work on the "mechanics of machinery" and the basics of machine lathe and milling machine were learned. Frequent liberty in Waukegan and Chicago was enjoyed. This phase of school was about a month in length, then we were off to Ford Motor Co.'s. River Rouge Plant, at Dearborn, Michigan. Two months of intensive, hands-on work in the apprentice school and general plant, under the watchful eye and tutelage of Ford employees was very rewarding and enjoyable. There, because of Henry Ford's aversion to cigarette smoking in his factories, I was initiated in the fine art of chewing tobacco without getting sick! On December 7th, we had just returned to barracks from Chapel, or noon chow, I don't recall which, when we learned that we were no longer just kids, looking for adven-

41

ture. The amazing change at the plant, almost overnight, from civilian auto production to almost 100% military production, was difficult to comprehend. The attitude of us "kids" changed just as rapidly. An awareness that from now on it was not going to be all fun and games. Even though we had plenty of light moments, we were all much more serious in our daily demeanor and discussions. Three quarters of our school term was completed and now we were real anxious to learn just what the immediate future held, for us."

"Now it was time to go back to Great Lakes for final exams, graduation, and assignment to our first real duty stations. Graduate, we did, all 116 of us, with no drop-outs or flunk-outs. I don't recall how Christmas was spent that year, but I'm almost positive that Thanksgiving Dinner was in the mess hall at the River Rouge Plant. My first year away from home for the Holidays! Oh--I mustn't forget----being an "old salt" now, with another stripe on the cuff of my dress blue jumper, I had to go to Detroit and get tattooed while we were in Dearborn!"

"Finally, duty assignments were being posted. It turned out that twelve or fourteen of us were all to report for duty on ships in Casco Bay or Boston. At Great Lakes, the train backed off the main line, right into the base, and loaded our sorry butts for the trip east. My next remembrance is of waking up to a lot of shouting outside the train. Peering into the darkness, I could see that the train cars had been backed right on the pier in Portland, Maine, Upon falling in for muster, we were assigned to various launches for transport to our ships. I was told that my ship, the USS Livermore, was at sea and that I was being sent to the Edison as a passenger, for later transfer to Livermore, when we next met. For the duration of the war and two years afterward, I never even saw the Livermore."

Stragglers in Convoys

One type of event that was sure to be in an escort ship's log would be an assignment to bring up a straggler. With her shakedown behind her, the USS Edison served in escort duty, both with convoys and for ships proceeding singly with important cargoes that required priority. In the Atlantic, the primary duty in these escort operations was defending against the submarine. Except for the mutual danger of enemy submarines, escort warships, and the ships they convoyed appeared to have little in common. To lend some perspective to the relationships between the convoyed merchantman and the escort ship, let me comment here on an essential attribute they shared. They were both surface vessels. The Convoy Commander, usually aboard a ship being convoyed, and the Escort Commander in overall command who was usually embarked on one of the screening warships, both knew that a convoyed ship which dropped back became an inviting U-boat target in the next period of darkness. The U-boats would surface to charge batteries, and get up ahead of the "base course", the mean direction of advance of the convoy, into torpedo firing position.

The Convoy Commander also knew that his convoy became more vulnerable if a screening vessel had to be dropped from the screen to escort a lagging convoy ship. It was a game of numbers. 100 ships in a convoy with seven escorts went to 99 ships and six escorts when a screening vessel was deployed one on one with a convoy ship out of station. Still, the initial defense tactic would be to do just that. The screening vessel so ordered back had a mission, to get the convoyed ship back into formation in the convoy as fast as humanly possible.

A destroyer skipper, ordered back by the Escort Commander to encourage a convoy laggard back into formation, was dealing with a skipper of another surface vessel. One commanding officer's career had been in the military chain of command. The other commanding officer, in the oft-encountered situation when U.S. merchantmen were in convoy, followed practices learned while operating under guidelines of the U.S. Maritime Commission. Naval warships follow protocol and discipline different from merchant vessels. But for surface vessels in a seaway, Navy or merchant, it is also helpful to consider their similarities. Both are surface vessels that face basic constraints. Each must deal with the same two environments and each has limited control over those environments. It helps to understand something about control options.

Air, Sub and Surface Vessel: Stability Control

An airplane has thrust, rudder, elevator and ailerons. These function beautifully *in the air medium* for which they are designed. An airplane is, at best, ungainly when taxiing around an airport. Thrust can act like the fourth control for an aircraft. In descent to a runway, if the plane gets a little too low, an application of power can cut the rate of descent immediately. The application of "up" elevator also does this, but that would force the plane out of its landing attitude and might even cause it to stall. The thrust available to an aircraft over and above that necessary to maintain level flight sets the aircraft apart from the water-borne vessel.

A submarine has bow and stern planes, rudder, and thrust. These operate best *in the water medium* for which the submarine is designed. On the surface, a submarine's maneuverability is reduced to that of a somewhat sluggish surface vessel. In the water medium, with its planes set toward deeper or shallower submergence, a combination of rudder and thrust can provide roll control. This makes the sub, while submerged in its water medium, a little more like the aircraft in its air medium. "Each is optimized for its primary medium.

The surface vessel, facing both wind and sea as conditions of its operation, is consigned to operate in two media while optimized for neither. It has thrust and rudder. Roll is at the whim of the sea. (Ships can have roll stabilizers, but these ships were rare.) The surface warship has to fight against enemy airplanes and submarines, each of which has the advantage of better control in its environment. General Billy Mitchell advocated doing away with a surface Navy. Some U.S. submarine zealots have been heard suggesting the same. The merchant cargo ship and the naval screening vessel are more alike than different in coping with their elements. Now, let us consider ways in which they differ from each other.

The Cargo Ship and the Destroyer

Destroyers have good control of their ballast. They can ingest seawater to fill fuel tanks that have been emptied from days of steaming. The result is that their "trim" can be controlled for best sea keeping. Merchant ships are designed to carry cargo. In World War II, U.S. flag merchant ships ranging from World War I leftover "Hog Islanders", to World War II Liberty ships and Victory ships, often sailed in mixed convoys with vessels of foreign registry. After their cargo was offloaded, most of these ships had some capacity to trim using fuel tanks but the major cargo spaces could not be flooded to give best trim.

Often referred to simply as a "Liberty", the Liberty ship will be mentioned frequently because it was the backbone ship in the U.S. cargo fleet in World War II. U.S. shipyards got them into production early and simply replaced tonnage faster than the U-boats could eliminate it. With smoother lines and an updated propulsion system, Victory ships started coming down the building ways in the latter part of the war.

In rough weather, particularly off Iceland, Edison and her convoyed charges occasionally spent days making zero net advance back toward the Western Atlantic. I can vividly remember convoys of ships whose propellers were rotating half up out of water. Any additional internal power plant difficulty and these "in ballast" convoy merchantmen would actually lose ground to the wind and sea and fall back out of position.

On one occasion the Edison's Capt.W.R. Headden was directed to take Edison back astern of the convoy to urge a straggling convoy ship to get back up into position. The bullhorn was a bridge-operated loudspeaker often used for skipper-to-skipper communication when ships were very close to each other. After a period of advisories over the bull horn in conciliatory tones, without results, the skipper-to-skipper communication using bullhorns grew more heated. Capt. Headden: "How many men do you have on watch in the fireroom?" The answer was followed by Capt. Headden telling the merchant skipper to wake up the rest of his fire-room watch standers and *get them all* on duty. In every case during my tour aboard Edison that this badgering was resorted to, it worked. The merchantman would coax a few more "turns" per minute on the main propeller shaft and the straggler would gradually pull back up into position. One particularly outraged merchant skipper's parting shot to Capt. Headden at being bullied like this, was, "Washington will hear about this!" All Edison men within earshot undoubtedly approved.

I mentioned earlier that the airplane has an excess of thrust available over that needed for steady state cruising. The destroyer and most naval warships have this advantage over the merchantman. In coaxing a convoy straggler back into position, the two skippers involved would be aware of this difference and it is not surprising that a merchant ship's Master might be upset if the escort vessel's Captain seemed a little overbearing in exchanges like the one above. *The stakes were very high.* That was the justification.

Readiness

Life aboard a warship is about getting ready and in wartime, even more so. I served aboard the USS New York on my Naval Academy class's youngster cruise ("youngsters' are Academy midshipmen who have completed their first year academic schedule successfully). This took place during the three months of the summer of 1940. War had come to Europe but the U.S. was not yet formally at war. Our Midshipman Cruise itinerary and ports-of-call list was altered drastically due to the hostilities in Europe.

In most transits, the long days at sea are more quickly forgotten so that memories dwell on the times devoted to getting ready to leave port or to enter port. It seemed to the work parties that the ship always wanted to make a good impression at the next port of call. At sea, then, on the USS New York, midshipmen would be holystoning the wooden deck. Or painting the hull. Up the chain of command, the ship's company would be launching and retrieving SOC scout planes. On approach to port, the entire crew would be sent to anchor detail, or in one rarer event, to a flying moor detail in the lower Hudson River with USS Arkansas and USS Texas. (The New York, Texas and Arkansas were designated as the "Atlantic Squadron" in 1940. The USS Texas of this story is the other of the two World War II ships with which I served that I could still visit; it is maintained for visiting in Texas.)

Throwing chips off the bow to help the USS New York's Captain Daniel Barbey conn the ship to the precision re-

quired for a smart moor was training that I would never specifically use again. But the manner in which trained crews
could bring three huge vessels into an anchorage in which all
three would drop anchor in formation and with precision is a
seamanship lesson that I have never forgotten.

Small Talk

On the USS New York in that "neutrality" period, we
midshipmen, lowest of the low, could still derive some ani-
mated conversation from reflections on the events of
"yesterday". These are the discussions that occur after an
event that sustain the event as a subject of conversation. One
such event on the USS New York was the boiler room personnel blowing tubes when all the officers in their white
service uniforms were sitting on the quarterdeck watching
the evening movie. Then, a sudden wind shift occurs, dousing the aforesaid officers in their immaculate whites with
black soot. Funneee! Do not say it out loud but enjoy the
quiet talk. That was a midshipman's cruise while the U.S.
was still at peace.

I joined the Edison in wartime and thought I would be
able to listen in to small talk about this or that event that had
occurred in the year since her commissioning. Not a word.
Everyone, including the most garrulous sailors, remained silent on the events of the year I missed. Past exploits were not
discussed. The talk on everyone's lips was running toward
tomorrow and it swept everyone with it. The newcomer is the
stranger and is in no position to demand even the smallest
accounting. Ship's company knew in a general sense where
the ship was going next, but I was in the dark even on that. It
is also pertinent to note that when we were in port personnel
were leaving every day and more personnel were coming
aboard. I was not alone in being uninformed. In terms of dis-

covery by the reader, I hope that these paragraphs on the year I missed of the Edison's travels will seem no different than those that come from the later on-the-scene observations. The early ship tales that I had wanted to hear from my shipmates have come to me much as the whole story comes to you, the reader, almost sixty years later.

There is always an exception. Let me jump ahead once again to recall here one event in which I did benefit from the past experience of an Edison shipmate after I reported aboard. Just as I became the immediate O.O.D in port the moment I reported aboard, I also became the immediate First Division Officer, with no indoctrination period. Formally, I succeeded nobody. But, there had been a predecessor, as I determined later. The First Division on a destroyer is the foc'sle division, and it was customary to assemble on the forecastle for "quarters" underway, if the sea was not too rough. This was a required assembly every time we left or entered port. Up on the bow, there are no windbreaks from the salt air sweeping over the ship. I learned that there had actually been a man in charge of the Division. He was Chief Boatswains Mate Carajohn, a very senior petty officer in the regular Navy. He was the BMC for the entire ship and likely had been running the First Division himself since the ship went into commission. And doing it well. Prior to "falling in ranks" or after "falling out", there might be moments for pleasantries or relaxation. Smoking a cigarette is a low-keyed way to pass this time without emphasizing your absolute void of knowledge based on experience. Smoking relates you to somebody and, aboard a Navy destroyer nearly sixty years ago, it was a connection to most of the crew. The only trouble I was demonstrating in smoking up on the bow of the Edison was that I could not get the cigarette lighted. The first bit of underway lore offered to this new Ensign was how to light a cigarette on the bow of a destroyer moving smartly in a seaway. The teacher? None other than the Chief himself. One quick lesson, one bit of "how to" information was quickly and warmly imparted and quickly learned and practiced (I could do it today and I have not smoked for 45 years and have not been on the foc'sle of a moving or still destroyer for 54 years). Most importantly, the Chief broke the ice. I will look for him in heaven if we both make it.

Beginning with the destroyer's origins in World War I, destroyer constructors emphasized speed over endurance. The early destroyers of World War I, emphasized torpedo launchers. Deck guns were few and of small caliber. The early World War I torpedo boat actually evolved into the first destroyers.

The next two photos show late World War I destroyers (known as 4-pipers) nested at the United States Naval Academy in 1940 or 1941. These destroyers were coming out of mothballs and some would soon be transferred to the British in what has been characterized as a "bases for destroyers" swap between the U.S. and Great Britain.

The two illustrations show the same nest of three 4-stack destroyers, hull numbers 341, 221 and 93, taken from different angles. I took these pictures myself but did not date them. The fact that the portholes had not been blanked out suggests the earlier of the choice of two dates. One of the first "getting serious" steps taken on Edison after her launch was to completely blank out her lower course of portholes.

Illustration 8-Nested World War I Destroyers

Illustration 9-Same Nest in Profile

From these 4-piper destroyers of World War I, the destroyer evolved into a ship with a dual-purpose (surface and AA) main battery of 5" guns that were central director controlled. (Each gun could also be controlled individually; this was called "local control.") Eight, ten or twelve mounted torpedoes were still carried, and the crude method of dropping depth charges ("ash cans") on submarine targets was improved slightly by adding K-guns to launch 300pound charges abeam in addition to launching 600pounders from racks astern by simply rolling them overboard.

During World War II in the Pacific, U.S. destroyers engaged in several mass torpedo attacks against Japanese warships. There was no such action by U.S. forces in the War in the Atlantic. The German Navy remained mostly a surface "threat." There were forays like the sea raiding German pocket battleship Graf Spee sunk by British cruisers near Montevideo in the South Atlantic. The German battleship Bismarck was caught and sunk in North Atlantic waters after she had sunk the HMS Hood. Otherwise, German Navy surface units remained pretty well bottled up in their home waters. British air and surface units stood watch. And wherever found, German warships like the Scharnhorst, Gneisnau, Prinz Eugen and the Tirpitz were constantly subjected to attack by RAF and Royal Navy air units.

The existence of these German Navy surface warships meant that there was always the *potential* for surface action in the Atlantic. The British squared off against the Italians in surface actions in the Mediterranean. The U.S. Navy was engaged in surface actions against the French during the North African landings. In November 1942, the French battleship Jean Bart, tied up at the dock in Casablanca, registered some very close main battery shell straddles of the USS Augusta off shore. We will get to that in Chapters Five and Six. Still, a U.S. destroyer in Atlantic or Mediterranean waters, except for the November 1942 landings in North Africa, was not likely to be surprised with surface action. (Submarines were an exception. U.S. destroyers on many occasions encountered surfaced U-boats, suddenly appearing out of the fog and at close quarters. Both vessels would be so taken by surprise that the fleeting encounters did not provide enough reaction time for offensive action. Radar upgrading in the U.S. Navy virtually eliminated surprise encounters of this kind in the latter part of the war.)

Most Likely Destroyer Missions in World War II

Q. "What does a destroyer do?"

A. With respect to World War II, a first response to this question might be, "Tell me what ocean you are in."

The missions of the Atlantic destroyer, in order of priority, were:

- ASW defense
- Shore Bombardment in support of troop landings
- AA protection. Defense of main forces in an assault landing area or underway steaming
- Rescue at sea

If a Pacific destroyer man responded to the destroyer mission priority question, it is quite likely that the answer would contain different missions and that these would be prioritized differently. One example would be the dangerous picket duty that spelled glory and tragedy for a number of U.S. destroyers in the Pacific.

Two numerically large classes (by numbers of ships built) of U.S. destroyers entering service just before and during World War II provided the bulk of U.S. combat destroyer deployments. These were the Benson/Livermore class of

53

which Edison was one, and the Fletcher class that delivered its main blows against the Japanese in the Pacific. This latter class was made famous by Captain (later Admiral) Arleigh Burke and the phrase, "31-knot Burke". The Fletchers differed mainly from the Edison in being larger (2100 tons vs. Benson's 1630 tons, nominal tonnage) and being flush deckers while the Bensons were foc'sle deck ships. Fletchers had the same 50,000 shaft horsepower as the Edison. The "31-knot Burke" adage was so tied to the Fletchers that the fact that the Bensons were actually the faster ships (same horsepower pushing a smaller vessel) is often overlooked. With four boilers on the line, the Edison, the Corry and others recorded 36 knots. Even split plant, with two boilers on the line, when her hull was clean, Edison could do 31 knots.

Both the Fletchers and the Bensons were capable of the same missions. The two classes had about the same armament (the Fletchers carried the fifth 5"/38 cal. gun that the Benson's had shed to lower topside weight). Franklin Roosevelt's plea for a "two-ocean" Navy was not an effort to obtain special destroyers for one ocean or another. The builders were not constructing destroyers for Pacific or Atlantic duty. That degree of construction refinement, even if desired, was not practicable. Since Roosevelt and Churchill had agreed to first concentrate on winning the war against Germany, the immediately available modern destroyers, the Bensons, went mostly to the Atlantic. It was a surprise to me to learn, in preparation for this story, that even after the major U.S. Navy losses at Pearl Harbor, a number of U.S. surface warships were sent back from the Pacific to the Atlantic to participate in the effort against Germany and Italy. After the run of building Benson/Livermores was completed, destroyer construction in World War II centered on the Fletcher class and a later Sumner class of 2200 tonners. One could certainly infer that the Fletcher's fifth main battery AA gun, and in the case of the Sumners, a sixth gun, made their assignment to the Pacific, with its Kamikaze attack threat, most logical. It was more, though, a case of timing. The assignments of Fletchers and then Sumners to the Pacific had more to do with a lessening of need in the Atlantic as the tide of battle swung in Allied favor, and the U.S. resolve to then undertake ever more ambitious operations in the Pacific.

There were systems developed for the theatre of war in which they were to be used. For the Atlantic/Mediterranean theatre, the FXR, a device we called "foxer", consisted of two small parallel bars towed on a long cable by a destroyer to create sound in a certain frequency band. The sound was designed to divert a German acoustic homing torpedo away from the destroyer propeller noises and leave the torpedo to explode harmlessly well back in the target ships' wake. The F8F Bearcat aircraft was a fast re-design of the Grumman F6F Hellcat. The F8F was designed to reach 10,000 feet in record time and intercept Japan's Kamikaze aircraft. Another coincidence in my military career occurred because of the Kamikaze. I was ordered to primary flight training at Ottumwa, Iowa Naval Air Station after leaving the USS Edison in October 1944. I was pretty good at instrument flight but not a natural born seat of the pants pilot. The excess of men ordered to flight training in that period forced the naval training command to be "very selective", and many student pilots were being "washed out". We flew Stearman aircraft (designator, N2S), a yellow biplane with a 220 horsepower Lycoming or Continental engine. I was up for a C-stage check, primarily acrobatic flying, including precision "figure-8s" around two pylons on the ground. I was very poor at this maneuver and expected to be washed out. When the kamikazes struck our ships in the Pacific, word came down that more pilots would actually be needed! I escaped one of the in-training pilot "purges." Later, I flew the F8Fs myself, and never made the connection between that and my primary flight training success until reviewing events for this story.)

The armaments and other important configuration elements like radar and sonar were pretty much the same for the two numerically dominant classes of World War II destroyers. The distinction of the "Atlantic" destroyer rested pretty much on *which of the ship's capabilities to emphasize for training*, done mostly at sea. ASW defense, and main battery offense, took center stage for training underway for an Atlantic destroyer. Shifting to main battery AA defense from shore bombardment during an engagement in progress was a challenging transition. It was one that I as the main battery director officer, failed to implement properly on one occasion that I remember. I failed to remove a "right 5 mil" shore bombardment aiming spot. We had shifted on short notice to an anti-aircraft target. The Chief Fire Controlman (the same Chief Jackson), using the stereo rangefinder, opened up on a Dornier 217 aircraft right on in range, and leading the German plane by 5 mils, exactly the shore bombardment spot I failed to remove.

Rescue at sea gave every destroyer Commanding Officer fits of sleeplessness. I observed two of our Edison skippers wrestle with the rescue-at-sea subject. One had faced actual World War II experience with sea rescue, and with the dangers involved, before coming aboard Edison.

In submarine infested waters, no commanding officer wanted to put his own ship at risk by standing dead in the water attempting to pick up survivors. Sometimes that was the only way it could be done, especially for men in the water who had become exhausted and could not assist in their own rescue. Another hazard was the possibility that depth charges would be used by other destroyers in the area that were running down sound contacts on submarines. The human body in the water was very vulnerable to the shock wave of a depth charge explosion.

My second Edison skipper, Captain Pearce, had a special raft type rig constructed by our shipfitters to aid victims in the water. It was tested inside the entrance channel at Mers-El-Kebir near Oran, Algeria. In that case, the test effort, though motivated by deep human compassion, went awry. The large CO_2 cylinders, propelling the rig toward the test specimen representing the person in distress in the water, ran out of thrust (gas) much too soon. Moreover, the harbor watch personnel sounded an alarm that an enemy sub had gotten inside the net stretched across the harbor entrance. No amount of explaining could have cleared this up. Edison personnel remained prudently silent.

While I was aboard, and while the ship was momentarily hove to, the Edison rescued friend and enemy at sea. A lone U.S. sailor on a piece of flotsam from his torpedoed ship near Casablanca was picked up paddling energetically toward New York, a few thousand sea miles away. When USS Woolsey, USS Trippe and USS Edison engaged the crippled U-73 off Oran, Algeria with heavy 5" gun salvos, after Woolsey's depth charge attack forced her to surface, the gunfire forced the sub's crew to abandon ship. 12 German enlisted men were picked up alive by Edison, and the body of a U-73 Warrant Officer was recovered. Resuscitation efforts for him were not successful. In later Pacific Ocean duty, the Edison rescued a sailor who had gone overboard from the USS Dawson in rough weather.

A new class of escort vessel, the Destroyer Escort (DE), arrived in 1942 in sufficient numbers to take some of the load off the Atlantic destroyers for ASW defense. Generally diesel powered, the DE was smaller and did not carry the offensive gunnery systems of the destroyer. The DE freed up destroyers for such missions as surface shore bombardment. Also, in World War II, though not employed as extensively by the U.S. in the Atlantic/Mediterranean theater as in the Pacific, the light torpedo boat from which early destroyers evolved, made its reappearance. Readers may have read about John F. Kennedy and PT 109 in the Pacific. German and Italian light torpedo boats attempted to intervene in landing assaults the Allies launched in the Mediterranean. Their attacks were often countered by U.S. and British torpedo boats.

German submarines were aggressive and pressed attacks home. German aircraft used standoff weapons to press attacks home but rarely committed themselves to pressed-home attacks against armed surface warships. The Japanese, both air and surface, were much more aggressive and willing to give themselves up in pressed home attacks. These truths, learned mostly in on-the-job experience, dictated the training emphasis for U.S. destroyers serving in the Atlantic and the Mediterranean. Notwithstanding the later addition of a remarkable surface radar system, lookouts remained the absolute quintessential element of vigilance. Edison devoted considerable effort to lookout training and it paid off.

Merchant Losses

In later chapters there will be more specific detail covering episodes involving terrible losses of merchant ships and personnel. I would just offer a comment here about the gravity of the enormous losses suffered by Britain and the U.S. While destroyer sailors saw many a merchantman hit by a torpedo, and each brought its feeling of horror, we could not even then imagine what these losses were adding up to. Examining tallies published after the war was over brought the immediate wonder that our leadership did not lose heart. An Exxon Valdez incident along the East Coast of the U.S. during the World War II would not have stimulated a single news article. I am not referring to censorship or security considerations, only to newsworthiness. East Coast and Gulf beaches were black with oil. There were no processes for cleanup and even if there had been, a busy wartime nation could not have taken the time to pursue organized cleanup operations. Nature did the cleaning. And did it slowly. I can only conjecture that for each defined need for a cargo of supplies, two cargoes sailed. While important exceptions will be covered, our troops for the main part were transported in high-speed ocean liners with escorts only for harbor departure and at arrival landfall. This proved to be highly successful.

Edison Leaves Her Tether for Duty in the Atlantic

The Edison commissioning detail, pictured in a photo taken on her fantail during the ceremony on 31 January 1941 in the Brooklyn Navy Yard, reveals eight officers, ten chief petty officers (CPOs) and about 100 sailors in the "ranks", from first class petty officers to apprentice seamen. The ranks continued to grow numerically, until Edison achieved her assigned complement. In officer grades, though there was no official limit, when the number grew beyond 20, the sleeping spaces became crowded and the "hot bunk" routine began. But, this was still two years in the future.

Just as he had preplanned with OpNav, Captain Al Murdaugh (these accounts use "skipper" and "Captain" interchangeably to denote "Commanding Officer") got Edison to sea on February 17, 1941, on "boilers 3 and 4" according to the ship's log. She went to Newport, Rhode Island, to receive her ten 21" torpedoes, then to exercise there for torpedo practice. Underway at sea again, Edison put in at Norfolk, Virginia on 3 March 1941. She went then to Guantanamo Bay, Cuba for her official, but gun-less, shake down, leaving Norfolk on 5 March. She put in at Port au Prince, British West Indies, on 15 March and left for Charleston, South Carolina on the 17th. On 28 March, she left for New York and returned to the Brooklyn Navy Yard on 31 March for some engineering repairs and for installation of her missing 5"/38 cal. gun battery. This work took until 12 May 1941.

Beginning the 12th of May 1941, the Edison went to Norfolk, back to Brooklyn and back to Norfolk, and while underway accomplished the main battery gunnery exercises missed on her first shake down. On 31 May 1941, Edison left Norfolk for Bermuda, arriving there on 2 June. Her two-phased shake down now considered over, Edison escorted the carrier, USS Wasp, from Bermuda to Norfolk in late June. In July 1941, Edison began mail trips between Boston and Argentia. Her first recorded effort in her assignment to Destroyer Division 25 was to escort the new battleships, USS North Carolina and USS Washington, on their shakedown cruises, to Guantanamo Bay and Port-au-Prince Haiti. Woolsey 437, Ludlow 438 and Edison 439 were regulars in DesDiv 25. The fourth slot was filled at different times by one of a number of destroyers depending on availability, but the USS Bristol was most often in company. DesDiv 25 left the West Indies and arrived in Rockland, Maine in late September 1941.

The Edison had no permanent homeport for repairs. The porting assignments were made on an ad hoc basis depending on what facility was required and what facility was available. Considerations ranged from-dry docking for hull repairs, to ordnance support, electronics installations, and so on. Ordinary supplies and victualling could be handled in most major ports of call. As to supplies, it is an oddity in my recall, but clean rags for the engineering spaces were on the list in every port. Edison's (and DesDiv 25's) operational home port became Portland, Maine using Casco Bay, under the oversight of Commander Destroyers Atlantic Fleet (ComDesLant), whose flag was afloat in Casco Bay on USS Denebola. By October 1941, Edison shifted from Rockland to Portland, Maine, usually an anchorage berth, as there was limited pier berthing there. It was generally a long trip in the Edison whaleboat to Portland for liberty. This porting assignment also marked the beginning of Edison's tenure in the North Atlantic Neutrality Patrol, covering the open sea rim defined by Boston, Massachusetts, Newfoundland, Nova Scotia and Iceland. Edison left Casco Bay on 31 October 1941, making port in Argentia, Newfoundland on 2 November and proceeding then to Reykjavik, Iceland, where she arrived on 6 November.

In Chapter One, we found the destroyer USS Charles F. Hughes entering Reykjavik on July 8, 1941 after an open sea rescue of Red Cross nurses. These nurses and other survivors had been found in a lifeboat with the Master of their ship, which had been torpedoed. When Edison first entered this Icelandic port in November of 1941, it was with the USS Charles F. Hughes.

These months proved crucial in World War II. The Atlantic Charter was developed. President Roosevelt, who had arrived in USS Augusta, flying the flag of CincLant (Rear Admiral E. J. King), and Prime Minister Churchill who had arrived on HMS Prince of Wales, put this critical document to pen on August 9 and August 10, 1941 in Placentia Bay, Argentia, Newfoundland. The warships that brought these leaders to this conference had transited increasingly dangerous U-boat waters.

The tabulations in Chapter One, especially the summaries of U.S. Navy activity in 1940 and 1941 cannot do justice to the unprecedented our naval build up. The U.S. did not have a string of overseas colonial bases like those available to the navies of Britain, Germany, and Italy. Our warships had been accustomed to long transits at sea with underway replenishment. That training would prove to be critically important in the counter offensives undertaken in World War II. But in 1940-41, with our nation on the defensive, the U.S. began commissioning new bases (Lend/Lease and others) for its new warships. The major impact would be in the Atlantic. The bulk of U.S. naval forces between wars had been allotted to the Pacific. The de facto assumption had been that Britain, our most reliable ally, could stand guard over the Atlantic. The Pacific theater, counting its losses at Pearl Harbor, the Philippines and elsewhere, and the assignment of a considerable number of Pacific warships to the Atlantic, would actually undergo a build down of surface warship strength before the huge 1943-1945 build up to V-J day in August 1945.

Operational losses (non-enemy action losses, but training and inexperience losses etc.) would occur in the Atlantic and Mediterranean, and will appear in our story. Such losses must be viewed in the context of a wave of new sea traffic, of seamen unfamiliar with approaches to new ports, and the enormous increases in personnel who had little or no experience. This familiarization effort involving thousands of new seafarers occurred under the intense periscope scrutiny of wolfpack commanders devising fresh tactics every month.

CONVOY INDOCTRINATION

Atlantic Convoys Before Pearl Harbor.

Three convoy experiences of the period have been selected for retelling. The factual base for these sea tales can be found in "United States Destroyer Operations in World War II", a United States Naval Institute publication by Theodore Roscoe. The material which is used for reference began on page 34 of the 1953 edition and includes the following three paragraphs taken almost verbatim from Roscoe's book. I have left open spaces between paragraphs to denote the material from this Naval Institute publication.

Convoy HX-150, with 44 merchantmen underway from Halifax on September 16, 1941, was the first to use U.S. escorts, which relieved Canadian escorts 350 miles east of Halifax on September 17. Captain Morton L. Deyo in USS Ericsson commanded the escort screen. (Ericsson was the Edison's sister ship.) The convoy was disposed in nine columns, with distance between columns set at 600 yards. Ericsson's station was 2,000 yards directly ahead of the convoy. The other four destroyers, a mix of one Benson class and three 4-pipers, patrolled 500-2000 yards from the outer ships in the convoy. Column distances were tightened at night. On clear nights the destroyers continued their patrols, but on foggy nights they were to "keep station". No U-boats were encountered to the point in mid-ocean where British destroyers took over. Stragglers were a constant challenge. On the night of September 24-25, nearing a point in the Atlantic called "Torpedo Junction", destroyer Eberle of the screen was dispatched by Captain Deyo to the aid of the SS Nigaristan which was manned by a crew from the Levant. She was afire. A smolder had suddenly fired up in the ship's bunkers. The barometer read 28.6 inches of mercury (low), and a gale wind was blowing. Eberle, the other Benson class ship in the

63

screen, closed smartly. The freighter's crew had taken to the lifeboats and in this raging sea, Eberle managed to get all 63 Nigaristan crewmen safely aboard. This was accomplished despite the fact that a member of the Nigaristan's black gang had gone overboard from one of the lifeboats. Ensign L.C. Savage of Eberle went into the water between the lifeboat and Eberle, and using a bowline, secured the distressed seaman. Savage then fended off the lifeboat, and both were hauled aboard Eberle.

Convoy ON-18 westbound from relieving a British convoy screen, passed HX-150 that night. Escorts in ON-18 were Madison, Gleaves, Hughes, Simpson and Lansdale. These were all Benson class 1630-ton destroyers of the class of 1940 or early 1941. ON-18, too, made the passage without encountering enemy submarines.

The next passage of convoys ran into trouble. The trouble led to an assignment for Edison. Convoy SC-48 sailed from Canada on October 10, 1941. Terrible weather and an abnormal number of stragglers, 11 of the 50 merchantmen, held the speed of advance to 7 ½ knots. A U-boat wolfpack struck during the night of October 15. The Canadian destroyer Columbia and four Canadian corvettes escorting SC-48 had more than they could handle. Three ships had been torpedoed and sunk when a call for help went into Reykjavik, 400 miles to the north. Captain L.H. Thebaud, ComDesRon 27 in Plunkett, with Livermore and Kearny, all 1630-tonners and the Decatur, a World War I 4-piper, answered the call. Additional help came from the 4-piper USS Greer, the British destroyer Broadwater and the Free French corvette Lobelia, all ordered from other duties. The Reykjavik group of destroyers arrived just before sunset on the 16th and found an exhausted

Canadian screen and her shaken merchant convoy, waiting for another night of U-boat horror. Kearny, Livermore, Decatur and Plunkett formed a close screen, less than a mile from the convoy. In three waves of attacks beginning about 2200 and closing about 0200 on the 17th, the U-boats found their marks in the convoy with torpedoes. First a merchantman, then two more, then four more, received deathblows. In the last wave, Kearny made her way into the convoy, close to a burning tanker. A sudden blaze from the tanker illuminated a British corvette picking up survivors. Kearny slowed and turned to avoid interference. With the scene now well lighted, a U-boat fired a spread of three torpedoes at Kearny. The center one hit in the #1 fire room. Men died from fire, impact, and seawater. The damage control officer and the Chief Motor Machinist shored up and saved the forward engine room bulkhead. The "split-plant" experience enabled Kearny to keep way on while a Quartermaster in the locked after steering engine room compartment answered rudder calls. The 4-piper Greer rallied alongside Kearny to give aid. Kearny's skipper told Greer he could make Iceland. Despite criticisms of this Benson class for topside weight, the class proved resilient with double bottoms and well designed watertight integrity.

Benson class destroyers often succumbed to a single torpedo; Kearny did not. Her crew responded magnificently. The Navy repair ship Vulcan in Iceland performed a near miracle to get Kearny back to sea. The gaping hole in her starboard side just forward of the number one stack and under the starboard wing of the bridge could have finished her. If a torpedo did not ignite a magazine and did not break the keel, two big "ifs", this class of destroyers could survive.

Edison receives an assignment

Admiral Murdaugh, who as Lieutenant Commander Murdaugh was Edison's first CO, had this to say in a letter that appeared in the September 1971 issue of Robert Cloyd's Edison News:

"When the Kearny was torpedoed on 17 October, we were sent out to replace her, and from then on it was all convoy except the welcome short break escorting the HMS Duke of York from Bermuda." Murdaugh's letter continued with,

"Maybe some day your readers would like to have the story of the defense of Convoy ON-67, which ...was officially classed as one of the major engagements of the war, carrying its own battle star. It can be found in Roscoe, Destroyer Operations in World War II (U.S. Naval Institute 1953) pages 69-71, and Morison, History of U.S. Naval Operations in World War II, Vol. 1, The Battle of the Atlantic, (Little Brown & Co., 1947) pages 121-2."

Boston, Portland, Newfoundland and Iceland were Edison ports of call while involved in North Atlantic Neutrality Patrol duties in the late fall of 1941. Edison made Argentia, Newfoundland on 21 November. There was a Boston departure on 2 December for Argentia and a Boston arrival on 28 December. Then her diary shows Portland (Casco Bay) on 5 January 1942, and Bermuda on 14 January 1942. She was in Argentia on 28 January, Iceland on 12 February, and departed for Halifax, Nova Scotia, on 16 February. The 14-28 January 1942 period included escorting HMS Duke of York from Bermuda to mid-ocean. No immediate change in escort patterns occurred as the result of the war declarations between Axis and Allied powers triggered by Pearl Harbor. The North Atlantic convoy practice changed gradually in early 1942, from mid-ocean handoffs, to U.S. warships convoying right into and out of United Kingdom ports.

Convoy ON-67

In recounting the story of Convoy ON-67, I have made use of the two references cited by Admiral Murdaugh in his letter to the Edison News. Actually, I have had these two essential sources in my library since these books became available, Samuel Eliot Morison's Battle of the Atlantic volume in 1947 and Theodore Roscoe's Destroyer Operations volume in 1953. The text for the latter was researched and edited for technical accuracy by Rear Admiral Thomas Wattles, who made use of official Navy sources. I knew this officer as Commander Wattles, the Executive Officer of Bancroft Hall at the Naval Academy, during my final year as a midshipman. It was from the loudspeaker carrying Commander Wattles' voice that most midshipmen living in Bancroft Hall at the Naval Academy on December 7, 1941 first learned of Pearl Harbor.

Edison, with Commander Murdaugh commanding and doing double duty as the Convoy Escort Commander, left Hvalfjordur, Iceland 16 February 1942, along with Nicholson (Benson class), Lea and Bernadou, both re-commissioned World War I 4-pipers. This force was to rendezvous at the mid-ocean passage point of convoy ON-67, westbound from the United Kingdom, and take this group of 35 ships on into Halifax. Meeting up with the convoy on 19 February, the escorts took up a 4,000-yard screen, patrolling in a semi-circle at 12 ½ knots ahead of an 8 1/2-knot convoy. Extra resources were the HMCS Algoma, which was to stay on from the UK escort group as long as her fuel permitted, and, in the convoy itself, the British rescue ship SS Toward, carrying special ocean-tested rescue gear and a High Frequency Radio Direction Finder, commonly called Huff-Duff. For the escort screen, only Nicholson's radar was working properly.

On the morning of the 21st, on course 204 True, with ten miles visibility, tell tale smoke from the convoy broadcast the convoy's presence over a wide span of ocean. At noon, the convoy entered fog. Edison had a sound contact, and dropped a small pattern of depth charges. At dusk, the Toward reported intercepting probable submarine radio traffic on bearing 107 True. The Lea made a short search out on the bearing but discovered nothing. The convoy was being shadowed and at 0305 on the 22nd, the shadowers struck. Two convoy ships were hit from torpedoes fired from the after quarter of the convoy, from a sector sparsely covered by a screen that was in its night formation ahead of the convoy. Nicholson fell back and joined Toward and Algoma in rescue of survivors. Toward's big dip net proved especially effective.

According to a footnote in Morison's Volume 1, "The Battle of the Atlantic", the SS Toward and the SS Rathlin (not present in ON-67) were the first two of a class of specially designed convoy rescue ships. A surgeon was embarked in each, the sick bay was well staffed, and accommodations had been designed for several hundred survivors. The dip net feature consisted of a large net with its own flotation that could be hoisted over the side and put into the water for "waterlogged and oil-smeared survivors."

On the afternoon of the 22nd, the convoy changed course to 240 True and four hours later to 200 True. ON-67 had caught a respite. With two ships sunk, the convoy nursed its wounds into the 23rd. At 1210, on 23 February, Edison reported another sound contact. Moving forward directly ahead of column 8 of the convoy, Edison dropped a pattern of depth charges. The contact had been evaluated "very definite" so Edison stayed with it until the convoy had passed well beyond the area. Unfortunately, the screw noises of 30 or more ships mask the noise of a single quiet submarine and Edison finally gave up and rejoined her convoy station at 25 knots. Later that afternoon, Bernadou picked up a sound contact on the convoy's port beam. It evaporated. Despite frequent course changes ordered by Commander Murdaugh to avoid ambush, it seemed likely that the enemy was not through with ON-67. While the first attack on the early hours of the 22nd probably came from one submarine, by the 24th a pack had assembled. At 0030 on the 24th, the second attack came and was pressed home in waves until 0645. Four merchantmen were torpedoed. Two were sunk and two were left momentarily dead in the water before emergency repairs enabled them to gain some headway. It was estimated that five to six subs participated, working from both quarters. The convoy resorted to the use of "snowflake" illumination, to help the merchantmen's Armed Guard gunners find surfaced subs for targets. Murdaugh, in emergency radio messages to the Chief of Naval Operations, recommended a drastic convoy course change to 285 True. Several hours later, after the events of the next paragraph, this course change was approved.

On the afternoon of the 24th, it became clear that what ON-67's commanders feared was, in fact, occurring. Toward picked up more "radio traffic" on her high frequency radio direction finder. On a sweep of one of the reported bearings 15 miles ahead, Nicholson sighted two U-boats and forced them to submerge, keeping them down until after dark. Lea was sent out on the starboard flank of the convoy to run down another radio bearing reported by Toward. At 20 miles out, Lea found a surfaced submarine, which she forced down and depth charged. Again, the wolfpack surfaced after dark and moved ahead to get into attack position. Edison made sound contact on the convoy's starboard bow shortly after nightfall and moments later her lookouts spotted a U-boat silhouette in a sudden shaft of moonlight. Too fast for the deck guns, the sub slithered away and Edison fired a pattern of depth charges. Five more patterns followed and sound contact could not be regained. After a sustained period of search, Murdaugh ordered his ship to return to station on the convoy. On the way back, at a distance of 200 yards, Edison came across a submarine in the night surface gloom-with no sound contact at all having been registered on the ephemeral target. Edison dropped a warning charge and engaged in suppression between the convoy and point of submergence until dawn of the 25th of February.

The escorts of ON-67 were learning valuable lessons about U-boat tactics and developing, on the spot, counter tactics in suppression. The value of Toward's radio direction finder and of her rescue gear had been demonstrated. The night of 24-25 February passed without the U-boats making an attack. Fog set in at 1410 on the 25th and escorts were called in from ranging forays. Then, Bernadou, running down another HF-DF report from Toward, made sound contact and dropped a pattern of charges just after 1500. Fog enveloped the convoy all that night and in the morning hours of the 26th, rough weather set in. The U.S. Coast Guard Cutter Spencer was a welcome addition to the screen that morning. Convoy ON-67 had passed through her danger period and the rest of the trip was without incident.

Four of the merchant vessels entrusted to the U.S. escorts were on the bottom and quite likely no subs had been sunk in the counter attacks. In a commendatory citation to Commander Murdaugh, Admiral Bristol (stationed in Argentia) closed his remarks with, "Commander Murdaugh outmaneuvered and outfought a concentration of enemy ships and effectively broke up the enemy's efforts." The record certainly supports those words. The U.S. high command must have agreed, too. Stars to wear on service ribbons were a rare recognition. Such recognition usually came only from participation in some huge invasion force that had a demonstrated bearing on the course of the War.

The early months of 1942 in the North Atlantic saw a lower incidence of aggressive wolfpack attacks. There was a good reason. The coastal waters of the U.S. and the Caribbean proved to be easier hunting grounds for Doenitz's submarines. In the next chapter, the author will take his place with the millions of U.S. service personnel taking up duties for their country.

JOINING THE WAR AT SEA

Chapter Four - Fog at Sea; Inauspicious Beginning

"The graduation of the Class of 1943 from the U.S. Naval Academy was scheduled for June 19, 1942. Orders dated June 1, 1942 directed Ensign Franklyn E. Dailey Jr., USN, to report, on graduation, for duty aboard the USS. Edison, DD439. Though I would not be an Ensign until June 19, the orders affirmed the fact that I would really graduate. In 1942, one needed all the "affirmations" that one could get.

Illustration 10-An Ensign's Orders

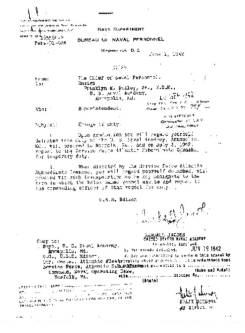

Military training experiences furnish a bond between servicemen of all ranks and ratings. There is some trepidation connected with beginning any new life involving a complete change in the cast of characters. Then, there was the war one is going to serve in. Perhaps the immediate ordeals of training are designed to take one's mind off these very basic changes in life. There is another ordeal that one faces after "graduation" from any military training school. It involves the challenge of getting to the unit in which one's first service is to be performed. I experienced what thousands of inductees, enlistees, reservists, guardsmen and other school graduates faced as they moved to their first operational duty. The military man moves with his life and all his possessions in tow. The first step is taken with utmost seriousness. The neophyte regards that first set of orders as the sure link between his training command and his first operational command. A shadow of doubt creeps in as "endorsements" to those orders pile on and the goal of actually reaching one's duty station seems to get further away. The sequence of endorsements that took me to the Edison involved challenges that appear laughable now, but were perplexing then. The original orders directed me to report to the Service Force, Atlantic Fleet Subordinate Command, located at the Naval Operating Base (NOB), Norfolk, Virginia.

"Yes", the Edison had been seen there I was told, but "It is not here now." Meanwhile, a week at Firefighters School and then a week at Gunnery School would keep me occupied. Learning to fight fire aboard ship was an important use of time and I made the most of it. The Gunnery School at Dam Neck, Virginia was a hands-on course in firing the U.S. Navy's 1.1inch rapid fire AA gun. It proved a waste of time insofar as most of us never saw the gun again. In the NOB barracks where I was bunked, I developed conjunctivitis in both eyes and an infected cyst on my tailbone. Medical prognosis: "There is a war on and there is no time for us to deal with such ailments."

Over a full career in the military, I learned that it was not realistic to expect training in shore-based schools to synchronize with the real military world. Training courses and training commands were always a step or two behind events. Short shipyard "availability" periods found frontline World War II ships on which the Navy-designed 1.1inch guns were summarily flame cut out of their gun tubs and replaced by Swedish Bofors 40mm AA guns just as the .50 caliber machine guns had been replaced by Swiss Oerlikon 20mm AA guns. I would soon discover that the only pieces of ordnance that I studied at the U.S. Naval Academy that proved relevant to my tour aboard the Edison were to be found in the Edison's gun locker. These were the .45 automatics for boarding party and sentry duty and 30 "ought six" Springfield rifles of my midshipman rifle range days. The latter were used aboard ship mainly to sink moored mines that had been cut loose by the minesweepers and had then floated to the surface.

While the U.S. Navy's original outfitting of smaller caliber AA guns on its fighting ships was prudently upgraded with ordnance designed outside the U.S., the U.S. designed main battery (on destroyers) of 5"/ 38 caliber Dual Purpose (DP) guns proved to be the envy of all the world's navies. From personal experience, I learned later that the 5"/38s were especially feared by German armored divisions, infantrymen and airmen.

The routing of personnel in wartime was, at best, circuitous. There came to be a general belief among those traveling on orders, whether true or not, that the destinations written into orders for military personnel were designed to fool the enemy. It often fooled the traveler. I discovered later that the

Edison was already at the South Boston (Massachusetts) Navy Yard when I received an endorsement on my original orders in Norfolk to proceed to the Third Naval District at 90 Church Street in New York City. Those orders led me to expect to find the ship at the Brooklyn Navy Yard. At the Federal Building at 90 Church Street in New York City, I was immediately given new orders to proceed without delay to the First Naval District at the Fargo Building in Boston, Massachusetts. My trip routing from Norfolk to New York had taken me onto the Pennsylvania Railroad, beginning with a train ferry to Kiptopeake, Virginia and there to pick up a locomotive that pulled us up the Eastern Shore to join the main line near Baltimore and then on into New York. My Naval Academy-issue Cruise Box traveled in the baggage car. At New York, that Cruise Box was nowhere to be found. After midnight, in a section of the subterranean labyrinth under Manhattan, I found a patient and quite elderly (called back to service) railroad telegrapher who keyed out an all points bulletin for the Cruise Box to get it redirected to Boston. It actually came aboard the Edison before we sailed, but I embarked on the New Haven Railroad for Boston without it. That box contained my dress blue uniform, my service dress whites, and my sword. In over 30 years of officer service, I never wore those uniforms and never used the sword for other than cake cutting at family weddings. I never even acquired the gold tassel for the sword handle that signified that the midshipman-issue sword was now being worn by a commissioned officer. But I could not see that far ahead, and I was immensely relieved to be intact dress-wise as I reported to the Edison and thankful for the assist given by that kind telegrapher. Most of that "stuff" was soon on its way to my home of record in Rochester, N.Y.

FOG AT SEA; INAUSPICIOUS BEGINNING

On reporting aboard the Edison at 1000 hours (10 a.m. local time) on July 30, 1942 in the South Boston Navy Yard. I was welcomed at the quarterdeck by Lieutenant (jg) Stanley R. Craw, USNR, who handed me the Officer-of-the-Deck (OOD) arm brassard, the gun belt and .45 cal. gun and holster, and had me sign the log as his relief as OOD in port. He also told me that the Executive Officer would see me soon. I was a little apprehensive about meeting the senior officers but I had had little time and no basis on which to reflect where these men and their ship had already been. Warren Blake, an electrician aboard, supplied this paragraph with an e-mail to me in 1998, very informative, even if 56 years too late for my meeting with Edison's Executive Officer.

"Memories of Boston, Portland, Halifax and Argentia, as well as Iceland, during the early part of 1942, were of the "frigid" variety. Pulling in to port with several inches of ice from main deck almost to masthead. The long convoy hauls where tedium could have set in were it not for GQ every morning at dawn, and the constant submarine alerts accompanied very often with depth charge attacks. You slept fully clothed, wearing your life belt, and when you had quartering seas and the can would "corkscrew", you slept (or tried to) with arm and leg on one side braced against your bunk chains, and on the other side, against the stanchions supporting the bunks. During calmer seas though, the bunks were quite comfortable compared to a hammock! (From the day I entered "boot camp" until I signed on as Ship's company in Edison and finally got a bunk, I had spent about six months in a hammock.)"

We had left Warren Blake's story in an earlier chapter as he arrived aboard Edison for transit to the USS Livermore. In a later e-mail, Warren informed me that he was "augmented" by Edison as a crewmember and he translated that word to mean "kidnapped". In olden days, he would perhaps have been considered "impressed" or even "shanghied."

It was not long before an incident occurred on that first deck watch in port and I was its focus. Outboard in the nest of destroyers at this South Boston Navy Yard dock was a destroyer flying the flag of a Division Commander.

I had less than an hour of experience in my new assignment as part of the Edison's ship's company. I was not yet fully aware that destroyers were organized into *divisions* (of four destroyers). Nor had it come home to me that *squadrons* consisted of nine destroyers, containing two divisions of four destroyers each plus a destroyer flying the flag of a Squadron Commander. The short title for the Destroyer Squadron to which the Edison was assigned was DesRon 13, and DesRon 13's flagship was the USS Buck. But this nest included destroyers from another division and Edison was inboard alongside the dock. Shortly after I relieved Lt. (jg) Craw on my very first watch, a Division Commander (three gold stripes) came up our gangplank to cross over to his ship. I did know that the protocol involved his saluting the flag, and saluting the quarterdeck to ask permission to come aboard. I did not know that the protocol was attenuated in practice to a quick motion that all but compressed the two salutes into a single salute. Nor did I know that I was to get my hand up in salute to him (a senior officer) as quickly as he raised his or, preferably, just before he got into the salute. This custom violated the protocol I had been taught but cut down on the amount of saluting and gave the senior officer his due. I returned his salute, thereby violating the practice but not the protocol. He sent a complaint to our skipper concerning my exercise of the custom. I was in the first hour of about thirty years of naval duty. My skipper was junior to this Division Commander. My Executive Officer (XO) straightened me out on how it was done, in a very nice way. Later I learned that on direction from my skipper, our XO responded formally to the complaint by telling that Division Commander that Dailey had done it according to the book. And so I met my first wartime Captain and his Executive Officer. These were men who would stick by you.

Alongside a dock near the Edison in South Boston, in early August 1942, was the USS Massachusetts, then a new battleship. An Academy roommate of mine, David Shonerd, had an older brother on the Massachusetts. Dave's father (a senior naval officer when I was a midshipman) and mother were very kind to me and always included me in the party when they visited Dave and took him for Sunday dinner "out in town" in Annapolis. So, not made bashful by my setback on naval customs at the Edison's gangplank, I got up enough courage to call on Lieutenant Henry Shonerd, USN, aboard the Massachusetts. The visit took place before Edison left Boston. In the course of shipboard duty in my wartime tour aboard Edison, I saw many famous warships, including destroyers, cruisers and battleships. For various duty reasons, I actually went on board a good number of them, British, French and our own. The USS Massachusetts is one of just two World War II ships that I could re-visit today. She is at Fall River, Massachusetts and is maintained for visiting.

Two of the first of my Naval Academy classmates to die in 1942 after our June 19, 1942 graduation perished in the Coconut Grove nightclub fire in Boston, Massachusetts. No enemy action. The first action episode which occurred during my tour aboard Edison involved just two adversaries, the elements, and our men and machinery. No enemy action. This episode began just before my relief of a midwatch. The date was August 22, 1942 and the scene was Convoy AT-20 out of Halifax, Nova Scotia, bound for Greenock, Scotland.

Task Force 37, Rear Admiral Lyal A. Davidson commanding, suffered grievous casualties. That story will be told later in the chapter.

Technology and Tactics; Still Catching Up
   Until the outfitting of U.S. destroyers in late 1942 and early 1943 with Raytheon Corporation's SG radar (an X-band radar system with its Plan Position Indicator (PPI) oscilloscope in the pilothouse), fog at sea raised hell for all ships involved in escort of convoy duty. The escorted ships and the escorts were both blind. Enemy submarines could maneuver almost with impunity outside the lookout surveillance of the convoy and its escorts. A fast convoy, with a speed of advance of 15 knots or better, had speed as its best defense, but would have to slow in a fog. A slow or a slowed convoy, 8 knots or less, became extremely vulnerable. The subs had the speed-of-advance advantage as long as they could run on the surface and avoid lookout detection. This enabled them to get into relative positions ahead of the convoy's mean direction of advance. Thus positioned, they then had their choice of closing angle. We saw in the story of ON-67, that with screens deployed ahead, submarine tactics using the quarters for attacks were successful. Their torpedoes, at say 45 knots speed in pressed home attacks, could find a seven or eight knot merchantman, and score hits.
   We also saw how Captain Murdaugh's ON-67 screen, using a relatively new tool, the high frequency radio detection finder, pioneered new tactics to run out on the intercepted radio signal bearing, and at least keep the submarines down, where their speed advantage over the convoy was markedly reduced. Most convoys in mid-1942 did not have the HF/DF equipment on any ship, escort or convoy. Military radio installations based on land also sent information, often

based on HF/DF bearings determined from intercepted wolf-pack radio traffic, to our ships at sea. These left the seaborne commander a wider area to search as bearing information at these longer ranges simply provided a line on the chart from which the contact could have emanated. But, information that radio traffic from enemy subs at sea was being picked up was always valuable to the embarked forces.

High frequency sonar pinging and echo detection did not provide a long -range submarine detection capability. Even after detection of a submarine, perfecting the use of sonar for a depth charge attack required a lot of training. In World War II, the critical technology advances for the essential longer-range detection of submarines were, in the order of their appearance at sea:

HF/DF first, SG radar second, and friendly air surveillance for convoy transit, third.

In its impact, the SG radar was the major addition to the World War II destroyer. The sub did not have to generate radio traffic to be detected; it only had to "be". If it surfaced or partly surfaced, SG radar would "see" it. The SG radar provided range, and bearing. Putting these advances in context, with the advantage of hindsight, ON-67's escort screen experience in the application of HF/DF was a very important step along the way. All three of the system introductions listed above meant an ability to "see beyond the lookouts". Lookouts could see beyond the sonar in reasonable visibility.

Later in the War, we had all three of these technology advances working together. But that time was yet to come and the losses we would incur before our technology advances and our training could be teamed up would be extensive.

Even with the advances in technology, weather was always a critical factor in operations. A roiled sea is something that a good surface ship has to learn to adapt to. Even an experienced seaborne Commodore might feel "bilious", as ours confessed he was to us over the TBS in mid-Atlantic on the way to the landings at Fedala, near Casablanca. (TBS was a crystal controlled Very High Frequency, line of sight, voice communication system. My recollection was that the crystal frequencies available were in the 68-72 MHz range.) In turbulent waters, submarines do not take to the layer just beneath the surface much better than surface vessels. These rough waters, encountered frequently in the North Atlantic, usually spelled a period of reduced activity for torpedo attacks by enemy submarines. Subs and fog thrive in calm waters. And it needs saying once more, in good weather or bad, the lookouts, whether the first source of warning or confirmation of that source, always served an essential role.

AT-20 Encounters Fog

In the fog, a day out of Halifax, Nova Scotia in August 1942, no screening destroyers and no ships in convoy AT-20 yet had anything like SG radar. The following lines are quoted from Theodore Roscoe's U.S. Naval Institute book, "United States Destroyer Operations in World War II." The lines relate to an earlier 1942 operation in these same North Atlantic waters with destroyer crews at their battle stations.

"The fog was nasty--cotton-thick in patches, but thinning here and there into open spaces (fog-dogs in the vernacular) which appeared unexpectedly, like clearings in a misty forest. One minute a ship was plowing blindly through an opalescent cloud. Next minute she was in the clear, exposed."

Convoy AT-20, with troops and supplies bound for Scotland, was, as convoys go, of the fast variety, with an anticipated 15 knots speed of advance. Fog forced the Convoy Commander to slow the convoy and to order the launching of towing spars into the water behind each convoy vessel. Under towing spar conditions, all ships in the convoy close up into a tighter formation so that the conning officers in each ship (except ships in the lead flank) keep station on the towing spar of the ship ahead. Forward lookouts strain to keep the spar in sight. The merchantman's helmsman must respond smartly to the conning officer's rudder commands in order to keep the ship in column. The towing spar must not be overrun, yet the vessel must hold position and not lose sight of the spar. The engines are being controlled by "turns", called for over voice tubes with feedback (confirmation) by means of an engine-turns indicator that shows the exact number of turns per minute on a propeller shaft. Annunciators (a brass mechanical handle-or set of handles, one for each engine/propeller), perched on a stanchion at waist level on the bridge, transmit fundamental speed changes from bridge to the engine room (ER) which, depending on handle position, call for "slow", "standard" or "flank" speed ahead, or astern. The annunciator method of speed control is not precise enough for minute-to-minute use, especially in a formation of ships in fog.

AT-20 was a troop convoy. The Task Force Commander's flag flew on the USS Philadelphia. That cruiser was one of four of the new 15-gun (6inchers) class of light cruisers that served with distinction in the War in the Atlantic. Edison served with three of these ships, Brooklyn, Savannah and Philadelphia. I saw enough of these three to observe their excellent sea-keeping qualities. They had big box sterns, and we'll hear more about the stern of Philadelphia in a later chapter on Salerno. The USS New York, my midshipman cruise battleship, was part of TF 37. Since Philadelphia and New York did not run down enemy submarine contacts, it had to be obvious that they were along for another purpose.

That purpose was more than to give an Admiral a comfortable place to ride.

Brooklyn and New York both had catapults and deck spaces for scout planes, like the Navy's SOCs (Curtiss observation seaplanes) or OS/2Us (Vought observation seaplanes). One might suppose that these would be handy for submarine surveillance. The North Atlantic was not a kind area for deployment of these aircraft. Recovery of them was effected by creating a knuckle in the wake of the parent ship to create a smoothed off place in the water for a light seaplane to land, a technique which I had witnessed frequently with the battleships New York, Texas and Arkansas on the midshipman cruise. This maneuver tied up a big ship and plane guard destroyers. The tradeoff rarely seemed acceptable to task force commanders in wartime conditions in foggy waters infested with enemy submarines. So, the primary reason for the use of cruisers and battleships in North Atlantic convoys, especially when troops were being convoyed, was the threat that heavily gunned German warships might be at large in the ocean.

Troopships were generally afforded passage in faster convoys. With several troopships in a convoy one could be sure that convoy escorts would be provided that could give an account of themselves against all threats. Although the CIC-Combat Information Center aboard U.S. Navy warships had not yet been implemented in early 1942, the larger warships carried more radio equipment and had larger plotting rooms. The ratio of ASW escorts to convoy ships was also higher in convoys with troop ships. These would have eight to fifteen ships in convoy, with escorts numbering nine or more, in addition to the "heavy" firepower represented by a cruiser and a battleship.

FOG AT SEA; INAUSPICIOUS BEGINNING

By July 1942, the enemy submarine wolfpack forces had been expanded in the North Atlantic. Every merchant convoy in August was attacked, and one convoy, eastbound SC-94, was attacked by two wolfpacks on separate nights. 24 ships went down in August in this area, 28 in September, 25 in October and 29 in November of 1942. Acoustic homing torpedoes had entered the U-boat arsenal. Also, by this time large supply submarines had begun to replenish the German sub fleet to keep it at sea. With new wolfpacks on the prowl off South America, in the Caribbean and Gulf, in addition to the mid-Atlantic and North Atlantic, the pressure on convoy defense planners to obtain escorts entered a crucial phase. The North Atlantic troop convoys carrying Army units to Britain kept the highest priority. In order to provide modern destroyers of the Benson class for troop convoys, the British Navy and the Canadian Navy re-assumed primary responsibility for the full transit of supply ship merchant convoys. There was occasionally an extra detachment of escort ships in Iceland to sally forth on call.

The result was that the fast trans-Atlantic AT troop convoys, heavily escorted, ran the wolfpacks without casualties due to enemy action. Not a ship underwent torpedo attack. Still, the submarine attack threat was paramount in the minds of the escort force commanders and any "trouble" whose source was not immediately apparent had first to be evaluated as potentially submarine-caused.

The North Atlantic took its toll of troopships. We will come back to an August 1942 submarine sinking of the Army transport Chatham, and will examine the events in which two other troopships which were sunk in 1943, after recalling what happened to AT-20.

Screen Commander for AT-20 was Captain John B. Heffernan, flying the pennant of ComDesRon 13, on the USS

Buck. DesRon 13 was as close to its full complement of as-signed destroyers for the transit of convoy AT-20 as I would experience in 27 months aboard Edison. The destroyers Ludlow, Woolsey, Edison, Bristol, Swanson, Nicholson and Ingraham were assigned to the screen. These ships, all of the Benson class, and all initially assigned to DesRon 13, joined active war service in the Atlantic at about the same time.

AT-20's 10-ship troop convoy was formed up and stand-ing eastward from Halifax by 0600 on 22 August. Just before 1800 that evening, troopship Letitia reported a radar contact which Swanson and Ingraham investigated. Sonar noise, pos-sibly porpoises, delayed their return. They were unable to determine the source of the original radar contact. At 2200 fog added to the complexity of a convoy attempting to re-sume its original screen sector alignment, which had been modified during the sweeps by Swanson and Ingraham.

At 2205, CTF 37, Rear Admiral Davidson, used the TBS voice radio to direct the USS Buck to go close aboard Letitia and escort her to her assigned station 1,000 yards on Phila-delphia's starboard beam. With visibility now near zero, and with the primary station-keeping resource, the towing spars, streamed, Buck actually had to get into bull horn range of Letitia to help direct her to the assigned position.

At 2225, now in a crossing position in a convoy column, a Buck lookout's shout was too late, as the transport Awatea, suddenly visible at 30 yards, rammed Buck's starboard quarter. The steep prow of Awatea nearly severed Buck. A 300pound depth charge from one of Buck's K-guns dropped over the side and exploded, damaging Buck's port propeller. Buck broke away, badly hurt, and helpless.

Ordered to investigate a "collision in the convoy", (only later determined to be the collision of Buck and Awatea), the destroyer Ingraham, in that same blinding fog as she entered the convoy's path, got into a crossing situation ahead of the Navy oiler, USS Chemung. The Chemung's bow cut a huge gash in Ingraham. Lying almost on her side, Ingraham blew up with an orange flash of such intensity that it cut through the fog and was visible on Edison's bridge. Ensign R.F. (Dick) Hofer, the junior watch officer on Edison's bridge, reported the flash in Edison's log at 2235 by Edison's chronometer. Because I was so new at watch standing underway, I was up on the bridge early to prepare to relieve Dick Hofer, and was just getting night-vision adjusted when I too saw the flash.

Just ten men and one officer survived on the Ingraham. The officer was my classmate from the Naval Academy, Ensign Melvin Brown. He would have had orders very similar to the orders reproduced on the first page of this chapter. Ensign Brown was in the Ingraham's Mark 37 director when the ship rolled over. He survived drowning mainly because he was wearing a kapok life jacket with a ring that curled from its vest on the chest up around and behind the neck. This jacket could hold an unconscious man's head out of water. In the late spring of 1997, just after I had determined to contact Mel Brown personally about his Ingraham experience for inclusion in this story, I read of his death in Shipmate, a magazine published by the Naval Academy Alumni Association.

The death toll on Ingraham was nearly 250 men. I will express more than once in this story how ill at ease it makes me to report death with such nominal figures. Each death is a significant loss. The fact of its occurrence in the defense of one's country certainly deserves accurate and specific recognition. A list of a ship's embarked personnel, left ashore with a responsible party on the ship's departure from its last port, furnishes the most accurate information on which to notify bereaved families. Loss reports came so rapidly in World War II that news sources had to use estimated loss figures contained in preliminary Navy or Army service announcements. It was rare that more accurate follow up reports got into the press because a new loss to announce would already be at hand. Despite the numbing down that the regularity of loss numbers caused, Ingraham's loss of life was exceptionally large, even for a sunken ship. There were many more losses to come. We never got used to them.

While Ingraham's condition made her more likely than not to sink, given the catastrophic damage of the collision, it was the explosion that followed that robbed her crew of any chance to save her or themselves. The observation made earlier that this class of ships could survive torpedo damage did not leave anyone comfortable with the demonstrated vulnerability of destroyer classes to magazine detonation. A severed keel might not always prove catastrophic. Sea conditions and immediate aid could mean the difference there. In the war at sea, in addition to collision, triggers for magazine detonation included enemy torpedoes, mines, and bombs. While Atlantic destroyers demonstrated toughness in seakeeping, and proved themselves effective in handing out punishment, their proportionately large cargo of high explosives and the large space the explosive materials occupied, could set in motion a chain of events that could doom a ship.

Too often, a destroyer's own depth charges exacerbated earlier damage. One of the sources consulted in preparing this account noted that after the collision, and rolling over on her side, Ingraham's own depth charges went into the sea and exploded under her. This account stated that it was then that the telltale blast of magazine detonation occurred. The prevalent condition of fog, in combination with a convoy with precious troop cargo that had to sail on, meant that we may never be completely certain of the exact sequence of events that led to Ingraham's loss. Two destroyers were ordered to stand by to aid in survival but destroyers do not have investigating committees aboard.

Not all the damage had yet been done to AT-20. Thankfully, no more destroyers would be used in that dense fog to coax the convoy ships back to station. In a turn for the better, patches of clear visibility began to emerge from the wreathy fog shortly after midnight. Bristol and Edison were assigned to stay with the damaged ships while the convoy moved on. Edison found the Chemung on fire in her bosn's stores in the forward hold. Bristol found the Buck dead in the water with men trapped in the after steering engine room. The Awatea, a transport with 5,000 soldiers aboard, had disappeared.

Damage Assessments

We will first examine the Buck's problems. What is an after steering engine room? On Edison, as on the Buck, way aft was a hatch that gave personnel access down through the main deck to a very small stern-compartment, the steering engine room. Steel cables from the bridge (actually, from the helm on the bridge) come down each side of the ship and enter this room to turn the rudder. These cables wrap around a rudder-turning pulley, a wheel of large diameter. Deck-hands manned this tiny room as a regular underway watch station. Trained personnel could take direct control of the rudder in the event of a rupture in the cabling between the helm on the bridge and rudder, for whatever cause. Directions for moving the rudder in local control could come via the sound powered telephones or, if these were not working, by man-to-man voice relay. For watertight integrity purposes, this steering engine room compartment is dogged down during action episodes such as when the ship is at General

Quarters. Junior Officers are assigned training watches in the after steering engine room and I can personally attest to the claustrophobia that can come over anyone standing (crouching) a watch in this space. Dead in the water, with men trapped in her after steering engine room, is how Bristol found the Buck in that eerie calm sea. We will come back to solutions to the Buck's dilemma after dealing with Edison's handling of the fire challenge faced by the tanker, the USS Chemung.

Navy tankers (oilers) differ from the huge sea going tankers like the Exxon Valdez. In World War II, most large commercial tankers, though not then as large as their late 20th century counterparts, transported a primary cargo of say, bunker fuel oil, or crude oil. Others carried aviation gasoline, avgas as it is often called. The distinction is that, short of some small quantities of other petroleum distillate cargo for its own use, the commercial tanker carries one primary petroleum product. Not so Navy tankers. They have traditionally carried a mixed cargo of bunker fuel oil, avgas, and diesel oil. They also have aboard extra pumping gear and hoses for fueling warships and other ships in the train. The "train" can consist of other Navy auxiliaries like supply ships or attack transports. Each of the classes of Navy ships has different petroleum menu needs. Some, like destroyers, will not need avgas at all. But of all seagoing warships, the destroyer needs the most frequent feedings of primary fuel oil. Edison carried just over 140,000 gallons of #6 fuel oil and a few thousand gallons of diesel fuel. The daily fuel report was a "must do" report.

The Chemung, as noted, was on fire in her forward hold. The flammables here were mostly boatswain's stores, ropes and the like. The fact that she was a tanker, and had a mixed cargo of flammable petroleum derivatives, was certainly on the mind of her skipper and our skipper. She was almost dead in the water. Edison patrolled slowly around her. Edison was now in a clearing in the fog. Visibility was good, really too good, for the Chemung and we were being illuminated by her fire. We had no idea then of what had gone wrong in the convoy. We had none of the post mortem data contained in the earlier paragraphs. All Ensign Hofer had told me was that he heard an order over the TBS given to a destroyer to "close the convoy at high speed." Edison personnel could not, therefore, when dealing with the Chemung, even equate the huge ball of orange to the loss of the Ingraham. Submarines were on our mind. The skipper of the Chemung asked the Edison to come close aboard so that Edison could put out Chemung's fire.

Both Captain Headden and his Executive Officer, Lieutenant Commander Pearce, were on the Edison's bridge. Both had experience that I had not had, and experience that I did not even then know they had. I was kind of dumbstruck by the Chemung's request. I assumed we would probably do what the Chemung asked, and I worried about getting that fire out before it spread to the rest of the Chemung, or to us. Our Executive Officer "Hap" Pearce, as he was known, already had a Navy Cross for keeping the Marblehead, a U.S. cruiser, afloat in the South Pacific after Japanese aircraft had scored hits. He had then been instrumental in helping to rig an emergency rudder so that Marblehead could get back to the States, the long way around. Edison's CO and XO conferred briefly. Captain Headden then told the Chemung skipper, in brief, to "get your own fire out, and do it quickly so we can both get underway." That was not what I expected. In my naivete, I had expected we would go alongside and push as many fire nozzles as we could into any hole we could find in the forward section of the Chemung.

What Headden and Pearce knew that I did not know, was that ships like the Chemung had more than adequate fire fighting equipment aboard, certainly more than a destroyer had, and that Chemung had men trained to fight even more dangerous fires. I watched in amazement at the reaction on Chemung to Headden's orders. Both her deck crews and her boat crews quickly moved firefighting equipment and pumping equipment forward and attacked the fire vigorously. Chemung personnel had a stubborn type of stores fire under control before dawn. Edison and the Chemung then got underway toward Bristol and Buck, not too far away. Edison sailors were always glad to be underway. Both Headden and Pearce, while they served as Edison's Commanding Officers, believed in movement. In addition to movement, and to zig zag patterns as prescribed in MERSIGS (a British merchant signal book), Edison constantly fish tailed along any course, and regularly altered the degree-of-rudder changing signals. (Going alongside a dock in a battle area was a "no no". I had heard our senior officers talk about that.)

I cannot put an exact time on subsequent events, except to try to be accurate about the order in which these events occurred. Buck's difficulty was quite severe and in attempting to overcome it, more tragedy occurred. One propeller shaft had been severed and the screw had gone to the briny deep. The crew in the after steering engine room were in communication with their shipmates but apparently a wall of water surrounded their compartment. We arrived with Chemung back in the vicinity of Buck just after the second event in Buck's fearsome night. I can only assume from what happened that the low freeboard after main deck of the Buck was under water as the result of her collision with the Awatea. The dogged watertight door on Buck's after steering engine room hatch would keep water out of the compartment but it also meant that there was no airway for escape. There were other courses of action, in retrospect, that might have been taken with the USS Buck. But, the plan by this time called for getting damaged ships back to Halifax and for getting Edison and Bristol back to the escort-depleted convoy as soon as possible. Even presuming that the just passed events of the night of the 22-23 of August, 1942 had not originated with enemy submarine action, one could still expect submarines to take advantage of distressed ships.

So, Buck made the effort to see if the remaining propeller shaft could be turned over. That proved to make things worse. The partly severed stern vibrated off and plunged into the deep. Not only did this take the after steering engine crew down with it, but the 600 pound roll off charges in the stern racks may have exploded when they got to their set depth. Buck was now propeller-less. These events had occurred before the Edison/Chemung duo got into the Buck's vicinity.

Had the depth charges on the Ingraham also been set to go off at depth? Every watch on Edison drilled at least once in four hours in setting depth charge patterns and proficiency was recorded by the time to set the pattern, and report the pattern set. It was further a mark of proficiency to get them set them quickly back onto safe. These drills to set a pattern and then return the settings to "safe" took place in almost all sea conditions and in darkness. I came to the conclusion years later, that apparently there was no Destroyers Atlantic Fleet (DesLant) directive on depth charge procedures that all destroyers had to follow.

The Awatea, with her 5,000 troops embarked, and bow damaged, did not return to AT-20. Some said she went back to Halifax. Others said she went on her own to Greenock.

Fortunately, we have an Awatea eyewitness. John Henry Valcour was a U.S. Army tank driver. He was embarked in

Awatea for transport to the British Isles. Through his son, Stewart Valcour, he informed me by e-mail in 1997 that after the collision, the bow of the Awatea was so severely damaged that the ship returned to Halifax at a speed of 3 knots. As the result of the near tragedy for the transport, the embarked Army personnel were given one month's leave. This leave was shortened to two weeks, then one week and finally three days. These foreshortened leaves were typical of World War II and many men in similar circumstances remained on leave ("out of touch") for the original period. Stewart Valcour told me that his father then served in the tank forces in North Africa and Italy and was in Holland when that country was liberated. Awatea was capable of ocean liner speeds approaching 20 knots. The faster ship's skippers always chafed at convoy speeds, which seemed to them to make their ship more vulnerable than going it alone. Awatea was not lost, thank God. AT-20 losses were already steep.

A mini-convoy was made up, Chemung with Buck in tow, Bristol and Edison screening. Bristol's skipper was Senior Officer Present Afloat (SOPA). Course was set to Halifax, and even with our slow speed of advance, we were back off Halifax in less than two days. Bristol and Edison turned their injured charges over to patrol boats out of Halifax, and made their way back to AT-20 at high speed. Calm seas prevailed, yet it took nearly four days at 25 knots for Edison to resume station in its assigned sector with AT-20. I had mixed emotions after these days, my first at sea in war conditions, and a lot of questions, most of which I kept to myself.

Theodore Roscoe's book, Destroyer Operations in World War II, did not become available until 1953. The striking similarities between ASW work in the North Atlantic in the two world wars did not end with the escort help we managed to give the British in our own interest during the "short of

94

war" periods. Here are three brief, consecutive, paragraphs from page 9 of Chapter 1 of United States Destroyer Operations in World War II, a US Naval Institute book by Theodore Roscoe. Please note that the period covered was 1898-1917. The U.S. warships involved were all World War I destroyers.

"Jacob Jones was the first United States warship to fall victim to a long-range torpedo. And she was the only American warship torpedoed during World War I (although the enemy torpedoed an American revenue cutter, an empty transport, and an armed yacht)."

"A second destroyer, the U.S.S. Chauncey, was lost through collision. The wonder was that, operating blindly with unlighted convoys, and working in all sorts of Atlantic weather, more of these fast moving American four-pipers were not sunk due fatal collisions."

"Heavy casualties were suffered by the U.S.S. Manley in March 1918 when she was jostled against a British cruiser while coming alongside in rough seas. Eighteen of the destroyer's depth charges exploded, wrecking her stern and killing or wounding 56 of her crew. In October 1918 the destroyer Shaw (Commander W. A. Glassford), her steering gear jammed, had her bow sheared off by the liner Aquitania. The liner sliced into the destroyer just forward of the bridge; twelve bluejackets were killed."

An interesting sidelight to this last paragraph was came to me when my Naval Academy classmate David Shonerd wrote to inform me that his father, Commander H. G. Shonerd when I later knew him, was aboard the Shaw in transit waiting to relieve Commander Glassford. as Commanding Officer of the Shaw. Commander Shonerd received the Navy Cross for valor in assisting in the saving of the damaged Shaw.

If these paragraphs from the World War I forepart of Roscoe's book on World War II had been available in 1940 instead of 13 years later when the Roscoe book was published, they would have made compelling reading for North Atlantic sea commanders in World War II. The three quoted paragraphs, coming one right after the other in Roscoe's book, were directly relevant to Edison's early World War II service in North Atlantic waters, and the Manley and Shaw incidents bore an eerie pertinence to the events which beset convoy AT-20 on August 22-23, 1942.

Some of our troop transports were sunk in North Atlantic waters, though none was lost in the fairly exclusive faster troop convoys. AT-20 type convoys were the most effective troop convoys for getting soldiers to get to their assigned duties across the Atlantic, but there was still a better way, no convoy at all! Taking a page out of World War I experience, on 2 August 1942, the U.S. and Britain agreed to use big, fast luxury liners to move troops across the Atlantic without escort vessels. In his Volume I of the History of United States Navy Operations in World War II, Volume 1, The Battle of the Atlantic, Samuel Eliot Morison mentions the French SS Pasteur, the Canadian Empress of Scotland, and the Cunard Queens, Mary and Elizabeth. The American SS Mariposa was used but did not operate under British command. The Queen Mary at 81,000 tons and the Queen Elizabeth at 85,000-tons, could each sustain 26.5 knots and make the trip in less than five days. In 1942, these ships made ten eastbound trips and in the first six months of 1943, twenty trips, all loaded with Canadian and American troops. They were not escorted for the main part of their crossings, never lost a man, and were much more expeditious and cost effective in moving manpower than the best of the escorted troop convoys.

Slow and Slower Troop Convoys

The least effective way to get troops to advanced stations overseas in World War II were the slow convoys and mixed slow and in my words, "slightly faster than slow" convoys. One such convoy, SG-6 left Sydney, Cape Breton on 25 August 1942. The first and faster group had the USCGC (US Coast Guard Cutter) Mojave escorting the US Army transport, Chatham. The second or slow group had the cutters Algonquin and Mohawk escorting three merchantmen plus the Navy oiler Laramie, and USS Harjurand, a coal-burning auxiliary with a maximum speed of 7 knots. Cape Breton is north of Nova Scotia. Once clear of the port, Sydney looks NNW into the Gulf of St. Lawrence or East into the Atlantic Ocean. The route chosen took these ships into the Gulf of St. Lawrence. The "G" in SG indicated a destination of Greenland. Air coverage was available on the 25th and 26th but not on the 27th. At 0915 on the 27th, Chatham was torpedoed, while making 9 knots. The action occurred in the Strait of Belle Isle. A large number of the crew of 139 men and of the 430 Canadian and American soldiers in transit were saved by the Mojave and a small Canadian patrol boat. Two planes that spotted survivors aided the rescue effort. Author Samuel Eliot Morison's account provides a footnote which states that 9 or 10 were killed in the torpedo explosion and 16 or 17 were listed as missing. According to Morison, the Mojave went back to Sydney with survivors but failed to radio information on the sinking in the Strait of Belle Isle, or to in-

form anyone that the probable cause was a submarine torpedo.

The slow group, therefore, had received no information on
the fate of the "fast group" earlier in the day. The slow group
took the same routing and at 2132 on the 27th, close to where
Chatham went down, the tanker USS Laramie was hit, and
the SS Arlyn was sunk, both by torpedoes. According to
Morison's account, the Arlyn carried 400 tons of explosives
and her crew "rushed to the boats", leaving the Naval Armed
Guard to swim. The Laramie, AO-16, had been built in the
Cramp shipyard in Philadelphia and commissioned in late
December 1921. She was decommissioned in 1922 and re-
commissioned in 1940. When standing out of Sydney with
the slow group of SG-6, in convoy, she was carrying 361,000
gallons of avgas, 55,000 barrels of oil and general cargo that
included depth charges. Hit on the port side forward, four
men in the crew's quarters were killed and a hole over 40
feet long caused extensive flooding. The port gasoline tank
was opened and the volatile liquid let off explosive fumes.
Down over 35 feet in the bow, with gasoline ankle deep on
the forward gun tubs, it was a miracle that no fire broke out.
Further, Laramie still had power. Steam smothering was effectively employed in the compartments that had not been
ruptured and pumping of liquid cargo corrected the list and
raised the ship's head somewhat. USCGC Mohawk escorted
Laramie back to Sydney for emergency repairs and she later
made it into Boston for repairs that let her resume duties in
the movement of petroleum cargo mainly in the western and
southern Atlantic. She survived the war but not a metals rec-
lamation company in Baltimore in 1947.

In late January 1943, convoy SG-19 stood out of St. John,
Newfoundland for Greenland. There were two merchantmen
and the U.S. Army transport Dorchester in the convoy es-

corted by U.S. Coast Guard cutters Tampa, Escanaba and Comanche. In this period, Coast Guard Cutters were being equipped with radar only when they went in for overhaul. The argument was made that the need for escorts overrode all requirements except the occasion for scheduled ship overhaul. Radar had not yet made the list of essentials in command thinking. An analogy would be that as long as the airplane can fly, we'll keep it flying but when it needs maintenance, then we'll upgrade the instruments.

On 3 February 1943, at 0355 Greenwich Central Time, with Dorchester and convoy SG-19 just 150 miles from landfall at Cape Farewell, Greenland, making 10 knots, a German sub determined that Dorchester, a 351 foot single stack passenger vessel of 5600 tons, was the prize of the group. Approaching from her starboard quarter, the sub torpedoed her. The hull was opened up and Dorchester flooded rapidly through her engine room. She immediately lost way. Two lifeboats were destroyed in the impact. With 14 boats aboard, just two were floated in good order. Her master, who did not survive, ordered abandon ship three minutes after the torpedoing. She went down, bow first, in 25 minutes. USCG Escanaba picked up 56 survivors from one lifeboat and USCG Comanche found another with survivors. Both stayed in the vicinity for several hours picking up men from the water and from rafts, Escanaba rescuing 132 in all and Comanche 97. Survivors told of some boats being launched and foundering from overcrowding. Ship's crew managed to cut loose some of Dorchester's life rafts so that these would float clear when she sank. In frigid waters, with no radio distress call and no effective abandon ship procedure, only 229 of the 904 aboard Dorchester survived. Of the 904, 130 men were in of ship's company and 23 were in the Naval Armed Guard. Many, not recognizing their serious plight, went down with the ship.

The sight of hundreds of dead bodies held up by life jackets was sobering to men on the vessels of the Greenland Patrol that came to assist. Heroism survived. This was the ship whose four embarked chaplains gave up their life jackets (and their lives) for soldiers who had no jackets. Captain Arthur R. Moore's compilation of U.S. Merchant Marine losses during World War II, 1941-1945, credits the German submarine U-223 with the Dorchester's sinking which occurred 150 miles west of Cape Farewell, Greenland. U-223 was later sunk north of Palermo, Sicily by HMS warships Laforey, Tumult, Hambledon and Glencathra.

On 7 February, 1943, in convoy SC-118 out of New York bound for Iceland, troopship SS Mallory with 384 US servicemen, a merchant crew of 77 and an Armed Guard of 34, was torpedoed just south of Greenland. Again, discipline was poor, and with no orders from the bridge, less than half the lifeboats made it into the water. Personnel loss was about 60% of those aboard. According to Sandi Tkaczuk whose grandfather Sam Raffe was a civilian plumber on the Mallory, U-402, captained by Siegfried Freiherr von Forstner, sank the Mallory.

We have provided some sense of the troop convoy picture for 1942 and early 1943. Mallory was the last to go down in this sequence. These convoys in the Atlantic generally took troops and specialists to stations under U.S. control or to the British Isles. These were build-up forces and in the beginning, defense forces for the areas they manned.

Large troopships also moved in convoys that were part of the initial assault force convoys for the Atlantic/Mediterranean counter offensives that began in late 1942. These convoys were not only heavily escorted but they moved across the Atlantic in the vicinity of convoys made up entirely of warships. If you were aboard a vessel moving in conjunction with heavily armed naval task forces to an Atlantic or Mediterranean invasion site, you were pretty safe during the transit. We will return to the subject of some merchantmen losses that occurred in the Mediterranean later in this narrative.

Merchant cargo shipping continued to take a heavy pounding in Atlantic waters. Some U.S. escorts (not the Edison) managed to get some reverse lend lease from the RAF in the form of radar equipment which they jury rigged and then nursed along, because support for it was not available. It was not "officially" part of a U.S. ship's configuration. Edison made one more early fall 1942 round trip to the British Isles in convoy duty and then prepared for new duties. These new duties culminated in the landings in North Africa in November 1942. Not many on board, and certainly not a new Ensign, knew of these plans.

Mentoring

Off watch, my assigned mentor was the Edison's Gunnery Officer, Lieutenant G.S. "Beppo" Lambert. Lambert's tutoring involved having me diagram, from close (nose length) observation, every nook and cranny of Edison's hull. I was assigned to the Ordnance Division when I had no duties as First Division Officer. Beppo wanted me to know my ship before touching a piece of her ordnance. I did get to know the magazines, and was terribly embarrassed later by what I let happen in two of them alongside a dock in Bayonne, New Jersey, when yard workmen one day tested the fire mains. As OOD in port, I met Captain Pearce the next morning at the quarterdeck, coming back from his leave, and he immediately noted that we "seemed low in the water". We were. Two after powder magazines (no ammo, thank God, we had lightered it off at Gravesend Bay) were flooded. The workmen had tested the fire mains all too successfully and I had failed to notice that we had settled into the water because the valves had not been shut off.

Another mentor was Lt. (jg) Craw, who helped me transition from Naval Academy "p-works", exercises in piloting and navigation, to the real thing on Edison. The "p" in p-works stood for "practical". By the time I left the ship two years later, Craw was my XO. He was the first of the reserve officers who were on board when I reported for duty to make it to this high position. The Navy no longer had to send for an Academy trained officer for these billets. (That supply was exhausted, anyway.)

I learned that while the training you received to prepare you for shipboard responsibility helped, it was how fast you could profit by experience, which was everywhere at hand, that would determine if you became a key player. Whether in ASW work in convoys, in shore bombardments, or in defending against enemy aircraft, the ability to make each new experience count influenced your next assignment and your performance in it. Improved escort of convoy results came with new technology, of course. But cohesion in effort, between ships in a command and between men and officers on a ship, came as the result of actual experience.

"Abe" Simon came aboard as an Apprentice Seaman. This man was a successful businessman and family man, yet found reading and writing to be a challenge. Topside aft, underway or in port, his shipmates conducted "school" for Abe. He learned to recognize the key words necessary for his survival, and for his part in the ship's survival. On the bridge, Parris the Signalman, and Davenport the Quartermaster, unselfishly taught me some essentials of communication and navigation. I avoided learning the essentials of card playing for money from Parris. He was usually the only rich man when we made port. The 8-12 morning watch was a particularly good time for a young watch officer underway. When Captain Headden, and later Captain Pearce, emerged in the morning from the skipper's bunkroom on the bridge, after a good night's sleep, the conning officer generally was assigned some new challenge. I recall that one morning coming into Portland, Maine (the rocky coast of Maine), Captain Headden let me (insisted that I) con the ship right on into port. He was gentle in remarking on the bearing change of successive buoys, in making sure that I understood which ones were "on our side" and which marked the center of the channel. He let me take Edison much further in than I thought he would let me go, or for that matter, further than I thought I should be trusted to take her.

Learning the Hard Way

Despite its North Atlantic convoy experience in World War I, the U.S. Navy did not make ASW a priority peacetime training objective in the 1918-1935 period. The naval treaties defining the permissible makeup of the fleets of Britain, the U.S. and Japan, in a stipulated 5-5-3 ratio for capital ships, absorbed most of our Navy's construction attention. Between-wars sonar equipment design and training did not in any way anticipate a future U-boat offensive. Almost the same could be said for amphibious operations, though some constrained budget exercises had been undertaken between wars. The mystery surrounding the radar early warning contacts made on Japanese aircraft descending on Pearl Harbor, and the breakdown in reporting those contacts to someone who could believe, and act, was part of a general lack of knowledge about radar. There were few radar "zealots" among our senior officers in both the Army and the Navy.

There were certainly technology believers. These persons were not likely to be in influential positions. We often failed to motivate that vital second circle of parties who could fan out and spread the word. The U.S. radar development program was very active. The United States armed forces were training people in the use of radar while continuing a very active development and building program. Perhaps the early systems could have used a hand that came up out of the oscilloscope to grab an observer by the neck. Even when tremendously improved systems became available, no groundswell developed to get it, to use it, and to "spread the word" about it. All of this is the burden carried by any outstanding technology developed in layers of military secrecy. We needed both the radar and the believer, and the believer had to be someone in a position to stimulate action. Watching illuminated traces on the early A-scopes and B-scopes did not stimulate missionary effort. Not quite overnight, not quite as fast as we would like to have seen with the advantage of hindsight, SG radar's outstanding results began to generate a consistent murmur about its efficacy. The SG radar's startlingly understandable PPI-scope presentation did, in effect, have the hand that reached out and said, "There it (the target) is. Go get it!" SG radar did the job operationally. Finally, the "word" got out.

I have mentioned the discipline Edison practiced in setting depth charge patterns. I wish I knew who on the Edison to credit for the decision to leave them set on "safe" and train the watch standers constantly to set the firing patterns properly under time pressure. I do know that the same lookouts Edison depended on to watch for ship's topmasts on the distant horizon, or periscopes closer aboard, usually set the patterns for the first attack on a submarine contact. Jack Sotis was an Edison torpedoman in charge of the after lookout watch in one of Edison's watch-in-three rotations. His deck watch and my bridge watch often coincided. Jack Sotis is an example of the type of man who showed constant leadership and the ability to execute. His watch crew could set depth charge patterns in seconds. That watch crew became the standard for other watch crews. We all learned from Jack. Edison came through almost unscathed because of men like Jack Sotis.

An Officer Is Detached

Lieutenant Lambert had been an Edison plank owner. He was the ship's First Lieutenant at commissioning and later became its Gunnery Officer. When he left the Edison, he became the Executive Officer of the USS Buck. This change of duty occurred after Buck's difficulties in August of 1942, described earlier in this Chapter. Lambert graduated with the Naval Academy Class of 1935, where he was a key player on a famous football team with players named Slade Cutter and Buzz Bories.

The photograph reproduced in the next illustration shows Lieutenant Commander Lambert, in the center, facing the camera. I found it in a book called Destroyers, by Anthony Preston, published in 1982 by Galahad Books, a division of A&W Publishers, Inc. This is a beautifully illustrated book. It was a gift to me in 1982 from my employer at that time, Manfred R. Kuehnle. The discovery of this particular photo came in 1997 only after I had begun to prepare this chapter. The photo's caption requires attention. The caption: "An unusually happy scene between the victors and the vanquished as officers of the USS Buck (DD420) interrogate several U-boat survivors." These were not, in fact, U-boat survivors, but were survivors of the Italian submarine, Argento. The Buck had just sunk the Argento and picked up the men pictured. On the left in the photo is Lieutenant Commander M..J. Klein, Commanding Officer of the USS Buck. I discovered other photos later that identified the Italians in the picture as officers of the Italian submarine. The Buck itself fell victim to a U-boat just four days after sinking the Argento.

Illustration 11-LCDR Lambert on USS Buck

Comings, and Goings, and Stayings

Lt. (jg) James Abner "Jake" Boyd, USNA '38, came aboard in early 1942 and later succeeded Lambert as Edison's Gunnery Officer. When Captain Headden left on 28 February 1943, after the landings in North Africa and the securing of Oran, Algeria and its adjacent port of Mers-El-Kebir, Lieutenant Commander Hepburn A. Pearce, USNA '31 became CO and Boyd fleeted up to become XO, replacing Pearce. Dick Hofer, '42, who had reported aboard on 3 January 1942 from graduation of his Naval Academy class of 1942 in December of 1941, succeeded Boyd as Edison's Gunnery Officer. Stanley Craw had been performing navigation duties all along. He often assisted Boyd when the latter was both XO and Navigator. Craw was that valuable officer who could step in and do almost any job on the ship. When an assigned officer was detached for special, temporary duty, Craw could take over. When there was a gap between a departure and an arrival, Craw could take over. I accepted all of this as routine procedure when I was aboard Edison. Later, I realized that very talented people made this possible.

I was not a participant in the planning for personnel assignments. Enlisted men and officers were coming and going and in war duty times there were precious few moments to reflect on either the addition in personnel or the loss of a key person who had orders to another ship. I can relate that I was confident at all time with the leadership and devotion to duty in Edison's officer and enlisted complement. Possibly 500 of the 940 who served aboard came or went when I was there. Only one incident occurred in my 27 months of duty to mar the record and I will go into that in a later chapter. I had to assume that the CO and XO huddled on personnel matters. I can remember that Bridges the Chief Radioman, Jackson, the Chief Fire Controlman, and Kerns the Chief Gunner's Mate,

107

were all overdue for transfer at the same time. Captain Pearce made it clear, in a constructive way, that these dedicated and highly experienced men would not be getting transferred over his signature, but would only be going after he, Captain Pearce himself, had been transferred. This was an affirmation of Pearce's recognition of their talents. It was also an affirmation of Pearce's instinct for Edison's, and his own, survival. Chief Torpedoman Kovalyak was another long serving key person on Edison. Kovalyak doubled as Master-At Arms.

Sharing the personnel-wealth was not a demonstrated virtue in DesLant destroyer commanders. Differing greatly in temperament, the men who commanded these destroyers shared possessive instincts for the best men available.

Chapter Five - Coming to Africa

A New Phase

I am aware that there are times in this narrative, especially when it shifts from present tense to past tense and then back again, that the reader may wish that I had stuck to one perspective or the other, either being there or, looking back. As a participant, I did not at the time have the perspective that I gained from reflections in later years. For example, the preparations for the landings in North Africa opened a new phase in the Edison's life, and mine. I had many questions then about tactics in the North Atlantic, not I must say of any coherent sense of how things might have been different, but just half-formed puzzlement. The human has the capacity to set questions aside, to submerge them slightly, and move on. Going into the next phase of Edison's seagoing operations, I had no sense then that we were about to proceed to the next phase in the war history of the Edison. It was all new to me. I, like my shipmates, just raced to keep up with challenges of new responsibilities.

The Edison entered its preparation phase for the Casablanca operation in October of 1942 configured exactly as it had participated in North Atlantic convoy operations. A few Navy warships, we learned later, had a new radar system installed for this next operation. But for most destroyers, the SC radar was our electronic aircraft detection system. Its antenna, atop the mainmast, reminded one of the wire grid formed by the two frames of the grilling basket that enclose hamburgers for grilling, with the ship's mast replacing the handle. Scale that hamburger wire frame up about five times and you had the SC radar antenna. We used it constantly, but I do not recall that it ever detected enemy target aircraft where that detection made a sufficient difference in Edison's ready condition to be noted as such. Occasionally, and this was useful, it confirmed what we already knew was supposed to happen with respect to our own planes.

That knowledge often came from operations plans. Positive confirmation of aircraft identity with an electronic tool like IFF, meaning Identification Friend or Foe, was not available. Later in the war, our aircraft were outfitted with transponders that would respond to our ground or ship-based radar query signals, but I do not believe that Edison's SC radar system was ever upgraded to this capability while I was aboard. My own impression of SC radar was that it was just one step beyond the CXAM, an experimental radar (the antenna looked like an old fashioned bedspring) which was carried by the USS New York on the 1940 USNA midshipman youngster cruise. Third Class (Youngster) Midshipmen of 1940 were too low on any priority list to be informed about what CXAM was all about. We divined that the X was for experimental.

Edison attempted, as did other destroyers, to make use of the Westinghouse FD fire control radar for detection purposes. I do not recall much success, and was left with the impression that there was little enthusiasm even for the AA target acquisition efficacy of early designs of the FD radar. It could sharpen bearing and range information on prominent objects in low visibility. The FD radar was certainly not designed for detection purposes. In fact, it had to be constantly justified in the eyes of Chief Fire Controlman Jackson for gunnery purposes in competition with optics. Edison did not fire on aircraft with its main battery under night or cloud obscuration conditions. We had no way of knowing, even if we could hear planes above the cloud cover, whether they were friend or foe. And when we were sure by their hostile actions that they were enemy aircraft, even on clear nights when the FD might compete with our optical systems, firing at an enemy aircraft would immediately give our position away to them. That was a tradeoff that Edison would not make. We fired one night off Italy when an enemy aircraft silhouette was clearly revealed by moonlight. This aircraft was not only visually identifiable as an enemy aircraft, but that identification was confirmed because it was in the act of dropping torpedoes pointed where Edison was heading. (We did not hit him. Thanks again to our lookouts, we made an emergency course change, and he did not hit us.) Radar was not a factor for Edison at Casablanca and even though there were some units of a vastly improved radar system deployed at Casablanca, the "newness" factor kept such systems from being fully used. Radar was not a factor at Casablanca.

The sonar was constantly being improved, one small step at a time, in every yard availability period. The greatest difference here though, came as the result of training. The British and the US agreed, with emphasis on "agreed", that training in sonar and sonar tactics was vitally important. In UK ports (the British called it ASDIC) or in US ports, Edison officers and men went to sonar schools at every opportunity. Junior officers went if there was a slot available, but to its credit, the Navy demanded that its senior officers and most proficient sonar operators, be constantly improving their ability to get better performance out of the equipment itself and to use the equipment tactically to greatest advantage. By senior officers, I mean the conning officers, the CO or XO at battle stations, and the qualified senior watch standers underway. A depth charge attack, with good information available, was best executed quickly, so the watch crew often executed the first attack, before the ship could get to battle stations.

Later, during the heat of the Mediterranean campaign, our sonarmen could find the edge of a minefield, a fantastic bonus resulting from the honing of their skills, one that I believe saved Edison on more than one occasion. It also permitted us to penetrate through a minefield and engage in close support shore bombardment.

By the end of October 1942, Edison was not advanced greatly in gunnery proficiency from when I first came aboard. Her baptism here was yet to come. But since I brought up the question of mines, let me anticipate the landings in North Africa by stating that mines advanced to co-equal status in my mind with submarines, as deadly menaces in our operations in the Mediterranean. I am sure that minesweeping had been accomplished in our approaches to rivers and harbors in the UK at the end of a convoy trip, and even at our own bases in Iceland. But I did not see the minesweepers do their thing. Usually, we entered at night and I did not see much of anything, except to marvel that the Captain, the Navigator and the Quartermaster could find their way around in some very complicated water passages in the western part of the British Isles.

The U.S. Navy's high command anticipated mines in the Mediterranean and its North African approaches. We had two classes of U.S. Navy sweepers, an all-metal hull fleet minesweeper AM class and a smaller wooden hull YM class. At North Africa, I can remember the USS Raven, USS Auk and USS Osprey of the fleet class. Lieutenant Commander Joseph Stryker, who had been a watch officer at the Naval Academy when I was a midshipman, commanded one of these fleet class minesweepers. Later, deeper into the Mediterranean, we were helped by British and French sweepers and by a large, motley, fleet of boats of mixed Mediterranean origin newly equipped with sweeping gear and pressed into service. Keeping the Tunisian War Channel clear of mines required round the clock sweeping.

Moored mines, found in large fields in enemy waters in the Mediterranean, were swept using paravanes, one on each quarter of the sweeper, which streamed out from the sweeper and supported cutters which would cut the cables to the moored mines. Most of these mines, when cut from their anchors, would rise to the surface, and float, still a menace but one you would occasionally see (those lookouts again). The minesweeper's service did not end with the end of the conflict in Europe. Mines, as ever-present dangers, survived the end of the war in both the Atlantic and the Pacific. Our mines were a major story in the Inland Sea of Japan.

The Pacific; Tense Months

In Chapter Four, we looked at some convoy difficulties in the North Atlantic in the late summer and fall of 1942. In the Pacific, the great sea battles of the Coral Sea, a defeat (counted by some a strategic victory though we lost the carrier Lexington), and Midway, a victory, took place in this crucial year. In both oceans, the U.S. Navy was reacting to enemy moves. For Midway, we might upgrade that characterization from reaction to counter-initiative. That was the picture at sea. In those same months, the U.S. was preparing to participate in actions where we would take the initiative. The invasion of northwest Africa occupied the Atlantic planners. The Pacific action that I most identify with landings in North Africa, as the beginning of U.S. counteroffensive operations, took place on Guadalcanal in August of 1942.

The Japanese decided in May 1942 to build an airstrip on Guadalcanal. (That decision led to the sea battle of the Coral

Sea.) Ninety miles long and thirty miles wide, this island in the British Solomon Islands had it all-mountains, jungles, quagmires and bugs and daily rainstorms. According to Richard Frank, in his book, "Guadalcanal", published in 1990, Admiral King determined that a base from which the Japanese could raid Fiji, New Caledonia and even Australia must be denied to them. Admiral Nimitz, with area operational responsibility, was of the same persuasion. In the background to an agreed priority for Europe, Admiral King and General Marshall did wonders in providing some landing forces for Pacific operations. On August 7, 1942, under General Vandegrift, 11,000 Marines began to land on Guadalcanal and 6,000 on Tulagi right alongside. On Guadalcanal, a small U.S. perimeter around the airfield was secured by nightfall. The Japanese mounted an all out suicidal assault on the Marines on Tulagi on the night of August 7. The U.S. warships supporting the amphibious assault were forced to leave their shore firing positions that night in the face of a superior Japanese naval force. The U.S. forces ashore were cut off from supplies and reinforcements and had to dig in each night against a series of attacks that lasted until December 1942. After furious sea battles between U.S. and Japanese ships, the U.S. finally got the upper hand locally and Army reinforcements began to come ashore in late 1942 and early 1943. When the last Japanese soldier evacuated in February 1943, our Marine and Army forces could tote up severe losses in dead and wounded in proportion to the number of men involved. (From Guadalcanal in 1942 to Okinawa in 1945, losses during Pacific assault landings would be heavy.) The U.S. did not hold a decisive edge in power in the sea and land effort in the Solomons in 1942. We eked out a victory over a stubborn foe. The foot soldiers labored under the physical strain of weather and terrain foreign to most Americans, and under the mental strain of being outnumbered on land and at times cut off from their lifeline, the supply and reinforcement train. King, Nimitz and Marshall made a fateful, courageous and correct decision about where to take a stand during a period in which the War for Europe would take precedence. The epitaph that a Marine etched on a mess kit placed on a buddy's grave in a Guadalcanal burial field says it all.

"And when he gets to Heaven, To St. Peter he will tell: One more Marine reporting, sir—I've served my time in Hell."

The Atlantic/Mediterranean Land Situation

We have dealt with actions at sea in the North Atlantic and touched on how the German submarines extended their reach to all parts of the Atlantic. The war on land in Europe had resulted in disaster for the Britain. Then, Rommel's Afrika Corps began to roll the British back toward the Suez from Libya in North Africa. After the capitulation of the French armed forces in France in 1940, a neutral French government was set up at Vichy, France, under Marshal Petain, a World War I hero. The Vichy French and the North African French, in Algeria and Morocco, and the West African French at Dakar, began a long slow dance with Germany, Britain, the U.S., and with their own free French nationals in Britain. United States military forces became involved in the Mediterranean part of this slow waltz. The French Naval Base at Toulon was under the nominal control of Vichy. It was kept in a non-threatening role to Hitler, yet its French Fleet units managed to refrain from fighting for him. Dancing together were French leaders who favored the Germans, leaders who tolerated the Germans, and leaders who waited for any opportunity to fight back. DeGaulle emerged in Britain as the leader of the French who had not surrendered and would not cooperate with the Germans and who would take part in covert and later overt operations against Hitler's forces in territory that Hitler actively controlled in France. The British identified with General DeGaulle's objectives, to remove Hitler from his occupied territory and defeat Germany. But in a way too complex to cover in this story, DeGaulle was sometimes an impediment to the strategy that the Allies practiced with "neutral" France.

When Hitler opened hostilities against Russia in mid-1941, he could no longer make territorial subjugation of French interests in North Africa a prime objective and did not need to as long as these forces appeared to stay neutral. The U.S. and Britain, after the fall of France, began a "good guy, bad guy" relationship with the Vichy French. The U.S. was the good guy, and for the balance of 1940 and all of 1941 up until Pearl Harbor, trafficked with the French under the eyes of the Germans. For most of that period there was no doubt insofar as North Atlantic convoy operations were concerned that hostilities with Germany had already begun. Roosevelt was the consummate strategist in this matter, and Churchill went along. Roosevelt, almost alone among his advisers, wanted the second front that Stalin was begging for to either begin in Western Europe in 1943, or failing that, in Africa in 1942. When the British made the strongest case that the invasion of Western Europe could not commence in 1943 and would have to be put back to 1944, the leadership discussions, political and military, came back to Roosevelt's idea to begin a second front in North Africa.

Some of the reading I have done for this story suggests that landings in North Africa were just as much Churchill's idea. Churchill knew that the top U.S. military leaders, who favored direct assault across the channel at the latest in 1943, would argue to shift their forces to the Pacific if forceful action in the Atlantic theater did not seem to be developing. Churchill agreed with the direct channel assault, but in the light of previous continental defeats suffered "on his watch" with insufficient forces, wanted to wait until the cross channel effort could be made with overwhelming forces. So Churchill may have made it appear that he was giving in to Roosevelt by approving the North African invasion. The capture of Tobruk by Rommel probably tipped the scales finally. It was good that political leaders could argue things out and then proceed. Compared with World War I, the second great world conflict became a model of cooperation among the Allied leaders.

The Discussion Period Is Over

The decision to proceed on the North African plan was made in July 1942. Roosevelt's decision to send modest relief supplies to help both Europeans and native Africans in North Africa, cut off as they were from most manufactured goods and some commodities by commerce that emphasized military supplies, paid off. Roosevelt's courting of French political and military leaders in Africa paid off. They were a mixed bag as to their persuasions and their loyalties, but just knowing who they were and what they believed helped the U.S. succeed in a role that often confounded it. In addition to General DeGaulle, French military/political figures with names like Darlan, Laval, Giraud, Weygand, Boisson, Nogues and Juin appeared in important roles. I have sliced through an enormous amount of political intrigue here and would refer the reader to the early pages of Chapter I of Morrison's Volume II, Operations in North African Waters. This Volume is the second listed in Morison's History of United States Naval Operations in World War II but was actually written before his Volume I which covered the North Atlantic. This occurred because Morison himself was embarked on the USS Brooklyn for TORCH, the code name the Allies gave to the North African landings. Morison likely did not want to set aside his first hand observations before returning to the geographically more challenging Volume I which dealt with The Battle of the Atlantic.

When France fell in 1940, Roosevelt sent Admiral Leahy as his Ambassador to the Vichy regime. After Pearl Harbor, Roosevelt recalled Leahy for "discussions" and then made the Admiral his own Chief of Staff for the balance of the war. Both Morison in Volume II of his History and Anne O'Hare McCormick in the New York Times, complimented Roosevelt for buying precious time (my words) in finding a way to conduct a non-threatening relationship with Vichy. I wonder how the press and the Congress would react if a U.S. President today made such an ambassadorial appointment as Leahy to the Vichy French. Would the U.S. manage to sound one voice (almost one voice, because some isolationists were still being heard in 1940 and 1941) as our people did 55 years ago?

For, Against, and Neutral

Summarizing, the Vichy government was in control of Tunisia, Algeria and French Morocco. There were no German occupation forces in these countries and no evident De-Gaullist core group. Libya, the Italian colony between Tunisia and an Egypt still under British control, was the scene of land warfare between forces of German General Rommel and the British General Auchinleck, who checked the Germans at the First Battle of El Alamein on July 2, 1942. Southern France, including the French Naval Base at Toulon was neutral under Vichy. Spain, with its Spanish Morocco, astride the Straits of Gibraltar, was neutral. Malta, after its heroic defense, survived to remain a critical base for the Allies. The British naval base at Gibraltar was the western anchor of Britain's Gibraltar-Suez lifeline, a lifeline that had been virtually closed since 1941. Italy, the Balkans, Greece, Crete and Libya were under Axis control. General Eisenhower would be the overall commander of the North Africa operation, with Admiral Cunningham RN as Allied Naval Commander. November 8, 1942 would be D-day.

U.S. Amphibious Forces

After the hiatus in major fleet training exercises that followed World War I, the U.S. Navy renewed amphibious training operations in 1933 with the creation of the Fleet Marine Force. The components of this Force were the 2nd Marine Brigade stationed in San Diego and the 1st Marine Brigade stationed on the Atlantic Coast. Each year from 1934, a training operation was conducted at Culebra Island east of Puerto Rico. This training included naval gunfire support. In 1941, Adm. E. J. King, Commander In Chief Atlantic Fleet (CincLant), was in charge of this exercise. For the first time Higgins landing craft were used in lieu of ships' boats. In his Volume II of History of US Naval Operations in World War II, author Samuel Eliot Morison records:

"No special landing craft for tanks and vehicles had yet been constructed, but their prototype, a 100-ton steel barge with an improvised ramp, propelled by four Navy launches secured one to each corner, transported to the beach tanks swung out from the ships' holds."

" After the fall of France the 1st Marine Brigade was held in a state of readiness at Guantanamo, and expanded to the

1st Division, USMC early in 1941. A part of this division was sent to Iceland. The rest of it on 13 June 1941 was combined with the 1st Infantry Division US Army, which had already enjoyed some amphibious training as the Emergency Striking Force, commanded by Major General Holland M. Smith USMC. General Smith formed a staff of Army, Navy and Marine Corps officers and continued training. After sundry name changes and reorganizations, during which both the Marines and the 1st Division were released for other duties, this Emergency Striking Force emerged as the Amphibious Force of the Atlantic Fleet."

Amphibious Operations by Type

There are two generic amphibious operations. One is shore to shore, which is pretty much what a substantial part of the Normandy landings turned out to be. The other is shore to ship, a transit, and then ship to shore. That describes the North African landings in 1942. In the training phase for what became TORCH, because decisions did not always filter down rapidly, the U.S. personnel were training for an impending operation expected to be shore to shore. The landing craft people did not have their training objective shifted to ship to shore until late August 1942.

A further distinction occurs in loading for the ship to shore amphibious operation. The vessels can be "combat loaded" or "transport loaded." The combat loaded ships would be the first ones in action as D-day and H-hour arrived for the North African invasion. The transport loaded ships could be off loaded with boats and lighters but worked best when we secured the port so that they could go alongside a dock and unload specialty troops and cargo. While in close proximity, an escort ship's personnel could tell which of his own forces' ships in the convoy had been combat loaded and which transport loaded. An enemy submarine captain, through his periscope a few thousand yards away, is not likely to make such a distinction. Both types would look to him like promising targets.

The combat loaded ships carried landing craft, crew for the landing craft, Army personnel making the landing and the vehicles necessary in the assault phase. For TORCH, the following landing craft were used:

(1) the original Higgins boat, 36-foot, plywood, with a square bow, Landing Craft Personnel (LCP).

(2) the LCP, (R) for Ramped, 36-foot, metal; the LCPs accommodated 36 troops, with a crew of three

(3) the LCV, 36-foot, metal, V for Vehicles; had a larger bow ramp than the LCP (R)

(4) the LCM, M for Mechanized, 50-foot, heavier metal, for one tank; an early model

The original plywood Higgins boats were holed easily on rocks and were used sparingly after the North African experience. Also, from this event on, ramps were a requirement to minimize troop exposure in the treacherous moments of hitting the beach, or shallow water, with heavy packs.

Close in Support; A Role for Destroyers

We are including only enough information in the foregoing paragraphs to cover the amphibious assault phase, which is the phase in which the destroyer played such a major part in World War II. The destroyer's role is our central theme and will be developed as the story goes along. It needs to be mentioned here that the minesweepers, in the initial phase of a landing operation, usually had sweeping duties that were even closer to the enemy guns than the destroyers. Often, just to defend themselves, the fleet type minesweepers would fire back at hostile shore batteries. But their mission was to clear the area of mines so that the fire support ships could get in.

The value of the destroyer in supporting assault landings could not have been realized without the communications teams that went ashore with the assault troops. Those teams, in effect, started the computer problem for the Edison's 5"/38 cal. gun battery and fire control. The shore parties furnished the initial land firing coordinates, observed the shell impact points, and then supplied corrective "spots", in, or out so many yards, and right or left so many yards, or mils (milliradians) if using angles for azimuth correction. Shore to ship communication skills developed only after some early frustrations. Such skills were largely absent during the North African landings.

At Little Creek, Virginia, an amphibious signal school was set up for Army Signal Corps and Navy Communications personnel. As it turned out, that school and Casablanca's successes and failures set the stage for how ship to shore fire control party communications would be continually improved in all subsequent landing operations.

The Navy shore fire contribution to the Army landings in North Africa and the Mediterranean perimeter had its origins in all-Navy exercises. One procedure evolved from scout planes that had been launched from cruisers or battleships. Their pilot or observer would "call fire" from their parent ships to support Marines in landing exercises. In the other teaming of forces, the intelligence might come from those same intrepid scout planes and the troops supported would still be Marines, but the weapons delivery, instead of shore bombardment from Navy ships, would be bombs from carrier based naval aircraft.

The adaptation of Navy weapons delivery to Army landings at Sicily, Salerno, Anzio and Southern France involved mainly changes in communications for the naval participants. The stage was set at North Africa where a naval aviator, an aviation radioman, and an SCR-193 radio set mounted on a jeep constituted one naval air liaison party. There were four such for TORCH and their original task was to obtain carrier-based air support for ground forces. These teams evolved into naval gunfire support teams with a destroyer or cruiser furnishing the firepower instead of the carrier. The first radios would not survive salt water dousing in the "swimming" stage when the landing craft could not make it to dry beach. In later Mediterranean landings, the team became mostly Army, with a spotting officer, a radioman and a man to crank the power unit to keep the radio going. When possible, an NLO (Navy Liaison Officer) completed the party. These came to be called a Shore Fire Control Party, or SFCP for short.

Assembly for TORCH

There were three Naval Task Forces.

The Eastern Naval Task Force, a Royal Navy operation, carried 23,000 British and 60,000 U.S. troops, all mounted from United Kingdom ports. Major General C.W. Ryder, USA, commanded the ground forces. Object: To capture Algiers, the capital of Algeria. The Central Naval Task Force, another Royal Navy operation, carried 39,000 U.S. ground troops, mounted from the UK. The troops were under the command of Major General L.R. Fredenhall, USA. Object: To capture Oran, Algeria. Militarily, these were larger operations than the Western Naval Task Force that proceeded to the northwest African coast on the Atlantic to take Casablanca. The Eastern and Central forces were more certain to see the Luftwaffe. They did not face a strong French Navy element though Toulon, just across the Mediterranean, contained such an element. Those interested in a full account of the part that North African operations played in World War II would want to pursue a more extensive examination of the subject than we will give here. Names like Eisenhower, Patton, Montgomery and Rommel became famous in this theater.

Our story will cover the Western Naval Task Force because Edison was part of that force. Here, the Sea Force as well as the landing force, were U.S. forces. Landings by the three Naval Task Forces were scheduled for the same time and were actually executed within minutes of each other.

The Western Force, to be escorted by the U.S. Navy, carried 35,000 US troops. The Western Naval Task Force, whose duty it was to deliver the landing forces safely to the beaches, was under the command of Rear Admiral H. Kent Hewitt. Hewitt had already been in command of the Amphibious Force, Atlantic Fleet. Beginning 1 September, 1942, Admiral Hewitt and his staff prepared for TORCH at the Nansemond Hotel, Ocean View, Virginia, near Norfolk. Transports Atlantic Fleet consisted of six divisions and included troop transports and cargo ships. To be embarked as personnel trained in the handling of landing craft were three thousand Navy and Coast-Guardsmen from Little Creek VA and Solomons Island, Maryland.

The Western Task Force units to be put ashore would be commanded by Major General George Patton who was appointed commander of the Western Landing Force of the Army on 24 August 1942. This Force's objective was to make Morocco, with its command of the Atlantic and of the approaches to the Mediterranean, an Allied bastion. This was also the western flank of a North Africa from which the Allies intended to expel all German forces. The core troops were initially the U.S. Army 9th Infantry Division and units of the 2nd Armored Division. A reinforced Regiment of the 9th Infantry Division, embarked in one of the six transport divisions, was sent to Great Britain to join the 1st Infantry Division for the assault near Algiers. The 3rd Infantry Division U.S. Army and a battalion of the 67th Armored Regiment joined the Landing Force under Patton's overall command. Intensive training at Solomons Island for day and night landings, and gunnery at Bloodsworth Island nearby, were nearly every day occurrences after the first of August 1942. Yet the time provided for this was later assessed to be about one third of the time needed.

Author Morison has summarized the challenge of amphibious operations as requiring "an organic unity rather than a temporary partnership". This was a tough challenge for the U.S. Army and the U.S. Navy in 1942, and very likely would be again today (1998).

I have given more space to the identification of Army units than a naval tale might require, but we will see these units as the nucleus of the entire effort to retake the Mediterranean. Some of these same units would later be part of the Normandy assault. The Army folk might object to my characterization, but these Army men and their leaders became the crack marines of the Atlantic/Mediterranean war.

Guadalcanal, in August 1942, was the first amphibious operation conducted by U.S. combat forces in forty-five years. North Africa was a huge jump upward in size and scope. It was bold. It was a fundamental projection of a force tasked to have and to hold territory. The transit involved 4,000 miles through wolfpack seas. It also involved some sleight of hand efforts by three U.S. World War I destroyers and their embarked forces to take the terrain-given strengths of the defenders and turn them to our advantage.

German intelligence knew that something was up. They never figured out the specific intentions of the three Naval Task Forces.

The Western Naval Task Force

The Task Groups of the Western Naval Task Force assembled in U.S. East Coast ports and in Bermuda. Once underway, Rear Admiral. Hewitt also became Commander Task Force 34. The Southern Attack Group of this force was to land at Safi, the southernmost penetration point of the Task Force, 150 miles from Casablanca. The Northern Attack Group was to effect a landing at Mehedia, north and east of Casablanca and much closer to it. Mehedia's U.S. ground commander did not arrive in the U.S. TORCH planning and training area until 19 September 1942. He came from England, where he had been on Royal Navy Admiral Mountbattens's staff as liaison for TORCH planning. His name was Brigadier General Lucian K. Truscott Jr. The Northern and Southern transport groups departed from Norfolk on 23 October 1942. The Center Attack Group would effect landings at Fedala, closest to Casablanca. Edison was assigned to this group. This group left Norfolk on October 24, 1942. The heavy fire support warships left Casco Bay, Maine the same day. Rendezvous of these underway groups was made at sea on the 26th and the Air Group carriers joined from Bermuda on the 28th.

Edison was part of the transport screen during the transit from Norfolk to Fedala, October 24 to November 7, 1942. Overall, there were thirty Benson class destroyers in various assignments, plus four single stack destroyers just a year or so older than the Bensons. The World War I 4-pipers Cole, Bernadou and Dallas had special missions; the first two of these had been physically modified to show no stacks at all.

A detailed list showing the assignments of Western Naval Task Force destroyers is shown on page 140 of Theodore Roscoe's Naval Institute book titled United States Destroyer Operations in World War II. Battleships Massachusetts, New York and Texas, fleet carrier USS Ranger and four carriers converted from tanker hulls, and seven cruisers played important roles in the all-U.S. Western Task Force. A minesweeping group and a minelaying group were in the force.

The USS Ranger (CV-4) and Four Converted Tankers

Converted tankers? In the context of 1943's Fast Carrier Task Forces, Pacific, the Ranger plus four tanker-hulls converted to "jeep" carriers sounds almost like a planner's afterthought. It was not. Consider that the Japanese had already sunk the carriers Lexington, Yorktown, Wasp and Hornet, and had damaged Saratoga and Enterprise. The later flood of World War II's Essex class carriers had yet to emerge from the shipyards. Therefore, Ranger, Sangamon, Suwannee, Chenango, and Santee can be seen as offering the Western Naval Task Force the Navy's precious reserve of available carriers.

In like vein, the Wichita, Tuscaloosa, Brooklyn, Savannah, Philadelphia, Augusta (Hewitt's flagship) and Cleveland were a formidable group of cruisers which would have been immediately welcomed by Admiral Nimitz in the Pacific. Fleet Oilers Chemung, Winooski, Housatonic, Merrimack and Kennebec were part of a vital supply train that could fuel oil-hungry destroyers underway.

U.S. men of war went to North Africa's Barbary Coast shortly after the U.S. was born. The British have been pre-eminent on the navigable waters of the Mediterranean all during the years of Empire.

The British Navy would spearhead the attack in the Mediterranean. The Americans would land on the Atlantic shore of Morocco. After its assembly at sea, the size of the seaborne force that my eyes could see stretched from horizon to horizon. I knew, too, from the planning documents, that I could see only a fraction of the immense Western Task Force. En route, Edison was part of ComDesron 13's inner screen, protecting the Center Attack Group Transports. We were in company with the destroyers Bristol, Woolsey, Tillman, Boyle and Rowan.

Define an objective and bring overwhelming force to bear.
Would the French fight? The answer turned out to be, "yes", and "no". We were to withhold fire, but when fired on, the signal "Play Ball" told us that the French were resisting. The plan has to be sound, and the leadership flexible enough to know when the plan called for improvisation. Five U.S. subs were to reconnoiter off shore for weather and to observe movement of local ships and forces that might knowingly or unknowingly impede the operation. The submarine, USS Shad, was to mark the departure point for boats in the Fedala landing forces. A U.S. destroyer sent ahead to find Shad the night before the landings could only determine that she was not there, and on the spot replaced her for this duty.

Few of these considerations entered the mind of an Ensign on his way to Africa on a U.S. destroyer late in 1942. Admiral Hewitt assembled 150 senior naval and military officers involved in the expedition at Norfolk on the day before departure. Many of them were finding out for the first time what TORCH was all about. Most of the rest of us began to find out after our ships cleared Hampton Roads.

COMING TO AFRICA

A Sea Transit Log

At this point, the Edison began its escort duties to make sure the transport ships got safely to Casablanca. Some of our charges were loaded with troops; some had military cargo and some carried oil. The author picks up an escort of his own for this historic trip. Assisting me in chronicling the trip to North Africa is Lt. (jg) Edward K. Meier, a shipmate in 1942, 1943 and 1944 on Edison. Ed became been a career lawyer in Wilmette, Illinois. He is (1998) retired in Vero Beach, Florida. Ed joined the Edison as an Ensign on 29 December 1941 and was a close friend during the time we shared on Edison. The historian's accounts of the sea journey to North Africa are all too brief on the transit of this, the largest armada of its kind ever assembled for a major sea voyage. Some even marked the 24 Oct. - 8 Nov., 1942 trip to Casablanca as "uneventful."

In my own reading of Ed Meier's reflections that follow, I see that many fundamentals that occurred to Ed on that trip escaped me entirely.

All dates in this transit sequence are late October and early November 1942. With almost no editing, then, here is Lieutenant (junior grade) Ed Meier's day by day view of events.

The 24th. Got underway at 7:30 this morning and spent the entire morning and part of the afternoon getting the convoy organized. Our group consists of about 50 ships, from battleships and carriers on down to minelayers. We have about 20 large troop transports with us, each carrying many tanks, invasion barges etc. It is the biggest aggregation I have ever seen. The Edison is patrolling the starboard bow of the inner screen and I have the mid-watch.

The 25th. A radio broadcast today reported that Admiral Darlan is now in Casablanca reviewing the French Fleet.

Evidently the French have quite a sizeable fleet down there and we probably will have quite an exciting time taking the place. I have been reading an intelligence report on Casablanca concerning its strategic importance to the Allies, the geographical and topographical layout and defenses, the type of ships and planes to be encountered and the makeup and psychological attitude of the people residing there.

The 26th. Three large cruisers and a couple more destroyers joined our group at daybreak today. Later on this afternoon, another large force consisting of two or three battleships, three or four aircraft carriers and several more destroyers also joined us. As the picture gradually takes form, this certainly is an undertaking of tremendous dimensions. The Navy Dept. has seen to it that this is no half-baked invasion. It ought to be sufficient to overcome the resistance the French are evidently planning to make. We are all in highest hopes that we can take them by surprise and quickly overcome their resistance, but naturally it is very probable that they already have information that we are coming in which case a pitched battle will result.

We are now in the Gulf Stream and it is quite warm. I stood my watch this afternoon in shirt sleeves and the temperature in the shade was 78 degrees F. It rained intermittently, but in general it was a pleasant day.

The 27th. My thoughts are with Mom and Pop a good deal of the time and I'm hoping and praying that all is going along well with Pop. It is a week and a half now since the operation and he should soon begin to show signs of considerable improvement. But from the extent of the surgical disturbance made necessary, it is necessarily a slow painful recovery. Pop has always been so fine and regular that it is a shame that this had to happen to him, but I am sure surgery was the only way out and that he can still enjoy life despite his physical handicap.

The weather the last few days has been wonderful and the nights lovely and balmy. Station keeping in the size convoy we have is quite a trick, due mainly to the large number of escort ships and the small sectors assigned to each. Particularly at night is station keeping difficult, but fortunately we have a full moon which helps out considerably. We are now northeast of Bermuda and from information we have (learned), a heavy force of battleships, cruisers and carriers will join us one of these days from that port.

(Comment: Ed Meier had been accustomed to the North Atlantic convoys in which three or four modern destroyers covering the entire 360 degrees around a convoy was considered a strong escort group. Also, from Bermuda for TORCH came just carriers and their screen. The battleships and cruisers had, in the main, already joined, but Admiral Hewitt's deceptive paths to North Africa required every group to make course changes designed to mask the actual destination. The groups were generally not in sight of one another, and proceeded as though each had its own destination. Author Samuel Eliot Morison, embarked on Brooklyn, stated that her pitometer log showed over 4,500 nautical miles for the 4,000 mile trip. If a cruiser's pit log showed 4,500 miles, any destroyer's log probably hit 5,000. For this reason, the "cans" fueled early in the trip and once again just before the landings so that no destroyer skipper would be feeling miserly about fuel as the action began.)

The 28th. The watches were dogged today and all in all I was on the bridge 12 hours, 00-0400, 1200-1600 and 2000-2400, besides 1 3/4 hours of general quarters. We have been having GQ every day from 9:30 to 11:15 for training purposes. The weather continues to be balmy and warm and I'm developing quite a suntan. Rain squalls, however, are very prevalent and are equally unpredictable, coming up in a moment's notice even when the sun is shining brightly. We were joined today with a task group of 4 aircraft carriers, plus additional escorting destroyers. Two converted 4-stackers, carrying commandos also joined us. These ships are heavily loaded with troops, have guns and masts removed. The plan is to run these ships up the river as far as they will go, run them aground and have the troops disembark.

(Comment: The four stackers were the Bernadou and the Cole. They had the stripped down silhouette. I believe Ed meant to note that they had stacks and masts removed. Each had specific objectives in the Safi landings; the Bernadou was to nose its bow onto a beach. It was the Dallas, not stripped down, at Mehedia, which pushed its way up a shallow, twisting river for quite a ways to reach its objective. Though we will stick mostly with the Edison during the fighting period of 8-11 Nov., we will also summarize the exploits of these four stackers and some other destroyers.)

The 29th. We've surely got a real fleet with us now - 3 battleships including the new Massachusetts, about 5 to 10 cruisers and about 30 destroyers plus plenty of transports and auxiliaries. Hughes said (that is Ensign Jim Hughes, from West Roxbury, Massachusetts) we should steam right up to Berlin; but even with all this stuff we may have a tough time if the French and Germans want to put up a stiff fight.

Spent quite a bit of time today studying maps and operational plans for getting our troops ashore and bombarding shore gun emplacements. We are to go within 3 or 4 miles of shore, just north of Fedala, which is some 10 miles north of Casablanca. We will be the central part of 3 landing groups, one of the other two forces being north of us and the other being south of us and south of Casablanca. The troops after disembarking will converge on Casablanca.

The 30th. Today I was promoted officially to Lieutenant junior grade. Can't say that I feel like an astute naval officer but I do think I'm getting the hang of things aboard and the extra $20 per month may come in handy. The Captain (Headden) has signed the promotion papers and tomorrow Dr. Kemp will give me the necessary physical examination. All the destroyers and cruisers refueled while underway today. This is a very ticklish maneuver and it was fortunate that the sea was calm. I have just returned from watch and I can't remember when the sea has been calmer except possibly that night last February when we made submarine attacks (attacks on submarines) just about all night. A couple destroyers have had sound contacts, but it is my personal opinion that they were not submarines. The chances are however, that we will run into subs rather soon.

The 31st. Took the physical examination today and everything was found to be OK so I guess I'm a full-fledged J.G. A battle station has now been assigned to me and I will be in charge of secondary control back aft. In this capacity I will have charge of No. 3 and No. 4 guns in local control. We are now southwest of the Azores on course 135 True. The plot seems to be to head directly for Dakar and then change course north to Casablanca in order to throw off their defenses.

The next picture shows Ed Meier one promotion later in his naval career.

Illustration 12-Ed Meier, Lieutenant USNR

The 1st. Nothing of much consequence happened today and it was a beautiful warm, sunny Sunday with the temperatures ranging in the mid-70s. It was holiday routine and we did not have our usual general quarters at 9:30. Planes are constantly overhead ranging out on wide patrols during the day. At 9:00 this evening we picked up an R.D.F. (Radio Direction Finder) bearing and on investigation by the Bristol it was found to be a Portuguese man of war operating out of the Azores. Our prearranged plan was to take neutral ships in for security, but for some reason we let this one go.

The 2nd. Stood the 4-8 watch this morning and the colors at daybreak were exquisite, ranging from deep purple thru various shades of red, blue and gray. The sea remains very calm as it has thru the entire trip. R.D.F bearings, presumably from submarines, continue to come in, and altho several of the ships have dropped depth charges, I rather doubt that any of the ships have had bona fide sound contacts.

Mail came aboard today from one of the destroyers which left the States a day after we. It was certainly good to hear from home and friends. In checking our position on the chart I find that we are considerably south of Casablanca and Fedala but only some 400 or 500 miles from the coast of Rio Diorio, Africa. Everything is going along smoothly altho hell is liable to pop loose just about any time in the form of submarines. This afternoon we took a wide sweep to starboard of the convoy to limit of visibility, returning to the convoy at dusk.

The 3rd. This afternoon we were to have towed a towing spar down the starboard side of the convoy to give the convoy target practice, but it got so rough that this was impossible. We pick up R.D.F. bearings frequently indicating that there are U-boats in the vicinity but since the bearings do not also give us range, we are helpless to track them down. We try to get cross bearings on them with other ships and in these cases we can approximate the distance and make an investigation.

The 4th. Stood the 0000-0400 watch this morning. What a grueling watch it was and the sea was plenty rough too. I had the conn at 0300 and we were supposed to have a course change from 355 degrees to 335 degrees. We changed course and seemed to be far out of position with all the other ships that had apparently not changed course. We found out later that they had canceled the change and had not notified us. It put us in a dangerous position since visibility was very poor and we had to do all our piloting by radar bearings and ranges.

(Comment: It was rare for this to occur when we were in company with an all Navy Task Force using Navy signals and communications. This did happen frequently when we were in merchant convoys using the British MERSIGS communications.)

Had typhoid and tetanus shots yesterday afternoon and apparently it hit my stomach and I came very close to being sick on the bridge tonight. It is starting to get rough.

The 5th. The arm still bothers me pretty much today and the stomach to seems to be upset. I didn't get sick but came pretty darn close to it. The sea has been quite rough and this has added to my discomfort. Stood the 8-12 watch last night and the convoy came into contact with two separate Portuguese ships. Instead of taking them into a friendly port, as was the prearranged plan, the boarding parties gave them instructions not to use their radios and sent them on courses so as not to interfere with our operations. I'm not quite satisfied with the way this was handled as these ships could very well give away our position and prejudice our safety and the outcome of our mission. (Author Samuel Eliot Morison stated that one or two had prize crews placed on board to prevent their broadcasting our position.)

The 6th. We refueled this morning and now have ample fuel supply for our operations. This evening we assumed base course 116 degrees and will probably take this course right into Casablanca. I was just thinking today that 3 weeks ago next Sunday I attended Church service at the Wilmette Baptist Church with Beck and Don and day after tomorrow our assault group will attack the city of Casablanca, Africa. It's hard to step from one type of peaceful life right into the most antagonistic and offensive type, but this is war and I was lucky to get home at all. Tomorrow morning we will undoubtedly go into Condition Two watches (watch and watch, 4 on and 4 off). From midnight on we will be at general quarters. Most of the officers and men are looking forward to this thing with a great deal of anticipation.

The 7th. We practiced our new battle station watches all morning and at noon, the word was passed that all hands should try to get as much rest as possible before the assault. Yesterday, Dr. Kemp put out a circular letter to the effect that everyone should take a shower and put on clean clothes before a battle as a precautionary measure against infection in case of a wound. I was back in the crew's compartment this afternoon and it resembled a fraternity house before a big dance. All hands were really scrubbing down. At midnight we go to battle stations for the assault, fingers crossed.

The 8th. Boy, what a day. The first troops hit the beach about 4:00 a.m. and immediately search lights were turned on by the French, but these were quickly extinguished by our machine gun fire. About 5:30 the shore batteries opened up and from then until about 9:00, our ships continuously laced the shore with heavy fire. The battleships and cruisers certainly did a job on those shore emplacements and a steady stream of fire poured from them. During this time we were out about 5 miles screening the transports. About 10:30 (a.m.) After the shore batteries had been silenced, another opened up at Fedala, which the Edison and two other destroyers silenced. We came in about 1 mile off the beach to do this. This battery had been firing on our troops just northwest of Cape Fedala and was really slicing them up.

About this time we received word that the French Army did not wish to fight. The (French) Navy however was a different story and at 11:00, the Brooklyn, Augusta, two other cans (if it has not come up before, destroyers were also tin cans usually shortened to cans) and the Edison, lit into a French cruiser and two destroyers. Our fire severely damaged them all and we came out unscathed. But about 4 other of our destroyers were damaged by shell fire from the beach.

Several shells hit quite close to us and shrapnel hit our port side. One shell sent a pillar of water skyward not more than 500 yards from our port bow. This afternoon, our cruisers severely damaged one more French cruiser and sunk or beached two destroyers. One French corvette was sunk by one of our destroyers.

We're all hoping that all goes well for our troops ashore and that they have already taken the Fedala airfield. Additional U.S. planes are due here tomorrow. Tonight we are screening the troopships which are moving close in to shore. The French Fleet has put up a gallant fight and for a while we had a real engagement.

The 9th. One French cruiser attempted to get out of Casablanca Harbor this morning and two of our cruisers drove her back in with gunfire; but other than this there was little excitement. The French Army has expressed a very cooperative attitude, but the Navy has altogether refused to discuss any peace terms. Therefore, tomorrow morning at 8:00 our battleships and cruisers will steam back and forth across the mouth of the harbor and reduce the ship and harbor installations to a shambles. We do not like to do this, but it is necessary since we need the harbor for disembarking troops and materials.

German planes were overhead today, but made no attack. Possibly tomorrow, since we heard over the radio that they did attack our ships and troops in Algiers. We are now in watch and watch which is plenty tough physically.

The 10th. Safi and Fedala fell to our forces yesterday and radio reports say that Algiers and Oran, together with their airfields fell to American and British forces. As yet we have not taken Casablanca altho city officials have already expressed their willingness to capitulate. Probably the only reason we have not already gone in is the resistance of the French Fleet and shore batteries in the harbor and vicinity. This morning, two French destroyers attempted to get out of the harbor. Immediately the Edison followed by the Augusta and 3 other destroyers piled right in at 30 knots and made a vicious attack. All in all we fired 369 rounds of 5inch shells at them and probably seriously damaged one of them. The Edison did most of the firing and drew most of the fire from the French ships and shore batteries. They had us straddled twice and shells were dropping in the water all around us, the nearest only about 100 yards away. It was really too close for comfort, but very exciting. Later this afternoon, the French Fleet having refused our ultimatum, our dive bombers attacked the harbor and we could see huge columns of smoke from the shore batteries.

The 11th. At 7:15 this morning I was aroused from sleep to the tune of beep-beep-beep-all hands man your battle stations. Apparently one or two of the battle scarred units of the French Fleet were intending to slip out of the harbor again.

This time we were all set to finish off the fleet, shore emplacements and the whole damn harbor and harbor facilities if necessary. All ships were fully ready and were starting to group for the coup de grace when word came over the TBS to cease fire. (I cannot help but notice that Ed, with this command of prose at age 27, under fire, used the word "coup de grace" for the French finale-and how about me at 77 ready with the word "finale"!) No one knew why, but later on over the radio, we learned that the naval authorities had reconsidered and had thrown in the sponge and were ready to confer on peace terms. It surely was about time.

This evening about 8:00, three ships were torpedoed: Hewes, a transport, sunk; and the Winooski, a tanker, and the Hambleton, a 4-stack destroyer, damaged. They certainly caught us with our pants down and in a very cocky mood.

(Comment: My records and my memory show Hambleton as a Benson/Livermore/Bristol class destroyer. She shows in Theodore Roscoe's United States Destroyer Operations in World War II as DD 455.)

The 12th. We escorted the Hambleton as she was towed into Casablanca today and got within a mile of the town. It is really a very pretty place, with modern buildings all very well kept. They are all white or of a light color, hence the name Casablanca. The Jean Bart and several destroyers and a cruiser and several merchantmen could be seen aground in the harbor.

This afternoon late we went into the transport area at Fedala to refuel from a tanker and at 5:45 as we were alongside her, two of the transports were torpedoed not more than 300 or 400 yards from us. General Quarters sounded and we got underway immediately. (I will return to this episode; we left Edison men aboard that tanker in our hurried departure.) Before we could get very far another transport was hit, right under my eyes. It quivered, shook, and nearly capsized. Within 10 or 15 seconds men were climbing down the sides into the water. One ship burned all night and sank about 3:00 this morning. (Would be the 13th.)

The 13th. Today was Friday the 13th. After the torpedoing last night the entire convoy got underway. Several other destroyers and we stayed and patrolled the Fedala-Casablanca area and this noon went out to the rendezvous and escorted part of the transports back to the Casablanca harbor. This evening we started out for the remainder and will probably pick them up tomorrow morning and bring them in for unloading.

That certainly was a pitiful sight last night to see those good ships torpedoed and sunk. Tears came to my eyes to see them in their helpless condition, but this is war and it is all part of the game. It is all a matter of give and take and we can't let it get us down. This morning the entire area was strewn with wreckage of all types and oil covered the surface. It was a disheartening sight.

The 14th. At 8:00 this morning we contacted the section of the convoy which has not gone into Casablanca for unloading. We are now some 150 miles northeast of our new base and will arrive there late tomorrow morning. (We) are hoping that as soon as the cargoes are unloaded, we will head back to the States. The Captain said today that if we all don't get leave, he will put all hands on the sick list and grant sick leave.

The 15th. Patrolling station on port bow of convoy bound for Casablanca. Early this morning the Electra was torpedoed and we picked up a survivor. (This is the one who was paddling a board toward New York.) For the remainder of the day we stood by her while salvage operations were conducted and about midnight, she was towed to Casablanca.

The 16th. On our usual 180 degrees, 000 degrees patrol outside Casablanca. Early this afternoon we went into the harbor and refueled. Boy, what havoc we raised in that place during the bombardment. About 10 ships are full of holes and resting on the bottom, including at least 2 cruisers and 4 destroyers. Other destroyers sunk by us were on the outside. The Edison had a pretty good hand in sinking three, one almost single-handed. The battleship Jean Bart is resting on the bottom.

The town itself seems to be very nice altho the reception granted to soldiers and sailors is still very hostile. Saw "Flight Lieutenant" tonight. We are now anchored in the mouth of the harbor and scuttlebutt has it that we will return to the States tomorrow.

(This is the end of the first portion of Ed Meier's reflections. We will return to his commentary on the Edison's trip home from the North African invasion. That trip had its own excitements.)

8-11 November 1942. The Author's Perspective, and Other Perspectives.

Here I will bring in other perspectives on the United States' North African actions. These actions were taken to gain our first initiative against the Axis forces in the Mediterranean and Europe.

Time Sensitive Landings with No Softening Planned

In all landings in the Pacific theaters, including the very first one at Guadalcanal, extensive pre-landing bombardments were conducted to soften up the defenses. This was not done at Casablanca in 1942. The TORCH timing was the most ticklish of all the assaults undertaken by the western forces against Hitler. The Western Task Force was at sea for two weeks before the landings. Two other seaborne forces from ports a continent apart had to transit other waters. All waters were unfriendly. The three forces were to strike a shoreline over a thousand miles long behaving as a single force with a single unified command. Despite resistance and some losses, the crux of the achievement was victory in the breathtaking scope of a plan that was successfully executed in all sectors, on time.

In the last four days before the Western Task Force would go ashore, the seas made up. A minelayer dropped out of formation due to excessive roll. The fifteen-foot surf forecast for Morocco on the 8th would preclude landings. This was the forecast from U.S. and British home-based meteorologists but the weather forecaster on board the Task Force opined that the storm was moving rapidly and the seas would moderate. He was right. (Two years later, General Eisenhower received such a moderating weather forecast for Normandy. He accepted it and it was right.)

SS Contessa departed Norfolk late, proceeded without escort, and then made the last turn to the Southern Task Group instead of its assignment to the Northern Task Group. This was corrected in time.

By the end of the sea journey, training had brought the signaling capabilities of the Task Force to the point that, practicing radio silence, any visual signal would reach every ship within 10 minutes. Historian Samuel Eliot Morison noted that if landing times became stretched out, that French naval forces from Dakar were only three days steaming from Casablanca. It is interesting that 10 minutes was cited for one figure of communications merit, and 3 days steaming was noted to express the proximity of French naval reinforcements. Ten minutes for one challenge, and three days for another, expressed crucial time intervals in 1942. Such intervals would not convey such meaning in 1998 where seconds and split seconds are reaction times.

The three Task Groups of the Western Naval Task Force, each led by their own minesweepers, and covered by their own air groups and seaborne artillery, the battleships, cruisers and destroyers, took position and commenced their roles. Unloading of the combat loaded transports was scheduled for midnight on the 7th, with four hours to make up into the boat lanes before departing for the beach. Earliest to reach this position was the Northern Group precisely at midnight and latest was the Southern Group fifty-three minutes later. This dark period was essential cover for furious offloading of troops and supplies into landing craft.

SG Radar Navigation Fix; Morocco Assault

A northeast set of the current moved our assault lanes off position. Samuel Eliot Morison's Volume II of the History of US Naval Operations in World War II informs us that a critically important SG radar on a ship that he did not identify, and that my research has failed to positively identify, detected a dead reckoning navigation error. As Admiral Hewitt's command and control ship for the Western Naval Task Force, that radar could well have been on the Augusta, his flagship. Attempting a late hour correction, emergency turns were effected in the assault craft mother ship columns. Darkness and the unanticipated maneuvers made for some confusion for the trailing transports in the Northern and Central Task groups. Their two locations were close enough to each other to be influenced by the same offshore current. As a consequence, organization of the two boat lanes for the Northern Group and the four boat lanes for the Central Group took extra time.

Dim lights ashore indicated that surprise was still with the attackers. Two accounts mentioned the pungent aroma of charcoal from Fedala, a characteristic smell we all noted while ashore in later months in North Africa.

A change of command takes place at this point insofar as the shore bound forces are concerned. In the Center Group, Captain Emmet on the transport Leonard Wood took over direct control of his group. I note this here because I feel that it was not fully recognized later on.

The times indicated are Greenwich. Local sunrise was 0655 with twilight almost an hour earlier. There were four boat lanes for the Center Group, at the head (south end) of which, closest to the beaches, stood the Benson-class destroyers Wilkes, Swanson, Ludlow and Murphy. The lanes pointed generally South, to the beach. Behind Wilkes in the western lane, was the Leonard Wood, first in her column to unload. Her scout boat was to head south for Red 2, the closest of the assault beaches to Cape Fedala, following her lead destroyer, the Wilkes, which would lead the landing boat column until turned away by shallow water. Similarly, with the same 0400 lead boat landing time, the Thomas Jefferson's boats were to head for Red 3 to the east of Red 2, behind the Swanson, with a lane heading from the Red 2 lane a bit to the SSE. From west to east, the Carroll's boats were for Blue 1 and the Dickman's for Blue 2, behind Ludlow and Murphy respectively. These last three lanes were parallel and avoided rocks located at the beach in the arc east of the Wood's Red 2 beach.

At the seaward end of Cape Fedala was the Batterie des Passes, two French 75s (75millimeter guns). At the base of the cape was a pair of 100mm guns. At Chergui, 3 miles north, Pont Blondin had a heavy battery of four 138.6mm guns which could cover an arc from the transport area to the control destroyers to the landing beaches. Down from the town of Fedala was a mobile 75mm AA battery. The beaches were in a two-mile crescent open to the sea on the north. Rock formations punctuated the beaches. The 138.6mm guns had a range of over 15,000 yards, more than matching a destroyer's effective range.

At the eastern end of the crescent was the Sherki headland and to the west, next to beach Red that was not to be used in the assault phase, was Cape Fedala. Just behind the Cape and Red 2 beach to the south was the town of Fedala.

The transport area can be visualized by considering the transports Leonard Wood, the Thomas Jefferson, the Carroll and the Joseph Dickman on an east to west line. Just to the seaward of a control destroyer, each was at the head of its own transport column, four ships deep extending north behind them. This group, twelve transports and three cargo ships plus a fleet oiler, defined a 2-mile square, six miles north of the beaches. They could lie to or anchor, at their option. While the lead transports had sufficient boats for most of their embarked assault troops, each had to borrow some boats from the transports astern for complete debarkation.

The scout boats were first to leave to mark the beaches. These had five men, one in command, and a mix of Navy, or Coast Guard personnel for the boat crew, plus Army enlisted men. These boats had engine silencers and a special compass. There were infrared flashlights and a radio set. The men carried submachine guns and automatics. They had to mark their beach, and anchor at a specific position. At H minus 25 minutes they were to point their flashlights seaward, and at H minus 10 they were to fire flares to identify their beach. (Two red flares would mean Red 2.) The control destroyers had to be one half mile south of their designated lane by 0200, defining the rendezvous area. On signal, each destroyer began to lead the boats in at 8 knots. Two miles off shore, the destroyers would anchor, defining the line of departure. At Captain Emmet's command, the assault wave boats would depart for the beach. The scout boats' flashlights were now their beacons. Some lanes might have armed support boats if required. At the break of morning twilight, the destroyers would mark their lane departure points with buoys and colored streamers. Scheduled arrival time for the assault wave was 0415. It would be pitch dark and the tide would be going out. The destroyers would proceed to their designated gun fire support positions.

Our Troops Go Ashore At Fedala

It will not go down as a textbook operation. The first line of transports began unloading on schedule. The decision to use all the small landing craft and all of the tank lighters (forty-four) in the initial waves, led to traffic jams in the water before departing for beaches. The task of the lead transports to load over fifty boats each, while borrowing boats two or three miles away, and have them in the water at the line of departure at 0400, would have been a daunting task even with experienced coxswains. Our boat crews for North Africa simply did not have the experience that the plan demanded. Adding to the loading difficulties, the rear of the transport columns straggled to position at the tail end of the emergency turns just past midnight and could not get the borrowed boats up to the head of the column on time. Just over three fifths of the boat lanes were populated according to plan when they left for the beach. Leonard Wood came closest with all her boats in the water before 0200 but that was not enough time for men, in the dark, to get down in loading nets to the boats and be ready to go. H-hour was postponed to 0500. The General of the 3rd Infantry Division commented in Samuel Eliot Morison's History, "Failure of ships to arrive in the transport area, as scheduled, completely upset the timing of the boat employment plan."

All Scout Boats except the Jefferson's (it had engine trouble) were ready alongside Wood and departed at 0145. With the Wood's boat in the lead, they looked over their assigned beaches and each selected its position. They did not find out about the one-hour postponement. On signal from the skipper of the USS Wilkes, the destroyers moved in at the head of their first assault waves to their anchor points. Scout Boat light flashes confirmed to the destroyers that a "follow the leader boat procession" would find the correct course. The assault waves left at 0500 and were on the beaches between 0515 and 0525. Successive landing waves came in five to ten minute intervals. Thankfully, the sea waves were negligible for the boats that actually found their assigned beaches.

Except for two boats which missed the control destroyer and landed and broke up on rocks to the east of Sherki Headland, the Blue 2 boats, at the narrowest beach under the headland, did well. Some of their boats retracted before it was light and got back to their transport by 0630.

At the next beach to the west, Beach Blue, the effort did not go well. There was surf created by ledge rock. The test of seamanship here was too demanding and 18 of the 29 boats in the initial attack waves were put out of commission and five more lost in the second landing here. The U.S., a producer nation, was put to the test by the very heavy loss of landing craft. By day's early light on November 8, this beach presented a disheartening scene to local commanders. To the credit of people who did not give up, salvage efforts regained some of the losses. But the salvage did not take place until the assault phase was over. The Scout Boat for this beach became a total loss on Beach Red 3.

The Jefferson's troops were to go to Red 3, just west of Blue. One of Jefferson's loading nets gave way and soldiers were flung into the sea. Jefferson's Scout Boat, with its engines now working, had missed the scout boat assembly at the Leonard Wood where courses to the beach had been given out. This boat went in on her own, to a beach east of Sherki, off its assigned position about 2 miles. The Ensign in charge of the first wave had the good sense to turn away from high surf there and led his small group back to the misplaced Scout Boat and all made their way west. Again, the assault wave boats lost contact with the Scout Boat in the darkness, turned east and made a rock landing at almost 0600, three miles east of their proper position. They lost two thirds of their landing craft. The next wave landing there lost half its boats. A third wave with vehicles aboard made an unplanned landing but got ashore in good shape, though out of position. The Jefferson Scout Boat finally found Red 3, and got the Swanson, which had also gone to the wrong position, to move. Wave four went to the right place but wave five went back to the wrong beach. Out of 33 boats, Jefferson lost 17. Of the 16 which made the two-way trip, six needed repairs.

Heavy defender firing began after 0600 and a hiatus in the assault landings ensued.

Wood's Scout Boat had been directed to mark the eastern end of Red 2, the westernmost beach for the assault phase. This position marked a reef and the assault boats were to leave the Scout Boat's marker position to their port as they made their way in. Approached by a "mystery boat", according to Morison's account, the Wood's Scout Boat let go its anchor and drifted away from its reef-marking position. The first Wood boat waves, taking their position from their scout boat's signals, turned SE and approached the beach on an oblique line and, with the confidence given by the scout boat's signals, ran full bore onto the rocks between Red 2 and Red 3. While some managed to retract, others left their troops to scramble over rocks with loss of equipment. According to Morison's account, 21 of 32 of Wood's assault phase boats were lost.

If one evaluates progress by survival of assault landing craft, the numbers for the initial waves were disheartening. None of the accounts I have read covers the resulting number of soldiers and sailors drowned or disabled. There is no account available on the loss of the soldiers' precious equipment, the tools for their own defense or for the attack at hand. In the Wood's case, as with the Jefferson, both scout boats and control destroyers were out of position.

It can reasonably be inferred that Admiral Hewitt and the Augusta determined late on the 7th of November that a set in current northeast threw off the dead reckoning, and ordered a late course change to put the Fedala transports of Captain Emmet's group in proper position. Bob Swanson, whose father served on Augusta during the North African operations, publishes a USS Augusta website. Posted there is Augusta's action report that Bob Swanson obtained from the National Archives. From this action report one learns that the Augusta had the latest equipment available, including the SG radar. Use of this radar system enabled the transports to proceed to the correct point of departure for the landing craft. Much like the destroyers, the Augusta turned to other duties once the Task Group arrived at the jump off point. Augusta went where gunfire support was needed, Augusta went where exercise of command and control was needed. Augusta went where the Task Force Commander needed to be.

I have made almost a regular mention of the SG radar in this story and in upcoming pages will bring this 1942 technology advance into the story again and again. Once the radar arrived, its employment was the key to success. When just one or two ships in a given force had this highly versatile equipment, and these ships could not be everyplace at once, any more than the equipment was designed to be passed from ship to ship for optimum use, its non-availability came, and comes once again, into question. While such questions will arise in the readers' minds, just as in my own, I have come to understand that there was a transition period in which SG was available but scarce. Looking for the silver lining, the scarcity period caused the U.S. to redouble its radar production efforts and caused responsible fleet commanders to realize at once where and how SG radar *made a difference.*

The set in current persisted along the assault sectors of the North African coast and the boat lanes ran into beach identification problems. Did just one U.S. Navy ship have SG radar at North Africa? There was a persistent scuttlebutt at the time suggesting that SG radar equipment was available on more than one U.S. ship at Casablanca. Morison's History mentions the SG radar at Casablanca only once. A reason for reflecting on SG radar availability at Casablanca will come up again before we are done with operations in the 8-12 November 1942 period. TORCH was not the only operation where the subject came up.

John Weld was a Lieutenant USNR on the staff of Rear Admiral Richmond Kelly Turner. Turner was Commander Amphibious Force, South Pacific, in 1942 for the landings on Guadalcanal. Although John Weld was married to my sister for many years, I had not heard from him for quite some time until two long distance phone calls in October 1997. John had discovered my comments about the use of SG radar at Casablanca in the web edition of this story. John Weld pointed out to me that Richard Frank in his book,

"Guadalcanal", made some important points concerning U.S. warships in the South Pacific that were equipped with SG radar and warships that did not have it. In 618 pages, Author Frank's index shows 11 entries for "SG radar." I will make an excerpt from the first of the entries, on author Frank's page 294 in Chapter 12, "The Battle of Cape Esperance."

"The one serious deficiency in Scott's calculations (Rear Admiral Norman Scott, in command of four cruisers and five destroyers) was his selection of a flagship. Heavy cruisers *Salt Lake City* and *San Francisco* were nominally his most powerful units, and Scott hoisted his flag in the latter. However, the mastheads of these vessels supported only metric-wave SC search radars of much inferior performance to that of the newer centimetric SG radars sported by both his light cruisers..........Because of the erratic performance of the SC radar (ordered turned off to avoid being picked up by Japanese listening countermeasure equipment, which, as it turned out, the Japanese did not have) the American Admiral did not regard its (the SC radar's) loss as grave, and as he was ignorant of the enormous improvement in technology represented by SG radar, he did not switch his flag to one of his light cruisers, the *Helena* or the *Boise.*"

An assessment of the situation after the first hour at Fedala was that 3500 troops had been successfully landed by morning twilight, which marked the beginning of French resistance. Initial beachhead objectives had been secured. After the gun battles (which we will get back to after looking in on the early progress at Safi and Mehedia), the assault waves resumed landing at Fedala. By nightfall of the 8th, over 7000 U.S. troops were ashore and had a pretty good handle on the ground situation at Fedala. Accounts of the actions of the

Eastern and Central Task Forces, attacking Algiers and Oran respectively, are not available in the detail that historians have provided to us for Fedala (Casablanca), Safi and Mehedia. It is generally understood that the losses in landing craft in the Mediterranean landings were even more severe than the losses in the Atlantic landings.

Safi

The Southern Attack Group of the Western Task Force broke off from the main group early in the morning of the 7th of November. Rear Admiral Davidson on USS Philadelphia, the USS New York, the carrier Santee, and a number of destroyers with their transports headed for Safi, 150 miles down the West African coast from Casablanca. Converted World War I destroyers Bernadou and Cole had key roles. French Navy-manned coastal batteries defended Safi to the north and an Army battery of 155mm guns defended to the south. Philadelphia and New York each took a position to get a firing line to those batteries. Three Benson class destroyers, Mervine, Knight and Beatty were the close in fire support for the landing parties. Destroyers Quick and Doran screened the transports and destroyers Rodman and Emmons screened Santee. With H-hour set for 0400, the two World War I 4-pipers peeled off for the harbor at 0330. Despite Mervine's hull being gashed by a Spanish fishing vessel at 2145 on the 7th, lights in the harbor suggested no alarms there.

Again, a little Scout Boat led the assault craft parade behind the converted destroyers. With assault companies of the U.S. 47th Infantry aboard, Bernadou was to touch bottom at the head end of the small harbor and her force was to seize and to hold the harbor area. Cole would go alongside the mole and her force was to grab and secure the loading cranes and machinery. Cole was to set it up so that the transport

Lakehurst could go alongside the mole and disgorge tanks which would form up ashore and head for Casablanca. North African coastal surf predictions precluded getting the tanks in via single barge and ramp landings on a beach.

Bernadou was challenged by defenders at 0410 just short of the breakwater and gave an innocuous answer. At 0428 as Bernadou rounded the north end of the mole, a shore battery belched fire. French 75s and machine guns raked the harbor and Bernadou announced a "Play ball" over her TBS. Her 3 inchers and her 20mm guns began to fire at gun flashes. Bernadou and Cole were straddled a number of times but Bernadou's counter fire and Mervine's 5"/38 cal. fire silenced Batterie des Passes 2000 yards north of Safi after six minutes of exchanges. Four 130mm naval rifles on a commanding headland three miles northwest of Safi then started firing into the transport area. New York, Philadelphia, Mervine and Beatty were straddled, but by 0715 the Batterie Railleuse was silenced. The harbor work was going like a day at the local shipyard when Cole was asked to take a signal station, on the hill overlooking the mole, under fire because troop advance there was hampered by small arms fire. With four 3" 50 cal. shells, Cole silenced this sniper fire. Coastal batteries were silenced by 1300 and the Lakehurst came alongside and unloaded tanks. Our tanks were underway to Casablanca with accompanying troops by the next morning. There were 150 French aircraft reported to be available to repulse the three landings of the Western Task Force. These planes were a distraction. They did not play a critical role though they made a brief attack on the 9th. By the afternoon of 9 November, Rear Admiral Davidson was confident enough to release New York and two high-speed minesweepers to the task group at Fedala. By the evening of the 10th, Philadelphia, Knight, Cowie, Cole and Bernadou commenced an offshore group escort for tanks and troops on the road to Casablanca. Sixty miles off shore, Santee was fired on by a submarine (could have been French or German, but my guess would be a German U-boat) which missed with two torpedoes.

Mehedia

This objective proved a tougher nut to crack. The 4-piper Dallas took Army Ranger troops aboard in the darkness before H-hour at 0400 on the 8th. Those men were to take the airfield at Port Lyautey. This field was a major objective of the Western Task Force. (The Douglas DC-4 aircraft was just coming into military service, as a C-54 to the Army Air Force and the R5-D to the Navy. Using a route with Lyautey as its continental African terminus, this 4-engine transport plane could fly to the Azores, thence to Newfoundland and then on into a U.S. base.) The Lyautey airfield was nine miles upstream on the Oued Sebou. (The Sebou River. These rivers in North Africa were alternatively called Oued, or Wadi. I never understood the distinction.) The Sebou twisted and turned, was shallow, and a dredged, buoyed channel could not be expected. A river pilot was needed. Rene Malavergne, a Free Frenchman who knew the river well, assisted by the XO of the Dallas, piloted her upstream, while her Captain commanded Dallas' furious resistance to the French Army, Navy and Legionnaire's efforts to sink her.

At 1900 on the 7th, destroyer Roe went ahead to find the U.S. station submarine, and failing to do so, marked her own position by radar and became the beacon ship for the Northern Attack Group. Three beaches were defined for the assault phase, one 4 miles north of the Sebou estuary, one three miles below (south) the river mouth and one hugging a jetty on the south side of the entrance channel. By one hour after midnight on the 8th, the full activity of unloading was in progress with personnel and vehicles moving onto their assigned assault platforms. The Rangers came from the Susan B. Anthony and proceeded to the Dallas. Shortly after the original H-hour of 0400 (it had been postponed one hour here for the same reason as at Fedala) the three fire support destroyers were in position. Kearny was to the north side of the estuary, Roe to the south, and Ericsson in the center where she could help wherever the extra firepower was needed. A stone fort was located in the estuary, and the south bank of the entrance was under the firing arcs of French 75s and a 138.6mm battery.

At 0500 the first assault waves passed the support destroyers and had landed on their beachheads before the defenders were alerted. Rifle fire then came from the fort onto the landing craft with a searchlight illuminating them. A shore battery then zeroed in on the landing craft going to Green Beach and destroyer Eberle was directed to respond and did so with two minutes of rapid continuous fire from her 5"/38 cal battery. Green Beach landings continued. Roe was taken under fire about 0630 from a battery and making speed on various headings fired back at a range of 5,000 yards. After a short halt in firing, aircraft strafed the Roe. Kearny and Eberle fired at aircraft strafing the landing boats and one plane was brought down.

The fort behind the native Kasbah was old and its 138mm guns were old too, but this fort kept firing at landing craft and into the channel. Despite intensive bombardment by Savannah's six inchers and Roe's five inchers, the fort continued to resist. Army troops were thrown back when the fort's garrison was reinforced. Dallas needed that fort reduced in order to begin her voyage upriver. Fumbling with a heavy net and boom across the river entrance under direct fire from large caliber guns was treacherous business. Finally, the large guns from the fort were silenced. A special Navy crew hacked through the net and Dallas lined up for a frontal ram of the boom. With rifle fire from the riverbank and heavy battery fire onto the channel point of entry chosen, Dallas was driven back.

A counter attack by Legionnaires from the fort had to be repulsed. Sangamon aircraft and Savannah's main battery dealt with French tanks on the road from Rabat south of Mehedia. In a very contested little acre of geography, the boom was finally cut in the wee hours of the 10th. The cut was made where Dallas had too much draft so she backed off and asked the engine room for full power. With the Kasbah guns reactivated, Dallas started forward just as a shell's geyser splashed ahead and another near miss lifted her stern, likely helping solve the draft problem. She got over the bar and pushed the cable aside. With engine turns for 25 knots and making six knots, Dallas was dredging her own channel. She made it to Lyautey, and embarked her Rangers in rubber boats just as French 75s came within 10 yards of her. Savannah's plane found the battery and silenced it with depth charges, the first time I have ever heard of them being used for this purpose. Rangers then captured the airfield. U.S. P-40 fighter/bomber aircraft were then ferried into the field from one of the carriers and established it as their base. Assault troops surrounded the Kasbah holdout citadel. The USS Savannah battered its walls and in the face of Sangamon bombers, it surrendered on the 11th, ending the defense of Mehedia. Casualties, as at Safi, were astonishingly light.

In the next Chapter, we will return to the French warship resistance at Casablanca. In several sorties, the French destroyers made smoke to confuse our fire. The next picture shows a U.S. Benson class destroyer making chemical smoke. U.S. destroyers did not use smoke at Casablanca but we did use it frequently in later operations during air attacks on convoys in the Mediterranean and during shore bombardment operations. The ship more on the defensive in a ship to ship melee was the one most likely to use smoke. Destroyers could combine chemical smoke from their smoke generators with black smoke made by the engineers in her power plant.

Illustration 13–Benson DD Makes Smoke

Chapter Six - French Navy Resistance at Casablanca

As some readers may know, this story appeared first in a World Wide Web edition at Universal Resource Locator (URL) www.daileyint.com. In December of 1997, I received a telephone call from a man who had just read substantially what appeared in the Web edition under the chapter heading above. The man was softly indignant. His main point was that the Jean Bart could not have been firing on U.S. warships because "the French were our Allies in World War II." It was inconceivable to him that the activity described in the story could actually have taken place. I attempted to recast those events for him but it was clear at the end of the call that I had not convinced him.

French Warships Head for Fedala

When we left our account of the action at Fedala on the evening of D-day, there were 9,000 troops ashore out of the planned 20,000. There was more work to do. The actions at Casablanca sorted out to a relatively short Fedala assault phase, and a full three-day Casablanca phase. The French Navy Casablanca sorties were first made to help support resistance to our landings at Fedala, then to defend Casablanca itself. A third phase then occurred as the result of submarine attacks by the main adversary, Nazi Germany.

Let me recap the forces available to Captain R.R. Emmet of the Center Attack Group. He had 15 transports and an oiler in his convoy, with destroyer protection assigned to Bristol, Woolsey, Edison, Tillman Boyle and Rowan. For boat lane control and fire support the following destroyers were assigned: Wilkes, Swanson, Ludlow and Murphy. Defending batteries would likely see these four destroyers first.

Well offshore, destroyers Ellyson, Forrest, Fitch, Corry and Hobson screened the carriers Ranger and Suwannee. A roving band of cruisers was available to move at will. These were the Brooklyn, the Cleveland, and the Augusta. In their screen were the destroyers Wainright, Mayrant, Rhind and Jenkins. Setting a pattern for many landings to come, U.S. minesweepers had come in ahead of the transport group and the assault fire support destroyers. These were the dispositions at the outset of the action. Reassignments were frequent once hostilities began.

Although there was no sea-launched commando penetration effort as at Safi and Mehedia, an incident did occur during the approach to Fedala late on the evening of the 7th. A two-ship convoy, a French coastal steamer escorted by a 600-ton corvette, came around Cape Fedala heading directly for our transport area. U.S. destroyer-minesweeper Hogan intercepted. A French Lieutenant, skipper of the corvette, was not to be deterred and changed course to ram the Hogan. Machine guns from the Hogan killed the Lieutenant and nine crewmembers on the corvette, which went dead in the water. U.S. minesweeper Auk put a prize crew on board the corvette and Hogan returned to her duties.

At just after 0600, batteries at Chergui and Fedala targeted the boat lane fire support destroyers. Division Commander E.R. Durgin on Wilkes ordered the four destroyers to take up their fire support roles. Wilkes and Swanson guns retorted to the Fedala batteries while Murphy and Ludlow responded to the heavier Blondin battery at Chergui. Commander Durgin radioed, "Batter up!" At 0620, a "Play Ball" was Captain Emmet's response. This response was passed throughout all U.S. forces at Casablanca.

In the first minute after Play Ball, the Murphy announced she was being straddled and asked for help from cruiser Brooklyn. By 0645, with Brooklyn and Swanson now firing on the Blondin battery, Murphy took a shell hit in her after engine room. Three were dead and seven were wounded. The Engineering Officer, Lieutenant Commander R.W. Curtis entered the space and with steam jets spouting, turned off the generator and stopped the arcing on the switchboard. He then made a search to assure himself that he had an accounting for all assigned personnel below.

Blondin was finally silenced but it took Brooklyn, Swanson, Ludlow and Murphy to do it. Brooklyn came all the way into the Joseph Dickman's boat lanes to fire at the Blondin battery. Augusta, with 8-inch guns, came into 12,000 yards range and silenced Batterie du Port, behind the Cape at about 25 minutes after 7 a.m. Battery fire on the beaches picked up again at 0830. Boyle, Edison, Ludlow, Bristol and Wilkes responded to gunfire from Fedala's guns during this period.

At 0825, two French destroyer leaders and five French destroyers sortieed from Casablanca heading along the coast toward the transport area at Fedala. While engaged with them, Ludlow was hit up forward by a 6.1-inch armor piercing shell. With four wounded, and on fire, Ludlow retired toward the transport screen to mend. Wilkes, Swanson, Brooklyn and Augusta began a concentrated firing period on the French ships with the longer range shells of Brooklyn and Augusta forcing the French to turn back. In evasive maneuvers on their return, the French ran into our Covering Group. We will return to this French Navy effort shortly, from the perspective of that U.S. Covering Group.

Just a few minutes past 1000, Batterie du Port reopened harassing fire on the Fedala beaches. Swanson and Edison responded until they were ordered to cease fire based on the erroneous information that our destroyers had fired on our own troops. ComDesRon 13, Captain John Heffernan, protested that he could see the guns of Batterie du Port firing on our men on the beaches and asked, "May I fire?" With a "Yes!" response, Heffernan ordered Wilkes, then on the most favorable bearing, to re-open fire on this battery. Wilkes followed with a high rate of fire and the battery shut down after four salvoes. But, again at 1035, the battery came to life once more. Bristol opened fire on it from 7,000 yards, and it was at 1130, at the U.S. Army's request, that firing ceased in this sector. In examining the damage later, it was discovered that one of the naval shore guns was disabled, and the fire control system demolished, but the other three guns, with plenty of ammunition still available, could still fire in local control. Our forces had resisted firing on two fixed 75mm guns, in a gun pit among oil tanks, because of an interest in saving and using the oil. Located on the point of the Cape, these guns had been the hardest to find and subdue. Destroyer fire had completely disabled these guns by 1100. Later, the oil tanks were found to be empty.

The 1130 cease-fire spelled the end of ground resistance at Fedala. Except for the naval gun batteries, Fedala had been lightly defended by about 200 French troops. French aircraft strafed Blue Beach at 1100, at noon, and again in the afternoon. At noon, the U.S. minelayer Miantonomah laid a minefield to the east of Cape Fedala as protection to our transport anchorage. The transports moved in closer in mid-afternoon, to an anchorage marking the original line of assault boat departure. It was not over for the transports.

In the Fedala landing phase, 45% of the assault landing boats had been wrecked or holed by strafing. With the surf rising, the Fedala beachmaster, Commander J.W. Jamison, did his utmost to re-direct boats to the harbor itself or to

Beach Red. His message took too many hours to reach all concerned and our forces continued to lose boats. U.S. Navy and U.S. Coast Guard amphibious personnel would need more training and experience. They would get it in training exercises and in subsequent Mediterranean or Normandy actions. They improved their landing technique, not just in major assaults but in repeated leapfrog landings after major assaults. Author Morison recounts in his History of United States Naval Operations in World War II that he later met some Fedala veterans who were fresh from landings at Saipan in the Pacific. They told him that the Fedala landings were the toughest of all because of darkness and surf. In addition to experience of the crews, doctrine would change. Softening up the defenders, and waiting until at least early light for the assault waves to hit the beach, would be lessons that took time to learn in the Mediterranean.

Just before noon on the 8th, U.S. Army forces ashore at Fedala called for a cease-fire from the naval gunnery. (By the afternoon of the 8th, nearly 17,000 troops were ashore, with full equipment, and fighting for Fedala was over. The destruction of landing craft had severely upset the rate at which we were able to put troops ashore, but thankfully, the Army ashore made do with less.)

The Air Group

The Air Group offshore, consisting of the U.S. cruiser Cleveland, the carriers Ranger and Suwannee, and the destroyers Ellyson, Corry and Hobson had had little to do on D-day directly in support of assault waves at Fedala. The Ranger launched Grumman F4F Wildcats at 0615. These planes headed for the Rabat and Rabat-Sale airdromes, headquarters for French air forces in Morocco. Encountering AA fire, they destroyed 21 planes on the ground at the two fields.

The second flight shot down a plane and the third destroyed more planes on the ground at Port Lyautey. One U.S. pilot was lost. Later flights went after batteries and French naval ships at Casablanca. Another fighter squadron from Ranger encountered 16 French planes airborne at Le Cazes airfield at Casablanca and lost four of its own planes as it shot down 8 French aircraft and destroyed 14 on the ground. This squadron also strafed the first group of French destroyers coming out of Casablanca. Ranger's Douglas SBD Dauntless dive-bombers reached 10,000 feet over Casablanca at 0700 in the 8th and bombed the sub basin in the harbor. Suwannee's planes maintained ASW and combat air patrol. With 18 knots maximum speed, converted tanker hull carriers like Suwannee needed a fresh breeze to launch planes. At Casablanca on November 8,1942, Suwannee often had to head for water where the chop indicated wind. We lost 44 planes, all causes, but many of our pilots and crewman were recovered.

The Covering Group - Heavier Stuff

At Casablanca harbor, the U.S. Covering Group objective was to hold the French warships in check while supporting the Fedala landings as needed. This group consisted of the battleship Massachusetts, just six months in commission, the cruisers Tuscaloosa and Wichita, and the destroyers Wainwright, Mayrant, Rhind and Jenkins. On a gun for gun basis, the battleship's role was to target a coastal battery at Point El Hank and to neutralize the French battleship, the Jean Bart. The latter, immobilized at dockside, had two available turrets, four 15inch guns in all, pointed to seaward. The French were noted for good optics and fire control. (While the French fire control with their land-based naval batteries worked fine, post-battle evaluations showed it was usually the fire control part of their systems that were knocked out first by our fire, while the guns themselves remained in firing condition.) Tuscaloosa and Wichita, U.S. heavy cruisers with 8inch guns, were to target other Casablanca shore batteries and make sure, along with Massachusetts, that no French subs, cruisers or destroyers got to sea. The Covering Group destroyers acted as an ASW and AA screen.

The French at Casablanca opened the D-day gunnery action at daylight. At 0610, nine U.S. scout planes were catapulted for spotting and ASW. These U.S. reconnaissance planes were fired on by French AA guns and challenged by French aircraft. The Covering Group's first targets involved AA fire against the French planes. The Point El Hank battery and the Jean Bart commenced firing at the ships at sea at a ten-mile range. Shell splashes appeared ahead of Massachusetts and she responded with her big guns shortly after 0700 on the 8th. Tuscaloosa began firing at El Hank and at the submarine pens in the harbor. The firing from El Hank and Jean Bart intensified, as more splashes moved closer to Massachusetts. U.S. destroyers in the Covering Group screen were out-ranged and had to hold fire. At 0815, large caliber gunfire from Casablanca was at its height. Then began the sortie of the French destroyer leaders Milan and Albatross, along with destroyers Frondeur, Fougueux. Brestois and Boulonnais, toward the Fedala transport area.

(With carrier aircraft available, in retrospect, it has to be marked as almost a matter of pride that our battleship and heavy cruisers would execute a maneuver, controlled by the wind direction, to catapult nine, almost defenseless, float planes for reconnaissance and spotting. During the 1930s these elegant triumphs of coordination between aircraft pilot and ship skipper had been perfected. The pilots surely wanted to do their part. The compromises to freedom of ship action, especially when retrieving their observation planes, became less and less acceptable as experience was gained in later actions of the U.S. Navy. In the fast carrier task forces in the Pacific, carrier airmen became skilled in the scout and observation duties of the "float-planes" of Casablanca.)

Directly after launching their planes, Massachusetts, Wichita and Tuscaloosa unfurled battle ensigns (oversize US flags), and increased battle formation speed to 25 knots. Massachusetts led the column, followed by the cruisers at 1000-yard distances. Four destroyers screened at 3000 yards ahead of the battleship. The fifteen-mile track of these ships roughly matched and paralleled the northeast to southwest line between Fedala and Casablanca. Author Morison's account in his Volume II, Operations in North African Waters is recommended reading. An excerpt follows:

"At 0640, when the formation had reached a position bearing about west northwest from Casablanca, distant 18,000 yards from Batterie El Hank and 20,000 yards from battleship Jean Bart's berth in the harbor, it began an easterly run, holding the same range. Ten minutes later, one of the USS Augusta's spotting planes reported two submarines standing out of Casablanca Harbor, and at 0651 radioed: "There is an anti-aircraft battery opening up on me from the beach. One burst came within twelve feet. Batter up!" Another U.S. spotting plane encountered 'bandits' at 0652 and signaled, 'Am coming in on starboard bow with couple hostile aircraft on my tail. Pick 'em off - I am the one in front!' The big ships opened up on these planes with their 5" batteries at 0701, and shot one down. The other retired; and almost simultaneously battleship Jean Bart and El Hank commenced firing. The coast defense guns straddled Massachusetts with their first salvo, and five or six splashes from Jean

Bart fell about 600 yards ahead of her starboard bow. Admiral Giffen (directly in charge of this group) lost no time in giving his group the 'Play Ball'. Massachusetts let go her first 16-inch salvo at 0704."

El Hank's 4-gun battery of 194mm guns was located just west of the harbor. This battery was modern and accurate. Another four-gun 138mm battery nearby looked eastward. A smaller, older battery at Table d'Aoukasha looked toward Fedala. Jean Bart's 15"guns and fire control were operative, though the ship was still being outfitted. The harbor and its approaches were covered well by gun batteries ashore.

Massachusetts and Tuscaloosa concentrated on Jean Bart while Wichita took El Hank under fire, using her own float plane to spot. Jean Bart took some heavy metal. Massachusetts unloaded 9 salvos, some with six guns firing some with all nine firing. (It depends on the bearing; it is not unusual for a maneuvering ship to have a turret unable to fire because its firing cutout cams are protecting the ship itself.) According to Morison's account, one Massachusetts shell exploded in an empty Jean Bart magazine, one wrecked her after control station and opened up a hole below the waterline. Two armor piercing shells hit but did not meet enough resistance to explode, and a fifth shell hit a glancing blow on the forward turret, causing the turret to lock up in train, (no movement possible in the horizontal plane) putting her entire available battery out for 48 hours. She was not a factor during the intense period of the landings at Fedala and for the central action period at Casablanca. Jean Bart's big guns could reach the transport area at extreme range. They were silenced in 16 minutes on the morning of the 8th.

Tuscaloosa concentrated on the submarine berths at Casablanca, and then shifted to the Table d'Aoukasha battery.

Wichita silenced El Hank temporarily with her 9-gun salvoes of 8" shells and then worked the submarine area over. This took the action to about half past seven in the morning and the Covering Group executed a course change to due west at a range of just over 25,000 yards. Firing was then resumed on all of the harbor ships and targets. Three subs were sunk at anchor. But eight French submarines had managed to get out and the shore batteries were still operational. No hits had been made on the Covering Group. By the end of this first phase of their firing at half past eight, the Covering Group was 16 miles northwest of Casablanca and 25 miles from the transport area. With the heavy guns of the U.S. ships now at a safe distance, the French Admiral Michelier ordered his destroyer squadrons to break up the landing area at Fedala. Their sortie actually began shortly after 8 a.m.

First French Sortie

First out were destroyer leaders Milan and Albatross, of 2500 tons, 423 feet at the waterline, with five 5.5" guns and four torpedo tubes, capable of 36 knots. Then came destroyers L'Alcyon, Brestois, Boulonnais, Fougueux and Frondeur. These were 1400 tonners, 331 feet long, with four 5.1 " guns, 6 torpedo tubes, and were also capable of 36 knots. Their Admiral was Gervais de Lafond in cruiser Primauguet. This cruiser did not depart the port until 1000. The segmentation of French resistance politics was so great that this Admiral did not know the nationality of the forces opposing him when he sortieed. A French general, Bethouart, who supported the U.S. and did know who the landing forces were, had been jailed for his truce-making efforts during the morning. Some reports spoke of anxious moments for the transports with this bold move of the French destroyers. I doubt that the transports and the assault boat crews had such awareness that morning. They, as one might say today, "had other problems." The French destroyers took beach Yellow, west of Cape Fedala, under fire first. This was not an assault wave beach but was designated for later waves and some boats were already there. The French also took Wilkes and Ludlow under fire. A Ludlow salvo started a fire on the Milan, but in turning at high speed, Ludlow herself was hit. As described earlier, Ludlow was then absent the action for repairs for about three hours. In leaving the scene Ludlow was straddled out to 24,000 yards. Admiral Hewitt ordered Augusta, Brooklyn, Wilkes and Swanson to intercept the French ships. With the two destroyers leading Augusta, Brooklyn then made a high-speed 300-degree turn to fall in astern of Augusta. All four US ships began firing at once. With the French ships down to just 8,000 yards from the transports, the ship to ship gunnery began at 18,000 yards. The French got off a good volume of fire but made no more hits and broke off at 0900. This is when Hewitt ordered Rear Admiral Giffen and his Covering Group in to intercept the French. That group reduced their range to the French ships at 27 knots, opened fire at 19,000 yards about 0915, and closed to 12,000 yards firing all the while.

A Second Go

The French ships used coordinated turns, smoke generation, and speed to cut the effectiveness of our optical range finders and allow their destroyer leaders to dart out and take a few shots and then hide once again behind destroyer-laid smoke. At 1000, Primaguet, 7300 tons, 600 feet long, eight 6" guns and twelve torpedo tubes joined the action. Two French destroyers moved north to make a torpedo attack on the Covering Group. In the lead, Fougueux, was hit by Massachusetts and Tuscaloosa from 22,000 yards, blew up and sank almost 7 miles north of the Casablanca breakwater. El Hank hit Massachusetts on the main deck forward but damage was light. Just minutes later, torpedoes were sighted on the port bow of Massachusetts and she turned in time to slide between the wakes of #3 and #4 of the spread. Four more torpedoes missed Tuscaloosa and as late as 1020, a torpedo passed 100 yards from Massachusetts. These were later assessed to be from the subs that successfully departed from Casablanca earlier in the morning.

The Covering Group was now in another run to the west and three French destroyers turned back toward the transport group. Admiral Hewitt ordered Brooklyn, Augusta and three destroyers to intercept. Recounting, up to this point, the French warships had been loose for quite awhile, had faced many aircraft attacks and some heavy shelling, and had lost just one of its nimble ships.

Brooklyn, to the east of Fedala at this point, steered directly toward the French surface forces and luckily threaded a spread of five torpedoes from the French sub, Amazone. Augusta was fueling one of her recovered observation-planes and was preparing to load General Patton into a boat for his landing ashore. Without Patton, the boat was cast loose and Augusta moved over toward Brooklyn. The latter ship came under fire from a French destroyer at about 1010. Augusta got into action 10 minutes later for this second morning engagement on the 8th of November. Wilkes, Swanson and Bristol screened the cruisers and were pitted against light cruiser Primaguet, destroyer leaders' Milan and Albatross and four French destroyers.

Our cruisers changed course at will and more or less independently of each other. This gave our screening destroyers quite a challenge. Sometimes, we were not screening at all. This was through no fault of our own. A high-speed course reversal would put us astern of the cruiser. I was not yet a conning officer for Condition TWO and for Condition ONE would have other duties. But, later at Salerno, I was the conning officer while screening cruisers that were firing at shore targets. It will be an item then to relate how these maneuvers effect a destroyer with two duties to perform, one to defend against aircraft, and one to screen against submarines. The Casablanca waters were full of splashes, but they were also full of torpedoes and destroyers escorting our heavier gunned warships had a complicated task. This time, Brooklyn was in the lead. She had fifteen 6" guns. Her gunnery tactic was to use one or two gun ranging salvos, to spot the effect, and then go to one or two minutes of rapid fire. By then, the French had turned northwest and were using smoke. At eight to nine miles range, the French ships seemed like small targets emerging from smoke then retiring into it. A 5" dud shell hit Brooklyn at 1045. The tenseness of this chase heightened when the masts of three ships appeared on the western horizon. It became clear that these ships on the horizon were firing, and large geysers of shell splashes appeared on Brooklyn's bow. At Dakar, the French had a battleship and two cruisers. Had those heavy French warships anticipated D-day at Casablanca and departed Dakar in time to participate in this action? No! The juxtaposition of splashes and masts was a coincidence. El Hank was the source of the Brooklyn near miss shell splashes. Our own Covering Group was firing as it re-entered the fray from its western swing. Massachusetts scored a direct hit on Boulonnais that rolled, suspended its roll momentarily, and then completely rolled over and sank.

Leaving Massachusetts to count what shells remained in her magazines (60% depleted), Tuscaloosa, now leading Wichita, and destroyer Rhind, closed the French to 14,000 yards, Brooklyn and Augusta were still pursuing from the east. Primaguet was holed five times below the waterline from Augusta and Brooklyn, and had an 8" shell on her #3 turret. She retired about 11 a.m. and anchored off shore. Milan had taken five hits, mostly 8" shells. Milan retired and anchored. Augusta scored a hit on Brestois. This French destroyer made it into the harbor, but after strafing from Ranger's planes, she later sank. The three French warships outside the harbor still underway were destroyer leader Albatros, and destroyers Frondeur and L'Alcyon. These ships organized for one more torpedo foray at 1115. Firing from Tuscaloosa and Wichita reduced the French ship maneuvering options to zig zags behind a smoke screen. Under continuous fire from El Hank, Wichita was hit about 1130 with light damage and 14 men wounded. Wichita then was missed by a three-torpedo spread from a French submarine. Tuscaloosa and Wichita hit Frondeur. Down by the stern, Frondeur made it back into port only to succumb to aircraft strafing. Shells hit Albatros twice at 1130 and she fought on with three guns, zigzagging in the smoke. One of Ranger's dive-bombers scored with two bombs that penetrated a fire room and an engine room. A hit from Augusta took out the other engine room. Albatros lost all way. Only L'Alcyon got back in unscathed.

Fedala conferences were being held. Casablanca conferences were being held. News of his defending troops' surrenders came sweeping up the road from Fedala. Still, Admiral Michelier kept his own counsel and had more fight in the forces left to him.

A Third Effort by French Fighting Ships on D-day

By noon, Brooklyn and Augusta had returned to their transport-guarding assignment. General Patton had been put ashore. The Covering Group was moving westward again to run down a false report of an unidentified cruiser. At shortly before one in the afternoon, La Grandiere, a 2000-ton ship with three 5.5" guns, left harbor at Casablanca with two minesweepers as escort. Again, the track was toward the transports. Two destroyers, Tempete and Simoun, which had not yet been in the open sea action, milled around the harbor entrance. In the face of shelling from Augusta and Brooklyn and their screening destroyers, La Grandiere, slightly damaged by our aircraft, returned, with her escorts to port. A tug attempting to tow Albatros was also bombed and strafed and finally helped beach Albatros near Primaguet and Milan. Primaguet came under almost continuous bombing attack in her exposed position with no shore based AA guns left to help her out. A hit on the bridge killed 9 officers, including her skipper.

Later in the afternoon, Massachusetts signaled that she had seven loaded 16" guns, and would make one more firing pass at El Hank. But, by the end of the 8th, El Hank stood firm. Massachusetts had only armor piercing shells left for her main battery, according to the Morison account. With no High Capacity (HC) point detonating ammo, only a direct hit on thick metal would do any real harm.

Samuel Eliot Morison's comment at the close of the first day at Casablanca included the following exchange:

The officer manning the engine room telephone on the destroyer Wilkes heard loud reports, then calls for more speed. "What is going on up there?" he inquired. "Enemy cruiser chasing us!" was the reply. Before long he was thrown off his feet by a sudden change of course and even more speed was called for. "What's going on now?" he asked. "We're chasing the enemy cruiser!"

French Submarines

There had been 11 French submarines in Casablanca when action began. Three were sunk in the harbor and eight got out. We have covered most of the action accounts of those that got to sea. Let me summarize what has been learned from later assessments. Meduse was bombed by a Philadelphia plane and beached. Orphee made it back into Casablanca and survived. Le Tonnant made it to Cadiz and was scuttled there by her crew. Amazone and Antiope made it to Dakar. Three have never been fully accounted for. They were Sidi-Ferruch, Conquerant, and Sybille. According to Author Morison's Volume II, one of these three was depth-charged by U.S. destroyers and bombed by U.S. aircraft. What the French submarines that made it out of Casablanca might have accomplished in several torpedo attacks against our most important warships could have spelled disaster. Hindsight tells us that it was right to try to take them out of action before they could leave port. The uncertainties about French resistance and the fragmentary last minute reconnaissance information on the harbor sent our first air strikes off with tentative objectives. Those subs should have been a primary objective.

Troop Progress at Fedala

On the ninth, in a visit to Patton's newly established command post at Hotel Miramar in Fedala, Admiral Hewitt transferred command of all troops ashore to General Patton. Although a good percentage of our troops had made it to shore by the evening of the 8th, only a fraction of the cargo from the transports had been unloaded. Three of the Center Group's smaller cargo ships moved right into Fedala harbor by the end of D-day. Ferrying cargo to shore in landing boats proceeded on through the night of 8-9 November. Two sorties of single French aircraft dropped a few bombs, without effect. The swell, unusually low for the 8th, increased to normal on the 9th. All remaining transports in the roadstead were moved shoreward so that the closest was just 4,000 yards from the harbor. Bristol had captured a French trawler on the 8th, and with a prize crew aboard, ferried 200 soldiers per trip for two days and two nights. This made available a greater percentage of the surviving landing craft to use for moving supplies ashore. The beachmaster concentrated on Fedala harbor or beach Red in the rising surf. Even then, tank lighters foundered in the surf.

Personnel with inadequate skills training, exacerbated by poor planning of the way material had been loaded aboard ship, were factors which delayed the movement of men and materiel to the beach. The job got done. But, it would never be done this way again. With the wrong supplies at the wrong place, competition for specific needs made matters worse. Trucks were needed to move material away from the docks, but Patton needed the same trucks for his advance toward Casablanca. Transports Stanton and Thurston, and soon-to-be communications ship Ancon, got their complex signal and medical equipment ashore. Boat crews were exhausted with no time off from the night of the 7th until the morning of the 10th when all troops had made it ashore.

Aircraft duels occupied much of the 9th, with Ranger planes shooting down French Dewoitine aircraft and a Messerschmidt-109 which had strafed the beaches at Fedala. Thereafter, Port Lyautey airfield and columns of French reinforcements moving toward Casablanca, occupied the attention of our air group. The beaches and transport area were not further bothered from the air. By the 10th, Lyautey airfield and the Kasbah to the north were in U.S. hands and Safi had fallen. Battleship New York was ordered back to the

Center Group and General Harmon's tanks started north toward Mazagan from Safi on the road to Casablanca. The Army intended to assault Casablanca on the 11th.

Admiral Michelier improvised. Crews from his disabled ships joined a Senegalese battalion and formed a perimeter on the 10th. U.S. troops advancing west were met by naval gunfire from the Jean Bart's secondary batteries and the Ainsaba AA battery. Two French corvettes advanced along the coast firing into U.S. troops with 100mm guns and machine guns. Augusta, Edison, Boyle, Tillman and Rowan moved toward the corvettes, with Edison opening fire at 1130 on the lead corvette and Tillman on the other. Ten minutes later Augusta fired several salvos at a range of 18,000 yards. Using smoke, the corvettes retreated into the harbor.

Michelier's defense was soon split. Augusta's attention then became riveted on large splashes ahead. Jean Bart had repaired the 15-inch battery azimuth jam, but had cannily left the guns in the disabled position until ready to fire. Turning seaward, Augusta was straddled closely three times from Jean Bart's ten two-gun salvos as she opened the range to Jean Bart from 19,000 to 29,000 yards. Edison was with Augusta on that retirement. Our guns were out-ranged. From being ahead of Augusta on the inbound course, we were left behind her as she swept outbound, so we had much too close a look at one tight straddle of Augusta's fantail. Ranger dive-bombers using 1000-pound bombs scored three direct hits on Jean Bart in retaliation.

(Though now put out of action for good at Casablanca, the resilient Jean Bart was shortly floated, escorted to New York with the help of one of Edison's officers, Jake Boyd. In the U.S. she was refitted, and made available again, this time for the Allies.)

By the night of the 10th, US troops converged in a 180-degree arc around Casablanca awaiting only the Sherman tanks from Safi. A final attack was set for early on the 11th. By 0600, Augusta, New York, cruiser Cleveland and several destroyers, all with plenty of ammunition, took up firing positions. Before 0700, the French sent a flag of truce and the attack was called off. The French communication chain went from Darlan at Algiers, to General Nogues to Admiral Michelier and covered the entire TORCH objective. The fighting ashore for Morocco and Algeria was over. There may have been exceptions, but the French in North Africa immediately began cooperating in the effort to defeat Germany.

U-boats Find Sitting Ducks

Some of the following material on submarine attacks at Casablanca comes from my own personal observations but the important deliberations that were held on the U-boat threat are told in Morison's Volume II, Operations in North African Waters, pages 168-173. Success in almost all other respects of the Western Task Group's responsibility ended with a dark blot on the record. By the 10th of November, the USS Ranger had reported a spread of four torpedoes that missed, her lookouts had seen a conning tower and one of her screening destroyers, Ellyson, had seen a periscope. On the 11th, Suwannee aircraft sank a shore-hugging sub with depth charges. That submarine was later assessed to be one of the three French subs not accounted for after the French submarine deployment from Casablanca. At this point, it was the French submarines that had generated most of the threats.

By the afternoon of 11 November, dispatches told the Task Force gathered around Fedala that Atlantic U-boat concentrations had moved toward the Casablanca area. A warning to this effect went to all ships. Most of the Center Attack

Group transports were still anchored in Fedala Roads. Author Morison's Volume II, Operations in North African Waters, details important discussions about moving some or all transports into Casablanca. Those present agreed on the advisability of moving transports Bliss, Scott, Hewes and Rutledge that were at the beginning of their unloading. After a strong endorsement of the move by Captain Emmet, Admiral Hewitt decided against it because a D-day plus 5 convoy was just entering the area and would need all available space in Casablanca harbor. The only alternative mentioned in the discussions held on this matter was for the transports to remain at anchor off Fedala.

The decision not to move was made about half past six on 11 November, and an hour later, the Joseph Hewes, the tanker Winooski, and the destroyer Hambleton, waiting at anchor to fuel from Winooski, were torpedoed. Hewes went down quickly, taking her skipper and many of her crew, and almost all of her load. Winooski was hit in a fuel tank that had salt water ballast in it, the hole being about 25 feet on a side. Hambleton lost 20 men, but the survivors kept her afloat and she was towed into Casablanca and months later made it to the U.S. under her own power. According to Morison's account, the skipper of the Hambleton was bitter about the order he received to anchor to await fueling from a ship whose personnel had told him that they only fueled ships during certain daylight hours. Later assessments confirmed that these torpedoings had been a U-boat job, most likely one that had made it through the defensive minefield we had laid to the northeast. It was almost as if this sub had a representative present at the meeting after which it was decided the transports would not move.

Let me reset the transport scene. They were anchored in a rectangle just north of Fedala. One line of the rectangle was almost North-South and the other was East-West. Our mine-field was to the northeast. The inner screen found Bristol patrolling east-west to the north, and Murphy patrolling north-south to the west. A series of screening ships made up layers of inverted Ls, shaped north to the open sea and east away from Casablanca. The screen was five layers deep, with Edison covering the north-south line the furthest west. Bristol sighted the U-173 (later assessment supplied this specific identification) retiring to the north, employed its searchlight to first make sure it was not a landing craft, got off one five inch shell, and then made two depth charge attacks after the sub submerged. It escaped, for the moment.

Author Samuel Eliot Morison's account highlights that the Ranger, Suwannee and Chenango in company with Brooklyn and six destroyers stood off a determined wolf-pack of U-boats in an area well out to sea from the transport area. This occurred in the morning of the 12th. At almost this same time came word that Casablanca Harbor was ready to take 12 ships. Admiral Hewitt, according to author Samuel Eliot Morison, again declined to approve moving the Fedala transports. Three destroyers reported aggressive torpedo activity on the afternoon of the 12th. U-130 approached the transports from the east, and got shoreward of the minefield and into attack position. At about 6-p.m. local time, this submarine fired a spread of six torpedoes from the forward tubes and two from the aft tubes. Edward Rutledge, Tasker Bliss and Hugh Scott received two hits each. The time of these torpedoings was just 24 hours after USS Hambleton was hit, as she lay anchored near the Winooski.

In this second torpedo attack, Edison was alongside the tanker Winooski, with lines attached to her, and with a fueling hose connected in which oil flowed from the tanker to Edison. I had just mentioned to a Winooski sailor that the impact of the torpedo explosion the evening before must have been tremendous since I saw bandages on the foreheads of many Winooski seamen. He responded, "Oh no, we hardly felt the impact. We knew something had happened. We were all at the movie in total darkness with hard hats on. In the confusion, we butted each other with the hard hats and that is the reason for the bandages." Moments after my discussion with the Winooski crewmember, the explosions resounded as the three transports were hit. Edison cast off immediately from the Winooski, leaving oil flowing out of her dangling hose.

Until I reread Historian Morison's account 55 years later, I was not able to put into context the Hambleton's skipper's upset at the Winooski's refusal to fuel him on the 11th. In my brief, torpedo-interrupted, conversation with the Winooski sailor before the second U-boat raid on Fedala Roads, I learned that the Winooski crew had been at the movies during the attack on the day before. Fifty five years later I discovered that the Hambleton had been told to wait for the reason that it was past the time of day that the tanker performed fueling service. Perhaps the fueling of the Hambleton late in the afternoon of the 11th would have interfered with movie time on Winooski.

Bliss burned and sank after midnight on the 13th with heavy loss of life. Rutledge and Scott went down earlier. U-130 retired northeast and Captain Emmet ordered his remaining transports to get underway.

Later, on the 15th, the USS Electra, en-route without escort from its service with the Northern Task Group to Casablanca, was torpedoed 17 miles off Fedala. With the Navy tug Cherokee pulling, and minesweepers Raven and Stansbury pumping, and with some screening of this operation by Edison, the assist got Electra tied up to Casablanca's Jettee d'Allure, where she ended up on the bottom with only her main deck above water. Since Edison was off to other duties before Electra made it inside the breakwater, my original information that she was grounded outside Casablanca came from Morison's Volume II, Operations in North African Waters. I am happy to acknowledge a correction received in an e-mail of 15 February, 1998. The e-mail came from Commander W.D. Cook, SC, USNR, who was Electra's Supply Officer in 1942 when she was torpedoed. Commander Cook reports that Electra made it into the harbor and tied up at Jettee d'Allure. It was there that she settled onto the bottom leaving only the main deck above water. The USS Electra, AK 21, eventually made it back to the States and was repaired for future operations.

U-173 sank Hewes and reported in to the German Admiralty. She probably also hit the Electra but likely had not had time to get this report in to the German Admiralty. About noon on the 16th, destroyer Woolsey got a very good sound contact. Assisted by Swanson and Quick, Woolsey forced the presumed submarine to the bottom. Woolsey repeatedly caused oil and bubbles to come to the surface with her depth charging. This was off the entrance to Casablanca and this was an action that U-173 definitely did not report to its Admiralty. Woolsey proved very adept at sub finding, as we shall see in a later chapter.

Anchored Transports Make Good Targets

We learn from experience, but sometimes not fast enough. The issue of Casablanca dock space versus keeping the Fedala transports at anchorage appears to have dominated the conversation before the recommendation was made to Admiral Hewitt on the 11th. One wishes that someone present had suggested a third alternative, *"get the transports underway."*

This is what Captain Emmet *did on his own authority* after the second attack. He really had this authority before the first attack but seemed to have been put off by the discussion that led to a recommendation to Admiral Hewitt. It may have been that Captain Emmet did not anticipate Admiral Hewitt's rejection of precious Casablanca dock space for Fedala Roads transports and it took Emmet by surprise. Destroyers screening anchored transports are working at a disadvantage. There were plenty of destroyers to screen underway transports and at this, they had experience. The subs were bold, and once in close quarters almost any firing angle was going to find some cargo ship, especially in a symmetrical formation at anchor. In addition to heavy loss of life, and loss of nearly all their cargo, transport survivors numbering over 1,000 were taken ashore and tended to by medical personnel and men of the 3rd Infantry Division. Burn wounds were severe.

SG Radar

A persistent set of the current to the northeast drove Fedala Scout Boats and control destroyers out of position. This contributed to the heavy loss of precious landing craft, supplies, and even some troops. An SG radar fix earlier in the evening of the 7th corrected the Dead Reckoning (DR) position of the lane leading transports and provided course change information to get to the correct initial point. With some delay caused by this last minute change, the rest of the transports wheeled into their correct positions late. It could be argued that the DR position error was an accumulation of errors but, in retrospect, it was a local current whose effect had not been entered into the original DR solution. The current remained to push the landing craft and the control destroyers out of position as they closed the beaches. In the darkness there were many unknowns to the Scout Boats. Not being aware of their faulty station-keeping was just one of the more aggravating unknowns. Continued use of an SG radar for more precise local navigation close to shore would have helped the entire operation. Author Morison confirmed that there was at least one SG radar on some naval ship at Casablanca. Perhaps there were more.

A rumor prevalent in destroyer circles just after TORCH was that there was an SG radar on one of the screening ships. With the visual sightings of conning towers and periscopes, and sound contacts, one speculates that SG radar contacts on submarines could have provided U.S. seaborne forces a real advantage at Casablanca. A richly populated area of anchored transports, and three days to find out that something was going on, would draw the attention of the German U-boat fleet. The evaluation boils down to a set of conjectures: (1) there was no SG radar on a screen destroyer, or (2) there was an SG radar and no one realized what a tool it could be, or (3) there was an SG radar, contacts were reported, and disbelieved.

Except for the torpedoing of the Hambleton, U.S. destroyers came out of TORCH with few casualties and with a lot of experience. The planning assignments at Fedala required four destroyers to head up the four landing craft assault lanes, and then take up position for counter-fire as needed. There was no assigned shore fire control party. Counter-fire requirements passed through a varied series of communication channels so that only direct feedback was from optical observation from the firing ship. Destroyers were recruited on the spot for sorties, alone or with cruisers, in toward the beach in response to French sorties toward the transports. A few times destroyers elected direct fire on their own when an enemy gun was clearly seen to be firing, but this was not a preferred mode by our troops ashore, or even by the destroyer itself. Too much chance for error. In the future there would be Shore Fire Control Parties with designated ships to support them for indirect fire. Edison served well enough in her ad hoc fire support duties at Casablanca to be promoted to a designated fire support responsibility for the next fleet landing operations at Sicily. SG radar was on its way to the Edison for the navigation required in tight quarters. Those future fire support duties could have been purely chance assignments but it is my opinion that the Fleet Commanders evaluated past performance in making future assignments.

French Submarines and the U-boats

Although the French submarines from Casablanca did not sink any of our ships, they did give an account of themselves and only some extraordinary vigilance and maneuvering by our warships prevented the French torpedoes from creating extensive damage. The French did not have the experience of over two years at sea that the U-boat fleet had. Giving them credit for audacity, the French submarines like their surface counterparts at Casablanca, were pressing attacks home on major US warships, not largely unarmed merchantmen.

The U-boats were called in from the Atlantic. Morocco has an extensive, open, coast. Approach conditions were ideal for the U-boats and their orders were to defeat us by sinking our shipping. At Casablanca, that mission did not change. With their open sea experience and daring, they did extensive damage at Casablanca to our supply train.

While the two most aggressive U-boat skippers involved in Casablanca attacks soon paid with the loss of their vessels, in 1998 terms, their "risk/reward" ratio was good. U-boats were not defeated in World War II. They were out produced. Speculate that a so-called conventional war occurred again,

184

and that one of the two regional conflicts the U.S. plans to be prepared for involves the sea environment. If in such a conflict, an enemy employs World War II subs and mines, such weapons would cause the U.S. plenty of trouble. The Strait of Hormuz was a reminder.

The Trip Home
    Here is what we thought about.

Illustration 14-An Edison Ship's Party

Here is how we communicated with home.

Illustration 15-V-Mail

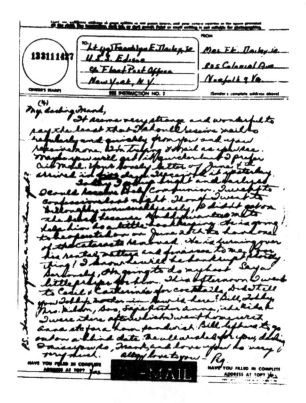

(The first half of November 1942 is now over. Edison returns to the routine of the convoy. There is one important difference from the previous convoy. This time, we are going back to the States. Ed Meier shares his return trip with us.)

The 17th. Got underway from the outer Casablanca harbor at 8:00 this morning and by 2:00 in the afternoon the convoy had formed up and was ready to put to sea. It is now midnight and I have just returned from watch on the bridge. The weather is delightful and the moon very bright. Temperatures in the evening range thru the 60's and low 70's. This type of weather is bad submarine weather, however, and we're all hoping for the best. In this connection, we received word today that a submarine was sunk in our (Fedala) mine field last night. This makes 3 or 4 sunk or damaged around Casablanca. The score isn't even with them yet, however.

The 18th. Nothing at all happened today. Stood my usual watches and played a couple of games of chess with Jake Boyd. We are all hoping that we will drop these transports off at Norfolk and then head for New York or Boston at 25 knots. The Commodore on the Bristol (ComDesRon 13) finds it very inconvenient to be in Norfolk so there is a good possibility of leaving there.

(A commentary on Norfolk: The author's wife grew up in Portsmouth, Virginia and in the Ocean View/Willoughby Spit area of Norfolk, Virginia. She has told me that the Navy people off the ships never liked it there. My guess is that there were just too many of them and the entertainment prospects compared with New York or Boston were not appealing. The Commodore in November of 1942 was Captain John B. Heffernan. After the war, as Rear Admiral, he became Director of Naval History. Finally, Jake Boyd from the Naval Academy class of 1938 was the games expert in the wardroom. I did not dare play chess against him but would try bridge, hearts, or cribbage. He always emphasized in cribbage that it was not who was ahead, but who had the last play. Jake was also a wonderful person, expert at everything he did, and willing to teach a younger officer.)

The 19th. Today was a beautiful, warm day and everything went along smoothly. Had a routine battle station drill this morning, the first since before the assault on Casablanca.

The sea is very calm--all the difference in the world from the North Atlantic.

The 20th. Nothing of importance happened today. The weather continues warm and pleasant but had a severe thunderstorm in the late afternoon.

The 21st. Refueled today while underway at 10 knots. It is a delicate maneuver and must be executed with precision. The barometer started to drop this morning and the storm which was expected came late in the afternoon.

(Comment: During General Quarters, the Deck Divisions largely melt away. Most of the men have assignments at some ordnance station. During fueling at sea, the deck divisions come into their own. On the bridge, the conning officer, helmsman and skipper are in tight communication with the engine-room. No fishtailing! The rudder is critical. On the main deck, the bos'n is in charge. The two principal connections with the tanker are the oil hose, and a tether to the tanker. Edison rides on the tether from the tanker, with just a turn or two on Edison's own engines lower than turns needed to exactly pace the tanker. So, Edison is being towed just slightly on the tanker's power. Ride the rope and not the oil hose. The bos'n has created a complex rig, and in addition to a smooth "ride" slightly at the expense of the tanker, his rig is designed to provide for a smooth, planned, disconnect or a quick emergency disconnect. The latter is not often required but when it is, it is done almost instantly based on eye movement of the skipper directly to the bos'n. The tool that accomplished the quick disconnect in those days was a simple axe. The bos'n must have created the rig properly, then he must swing that axe accurately. On one occasion, our tanks were full and we *could not get the tanker to stop pumping*. With oil all over the deck and flowing down our hatches, the bos'n not only exercised the quick disconnect but he also had to throw the oil hose into the sea.)

The picture that follows is the bos'n. His name was Francis Ducharme, and at the time of the picture was Boatswain's Mate First Class. He later made Chief.

Illustration 16-Francis Ducharme BM1/c

The 22nd. Boy, what a storm we had last night and all day today. The barometer dropped rapidly to 28.08 and the mountainous waves washed right over the ship. It was just as bad as those North Atlantic storms last winter. The moon came out clear and bright tonight and rain in the distance made a rainbow or rather a moonglow. It's the first time I have ever seen a phenomenon like that.

(Comment: That barometer reading refers to 28.08 inches of mercury. By coincidence, I was transposing Ed Meier's notes on September 12, 1997 and just three days earlier on 9/9/97, our East Coast USA weather forecaster told us that hurricane Erika had turned northeast and would miss Bermuda to the east. He reported that the eye of the hurricane had a pressure of 28.08 and the winds were then at 125 mph, a Class 3 hurricane. On that trip home from North Africa, and in flying Liberators and Privateers later on in the Navy, I have been in the "eye" of hurricanes about three or four times. The eye of one East Coast hurricane named Gloria in the late 1980s or early 90s passed right over my home in Massachusetts. What Ed Meier experienced in mid-Atlantic on November 22, 1942 was the "eye" of the hurricane. In those days, the "eye" was not a familiar term. I might also note that the Convoy Commodore on the way home told us over the TBS that he felt "bilious" in that storm and was turning command temporarily over to his #2. Ships that fueled later on the 21st of November had much more difficulty. In a later transit of the Atlantic, a cruiser skipper was quite finicky about going alongside the tanker in the pitching seas, and made a number of passes without hooking up. The Task Force commander relieved him on the spot and the cruiser's Executive Officer was put in command.)

The 23rd. The storm is beginning to abate altho it is still plenty rough. By noon the barometer rose to 28.50. News from all battle fronts seems to be excellent and it looks as though next year (1943) will be a big one for the Allies. With Rommel pushed out of Africa, which I believe will happen within the winter, the Allies should be able to knock Italy out of the war by early spring or early summer. And from there on, it will be an all out offensive against Germany. And with Germany on the run, Japan will not present much of a problem. I am extremely optimistic over the prospects of the war being pretty nearly over by this time next year.

The 24th. Nothing of importance occurred today. The storm has to a great extent spent itself and we can again enjoy a meal without spilling part of the food on the table.

(This concludes the summary of Lt. (jg) Meier's recollections about the North African invasion in November 1942. I am grateful that he shared his experiences. I must again admire how aware he was of the events in which he was participating, even though his end-of-war forecasting was too optimistic.)

Operations, December 1942 to June 1943

Edison made Norfolk, on the return from Casablanca, on December 1, 1942. We were then, as many aboard had hoped, ordered to New York. She returned to Norfolk to pick up a single tanker to convoy to Port Arthur, Texas, where Edison spent Christmas eve, 1942. Texas did not permit liquor to be sold in bars. One had to go to a state liquor store and buy a bottle and then go to a bottle club. Which we did. We were enjoying this freedom. There was really no entertainment as such. At the next table, a Texaco oil man and a Gulf oil man got into a big argument. By the time we were fully aware of their anger, the two were brandishing liquor bottles with the heads knocked off. Dick Hofer and I went out into a lumberyard next door and hid while the shore patrol and local police restored order. The trip in and out of the channel at Port Arthur, with a pilot aboard, was made in pitch darkness, a heavy layer of fog and dense clouds of bugs. I marked it as a place not to live.

On Christmas Day, 1942, we left for New York, arriving there on 2 January, 1943. We left with a convoy for Casablanca on 14 January, arriving without incident on 25 January. We patrolled outside the harbor. We also moored inside the sea wall, a new experience for us where the ship is perpendicular to the sea wall, stern lines are attached to the sea wall, and an anchor is dropped off the bow. The swells cause the largest lines to fray and break, and the anchor drags even though the ship is inside the sea wall. This can get on one's nerves. It kept the skipper and exec at full alert. We returned to New York on 13 February. Went to Casco Bay, Maine, on 25 February for type (destroyer) training, then left for New York on 2 March and joined a convoy for Casablanca on 5 March, arriving on the 18th. Sailed on 6 April with convoy for New York and made repairs in Brooklyn Navy Yard on 18 April, and left for Norfolk on 19 April.

After exercises in the Chesapeake, including emergency drills and gunnery, the Edison sailed for New York on 4 June and a rendezvous with a convoy to Mers El Kebir, Algeria. Full convoy underway by 10 June and made Mers El Kebir harbor on 21 June. This commenced a new phase of Edison's life, with a Mediterranean base at Mers El Kebir, Algeria and support when needed from repair ship, USS Vulcan, AR5.

On 8/17/98, I received an e-mail from Jerry Hawkins, whose father-in-law, Ralph Ault served in Companies E, F and Headquarters Company of the 1st Battalion, 157th Infantry of the 45th U.S. Infantry Division. This Division fought at Gela in Sicily, in the northern Sicily end run, at Salerno and at Anzio. From Ralph, Jerry learned that the 45th left Newport News, Virginia, combat loaded on troopships Anne Arundel, Barrett and Harry Lee, and were in convoy on 6/10/43. Jerry wondered if Edison were part of the screen for that convoy, and questioned whether it was unusual for

192

troops to be combat loaded leaving the States. Names like the Anne Arundel, Barrett, Harry Lee, Samuel Chase, Susan B. Anthony and Elizabeth Stanton are indelibly imprinted on my mind. The vividness of those names occurs not because I was a history major but because of World War II convoy experience with those ships. No, it was not unusual to be combat loaded right out of the States, witness the North African assault just covered. Sicily was coming up and Jerry Hawkins mentioned a practice landing at Arzeu after arriving at Oran. That tracks with Edison's experience. The 45th went to the Gela sector for the Sicily invasion while Edison went to Licata, the next sector north. Edison did participate in the Sicily end run and the Salerno and Anzio landings. These are all yet to come in this story. There is plenty of mention of the 45th Infantry Division.

Again, I failed to recognize at the time that we were entering an entirely new phase in the life of the USS Edison. The rest of my tour would find Edison a principal fire support ship for amphibious landings, with just occasional ASW convoy duty. When we got low on ammo or needed stateside repairs, we would be assigned escort duty for any convoy that was returning to the States.

By early winter of 1943, we had had a yard availability period during which the SG radar was installed. With that radar, the balance of power in the battle with U-boats shifted back a little toward our side. SG could "see" a periscope. It would also prove handy in close in support for assault landings.

Chapter Seven - Lake Bizerte and Sicily

1943; The U.S. is Now a Mediterranean Power

U.S. land and sea forces had reached near parity with the British in the Mediterranean by early 1943. The next time that an uncertainty occurred about who would fight and who would not, the situation worked out much more to our disadvantage than it had with the various political shades of the French military in Morocco. This would be at Salerno, and the Italian surrender provided the uncertainty. At Salerno, the Germans were able to take advantage of what we might have thought was bad news for them, Marshal Badoglio's surrender. But, we must first go to Lake Bizerte and to the assault beaches at Sicily before we come to Salerno.

Before setting out on her Mediterranean duties, it should be noted that Edison's third skipper took over on February 24, 1943. On that day, Lieutenant Commander Hepburn A. Pearce, Edison's Executive Officer relieved Commander William R. Headden. Lieutenant James Abner Boyd fleeted up to become XO of the Edison. Lt. (jg) Richard "Dick" Hofer became Gunnery Officer .The next four chapters will deal mostly with action-filled months for Edison in 1943 and 1944 in the Mediterranean land and sea war.

General Eisenhower remained Supreme Allied Commander in the Mediterranean for all of 1943 while the next in command, land, sea and air, were British. Allied naval forces remained under the command of Admiral of the Fleet Sir Andrew B. Cunningham RN, and later Admiral Sir John Cunningham RN, who succeeded him.

Command-wise, the sea matters went well. Not as much can be said for land and air commands. Even considering the testy nature of General Montgomery ("Monty"), the British were not always the problem. U.S. air forces, though then still a part of the U.S. Army, followed their own star.

U.S. Destroyers: New Roles

From January 1943 through October 1944, when I departed the Edison at Oran, there were no U.S. Navy air forces available for Mediterranean operations except for the cruiser spotting planes. Available Atlantic escort carriers were fully engaged in ASW Hunter/Killer efforts in the Atlantic Ocean. As larger carriers were commissioned in U.S. shipbuilding yards, they were sent to the Pacific, where there were fleet engagements to be fought, some related to the strategic island hopping counter offensive which began in the South Pacific. Although there was an Italian surface fleet, no more fleet battles were to be fought in the Mediterranean. Italian submarines were active in the days leading up to the invasion of Sicily.

Coordinated amphibious assaults characterized the remaining efforts in the Mediterranean conflict. These shaped the mission of U.S. destroyers. On defense, even accounting for some episodes of accurate German counter fire during and after landing assaults, it was the German submarines, mines and aircraft that became the prime concerns of Allied naval ship commanders. The French defending North Africa during TORCH scored more hits on naval vessels than German shore batteries did in the balance of the Mediterranean campaign. (The invasion of Normandy was not part of the Mediterranean campaign.)

Naval gunfire, particularly U.S. naval gunfire in support of troops ashore, came into its own in the Mediterranean. In Volume IX of his History of United States Naval Operations in World War II, author Samuel Eliot Morison (writing under the title, "Sicily, Salerno and Anzio", almost ten years after finishing Volume II on North Africa), finished the Mediterranean part of his history. He stated in his Preface to Volume IX, "Frequently in Italian and German sources, we find that this ferocious and devastating intervention of the Allied Navies was the crucial factor that forced Axis ground forces to retire." Morison was referring to naval gunfire.

Nineteenth century land surveys which the British had conducted, resulting in the British North African Purple Grid System, provided the frame of reference for Allied sea and land forces, especially for shore fire control of naval gunfire. I can recall dates in the 1860s on the charts we used for gunfire support. U.S. Navy units, for the most part, remained under the direct command of Vice Admiral Hewitt. Hewitt's Eighth Fleet was part of British Admiral Cunningham's combined Allied naval operational force. Those British "Purple Grid" maps were very hard to read under blackout conditions with red light for illumination.

It is appropriate to note that Historian Morison dedicated his Volume IX to Vice Admiral Lyal A. Davidson who died in 1950. We have already met the Admiral in this story and will meet him again in these next few chapters. Morison's dedication was most appropriate.

High Strategy in the First Six Months of 1943
By January 1943, U.S. land forces were moving in strength toward Tunisia from the east, while the British Eighth Army under General Montgomery was moving west, fresh from a victory at El Alamein. Although the siege of Stalingrad had been lifted, Germany had nearly 200 divisions putting pressure on the Russians. Pacific supply routes to Siberia, North Atlantic routes to Murmansk, and the extra long trip around the Cape of Good Hope to the Persian Gulf were

long and exposed to German interdiction. Allied losses of over 700,000 tons of shipping sunk in November 1942 showed some signs of easing with half that reported in December 1942. Roosevelt, Churchill and their senior military staffs met once again in Casablanca for just over a week beginning January 14, 1943. Stalin was invited but did not come. The argument over the cross channel invasion was renewed. The U.S. pressed for sooner, and the British for later.

The three binding concepts agreed to by Britain and the U.S. at Halifax in 1941 kept the Casablanca conference, with all of its contention, from tearing apart the coordinated effort thus far achieved. Those concepts were the priority to defeat Hitler before Japan, to persevere in ASW operations, and to give Stalin a second front which would drain pressure from Hitler's eastern front, or at least, make sure that Hitler had no additional forces to send against Russia. With the Japanese always in their minds, General Marshall and Admiral King wanted to keep enough pressure in the Pacific to prevent Japan's consolidation of its gains.

The U.S. wanted to put North Africa on hold after defeating Rommel there, and begin a buildup of forces for a cross channel invasion. The British wanted to go after Sardinia or Sicily and pursue the "soft underbelly" theory. The British wanted to win objectives one at a time while the Americans always wanted to be able to answer the question, "When we do that, what do we do next?" For the short term, with the agreement to invade Sicily next and with no follow-on objective stated, the British won the argument. The U.S. departed from the bargaining at the Casablanca Conference determined to point for and plan for a cross channel invasion. That invasion would be the "big one" irrespective of what further was accomplished in the Mediterranean. Eisenhower could only spare one day from the African Front to present his views at this Casablanca Conference.

In the final discussions, the British had favored occupation of Sardinia. According to Historian Morison, General Brehon Somervell, the U.S. supply chief, pointed out that the Straits of Sicily were still too dangerous for all but the most urgent convoys. He argued that gaining control of the Mediterranean sea lane gave unchallenged access to the Suez Canal, thus adding up to an equivalent of 225 freighters saved from the Cape of Good Hope route to India. Sicily became the decision. The broad outline furnished to General Eisenhower at the conclusion of the Casablanca Conference on January 22, 1943 called for a British Force mounted from the Near East and a U.S. force mounted from Africa, from the U.S., and from Britain.

The Axis forces in Tunisia, confronted by the British from the east, and a predominantly U.S. soldiered Allied force from the west, surrendered on 13 May 1943. Field Marshal Rommel got out, but many of his soldiers became POWs. This cemented North Africa in Allied hands while the north rim of the Mediterranean remained under Hitler's control. Malta stood fast as a British Mediterranean island outpost.

Transit Challenges to Sicily

From Cap Bon in Tunisia, the closest point of Sicily is just under 100 miles. This shortening of distances accompanied by home front progress in the design and production of more seaworthy landing craft meant that shore to shore amphibious operations would play a role in the Sicilian invasion. That same projection of 100 miles in distance meant that German bomber bases moved closer by the same amount. Just as occurred during the planning for the landings on the Atlantic coast of Morocco, U.S. planners for Sicily had to structure the Sicilian operation without the presence of many commanders scheduled to participate in it. Most of the field commanders were occupied with the action in Tunisia until the final month of planning for HUSKY, as the Sicilian invasion was named. Men like Eisenhower, Patton, Truscott and Allen were gaining recognition in discreetly written dispatches in which a little "name dropping" got by censors on the way to the U.S. news media. General Montgomery, too, from the British side was becoming a household name in the U.S.

Edison Takes Up Her New Post

A number of small assignments in and out of Mers El Kebir occurred between June 24 and June 30, 1943. On the 30th of June 1943, Edison participated in amphibious landing exercises at a beach called Arzeu, east of Oran. That beach had been involved in the TORCH landings at Oran on November 8, 1942 and some of the debris from that effort still littered the beach. Edison was introduced to the newly arrived U.S. 45th Infantry Division at the Arzeu practice landings. When the surf rolled on Mediterranean coasts, danger was present and our practice run at Arzeu resulted in some landing craft foundering casualties. U.S. forces were now in earnest practice for the invasion of Sicily. The Army had learned to lighten the pack somewhat for its soldiers. Aboard Edison, our gunners anticipated giving our troops the benefit of some suppression fire before they hit the beach. But, that was not to be.

On July 1, 1943, Edison departed for Bizerte, Tunisia. The anchorage in Lake Bizerte gave our crew a closer look at war than most cared for. The lake was still full of floating, dead bodies. Edison crewmembers had taken advantage of a brief authorization to swim. Swimming was terminated by signal light from another warship conveying orders to stay out of the water due to contamination.

Danger From Above

The night of July 6, 1943 brought Edison's first experience with what would become a daily occurrence, regular air raids by German bombers. I admired the progress that U.S. and Allied forces ashore had made during their battles against the Germans in North Africa. Of particular note was the air defense capability installed just since the local area had been subdued in mid-May. Powerful searchlights combed the sky for enemy planes. U.S. and British technicians had come to a foreign land in war conditions. Under daily threat, they made a connection with the local power grid seem routine. These achievements added to the pride I felt in our country. Sometimes the generators that the U.S. brought along filled in for local power facilities that had become battle casualties.

Selfishly, I liked any tool that helped preserve my life. Once two of those searchlights got an intersection on an aircraft, that pilot could not wiggle out of the beam. Then, he was a pretty good bet to get some serious flak. Our defending planes were aloft too, and if they stayed out of the Zone of the Interior, (ZI), a defined conical envelope with its apex on the ground, they would not be shot at by our ground based AA guns. We wore hard hats during these attacks, as the falling shrapnel was very dangerous. Only occasionally did U.S. warships augment ground based, air defense, fire in the confines of Lake Bizerte because of the communication and coordination difficulties. Edison's main battery was credited with one JU-88 (German Junkers, Model 88). We were pretty much under the protective umbrella of the British air defense commands while in Lake Bizerte. We were there to form up for a departure to Sicily.

Since the JU-88 is a plane we saw frequently, too frequently, it is pictured in Illustration 17. The aircraft photos are taken from recognition slides in the collection of Bill Rowan of Springfield, Massachusetts. (Commissioned an Ensign USNR out of the Kings Point Merchant Marine Academy, Bill went to the USS Doyen, PA-1, for service in the Pacific.)

The original Black and White (B&W) photos of ships and planes in the nearly 1,000 35mm glass slides in each U.S. ship's recognition training set were undoubtedly of high quality. Thousands of copies were made from the original set, one for each warship and one for each merchantman flying a U.S. flag with an Armed Guard crew aboard.

There is a tendency in photo reproduction to pick up Dmin, a higher minimum optical density, noticeable mostly as background. This makes everything appear darker. Add two layers of glass to create the slide and with constant feeding and discharging in projectors scratching the glass, the "target" plane or aircraft almost always looks dim, as in twilight or darkness. It turns out that without intention, the slide pictures come across to the viewer pretty much as an actual aircraft or ship might appear under less than ideal twilight conditions.

Illustration 17-German JU-88

A factor in the air defenses at Lake Bizerte were the British night fighter pilots, equipped with twin engine Beaufighters. Those were truly, friendly "friendlies."

Illustration 18-British Beaufighter

Lake Bizerte is a large lake. Again, U.S. ingenuity was called upon to open a wider channel to the Mediterranean for the enormous flotilla that assembled there for the Sicilian invasion in the summer of 1943. Air views in wartime photos published after the war showed an even larger assemblage than surface eyes could see at the time. If Marshal Goering's Luftwaffe, his Nazi air armada, was ever to play a part in denying further Allied penetration in the Mediterranean, it would have defined the concentration of targets in Lake Bizerte as the ideal place to make the point. That they did not was an indication that they could not, though their attacks seemed frequent enough to me at the time.

This force of warships and landing craft in Lake Bizerte were primarily for the Licata beach area, the northernmost of the three landing areas defined for the U.S. force landings on the Southwest coast of Sicily. Direct from the States, from England, and from all North African ports west of Bizerte, U.S. land and sea forces staged for the Gela and the Scoglitti beaches of Sicilian Invasion. These were the center and the southernmost landing areas in the U.S. sphere of responsibility for Sicily. The British were doing the same in the Eastern Mediterranean for their landings on the Southeast coast of Sicily, with the city of Syracuse one of their primary objectives. Once again, the whole could be touted as the largest such amphibious operation ever mounted. Edison was involved in a series of such firsts. Even Normandy, one year later, did not have an eight beaches-wide initial landing spread like Sicily.

Preparation Ends; Sicily Looms

JOSS was the code name for the Licata sector of landing operations under the immediate command of Rear Adm. Richard Conolly. DIME was the center attack force under

Rear Adm. Hall, with Gela its prime target. Rear Adm. Kirk commanded the southernmost CENT force, with Scoglitti the beach town in the center of the several beaches over which CENT troops would land. Admiral Hewitt, in overall command of the southwest Sicilian coast landings, "pleaded", according to author Samuel Eliot Morison, "to be allowed to deliver a pre-landing naval bombardment." He was turned down by an Army still in denial that naval bombardment could handle that task. Further, our own Army Air Force was not going to help neutralize beach defenses. Their decision came as a consequence of their self-defined sole objective of destruction or interdiction of enemy air forces. The two decisions leaving the enemy free of pre-landing fire suppression on the beaches presented quite a challenge for naval gunfire once our troops hit the beach.

Sicily is a triangle. From Marsala on its westernmost tip, southeast to Portopalo is a distance of 125 statute miles. This leg contains the Licata, Gela, and Scoglitti geography and beaches. From Portopalo on the Sicily's southern tip, north/northeast to the narrow Strait of Messina between Italy and Sicily, it is another 125 miles. Across the top of the triangle from Marsala to the Strait of Messina, roughly east to west, is about 180 miles. Edison would get to know the west side and the north side of this Sicilian triangle very well.

Storm!

An intense low-pressure cell suddenly built up in the North Tyrrhenian Sea where the Italian coast curves west toward Southern France. The water west and southwest of Sicily where we made our approach was churning with gale force winds during the approach on July 9, 1943. The larger landing craft, LSTs, Landing Ship Tanks, and LCTs, Landing Craft Tanks, and LCIs, Landing Craft Infantry took a pounding. The smaller personnel-bearing LCVPs, though now much improved from Casablanca, were tossed about like straws. We were close aboard many of these craft, actually at times looking almost directly down on them as we went by. Not one of the soldiers appeared fit for an assault operation. Terrible seasickness enveloped them all, as they lay flat, or across the gunwales puking into the sea. I imagined that it was the one time that these men, whose units would be chosen over and over again for assault landings, probably welcomed the landing itself, even though acutely aware of the enemy actions that they knew they would have to meet. The LST, bearing the alphabet letter S for Ship, was truly a ship. The Germans acknowledged as much by torpedoing them and by using advanced glider bombs against them. The LST could off-load a loaded LCT from its side into the sea.

U.S. Force Dispositions

JOSS, TF 86, was to put ashore the 3rd Division, Major General Lucian K. Truscott USA, commanding, along with two Ranger battalions in Princess ships. The Princess ships were neat little British pleasure steamers until commandeered for war. The 1st Infantry Division, commanded by Major General Terry Allen USA, along with a combat team of the 2nd Armored Division and one Ranger Battalion was the responsibility of TF 81, the DIME force at Gela. TF 85, the CENT force at Scoglitti, had the duty to deposit the 45th Infantry Division, under the command of Major General Troy Middleton, USA. The cruisers Brooklyn and Birmingham backed up JOSS at Licata, the cruisers Savannah and Boise stood ready behind the DIME force and the cruiser Philadelphia provided the heavy firepower for the CENT force. At Licata with Edison were seven other destroyers in dual roles of escort and gunfire support. At Gela, there were 13 destroyers and at Scoglitti, 16 destroyers had various assignments. In immediate "floating" reserve were the remaining two combat teams of the 2nd Armored Division, Major General Hugh Gaffey USA, commanding, along with one combat team of the 1st Division. These were part of the DIME force, and as matters developed, this is where they were needed. In Africa, a little over 100 sea miles away, the 9th Infantry Division was in General Reserve. General Patton commanded the overall Seventh Army of the Western Task Force.

Commander E. R. Durgin was now ComDesRon 13 with his pennant on the USS Buck. In DesDiv 25 were Woolsey, Ludlow, Edison, and Bristol supplemented by the destroyer USS Wilkes. In DesDiv 26, Commander V. Huber, were Nicholson, Swanson and Roe. Roe was a one-stacker like the Buck. Both Roe and Buck were built just one class before the rest, which were all two stack Benson/Livermores. Conolly's flag was on the USS Biscayne, which had been fitted with extra communications gear.

The warships named after U.S. cities in the Western Task Force were all light cruisers, with twelve or fifteen 6inch guns. The Wichita, Tuscaloosa and Augusta which had been with us for TORCH, all heavy cruisers with 8" guns, had been re-deployed to other areas. The British monitor Abercrombie was with the CENT force. I was not aware of the Abercrombie during the Sicilian action because Edison immediately moved northwest, then around Sicily's westernmost extremity and on toward Palermo harbor. This movement after the initial landings, in order to support the 3rd Division advance, separated us from the CENT force ships which stayed on for a more protracted effort in their initial assault area. I did get to see Abercrombie later in broad daylight at Salerno, and she was a unique site in my naval career. I was totally unprepared to see a monitor. I thought that the Monitor that fought for the Union in the U.S. Civil War was from a period long gone. The British obviously did not think so. Low in the water, Abercrombie's only purpose was to float two forward-looking large bore gun turrets to any battle scene she could get to. She looked like a battleship's forward section that was then sealed off to create a premature stern. She even had a tripod mast like the U.S. battleships New York and Texas. I do not know what her propulsion was. My guess was that she would need to be towed if she had to move with any speed.

If there was one difference in tactical objectives between TORCH at North Africa and HUSKY at Sicily, it was that at Sicily the capture of the airfields took precedence over capture of the harbors. For bringing up reserves, Allied naval forces were now within a half day's steaming of harbors in North Africa. At Casablanca, until that port was captured, our supply harbors were an ocean away on the east coast of the United States. On the other hand, penetration at Sicily meant that our forces were just a milk run from German air bases. We had no carriers, so needed to capture and put in service any enemy airfield that would fall. The airfield at Pantelleria, a small island off the southern coast of Sicily, became a preliminary target in the need to bring our land-based fighter aircraft to Sicily with more time over target. Some of the friendly force planes available over Sicily on D-day staged from the newly captured field on Pantelleria.

An Overview of the Landings at Licata

Storm or no, the landings took place as scheduled in the early morning of July 10, 1943. Though still rough, the seas began to abate at midnight. The boats headed for the beach at

0200. Some boats foundered in the high surf still running, although the heart of the storm had played itself out. Destroyers Swanson and Roe collided in the darkness. Damage was sufficient to later send them to the States for repair but not before they each played important roles at Licata beach. Defensive gunfire broke out about 0400. By dawn, the gunfire from attackers and defenders was heavy. Woolsey and Nicholson went close in to make smoke to shield the first boat assault waves. By 0730 the Beachmaster at Red Beach indicated that the smoke had worked, and that our counter fire had suppressed enemy fire on his beach. Woolsey had actually used 5" white phosphorus shells to cut off the sight lines of the defending artillery on the beach to the landing craft. By afternoon, the port at Licata was in our hands with naval casualties of 23 sailors lost and 118 wounded.

82nd Airborne Division paratroops in C-47s experienced rough conditions in the hours of darkness on July 11. British airborne troop carriers approached on unexpected navigation tracks on the 12th, missed their drop zones, and took fairly heavy small bore AA fire from our own landing craft just before drop. Airborne took a beating at Sicily, losing many lives even before facing enemy action. The lack of offshore AA discipline in our smaller craft was partly due to a planning failure to anticipate how things might go wrong, and consequent failure to prepare an emergency communication with a drill on the discipline that would be needed under such conditions. (An example might be the British MER-SIGS manual used with mixed-nation convoy ships at sea, where for example, two large red flares signaled an emergency turn for convoys.) Where the communications were in place and were ongoing as on destroyers and larger warships, Anti Aircraft fire discipline held at Sicily.

Edison's primary mission at Licata was fire support, "on call" from the assigned Army/Navy shore fire control party that stormed ashore at H-hour on D-day. Other missions were AA and ASW escort, though since the JOSS force had no transports, Edison's sole ASW escort duties were to screen the cruisers. At times, Edison patrolled independently ahead as our forces advanced and later we free-lanced by going up the coast on missions to draw enemy fire. Rarely did any U.S. warship employ direct fire on enemy targets during the landing phase when our own forces were intensely concentrated. Safety for our own troops from friendly fire was paramount. There were occasions when skippers thought they could get in some damaging licks as a result of what their own range finders could see, but gaps in the knowledge of what the actual situation was ashore spelled a potential for error. But when ranging ahead of the battle lines, there were opportunities for shelling forces in retreat. Later at Salerno, we were specifically asked by the USS Savannah's SFCP if we could see the line of German Tiger tanks advancing on our beachhead, and were requested aloud over voice circuits to go to direct fire if we could affirm the enemy disposition. But, that was an exception made when matters hung in the balance.

New Amphibious Tools Used at Licata

The final dry beach at Licata had in front of it a series of sandbars. The last sandbar on the tide of July 10, 1997 was followed by an exceptionally deep gully parallel to the beach. The LST's draft prevented it from making it across the last sandbar so six-foot steel pontoon segments were fabricated in the States along with hardware to buckle the segments together. In this way an LST could carry its own causeway. This enabled the LSTs to unload tanks or vehicles that would not be immediately inundated in deep water as they drove off the LST. Another method of dealing with this obstacle was a cutout section in the sides of some LSTs that enabled them to launch a loaded LCT at right angles to the fore and aft axis of the LST. The LCTs could make it over the last sandbar. Admiral Conolly also had the bulk of the newly available 158 foot LCIs, capable of carrying 200 men directly to the beach in better fashion than the smaller 36 foot LCVPs. Rocket launching landing craft dedicated to pre-landing defender suppression were not yet in the arsenal.

On the enemy side, afloat, the ten Italian and six German subs available in the central Mediterranean were directed to interdict our sea supply lines and avoid tangling with amphibious operations. Though we did not know this, most German E-boats, motor torpedo boats, and their Italian MAS counterparts had been withdrawn toward Messina. No Italian surface vessels larger than PTs sortieed from Italian ports to interfere with HUSKY. The Axis subs sank some important tonnage en route to HUSKY but paid heavily in surface attacks from Allied ASW craft that had an increasingly good opportunity to get to the scene of activity quickly. It was no longer the lonely North Atlantic. British motor torpedo boats operating off Messina were especially effective. British subs, too, scored kills on large Italian supply submarines running from Taranto through Messina to Naples. Mines were a threat at Porto Empodocle, just a little northwest of the JOSS sector at Licata.

Island Aircraft Carriers

Pantelleria, an island 60 miles off the southwest coast of Sicily surrendered, after heavy air and sea bombardments, on 11 June. American engineers, in just six days of work, fashioned a new airport on Gozo, an island next to Malta. With

211

these two new fields, Supermarine Spitfires, supporting both the British and American sectors of HUSKY, now had more precious time over the landing areas. This time became essential because the defenders could call on 800 aircraft, of which 500 were JU-88s and about 200 were ME-109 fighters.

Ship Transit Traffic Control

We have mentioned the storm. Even with calm seas, the control of sea traffic for this invasion would have placed heavy demands on communications at sea. The JOSS force, all shallow draft except the flagship and the naval warships, had an exceptionally challenging navigation problem. With his boats being blown before the wind to the east, Admiral Conolly felt required to disobey Western Task Force "no course change" orders three times on July 9. He used USS Swanson as a courier ship to Commander Durgin in Buck leading the slow JOSS convoy. Each time, Conolly ordered the slow group in Buck's charge to alter course "a point to the north". Starting from an initial course almost east from the coast of Tunisia toward Malta, this meant a "correction" when totaled of almost 34 degrees! The Admiral was right! Timid course changes would have meant inordinate delays in reaching Licata beach and certainly would have invited late hour traffic jams with sorting out and re-assembly challenges. By 2100 on the ninth of July, all tracks had converged at the proper point off Malta and had turned northward to their assigned landing beaches. By 2300, all radar-equipped ships had made landfalls on Sicily. The winds, though not yet the seas, had begun to moderate. There were delays, especially getting the slow LCTs with their tanks to the beaches, but Conolly's in-transit course change decisions enabled this group to play their role, though slightly late.

Time and Space Merge

Licata is at the western end of the shallow Gulf of Gela and Scoglitti is at the southern end. Bristol had been sent ahead late in the afternoon of the ninth to make contact with the British beacon submarine, Safari. Bristol made contact at about 2300 and took station as planned, beaming her searchlight due south. A U.S. PC boat (Patrol Craft) made contact with Bristol and took station five miles further offshore, with a blinker light operating to seaward. A series of patrol craft, taking bearings on the one ahead, marked each beach to the south. Air bombardment of Italian airfields was already underway. Brooklyn found Bristol at 2330, then covered the release of Conolly's western attack groups. Birmingham did the same for the easternmost groups. Conolly set the landings in motion at midnight. At 0300, the Buck, leading the slow convoy group of LCTs, became their landings traffic director. The moon set at 0030 and morning twilight began at 0510. A cool clear day was in prospect.

The Roe-Swanson collision, mentioned earlier, left the westernmost landing forces light on naval gunfire. USS Buck filled this breach, silencing field artillery firing on Beach Red. Brooklyn moved in and fired on batteries atop Mount Sole, then on batteries just behind Beach Red. General Truscott became impatient that his mobile artillery was being held offshore because the LCTs had been late. Admiral Conolly ordered all LCTs, now assembling for an orderly progression into the beach, to get in line abreast and hit the beach as fast as possible, while ordering Edison and Bristol to lay smoke to cover this broad advance. It worked. They all made it by just after 0800.

Beach Red, the furthermost to the west in the JOSS responsibility, ran northwest to southeast, and Roe and Swanson's fire support area was close in, in relatively shallow

213

water almost due west of Beach Red. Edison and Bristol were south in somewhat deeper water and on the border with Green Beaches to the east. The Green Beaches marked a turn of the Sicilian coastline eastward. At sea, between the Roe/Swanson fire support area and the Edison/Bristol area were the Gaffi attack group for Beach Red. This group had LCVP assembly closest to the beach, then a grouping of LCTs just outboard, then LCIs, and then another group of LCTs. This was designated as a "transport area" with the larger Landing Craft acting as transports. All had proceeded shore to shore from Lake Bizerte in Tunisia to Beach Red at Licata. The assault troops were the 7th RCT of the 3rd Division USA. Both Licata and Gela were astride roads to Palermo through valleys in Sicily's mountainous terrain. Both Licata and Gela had rivers with their river plains in front of the hills. Further west was the larger town of Empodocle, harboring expected (but, not realized) Italian motor torpedo boats. The nasty part of Empodocle was an extensive minefield offshore. The Allies employed PT boats in this area beginning in the evening of the ninth of July to fend off expected enemy PT boat attacks. It was while Roe and Swanson were maneuvering at high speed to investigate what turned out to be our own PT boats that Roe, changing course to miss the Empodocle mine field, struck Swanson with damage severe to both. The friendly PT boats were deployed directly under Admiral Hewitt's command and were operating unbeknownst to the JOSS destroyers under Conolly.

Brooklyn and Buck made up for the gap in shore fire support left by Roe and Swanson. It turns out that Licata SFCPs did not make many demands on the cruisers and destroyers offshore. The Edison and the U.S.minesweeper Sentinel supported the Molla landing group, for Green Beaches one and two. The Molla responsibility included LCI-32, carrying naval and military commanders assigned to go ashore, and the two Princess ships with their Ranger battalions to be landed by off loaded British landing craft. The Rangers made shore in two rocky coves and did not wait for their vehicles, which were on the LCTs that were late getting to the beaches. Rangers quickly seized the high ground on 500-foot Mt. Sole, one of the few promontories in all the Gulf of Gela. This hill was directly behind the Green Beaches. It provided an immediate observation point to assess all the Licata sector operations.

Despite the LCT delay, timing worked for the Molla group. The Rangers hit the beach at 0300. Just an hour later came the LCVPs off loaded from LSTs, carrying the 15th RCT of the 3rd Division. With this team able to take over a full possession of Mt. Sole, the Rangers pressed ahead, still without vehicles, into the outskirts of Licata itself.

The fleet minesweeper Sentinel became a casualty of repeated air attacks. She was holed astern in morning twilight at 0500 by a bomber which pressed its attack home. After four more devastating attacks in the next hour, Sentinel was in dire straits and was eventually abandoned and sank with loss of life. A U.S. sub-chaser and a PC stood by her, rescuing personnel. Of 101 men, 40 got safely off, 51 were wounded and ten were killed.

Where to Next?

Having the troops of the 3rd Infantry Division under General Lucian K. Truscott on the northwest flank of the U.S. sector invasion proved doubly beneficial. That the Licata landings were less opposed than those at Gela could be put down as lucky for the JOSS force. What then happened was the ability of our commanders and soldiers to take advantage of good fortune. The 3rd Division, once assured that the situation in the other U.S. sectors was in hand, was able to turn northward and threaten the port of Palermo. No matter how good a force gets at lightering and otherwise off-loading equipment and supplies to move through a beachhead, it is much easier to do supplies replenishment through a seaport. Palermo was a good port and we wanted it.

General Truscott, commanding the 3rd Infantry Division, pioneered the "Truscott Trot" for the occasion. The rear man in the column double times to the front of his column. I am sure he does not start out relishing the idea that double timing with a full pack is much fun. But, once a soldier gets the idea that as soon as he gets to the head of the column, he can resume walking, it must have played in his head that he wanted to get there. Result 1: The column moves forward faster than even a defense can pull back. Result 2: Despite the much longer distance the U.S. forces needed to traverse get to Messina than the British, it began to look like we could get there first. Palermo fell. The U.S. advance along the top of Sicily toward Messina resumed in a series of leapfrog amphibious assaults with the Edison and other destroyers assisting in the landing phase and subsequent fire support as artillery for the troops. Naval gunfire as artillery was long the accepted norm in the Marine Corps. In the Mediterranean, our seaborne artillery gradually earned its way into the full respect of Patton's Army.

Edison began to get some fan mail. From the Army! Nice things were said about our shooting. Those Generals were not all into self-glorification. We liked working for them and their troops, and they developed quite a bent towards us. We will collect and reproduce some of their actual dispatches later in this story. I only have a record of one dispatch we sent to a shore group. That one was not a "thank you" note but a request for coordinates on an enemy battery that was hammering us. My sense of gratitude for the Army's loyalty to us, some 55 years late, leads to the next paragraph.

"You took heavy casualties. You worked under great pressures that seamen do not face. You worked hard just getting from here to there. We had 50,000 Shaft Horsepower and water that was not always an enemy. I never heard you gripe about your lot. We were proud to have served you. So, this is a belated salute to the U.S. Army from a grateful sailor."

There were some clear moonlit nights along the north coast of Sicily. The German air force began using new stand-off weapons that we did not fully understand. We learned by experience that a descending colored flare could signify a bomb falling, a bomb whose tail vanes could be moved from controls in the parent bomber to improve the impact accuracy. The U.S. destroyer Mayrant took a bad hit and needed assistance getting into the harbor at Palermo.

Except for the tipped over Italian destroyer Genere in a drydock in Palermo, that harbor came into our hands in good shape. German harassment air attacks picked up in frequency and again those great Army searchlights ashore helped find and ultimately shoot down some planes. Offshore, we spent most of our time patrolling to interdict any German air, sea or sub-sea attacks. At night, even in the moonlight, we would only shoot at aircraft targets when we had the advantage of a good silhouette. Our lookouts found plenty for us to be concerned with.

Mines had been a factor at Licata and the sweepers had been very busy. While we did not find any concentrations of moored mines long the north coast of Sicily, we knew that even the best night lookout was unlikely to see a "floater."

This was a moored mine cut loose from its anchor by our sweepers. It was then still as dangerous as when moored unless it could be holed by rifle fire. Holing it with a bullet let it fill with water and it would sink to the bottom.

Submarines and German aircraft were the main threat on the route from Palermo to the Strait of Messina. Not only were the Luftwaffe's new standoff weapons not fully appraised, they could still bomb you directly. One did, but he passed on by the Edison.

I had become confident of my expertise as OOD underway. During the Licata to Messina effort, I began to stand watches during which the CO had enough confidence to catnap in his stateroom on the bridge. I still was taking everything that happened those days as it came, but I realized that these were important progress days for me. I liked conning a U.S. destroyer and gradually developed the confidence that I could take such a ship anyplace in the world. My proficiency at aircraft and ship identification in our training classes was recognized aboard ship. But, one moonlight evening at Palermo, I demonstrated that I had a lot to learn

Recognition training with 35mm B&W slides and short interval projection shutters, and exercising the 5" gun loading machine device, were the two most used training tools on a destroyer. You focused on something useful. You were distracted from worrying about the next German attack. I had been especially good in the *night* aircraft identification exercises. The next episode "was no drill!" Along one night came a single bogey, just as I was enjoying my newfound responsibility. I got a good glimpse of the plane in starlight if not in a full moonlight. I kept our ship "peaceful." There was no purpose in disclosing our existence even though I assessed our night caller as a friendly C-47, the civilian equivalent of which is the DC-3. The plane passed down the destroyer picket line toward the next U.S. destroyer. I "passed the word" to the OOD on that ship by voice. "A C-47 just passed down my port side." Moments later, I heard a muffled explosion some distance away and saw some water mushrooming into the air. Then came a laconic voice on our TBS receiver. "That C-47 was a JU-88! He just bombed us. Fortunately, he missed."

Illustration 19-C-47 "Gooney Bird"

Wow! Our skipper was asleep. No need to wake him up. But, the helmsman, the JOOD, and the bridge lookouts had heard this. What an embarrassment, to say the very least. I resolved to be more attentive in the recognition training sessions. Both planes are pictured in this chapter. I am not showing them side by side. I am still, I must admit, too embarrassed to do that. On separate pages they do look alike. It could have been a costly mistake. Also, it gave that JU-88 crew a chance to come back another day and try again.

Other forces that we worked with at various times were undergoing their own trials at Gela and at Scoglitti.

Gela; USS Maddox Sunk

Edison was not at Gela so this is pieced together from comments made at the time (scuttlebutt) and accounts from other historical narratives. This narrative is not going to be comprehensive in covering the landings at Gela, nor will it cover in any detail the combat phase of the landings at Scoglitti, or the British assault on the southeast coast targeted toward the cities of Syracuse and Augusta. Suffice it to note that progress was slow for British forces up the east coast of Sicily toward Messina as they encountered heavy resistance. British progress did have an effect on the Allies' hopes to seal off the Strait of Messina and therefore on Edison's deployment as the Seventh Army battle line in the west of Sicily moved toward the Strait of Messina.

Licata had been forecast to be the toughest assignment of the three landing areas for the U.S. forces. Using an all-landing craft assault force meant not only that those forces would be deployed from the nearest debarkation ports in North Africa but also reflected a desire to rapidly deploy and engage the enemy at the point where we expected defenses to be the strongest. As it developed at Licata, the enemy did not present the strongest resistance there and our landing strategy at Licata was pointedly successful.

Gela yielded stubbornly. German air chose to concentrate on the sea forces at Gela, both warships and transports. In the melee, a German dive-bomber got in on the stern of the destroyer USS Maddox with a very near miss, then a hit. These explosions did quite a bit of below-decks damage aft. Events proceeded unfavorably for Maddox, a Benson/Livermore 1630-ton destroyer like Edison. The stern went under, and a series of catastrophic explosions occurred under her hull, opening up so much space that she sank very fast, in about two minutes. The enemy bomb may or may not have set off "sympathetic" explosions of Maddox' ordnance but one observation, that depth charges physically separated from their deck hold down restraints, rolled off or fell off, is plausible. Then, quickly reaching depth at which set, these charges were a killing blow for Maddox. In this two minutes of eternity, 202 men perished; this was another indication that Maddox had no control of her fate after the near miss. One who lost his life was Ensign Eugene J. Canty, an Academy classmate who had joined Maddox about the same time I joined Edison.

Depth Charge History Seemed to Repeat

In Volume I: Warships, by Keatts and Farr, published by Gulf Publishing in 1990, the authors uncovered the uncannily similar fates of two U.S. destroyers named Jacob Jones. Both were four pipers of World War I design. The first Jacob Jones, DD 61, was an early German submarine torpedo casualty of World War I and her heavy loss of life came as the result of her own depth charge explosions killing or maiming men in the water. A second Jacob Jones of similar vintage design, DD 130, did not reach the fleet until World War I hostilities were over. She became the first U.S. destroyer casualty of World War II, meeting an almost identical end as her earlier namesake, again with loss of life heavy due to her own depth charges. I will reach forward to World War II in the South Pacific for the experience of a Fletcher class destroyer.

The following paragraphs in quotes are a recorded recollection of Ensign Bernard Frese, USN, who was the plotting room officer of the USS DeHaven, a Fletcher class destroyer.

In the action Frese relates, DeHaven was assigned to escort LCTs loaded with American troops to the north end of Guadalcanal. These troops were sent to cut off escape of Japanese troops. The DeHaven was the victim of Japanese bombers on 1 February 1943. Here is Frese's story of the DeHaven's ordeal: He was in the Plotting Room.

"Soon thereafter there was a jolt and an explosion. We had taken a direct hit amidships in the engineering spaces. We lost electric power immediately. The guns were helpless and the computer useless. ...Meanwhile the ship took a near miss on the port side and another hit forward....Suddenly, a brilliant white light appeared, coming from a point forward and slightly above the Plotting Room. There was no sound....The room turned fire red and everything started to move. ....somehow my legs were under the overturned computer....The room was filling with liquid which I thought came from the fuel tank abaft the Plotting Room. ...Then it occurred to me to open my belt and zip down my zipper.....I was finally free....Actually the ship was sinking but I didn't know it at the time.....I.saw that I was out of the Plotting Room with water up to my waist.....I dove in, wondering if a piece of jagged metal would slice me open....I heard another voice say, "There she goes!"....I saw the ship's propellers directly above my head and the ship ready to plunge to the bottom....I set a record doing the backstroke and getting out of the way......There were several underwater explosions but no churning of the water like a depth charge would make."

A sailor in a life jacket saved Frese. The man held him up until one of the LCTs took both of them aboard. He was covered over for dead by a succession of medical teams but, though badly burned, lives to this day. (October 11, 1998)

Questioned about the depth charges, Frese, now a Captain USN (Ret) recalled from discussions with other survivors (about half of the DeHaven's complement survived the sinking) that a brave sailor went around setting them all on safe in those few moments before the DeHaven sank.

Counterattack on Western Task Force Assault Troops

In two days of action on the Gela plain, an attack by the Hermann Goering Panzer Division heavy tanks with supporting Italian tanks, was broken up by heavy U.S. cruiser and destroyer fire. This attack got to within one thousand yards of the beaches. The cruiser Boise and destroyers Jeffers, Shubrick, Laub and Cowie left fourteen demolished tanks on the plain. The U.S. Navy finally got some of the U.S. Army's tanks ashore. These tanks assisted in taking out more enemy tanks at the turning point of this, the only promising counterattack mounted by the Germans and Italians against the Western Task Force.

Naval gunfire did its job at Sicily, but a lot of tuning up needed to be done in the new SFCP liaisons between Army troops and Navy warships. Communications and timing left much to be desired. Also, the use of Navy cruiser float planes for spotting, in the absence of any ground based aircraft assigned to landing support, proved exceptionally dangerous to those pilots and crewmembers. Their information was greatly needed, but these aircraft were no match for Luftwaffe fighters or ground based AA and took heavy casualties.

Gela Supplied the Fireworks

Luftwaffe aircraft hit the Robert Rowan, an ammunition ship which blew up and furnished a beacon for air attacks on the night of 10-11 July. Cruiser Boise, and destroyers McLanahan, Jeffers, Murphy, Benson, Plunkett and Niblack fought off numerous attacks. A near miss wounded 18 on the Benson including her skipper.

LCVPs; Two Views from July 1943

A feeling for what entering an off-loaded LCVP is like is provided in the book, United States Navy in World War II, compiled and edited by S. E. Smith for publisher William Morrow of New York. The following segments are from "Battle Stations" by John Mason Brown. He was a writer for the New York World Telegram newspaper. Brown signed up with the Navy at the outset of hostilities. Brown was on a transport at Sicily in 1943. Here, he was observing the lowering of his transport's landing craft. Destination of the landing craft is Scoglitti. This landing craft was off loaded from a transport, so has at least missed the worst of the storm that the JOSS landing craft to the north at Licata had experienced in the tossing Mediterranean all the way from Bizerte. Brown's transport had staged from a port that took her through Gibraltar. The transport's anchor crunched into the bottom off Scoglitti at 0045 on July 10, 1943.

"There's a hell of a lot of difference between our searchlights when they are looking for the enemy, and enemy searchlights when they are looking for us. 2:40 a.m. July 10, 1943."

"They (German aircraft) headed for our beaches, dropping flares over them. Then they turned wheel for us, still dropping flares. ....One of them has hung right over our Force like an old-fashioned light over a dining room table.....They are strange things, these German flares; disturbing but completely undisturbed. All the other lights are twitchy, nervous, explosive, darting. But these flares have a fearsome serenity.

The parachutes supporting them do more than rest on the air....They just hang there like fixtures. They appear to be eternal. 0445 July 10, 1943"

Novelist Jack Belden who rode into Gela with the DIME force, authored the next excerpts from the same book. He was aboard the transport Barnett as July 10, 1943 began. This is taken from his observations entitled, "Shoot Out That Goddam Light." Belden went into the beach in an LCVP.

"There was an immediate sense of gladness (from successfully going down a rope ladder in darkness and getting into a pitching boat) at getting started and a heightened awareness. When we got away from the shelter of the fleet, this feeling, however soon gave way to another. We became sick.....The rocking of the small landing craft was totally unlike anything we had experienced on the ship. It pitched rolled, swayed, bucked, jerked from side to side, spanked up and down, undulated, careened and insanely danced on the throbbing, pulsing, hissing sea. The sea itself flew at us, threw the bow in the air, then, as it came down, swashed over us in great roaring bucketfuls of water......The Ensign standing on the high stern of the boat ordered the sailor by the bow to close the half open ramp....At that moment there was a loud hissing sound...and a wave of water cascaded through the ramp....."Bail with your helmets!," called the Ensign in a voice of extreme irritation...(there followed what seemed an interminable time as the Ensign sought to find his landing wave's form-up circle)...we broke out of the circle formation and headed in a line toward a blue light, which, shining to seaward, was bobbing up and down some distance ahead......One by one they vomited, holding their heads away from their loosely clasped rifles, and moaned softly.....Astern our great fleet fled, diminishing, sinking beneath the waves......The boat pounded on......Instead of feeling myself part of a group of American soldiers going ashore on a carefully planned invasion, I saw myself and the men as strange phantoms flung out across the maw of the sea , into the blackness of eternity......Suddenly the light swung across the water, fastened on our boat, and illuminated us like actors on a darkened stage...'Why don't they shoot out that goddam searchlight?', growled a voice from the depths of the cavernous boat...'Steady there!', said the voice of Captain Paul Carney.

"Our engine gave a sudden full throated roar as the Ensign cut off the underwater exhaust. The boat leapt forward. The other boats behind us raced around to either side of us, and we sped forward like a charging football line....Ahead - directly ahead - two strings of dotted red lights were crossing each other. 'Machine guns!' the sailor shouted. I heard a sharp cracking sound..... Then I heard the engine break out in a terrible throbbing roar. At last there was a jerk and a bump and the boat came to a halt. 'Open ramp!', shouted the Ensign in the stern....The ramp jerked down farther until it was level with the water....Still no one moved. 'Get off!' Major Grant's voice was imperious. No one moved. 'Jump off!', he hollered again. 'You want to get killed here? Get on that beach!' With these words he leapt out into the darkness....Here it comes, I thought and jumped. The water struck me like a shock. I kept going down. My feet sank down and I touched bottom. My chin was just at the water. A sharp crackle burst the air nearby. The water was growing shallower....Ahead of me....figures were crawling on hands and knees up the slope...At last I was on dry land."

The Flare War

When I wrote the following observations a few years after World War II, I had not seen the searchlight comments of John Mason Brown or the flare comments of Jack Belden. The next sequence actually occurred and lasted perhaps 30 seconds. I am the secondary battery Anti Aircraft officer on the after deckhouse. We have been under air attack for an hour. Under the heading, "Night Air Attack", I wrote:

"The flares! Would they ever go out? The last one goes out. Relief. Then some ship hears aircraft engine noises and starts firing tracer bullets at them. All the flares go back on again. Under my breath, "O God! Why do our ships fire on "noises?" Woe is us. Trouble overhead. Mines in the water. Subs under the water. Go fast enough to keep your rudder effective. No faster. Minimum wake to provide the least aiming line for a bomb run. Fishtail, slowly. Wakes are phosphorescent and pick up starlight, moonlight and emit light of their own. Torpedoes make wakes. Be prepared to comb the wake of an enemy torpedo."

"Observe tight AA discipline. Lo, a Dornier 217 comes down the port side, between flare lanes. He sees us. We see him. He drops a torpedo to intersect our track. Lookouts jam the sound powered phones with torpedo wake reports. The skipper turns 30 degrees starboard. The torpedo wake parallels our course. The torpedo misses. I give our secondary battery permission to fire. The enemy aircraft is now exiting toward our port bow. The best chance to hit the 217 with machine guns is long gone. I am much too late giving permission to fire. Did my conservatism lose an advantage for us? I hope those flares go out."

The Armies Head For Messina

With the assault beaches secure by 12 July, the Allied forces were primed for a breakout. The British and Canadians to the east captured Augusta and Syracuse and headed north toward Mt. Etna. Patton's Army, with three important forces ashore, took three routes. One led west toward Marsala, another drove north into the mountainous interior, and the third raced across the island's shoulder to capture the port of Palermo on 22 July. Our sea forces met them there and were immediately attacked by more JU-88s.

In separate air attacks, destroyers Mayrant and Shubrick sustained heavy damage that forced them into Palermo where they endured more air attacks. Off shore, Shubrick took a near fatal hit in her after fire room, with a number of men left dead or wounded, and the ship without power. Mayrant had her forward engine room and after fire room completely flooded and ended up without power. Mayrant survived her bomb hits with 14 inches of freeboard. She too had men killed and wounded. Both ships were saved by a combination of U.S. mine-craft and sub-chaser help, and covering AA fire from cruisers and destroyers.

German and Italian ground combat forces fought strictly rear guard actions as soon as the assault beaches of Sicily were lost. Allied forces moved aggressively to keep them in engagement, not sure what German intentions were, whether to stand and fight at another line in Sicily, or to get across the Strait of Messina as fast as possible. With the benefit of hindsight, it is clear, that failing to stop the Allies at the beaches of Sicily, the Nazi commanders had made the successful retreat to Italy their prime objective. U.S. ground forces engaged in successful "make it up as you go along" leap frog amphibious efforts to insure that the Axis forces' retreat was as onerous as possible but there was no plan in place to deny them their escape across the Strait. The "what next" question had not been asked, or answered.

For this period, Edison's Official War History contains the following summary:

"Edison departed Bizerte for Sicily, where she arrived on 10 July. Air attacks were heavy during the landings here but Edison escaped without a scratch. She moved on to Realmonte, Sicily, on 12 July where she was assigned a fire control station to bombard enemy shore defenses. She remained in this vicinity until 19 July when she retired toward Algiers, Algeria, arriving on the 20th."

"Edison got underway the same day for Bizerte, but returned to Algiers on 23 July. On 26 July she arrived at Mers-el-Kebir and returned to the shores of Sicily on 31 July where she remained until 21 August. While there, an air attack developed at 0410 on 1 August but it was repelled without damage to the ships. Edison arrived back at Algiers on 22 August and patrolled along the northern coast of Africa until 7 September. On 7 September, DD 439 steamed from Bizerte en-route to the beaches of Italy for Operation Avalanche." (This was the code name for the landings at Salerno. This will be covered in the next chapter.)

On the 2nd of August 1943, the USS Buck and the USS Nicholson were escorting six vessels from Licata to Oran. At Oran, these destroyers would pick up ammo, fuel and other needed supplies. Buck found the Italian sub Argento on the surface off Pantelleria in the early evening. After challenging the Argento, which immediately submerged, Buck pursued sound contacts for two hours, dropping several patterns of depth charges when over the target. Argento was finally forced to surface astern of Buck and fired a torpedo which missed Buck. Buck's 5" gun battery inflicted heavy damage on Argento which managed to fire a second torpedo. This one also missed. Buck's shelling had fatally wounded Argento. With their submarine sinking, the Argento's crew abandoned ship. Buck's whaleboat saved all but three of the 49 aboard. The survivors included Argento's skipper. A photograph in an earlier chapter showed some of the Argento's survivors on Buck's bridge.

(The day-dated paragraphs that come next are quoted from Ed Meier's notes of the Edison's travels. This sequence covers the period after Sicily to and including the assault at the Bay of Salerno. The year is 1943. In the next sequence, the Edison has escorted the USS Philadelphia from Palermo, to Algiers, and thence to Oran and a berth for Edison at Mers-el-Kebir.)

"August 24. The neglect of the diary was due to a little bug which made me violently ill with food poisoning. Apparently I had consumed too much free wine and fruit at Luigi Lufo Raymondi's place in Palermo, as I was a very sick man for a day or so. (Edison men were constantly reminded not to eat raw fruits or vegetables in Sicily because of the practice of fertilizing the gardens and orchards with "night soil". Ed's indisposition may not have come from the wine.) Something is cooking by way of another Allied blow, but where and when we don't know. Perhaps Sardinia or Corsica."

"August 25. Went out with the Boise, Savannah, Mayo and Benson (Mayo and Benson were the first destroyers of the Benson/Livermore class) and had practice shore bombardment on a beach east of Arzeu. Returned to Mers-El-Kebir at sunset. For reasons of security I cannot as yet discuss the matter (of another Allied blow) but it is sufficient to say that it will be a daring step and we'll probably see plenty of opposition. The attitude among the officers and the men is a very restless one with mingled feelings about getting back to the States or getting another offensive started. My feeling is that I'd like to see a foothold established on the continent before shoving off, but it would seem that that would be only the beginning and that once a foothold is established we could not be released."

"August 26. Shifted berths this noon and tied up alongside the Savannah. Ed Doyle is on the Savannah and we had a nice long chat swapping war yarns and discussing things back home. This afternoon I went out to Ain El Turk, a lovely beach resort some 8 or 10 miles west of Oran and went swimming with two French girls whom I met out there. The water was wonderful. The drive out to Ain El Turk is very pretty, winding through the mountainous country. The style of buildings and the type of landscape and plant life remind people of California. Several prisoner of war camps along the way."

(Ain El Turk was also the location of a quickly established club. Some Italian POWs did the cooking. We established a duty driver practice. If you have escorted an LST and the motor pool could not get you a jeep, that friendly LST had already commandeered one that they said was "left over" from the last assault operation. They would loan it to you. The duty driver did not quite abstain but he stayed soberer than the passengers. Favorite Edison songs at the club were "My Wild Irish Rose" for skipper Pearce, "McNamara's

Band", often rendered on the foc'sle by Edison's Seaman First Class of that name, and the all hands favorite, "Vee'l Heil Heil Heil Right In Der Fuehrer's Face.")

"August 27. Got underway at 8:00 this morning for a practice amphibious operation with many transports, cruisers and destroyers. It will be a simulated capture of a city from the sea and the city designated is Arzeu, a French town 50 miles east of Oran."

"August 28. The simulated attack on Arzeu was carried out last night and I guess everything went off OK. The Edison was supposedly a fire support ship and since no firing was done, we were just along for the ride. Returned to port this evening and refueled. Tomorrow, the Nicholson and the Edison will go to Algiers for a 3-day availability alongside the Vulcan, a destroyer tender."

(Going alongside the Vulcan *in Algiers* runs counter to my recollections. My own recollection is that the Vulcan was mostly tied up at Mers-el-Kebir, next to Oran harbor; all my photos show her there. Technically, the USS Vulcan (AR-5) was a repair ship, but she doubled as a destroyer tender.)

The next Illustration is a photo of Edison's engineering officers, Kelly Hall and Joe Dwyer. Here they are posing in a rare moment topside, with the USS Vulcan as a backdrop. Edison was apparently airing bedding this day. A nuisance, but very necessary.

Illustration 20-Edison Engineers Hall and Dwyer

"August 29. Shoved off for Algiers at 0700 this morning and on the way stopped off at Arzeu to replenish our ammunition supply from the USS Mt. Baker. Left Arzeu about noon and ran up to Algiers (further east) at 25 knots arriving about 8:00 in the evening. Jim Hughes and I got permission to leave the ship and went over to the Allied Officers Club where we each downed a bottle of white wine. This of course put us in a jovial mood, but we were able to get back aboard ship before the 11:00 curfew."

(The author made one visit to that club which has been mentioned in books like "Ike The Soldier" by Merle Miller, about General Eisenhower. That club was also mentioned in Morison's Volume IX. I stood at the club bar for a few minutes before it dawned on me that the officer standing next to me was Douglas Fairbanks Jr. We exchanged a few pleasantries. In doing some reading for this story, I discovered that

233

Fairbanks is mentioned in Morison's Volume IX, "The Invasion of France", for specific participation in the Southern France operation which began August 15, 1944.)

"August 30. This afternoon I went ashore to line up some canteen supplies at the Army P.X. warehouse. After that I took a bus up to the top of the hill overlooking the city. It was a magnificent view, to gaze over the city's rooftops and out to the harbor and seaward. There is also a beautiful cathedral on the hill, the Cathedral de Notre Dame de Nord-Afrique."

"September 6. I got ashore several times (since the previous log entry, but still in Algiers) and one day took an escorted tour of Algiers. In centuries gone by Algiers was an important center for pirates, corsairs and slave traders. We were taken through the lovely palaces built by the people, also their forts, meeting halls etc. Other points of interest that we saw were a mosque, cathedral and of course the Casbah - meaning, fortress, in Arabic."

"Ran into Bill Love from Denison at the Red Cross Officer's Club a couple days ago. He is navigator of a Fortress bomber and had just completed 50 bombing missions and is being returned to the States on 20 days furlough. He certainly has had some exciting experiences on his missions over Germany, France, the Low Countries, Italy, Sicily, Pantelleria etc. I persuaded him to come along with us and after having had a glass or so of champagne we returned to the ship for dinner and then saw a French vaudeville show on the forecastle deck which Sullivan (Ensign John L. Jr.) had arranged. It was quite good and after the show had a little party in the wardroom. It was a very nice evening and I'm sure Bill enjoyed it."

"Right now we are escorting a large convoy of transports for the next operation which I am sure will make good reading for the people back home. I can now say that we are en route to Naples, Italy. Our force will strike south of Naples, near Salerno and Agropoli, while a British force will assail the beaches north of us. The two forces will converge on Naples after getting ashore. We expect considerable opposition, particularly from planes, although we might also see action with submarines, E-boats or even units of the Italian Navy which might try to interfere. It is going to be a large operation and we're looking forward to it with anticipation as well as with some apprehension. If all goes well, it will be a big step in finishing off the war."

"September 7. This morning early, the fire control force consisting of the Philadelphia, Boise, Savannah, Plunkett, Ludlow and Edison left the convoy and went ahead to Bizerte at 25 knots. We arrived there at noon and in time for the Captain (Pearce) and Hofer (the Gunnery Officer) to attend a gunnery conference. The convoy came past Bizerte a few hours later down the Tunisian War Channel (a continuously mine-swept channel through the shallows of the Mediterranean) and we rejoined. The bay outside Bizerte was completely filled with ships of all types and I was able to count about 75 and I'm sure there were many more that I could not see. This evening we headed northward to pass to the west of Sicily."

"September 8. Today is D-Day minus 1 and at time of writing it is about 1:00. We have passed between Sicily and the Island of Ustica and are still heading easterly. Soon, we will change course to the northwest in order to give the impression that we will strike at Sardinia. At 2230, we will rendezvous for the approach about 70 miles off Naples and in time for the assault at H hour or 3:30 tomorrow morning."

"This morning about 10:30 we were called to General Quarters on an enemy plane contact. No attack materialized and it was undoubtedly a reconnaissance plane giving us the once over. While at General Quarters, a flight of 40 Flying Fortresses winged overhead bound for targets in Italy. They certainly are doing a grand job and we're all hoping that they succeed in tearing up all Italian airports and also give the shore batteries a going over." (Research for this story makes it clear that these planes were not going after shore batteries as Ed had hoped.)

"The convoy is a large one consisting of some 70 ships for the assault. The Edison's duties are to screen the Savannah and provide fire support with her. The sea is calm and the day bright and clear. Moonset is about midnight and we're all hoping for a good dark night. We are told that (President) Roosevelt has a speech planned for tonight at about 10:00 New York time. That will just about coincide with our zero hour as we are 6 hours ahead of New York and zero hour is 0330. Churchill is still in the U.S., presumably in case of an Italian capitulation following the assault on Salerno."

(Our narrative will return to more of Ed Meier's day by day sequence again in Chapter Eight.)

Ed has mentioned "going ashore" at various ports. The Navy tried some physical fitness programs for warship crews during these long periods away from U.S. ports. These were delivered with more than a suggestion that the exercises and sports could act as a form of shore leave ("shore leave" and "liberty" were interchangeable terms) besides "being good for you.")

Liberty and Recreation

I thought at first to title this subject as leave and recreation. But then, I remembered that in World War II, leave meant just one thing, emergency leave. Too often this meant that a father or mother was sick, possibly dying, and the sailor could get home briefly to pay his respects and return to his ship. So, leave is not the right thought. Liberty is the better term for this story.

There were a number of gradations of liberty. Sometime in 1943, Ensign John L. Sullivan, USNR came aboard the Edison to help us keep fit. He was part of a multi-fleet effort led by Commander Gene Tunney, the famous U.S. heavyweight boxing champion who dethroned Jack Dempsey. Some of us received early wind of Tunney's program to make us fit. His fitness emissaries were often called "tunneyfish". I listened to Commander Tunney one day in cold Thompson Stadium at the U.S. Naval Academy, as he explained ("promoted" would be the current term) his fitness program. All midshipmen were required to be present for Gene Tunney's talk that day. After three years of marching to every meal, fitness, in a cold stadium, was a subject that the midshipmen could have done without, though they gave Tunney's program the benefit of a polite listen. (A later "all hands" affair at USNA featured Admiral Lord Louis Mountbatten of the Royal Navy as an inspiring speaker during lunch in the midshipmen Mess Hall. His talk was received with great enthusiasm.) Ensign John L. Sullivan had the proportions to be a direct descendant of his namesake, the heavyweight champion of the U.S. before Dempsey. Our Ensign "John L.", though not related to the Sullivan of boxing fame, was a big man, and likeable. Again, though, what he had to offer sailors were calisthenics on the foc'sle, or on the dock. So, a limited form of liberty was to get on the dock at Mers-el-

Kebir and stretch the muscles. The muscles needed stretching but there was little spirit for this among the troops. The messenger was fine-but the message was not too well received.

If liberty meant getting off the ship, the object was recreation. Not, as I have noted, compulsory calisthenics, which hardly involved liberty and certainly was not recreation. One step better would be a baseball game. The Tunney program provided balls, bats and mitts. Frankie Williams and Leonard Williams were two, young, educated and very talented black men whose World War II role meant being stewards in the officer's country. While shipboard amenities observed the seniority of officers by rank and enlisted men by rating, in a baseball game ashore all could participate based on skill. Frankie Williams was a premier softball pitcher. I need to provide a frame of reference for the term, "premier." In my civilian life before the Navy, I worked for the Eastman Kodak Company in Rochester, NY. At Kodak Park, in Greece, NY, Kodak had built a huge manufacturing facility for film. One of the public relations methods for keeping the name Kodak before the public was to sponsor a softball team. The Kodak Park softball team was a world champion and they had the world's premier softball pitcher, Harold "Shifty" Gears. Shifty had the most wins and the most no hit games; he held all the records. Frankie Williams of the USS Edison was in that class. Edison won all the games against the other ships. The unmistakable acknowledgment of Frankie's prowess was that the Edison center fielder sat on a chair in the outfield most of the time.

While swimming at a Mediterranean beach, in season, was perhaps the next echelon up in liberty and recreation, I will have to reserve my final general remarks on liberty and recreation to the occasions that got us to a bar, and to alcohol. I was an example of what some deprived sailors (I use the term "sailors" to mean all that sailed on Navy ships.) did when they got to a bar. I often drank too much. Not all of the officers and men drank, but since I did, I can recall mostly those who drank with me. It was a way of "blotting out" what we had experienced, and what we conjectured was coming next. I write this today, not as a matter of pride in any way. I have been completely dry, at the "suggestion" of my wife, for over 25 years.

When a DD's Ammo Is Expended

A destroyer in need of ammo moved into a category like a destroyer in need of fuel. The ship had to start economizing. In the fuel case, fueling at sea was an alternative that had been developed to a high skill in the U.S. Navy. In the ammo shortage, the only alternative was to go someplace where they had some. The Robert Rowan at Gela burned and exploded throughout the night after being bombed, revealing her cargo as an ammunition ship. Risking an ammo ship in the attack transport area signified that her mission was to supply ammunition to the troops that had landed. Such ships did not carry naval warship ammunition.

Naval warships were re-supplied from ammunition ships which all of us hoped were more discreetly located. This replenishment was not generally attempted in actual forward assault areas. Edison received ammo from the most motley collection of ships. At Ajaccio in Corsica, we took on ammo from the grimiest United Kingdom merchantman I had ever seen. Her crew was terrified at being this close to the Italian front and worked like beavers to get the projectiles and powder cartridges out of her hold. There was no cover of darkness. Time was of the essence. We were due back on a firing station as soon as we replenished the ammo. This evolution took place at high noon under a blazing sun. Our men moved right over onto the ammo ship, and worked side by side with its very limited crew. I hope the Bureau of Naval Ordnance never reads this. The five-inch projectiles were packaged two to a wooden box. To speed things up, we held the boxes over our head and broke them by smashing them down on the deck of that freighter. We stowed the projectiles in our magazines and tossed the wood over the side. There were three fuzes in those 5" projectiles and the designers required a certain sequence to ensue before any fuze would go off.

Ammo in reserve became a more important factor in the next three action campaigns of the USS Edison. At Salerno, for the Edison and the U.S. destroyer Rowan, the ammo level dictated passage through that narrow channel between life and death.

Chapter Eight - Salerno; Edison Makes Her Mark

Part I - Our Strength up; Strategy at Turning Point

Contested Strategies

The choice of Salerno as the next assault point was another step in the strategy to penetrate the soft underbelly of Europe. The U.S. Joint Chiefs of Staff (JCS) increasingly wanted to give its priority to a cross channel invasion into Western Europe. Prime Minister Churchill wanted to demonstrate the vulnerability any defender of central Europe would have in attacks from the south, originating from Italy eastward. He had taken this route in World War I campaigns and was defeated then. With strong and appropriately disposed forces from the south, Churchill made the argument that the Allies in World War II could accomplish decisive central European war objectives.

Prime Minister Churchill was not opposed to the cross channel invasion but it was not a 1943 priority for him. Increasingly, U.S. commanders got the impression that it might not even be a 1944 priority for the PM. Moving up the Italian peninsula fit Churchill's idea of the strategy that should be employed. Interestingly, the Southern France invasion of August 1944 found the U.S. and England switching sides on the importance of the Mediterranean. The south of France did not fit Churchill's soft underbelly focus but it did fit the U.S. concept of leverage once the cross-channel invasion of France had begun. Perhaps more importantly, the port capacity of the south of France would be absolutely necessary to support our millions of soldiers on continent Europe.

241

Trident and Quadrant

There were two conferences subsequent to the Casablanca Conference that dealt with Mediterranean matters. The first was the Trident Conference and it took place 12 May 1943 in Washington DC. It got off to a good start with word of the Axis surrender in Tunisia. The U-boat picture in the Atlantic had eased somewhat. The Germans on the eastern front had retreated under Russian pressure to the Donetz River basin. The U.S. was about to step up the war against the Japanese in the Solomon Islands. While most of the high level people who attended the Casablanca conference were present at Trident, neither General Eisenhower nor any of the other field commanders could come. Weary from fighting in North Africa, the active force commanders were attempting to meld their field experience into HUSKY (Sicily) plans.

Churchill's persistence won the immediate argument and an invasion of Italy went into planning. Landings at the Gulf (or Bay, as it was often referred to) of Salerno, Italy, just below Naples, would be the target. It was authorized officially on 26 July 1943. The Quadrant Conference in Quebec in August 1943 confirmed the decision. The operation's code name was to be AVALANCHE. What would happen after Salerno was not formally determined.

The U.S. Joint Chiefs of Staff

In reviewing history as preparation for this story, I have made a number of inferences to piece together the role of the topmost military command of the U.S., the Joint Chiefs of Staff (JCS). Of special interest to this narrative was the challenge of prioritizing manpower for Europe over the Pacific. Behind each move, one can see not just a JCS focus on the Normandy invasion and the consolidation of a viable Allied force position in Western Europe, but the JCS focus beyond Europe.

The Churchill/Roosevelt agreement that victory in Europe over Hitler had priority over Japan and the Pacific was always honored. That agreement was, without question, the greatest contribution that the two leaders could have made to the survival of the free world. After making it, these two political leaders took more interest in the war's tactics than the conduct of its strategy.

To the JCS, and my emphasis is on General Marshall and Admiral King, the strategic concomitant of the Churchill/Roosevelt agreement was never to forget that success in Europe was also the prerequisite for getting at the Japanese. While they did not exercise veto power over specific actions in the Mediterranean, the JCS had the ultimate power of allocation of resources. The two Chiefs grasped the reality of the U.S. as the arsenal of democracy, and their vision and grasp of a changing world grew with this new United States as it was blossoming into a world power. In providing sufficient forces for the Mediterranean up to and including the invasion of the south of France, the JCS exercised rationing control over essential components like Army divisions and Navy carriers. The JCS forced the political focus back to cross channel invasion plans for 1944 by the manner in which they rationed manpower. The operational persons on stage were Eisenhower, Montgomery, Patton, Clark, Tedder, Wilson, Alexander, the two Cunninghams, and Hewitt. The political leaders were Churchill and Roosevelt. But the men behind the scenes determining what future actions could be undertaken were the U.S. Joint Chiefs of Staff. They had Nimitz and MacArthur and the Pacific on their mind at all times. Marshall, King and Arnold were not always in the public eye, but they were tuned to the most fundamental changes in the world power structure.

Salerno; More than a Landing Operation

Salerno became the pivot for change. There was no "Salerno Conference" of historical significance at which the political and military leaders of Britain and the United States gathered to engrave any new essentials of strategy. All the alternatives had been discussed before. Those discussions and the arguing that attended them continued. But the resolve to do what we knew we had to do slowly hardened in this period. The steps to put a cross channel invasion onto a definite calendar began to be taken. Once in motion, there was no going backward. The U.S. high command simply used their omnipresence and made the moves that forward planning required.

The U.S. did subscribe to the Salerno assault landing decision. Later, the U.S. agreed to what became the Anzio siege. Anzio was not planned as a siege operation. U.S. commanders in Italy bear their share of responsibility for the fuzzy thinking that led to the Anzio standoff. I only bring these matters up here to remind myself that a Mediterranean destroyer's full dedication then was to the matter at hand, an assault landing against German defenders. There was a bigger picture but that was not available to a destroyer sailor when the events unfolded one at a time.

Key commanders and key invasion forces at Division strength began to show up on lists to go to England and make ready for the Normandy operation. One early nominee for such a move was British General Montgomery. Another important move in the offing was a change in General Eisenhower's responsibilities. When the British General Alexander would take over overall command of ground forces on the Italian peninsula and General Mark Clark would be established ashore as commander of the U.S. Fifth Army in Italy, the command structure in the Mediterranean sector would change. Ike's dual role, for active prosecution of the Mediterranean effort and for the planning and build up effort for Normandy, would cease. Ike would then become actively and continuously dedicated to preparations for the cross channel invasion.

Insofar as Italy was concerned, *after* Salerno, Ike became a negotiator for talents there that he felt he needed in England. For the Salerno assault itself, however, Ike was a negotiator for larger forces for that operation as he was still the senior military commander with operational responsibility in the Mediterranean. The U.S. Army First, Third, Ninth, 45th and Second Armored Divisions had already acquired valuable experience. After Sicily, some got a rest. The U.S. 36th Division was to get its baptism in the Salerno assault operation with the U.S. 45th Division in immediate reserve.

Salerno was a pivot, militarily, and strategically. Salerno was the last Mediterranean operation where the soft underbelly strategy edged out the cross channel strategy in priority. Casablanca, Sicily and Salerno were a phase; Salerno and Anzio were a phase. But at their common juncture, Salerno, the important force and command changes outlined above were about to take place that put cross channel into active planning for calendar 1944! This dynamic did not occur, even at the most private and secret war discussions, with any clarion statement. It was just that key divisions and key leadership would begin to leave the Mediterranean. The Mediterranean war would go on, but these changes foretold a pressure role for the Allied presence in Italy rather than a breakout strategy. Finally, as executed in August of 1944 almost a year later, the invasion of Southern France was part of the

cross channel invasion strategy. Though few have characterized it as such, Salerno, Normandy, and Southern France became the active prongs of the Allies' strategy.

Aftermath of Sicily

Palermo fell on 22 July 1943. Mussolini told the Italian
King (Victor Emmanuel) on July 25 that he, Mussolini, was
all through. Marshal Badoglio was appointed to head the
Italian government and its armed forces.

Beginning on 10 August, across planned water routes and
in planned stages, the Germans got 200,000 men out of Sicily
and safely across the Strait of Messina. This included a number of near intact Panzer Divisions. Although many Italian
soldiers had surrendered to the Allies in Sicily, the Italians,
too, evacuated many units intact. With 350,000 men available in Sicily at the beginning of the Allied invasion, and
with the reinforcements they had moved into Sicily from Italy, the Axis had made a major commitment there. Sustain-
ing that commitment by the German High Command was
predicated on their success in the field. With the fall of Palermo, Syracuse and Augusta in the early stages of the Allied
effort in Sicily, the German high command had one goal, to
extricate their forces and make their stand in Italy. Their plan
to extricate had been made as part of their plan to commit.

The Allies had no strategy in place to prevent this. The
opportunity was there. While uncertainty existed in Allied
minds concerning the war intentions of Italian surface Navy
forces, the Italian Navy was for the most part absent from
Axis defense activity. Britain and the U.S. had the naval
forces for interdiction of the Axis retreat across the Strait of
Messina. The one-operation-at-a-time syndrome infected Allied planning and many felt that a major opportunity had
been missed. Germany successfully executed an important,

controlled retreat and would have her forces available for another day. Even if Allied commanders had generated an ad hoc plan, the fact that their own air forces, both U.S. and British, were "out of the loop" pursuing their own war, meant that the complete echelon of the top Allied commanders, land, sea, and air were not even comparing notes. Our forces had made a successful landing in Sicily. Allied land forces went on from there with little variation from the originally planned routes and fought brave and clear to the Strait of Messina. The U.S. Army and U.S. Navy almost nightly conducted locally conceived leapfrog attacks along the north coast of Sicily on the road to Messina. Toward the end of the campaign in Sicily the Axis forces were moving out faster than we were moving in. A major foray into the heart of the Axis evacuation across the Strait of Messina was never conceived, let alone executed.

Oceans Apart, Salerno was more like the Pacific

This is not to say that Salerno and Tarawa were the same. Fortress Europe was a continent. Roosevelt and Churchill, though at issue on specifics, never deviated in any major way from the manpower priority given to the defeat of Hitler. Even with his monumental misjudgment of June 1941 in turning on his ally, Russia, Hitler still extracted a horrible death toll in his defense of Europe. The U.S. cemetery at Anzio is just one reminder of German effectiveness in defending Italy and keeping Allied forces there from sweeping up into Europe proper.

The Japanese Empire had no continent. It was a string of captured islands, some large, some small, with a limited continental stronghold or two thrown in where needed. The contest to dislodge the Japanese from these islands was first a strategy to terminate the expansion of Japanese hegemony,

247

and then one by one, and very selectively, to gain or gain back the key points the U.S. needed for the final assault on Japan itself. The carnage in most every landing the U.S. made in the road back was particularly horrible in terms of the percentage casualties to the numbers of troops involved on both sides. The U.S. was not dominant numerically in the beginning and the critically important U.S. tactic was to interdict by sea any attempt the Japanese undertook to bring in reinforcements.

Up until the invasion of Sicily, a main challenge for the Allies against Hitler was long supply lines. For his part, Hitler was still facing a large potential number of attack points that the Allies might choose. In North Africa and at Sicily, the Allies put ashore numerically stronger forces than the defenders could commit directly at the beachheads; the Allied attackers then tried to work fast enough so that the defenders could not move their defense-in-depth troops or armor fast enough to gain local superiority. At Salerno, the shorter perimeters of the defenses began to work more toward the German advantage. The uncertainties faced by the German high command of where we would attack became less. For the assault at Salerno, the land forces available at the points of attack moved toward parity. The defenders still had more air bases, though the Allies had captured enough of them to give a good account of itself in the air. It was in surface based sea forces that the Allies had the major advantage. The Italian Surrender just added to the uncertainty element present in all military strike operations.

Although the strategic balance was shifting toward the Allies, at Salerno the German defenders enjoyed something of the tactical parity that Japanese defenders of the Pacific islands enjoyed at the point of engagement. In troops and in armor, the defenders at the beaches of Salerno in the early hours had superior forces This would be the advantage the Japanese held in almost all the early contested landings in the Nimitz/ MacArthur rollback campaign in the Pacific. The differences were important. The Japanese could not fall back to some mountain stronghold. This undoubtedly increased their acknowledged ferocity in combat. The Japanese Navy could, and did, contest the combat sea forces that the U.S. employed in getting its assault forces to the beaches. The Japanese won their share of those sea battles but in no case did they prevent the U.S. attackers from gaining and holding the beachhead. Learning from Guadalcanal and Tarawa, the U.S. increased the intensity and duration of pre-landing bombardments. That lesson took longer to be learned in the Mediterranean. Hitler's U-boats took a heavy toll of Allied warships in the Mediterranean but in no case did this prevent the Allies from establishing and controlling the beachhead that was their initial objective.

At Salerno, the D-day toll in lives lost by soldiers and seamen was high, especially high as a percent of those engaged. Despite the fact that the issue at Salerno was in doubt all day on D-day, and the operation's immediate objectives in doubt until D+6, the Allied land forces fought their way in foot by foot. British and U.S. soldiers eventually achieved the breakout from the beachhead that was the objective of their concentrated effort. The Edison played a key role on D-day at the Bay of Salerno.

The Toe and The Boot

In its shape, the "foot" of the Italian Peninsula is characterized as a "toe" and a "boot." The Allies put in progress important tactical operations there in early September 1943. The British Eighth Army of British General Montgomery was entrusted with the move, which took place on 3 September. Landing craft, under cover of a heavy cross-strait British bombardment from sea and land, went ashore north of Reggio on the Italian peninsula's toe. A leapfrog operation up to Pizzo at the narrowest part of the foot engaged the tail end of the 29th Panzer Grenadiers moving north. This occurred on 8 September, the day the Italian armistice was announced. Admiral Cunningham was mindful of the Italian "fleet in being", an important segment of which was at Taranto. He suggested to General Eisenhower (according to Samuel Eliot Morison in Volume IX of United States Naval Operations in World War II in which he credits Admiral Cunningham's "A Sailor's Odyssey") that the British would supply the ships if Ike would supply the troops for the occupation of Taranto. He did supply all the ships except the USS Boise which was recruited away from D-day at Salerno to return to Bizerte and embark the last contingent of the British 1st Airborne Division which was committed to the Taranto occupation.

This was an interesting play, this "borrowing" of resources. Theoretically, Eisenhower "owned" all the operational forces in his area of responsibility. So he "loaned back" a British Division for Taranto. Cunningham, who was the overall sea commander, under Ike, in the Mediterranean, had to "borrow" a U.S. cruiser, which he had ticketed for the Salerno invasion, back from Ike, in order not to leave about 800 officers and men of the British 1st Airborne at Bizerte. Boise's aircraft were off loaded to provide space for nearly 100 jeeps. So, with British cruisers and minelayers pressed into service, supplemented by the USS Boise, the force sailed to Taranto on the evening of 8 September just as the AVA-LANCHE force gathered off the Bay of Salerno.

Cunningham brought along the British battleships HMS Howe and HMS King George V and a six- destroyer screen just in case the Italian warships objected. On the afternoon of

250

9 September, two Italian battleships and three cruisers stood out of Taranto. No shot was fired. The Italian fleet passed the British fleet and proceeded on its way to designated surrender ports. While planes pass in seconds, ships pass in hours. During those hours, a German observation plane might have taken an air photograph that would have provided German air intelligence officers any number of scenarios.

The British cruisers entered the outer Taranto harbor at dusk on September 9th, and took pilots aboard, according to Morison's fascinating story of this event. Those Italian harbor pilots must have had a busy day. An Axis fleet was leaving and an Allied fleet was coming!

"Buon giorno, pilota. Mi permetta di presentare il Capitano de Fregata, il signor Thebaud."

So begins and ends my two years study of Italian at the U.S. Naval Academy. It was intended for just the situation that Boise encountered at Taranto, but alas, I was up at Salerno unable to assist Captain Thebaud of the USS Boise in his dialogue with the Italian ship pilot.

The Taranto occupation was comparatively peaceful and Allied troops went on to occupy nearby Bari, an important Italian port on the Adriatic side of Italy, later the scene of one of the worst ammunition conflagrations of all time. Montgomery's Eighth Army made ready to move northward, out of Calabria as the general area is called. The Allied cruisers then departed Taranto, proceeded through the Strait of Messina, and joined the battle for the beaches at Salerno, already in progress.

Uncertainty

As had occurred with French Admiral Darlan in North Africa, secret negotiations between General Eisenhower's representative and a representative of the Badoglio government

251

took place before the Allied landings at Salerno. I am struck now by the bravery of these emissary/ negotiators who took enormous personal risks to pass through contested territory across enemy lines to conduct discussions. Also, those who did this on both sides never had a full hand to deal from. Anyone who wants to surrender wants to know that the other party has an irrevocable resolve to invade, and wants the essential detail on where it will take place. General Eisenhower's emissaries, Walter Bedell Smith for Italy and General Mark Clark for North Africa, were not delegated authority to reveal this information. Irrespective of any agreements negotiated, therefore, the ideal was not reached in either case that would give the tactical commander of the invasion forces any sort of knowledge-certain about the nature or predisposition of enemy forces.

And, who was the enemy, anyway? An agreement of sorts was reached with Badoglio on September 3, 1943, after which, in effect, Italy was out of the war. Surrender? Armistice? U.S. General Maxwell Taylor of the 82nd U.S. Airborne Division was also involved in an authorized side negotiation with the Italians about a paratroop drop on Rome. This was called off due to uncertainties on both the part of Eisenhower's representatives and Badoglio's about whether the other side was telling all that it knew. General Eisenhower chose to announce the original deal in the early evening of September 8, 1943. Forewarned as to time and frequency, many on the invasion ships listened to his broadcast. The desired result of "coming over" to the Allied side by intact units of the Italian Army and Air Force did not occur. The German hold on the peninsula was too strong. Many units of Italy's armed forces just sort of melted away. The Italian Navy did carry out the terms of the Armistice. Italian Navy units departed from north Italian ports and Corsica and

Sardinia and headed for designated Allied surrender ports. They took a fearful beating from the Luftwaffe. Many ships were lost, with great loss of life. Allied naval forces, occupied with the Salerno, could give them no help.

Allied Force Structure for Salerno

The naval force structure had not changed. Reporting to Eisenhower, Admiral Cunningham, RN, headed up the overall naval force structure. Admiral Hewitt, now in a flagship outfitted for task force communications, the USS Ancon, had the responsibility for all amphibious forces and for the bigger Royal Navy covering force ships. The Northern Attack Force was led by British Commodore Oliver RN and the Southern Attack Force aimed at its assigned beaches at Paestum was led by U.S. Rear Admiral Hall.

Aboard Ancon was General Mark Clark, commanding the newly designated U.S. 5th Army. His Army headquarters was to be put ashore in the U.S. sector, southeast of the British sector. An important new U.S. Army division, the 36th was in the assault wave. Clark had been picked by Eisenhower and reported directly to him once established ashore. The British X Corps for the Northern sector was commanded by Lieutenant General McCreery who replaced a British General wounded in a Bizerte air raid. Major General Dawley USA led U.S. troops in the Southern sector.

Montgomery's British 8th Army would be fighting northward from Messina to make a juncture with the Fifth Army. Eighth Army progress was being slowed by carefully executed German defense moves. Montgomery's slow progress became a factor in the German ability to make an all-out defense at the beachheads of Salerno.

The JCS (U.S. Joint Chiefs of Staff) had given back to Admiral Cunningham one of his British carriers and four of his British converted-hull escort carriers. This gave the Sea-fires, the carrier equivalent of the Spitfires, important time on station over Salerno. The land based Spitfires had 180 miles to fly from Sicily, giving them just about one half hour over the attack area. An aircraft fighter-director team under a U.S. Army Air Forces Brigadier General was embarked on the USS Ancon with Hewitt and his staff.

"Company" Overhead

While we had seen the scouting planes from the U.S. Navy cruisers and battleships at Casablanca, and from just our cruisers at Sicily, air combat had taken place mainly out of sight of Navy ships. At Salerno, we became more aware of what was going on upstairs. The Luftwaffe furnished their brand of entertainment to the ships at sea, delivered for the most part by Junkers JU-88s and Dornier DO-217s. These delivered bombs, torpedoes, and the new guided bombs. The next illustration is a DO-217 with a bomb under each wing. The starboard wing holds an HS-293 glide bomb.

Illustration 21-DO-217 with Bombs Loaded

For friendly high cover, the Supermarine Spitfire, with an elliptical wing readily visible in good weather at 20,000 feet, was a welcome partner. Sighting them buoyed our morale.

Illustration 22-British Supermarine Spitfire

The next picture is a U.S. Navy recognition shot of a Spitfire. Labeled a Spitfire XII, its wings are clipped. It was much harder to identify without the beautiful elliptical wing.

Illustration 23-Clipped Wing Spitfire XII

The Spits and the British Hawker Hurricanes were powered by the Rolls Royce Merlin engine, of just over 1,000 horsepower. This in-line, liquid cooled engine, was a breakthrough in engine design and provided fast, single-engine fighter performance for the British.

Legions of workers on the U.S. home front provided not only the steady supply of new warships needed for the ambitious Allied counteroffensives, but also mass-produced, aircraft. Here is a picture I found in Little Friends, a beautifully written and illustrated Random House publication. This young lady is working on a P-38 Lockheed Lightning. In the Mediterranean, these aircraft were used for low level bombing and strafing of enemy positions. In other war sectors, they escorted bombers.

Illustration 24-Production on P-38 Assembly Line

One day off Italy, two P-38s in perfect formation came roaring out of the foothills over the water making their exit from a low level land attack at less than 500 feet and not a half mile from Edison. The wingman in the formation then made a graceful, tangential descent at high speed, finally impacting the sea and sinking immediately. We were at the spot in seconds. Roiled, soiled water was all we could find. The pilot had undoubtedly been hit by flak and become unconscious. As he relaxed his hand on the stick and throttle, he flew to a graceful, sudden death. Here is a U.S. Navy recognition picture of the Lightning.

Illustration 25-Lockheed P-38 "Lightning"

Toward the end of the 1943-44 phase of the Italian campaign, the U.S. Army Air Forces got another fighter into mass production. That was the P-51 Mustang, which replaced P-40 Warhawks as both a low-level fighter-bomber and high altitude escort plane.

For its high altitude bomber escort mission, the P-51 had a longer range than the Spitfire. The long-range missions oc-

curred most often with raids over the continent that originated in Britain. The U.S. Navy recognition set from which
the Mustang slide was taken was a set made relatively early
in the war. The Mustang below is a drawing. We used it in
lieu of a photograph for our recognition training.

Illustration 26-U.S. P-51 "Mustang"

The P51 marked the end of the military reign of the liquid
cooled piston engine aircraft. Liquid cooling provided high
performance but also a possibility for catastrophic engine
failure. The Republic P-47 Thunderbolt, which we did not
see in the Mediterranean while I was there, joined the battle
for Western Europe with its air-cooled engine. All the U.S.
Navy carrier aircraft engines had been air-cooled for years,
though we did not see them in the Mediterranean either. This
changeover to air-cooled piston engines passed rather quickly
as Germany introduced all jet aircraft before the end of the
war. The piston engines for combat fighters were eliminated

after the end of World War II though used for fighter-bombers into the Korean conflict.

I ask the reader of this sea story to indulge the author one other discourse on aircraft. Both the Spitfire and the Hurricane were important and each had a mode of use in which it became pre-eminent. Though justly proud of both, the British favored their Hurricane over their Spitfire based on experience in the Battle of Britain. Where it counted the most in Mediterranean air warfare, my vote would go to the Spitfire. It was the only defense system working for us that could argue with the high altitude German bombers carrying guided weapons. Anything that could interfere with a German flight crew aiming one of those weapons at one of our ships meant the difference between life and death to us. The reader will have the opportunity to examine that assessment in upcoming action episodes.

Departure

Major convoys with heavy surface escort forces began to leave North African ports as early as 3 September, 1943. The principal assault convoy for the Southern Attack Force left Oran on 5 September and included the U.S. Army's 36th Infantry Division in 13 transports, escorted by Philadelphia, Savannah and 12 destroyers. Admiral Hewitt on USS Ancon, accompanied by HMS Palomares, and the U.S. destroyers Bristol, Nicholson and Edison left Algiers on 6 September.

Geography

The Bay of Salerno is shaped like a broad crescent, open to the southwest, with the beaches roughly on a northwest-southeast line. The American sector was to the south with four beaches, and the British were just to the northwest with six beaches. There was a gap between the assault sectors.

Salerno had the finest beaches we would find in the Mediterranean campaign and the Germans knew this too. The next harbor north was beautiful Naples, U-shaped and also open to the southwest. The Isle d'Ischia marks the entrance to Naples harbor to the north. To the south is the Isle of Capri. The Germans knew we would want Naples, one of the world's great harbors. The British forces moved into Salerno with Capri to their port side, and on the clear, golden sunset evening of the 8th during the approach, and on a perfect weather D-day itself, Capri was quite visible to the British.

The Human Equation

General Clark was interviewed by author Quentin Reynolds during the transit of the USS Ancon to Salerno on the 8th of September 1943. We will select just a few lines of that interview from the volume, United States Navy in World War II, compiled and edited by S. E. Smith and published by William Morrow.

"Reynolds: Are you apprehensive of what their air will do?

Clark: I'm scared stiff of what their air will do, but we hope to have two of their air fields by D plus 2 and then our fighters won't have that long pull from Sicily."

"Reynolds: When do you expect to establish headquarters ashore?

Clark: If everything goes according to plan-and it never does-I may get ashore on D plus 2."

Destroyer sailors might also be interested in how Commander D.H. Swinson, USNR, Ancon's Executive Officer, helped prepare his ship's company for General Quarters. This advice is found in a "Plan of the day for Thursday 9 September 1943" on USS Ancon (AGC4) as reported in the Morrow volume, United States Navy in World War II. "Food will be brought to General Quarters stations in food carriers by men detailed from ammunition parties. ......Gun platform crews will provide three fathoms of manila line for hoisting and lowering 10-gallon Aervoid coffee containers."

The discovery that coffee was available at General Quarters' stations on the USS Ancon reminded me of what Captain Headden on the USS Edison told us when he ordered the galley closed during General Quarters, "A hungry tiger is a fighting tiger."

Who Gets There First?

The assault waves of landing craft and the minesweepers were usually engaged before the backup fire support ships went into action. Some comments by Commander W. J. Burke and author William Bradford Huie in their joint offering, "The Panzers Were Waiting For Us" are a reminder of who gets there first. These excerpts are from S. E. Smith's compilation, "The United States Navy in World War II", published by William Morrow.

"About 0320, in pitch darkness, the rocket craft let go their barrage....They were fired in bunches, enveloping their craft in brilliant sheets of flame, then soaring high up, over and down toward the beach where thunderous explosions took place."(Author note: This pre-landing bombardment was new, the rockets were new, the craft that carried them were new, and the whoosh they gave off was terrifying.)

"At 0330...the first waves of the assault troops landed in their small craft...followed by waves of LCVPs, LCIs and LCTs....Sometime around 0430 four German artillery shells fell into the water near our causeway." (Burke and Huie were in an LST which had its causeways rigged)

"At 0525 our ship, with causeways rigged for "momentum beaching", was ordered to Green Beach. (This episode and its Green Beach were in the British sector.) We were following the course of the YM minesweepers. (YMs were the smaller U.S. wooden craft, not as big as the metal hulled fleet AM minesweepers.) About a mile off shore a large size Italian mine which had been swept to the surface, but not exploded, loomed in the path of the ship. The forward lookout saw the ominous round shape and a frantic effort was made to veer the ship to port, but not enough. The curved end of the in-board causeway hit and rode up over the mine before going off against the side of the ship.......There was a blinding flame, water towered up, objects were hurled aloft, then a blast of air and a deluge of water and oil fell on us....The explosion ripped into troop quarters killing and seriously injuring a number of British soldiers."

"....We grounded about 0600 without our causeways, some 250 feet off the shore line and about 11 feet of water at the bow ramp....It was immediately apparent that the beach had not yet been taken. Batteries of 88s and mortars had the range of the beach and kept up the shelling all through D-day. .....We decided to retract and attempt to put our cargo ashore.....via LCTs....When we were about a half mile off the beach, a British destroyer laid a smoke screen which protected us from further fire......"

Ensign M.T. Jacobs, a former TVA engineer, takes up the story of his LST. "We were carrying men of a Hampshire Regiment of the 46th British Division. On the tank deck we had six Shermans, with a lot of half-tracks, Bren gun carriers, and ducks .(these were the DUKWs which performed so well in all Mediterranean assaults)..It was a clear night with a million stars but no moon."

"The 16th Panzers were ready for us. When the small craft began hitting the beach, the Panzers opened up with every-thing they had. Big guns, 88s and machine guns. Our war-ships including the cruisers Savannah, Boise and Philadel-phia were with the Southern Attack Force off Paestum, and they returned the fire. (I doubt if the Boise, though originally scheduled to be present, had really made it back from her special mission at Taranto as early as D-day.) The Savannah had pulled to within a few hundred feet of our LST, and she was blasting with everything she had. German bombers started coming over, so even the guns on the LSTs started firing. God, it was hot! And right at that moment we got the order to prepare to launch the causeways."

"Off to my left as we were going in, I could see another LST with her set of causeways. That was Lieutenant Com-mander Burke, our officer-in-charge, with Mitchell and Look. ....When we were about a mile off the beach, the causeways ridden by Look and his men hit a loose mine, and there was one helluvan explosion. ....Look and most of his twenty-four men were blown off the causeway by that explo-sion...."

"About 0620-just before sunup-we hit the beach full speed....The beach condition was such that our LST slid right on up to the water's edge....we didn't need the causeways. All we had to do was throw a few sandbags under her ramp and spread the mat...We began unloading our LST and had her unloaded by 0800....That was the best beach we'll ever see for LST operations....Shellfire from the 88s was still bothering us on the beach.....Seven or eight Hampshires decided they'd brew up a spot of tea on the beach...They lit a fire and had the water boiling when one of them called to me. 'Say, chappie, come and have a spot o' tea.' I started walking toward them and was within fifty feet of them when a land mine went off right under that fire. ....when I got up every damn one of those Hampshires was dead and mangled...We stayed on the beach for ten days.. the bombing, shelling and fighting continued almost constantly...."

Part II - Edison in Action

Southern Attack Force; USS Philadelphia

The cruisers were able to lend an earlier hand to the landings in the British sector in the north because some progress was being made there, despite the mines and the vigorous defense ashore. The situation in the American sector landings to the south was behind schedule and deteriorating. The heavily mined approaches had interfered not just with the landing craft but more critically with access to fire support positions for the fire support destroyers and cruisers. Ashore, the situation grew desperate. Many SFCPs had been wiped out and those that survived were under fire and had difficulty establishing communication with their designated ship.

In seeking yet another report from the minesweeping commander, Rear Admiral Lyal Davidson got an unwelcome answer on the TBS voice circuit, "They're popping up all over the place. There is no channel for you yet." This was midmorning on the 9th and though I could not see the Admiral say these next words, I could understand his state of mind as I recall the gist of his response, "Stop talking (on this voice circuit) about mines popping up all over the place. I can accept your assessment that there is no safe channel. Just get on with your job. I am coming in." With that, the Admiral directed the skipper of the Philadelphia, Captain Hendren, to move through the minefield and get inshore of it for close and if necessary, with no SFCP contact, direct-observation fire support.

My battle station for secondary fire direction was on the after deckhouse. I did not get quite the intimate view of the Philadelphia that the crew on the Edison's bridge was about to see.

I am indebted to Drake Davis, webmaster for the USS Savannah website, for this next illustration. It is a view of the proud cruiser USS Philadelphia, CL-41.

Illustration 27-USS Philadelphia

What the Edison Did Then

Our skipper, "Hap" Pearce, listened carefully to Admiral Davidson's voice transmission over the TBS to the sweep commander and made his own plan on the spot. We had made contact with the USS Savannah's SFCP. They had more targets than Savannah itself could handle. When the Philadelphia made her bold move, we were close to her. Pearce knew that his sonarmen had developed moored mine detection experience off Porto Empodocle at Sicily. To him, the USS Philadelphia was by far the best minesweeper in sight! He gave orders to the helmsman and the engine room to have Edison fall in right behind Philadelphia. I had never seen the big box stern of a cruiser that size so close ahead. I had to look up at an angle of at least 45 degrees to read her lettering. I will never forget that scene. For the only time I can recall in the five attack landings in which we participated at North Africa and in the Mediterranean, I felt exhilaration as Edison made her move. Both ships made it in and then ensued the most action-filled, harrowing, and fulfilled day of Edison's life.

Lieutenant Stanley Craw was usually back on the after deckhouse with me when we were at General Quarters. I was there to provide some direction to the secondary guns, the 40s and the 20s. Lt. Craw was there primarily because he would become the after conning officer if our bridge controls were disabled or destroyed. He also helped with gunfire direction. After the Edison made her move to get inboard of the minefield and get into position for shore bombardment, the ship's control officers, Captain Pearce and Executive Officer Jake Boyd knew they'd be in for a busy day. We would be dodging bombs, counter fire from the beach, and mines. Edison's radar and sonar operators were able to help define a narrow operating zone between the minefield and the shore. Navigation information would need to be ultra-refined, and it would be much more time-sensitive than usual. Even the fathometer became a war tool! An extra hand was needed on the bridge. Stan Craw provided another capability for a stretched out General Quarters crew on the bridge. He was called to the bridge and I was left alone topside aft to observe what was about to unfold.

Lieutenant Dick Hofer, the Gunnery Officer and his main battery gun crews were magnificent that day. But equal billing on the Edison for D-Day at Salerno had to go to the Seamanship effort. This was not just another shoot from long distance. This was an all day gunnery effort in cramped quarters, at high speed. We were not casually lying off Bloodsworth Island in the Chesapeake or even off Cape Arzeu in Algeria. This was a total ship effort under combat conditions. I will insert below major excerpts from a typescript called "Salerno, First Day", which I wrote about 1960. The thoughts were then just over 15 years old. The action takes place in the Southern Attack Sector. The landing craft release point was about 6,000 yards (three nautical miles) from the shore, at the outer edge of the coordinates of the minefield. The sweepers worked tirelessly all day to sweep channels through the minefield.

The memorandum that I have reproduced below is taken from a 1960 typescript that I wrote and set aside. That typescript provides an interesting contrast to what the official War Diary of the USS Edison, written in Washington after the war, provides in the next 12 lines: Herewith, the War Diary.

"She screened the minesweepers while they cleared the fire support area. At 0510 on 8 September (War Diary error; should have been 9 September) DD 439's guns were trained inland for shore bombardment. Her targets were enemy troop concentrations, tanks, trucks, and artillery in the vicinity of Il Barizzo. Before leaving the area on 24 September (second error; Edison left on 10 September and returned several times before 24 September) en route to Mers-El-Kebir, two more air attacks developed though they were not pressed and all units escaped damage. All hands had an anxious moment (on 10 September) when a torpedo passed along Edison's port side only 100 yards abeam."

The Author's 1960 memorandum of a 1943 event

"It was early evening on 8 September 1943 when the watch relayed the news that Badoglio had surrendered. I must say there was an immediate disposition to question just what Badoglio could surrender. As the hours wore on, however, the official broadcast made it sound as though Badoglio had been able to effect, in the name of the King, a surrender of all of the Italian Armed Forces. The depth of the German military involvement in the Italian Peninsula was unknown to a Junior Grade Lieutenant aboard a U.S. destroyer. Early disbelief that anything could be won so easily gave way to a disposition to believe that matters would perhaps be somewhat easier on the morrow than had been anticipated. I believe that this statement accurately reflects the feeling of most of those men in the U.S. Armed Forces who were expecting to take part in the Salerno landings."

"The beautiful weather which had made the approach so much like a War College textbook amphibious operation, certainly also provided any defender with a period of time, beginning on the afternoon of September 8th, to calculate our strength and arrange his beach defenses. The morning of September 9th commenced and it remained to be seen if the defender would fight."

"Well, fight he did! Our minesweepers were the first forces in action, and they were totally engaged while dealing with the task of clearing dense mine fields. The story of our minesweeping operations in the Mediterranean Sea has never been comprehensively chronicled to my knowledge. By the time that H-Hour, D-Day, Salerno, arrived, it was apparent that the minesweepers had only just begun their task. My recollection is that some postponement of H-Hour was authorized. (Faulty. I can in 1998 find no corroboration of that.) The first waves to hit the beach (Southern Sector) were quite late."

"Even in the early light of morning some casualties in the seaborne forces were already apparent. Numerous vessels were on fire and others were settling low in the water. Our own visual observation of the troops hitting the beach, later confirmed by fragmentary radio reports, showed that they were in a murderous crossfire. As the morning wore on, our task force commander for gunfire support, Rear Admiral Lyal Davidson, became more and more impatient. His main concern, now that he had safely conducted his forces to the landing area, was to see that the troops got ashore. After the Admiral's fourth or fifth interrogation of the sweep commander over the TBS brought forth the response that the field was not swept, and that the mines were still popping up all over the place, Admiral Davidson himself exploded. The Admiral must have been thinking of the morale effect on his ships associated with these reports of mines. He knew that most of his fire support destroyers and cruisers would have to penetrate the minefield if they were to provide effective gunfire support to the now badly off-balance landing forces. The Admiral then told his Sweep Commander (it should be remembered that these sweep people had been heavily engaged for many hours and had really done a magnificent job) not to report again the status of the sweeping operation in terms of "mines popping up all over the place." Then the Admiral announced tersely, "I am coming through." Admiral Davidson was embarked on USS Philadelphia, and true to his word, Philadelphia immediately started in."

"The Philadelphia, the Brooklyn and the Savannah had been wonderful ships to us in the destroyer Navy. We had operated with them during convoy operations and then during amphibious operations commencing with the Casablanca landings, thence to Sicily and now Salerno. We would see them hammer away at Anzio and again at Southern France. This light cruiser class had been designed, I believe, to counter the Japanese 15-gun cruisers. Their big payoff in Mediterranean operations came as the result of the firepower of their six-inch guns in support of amphibious operations. AA-wise they were perhaps slightly deficient but hull integrity-wise, as Captain Cary and his crew so courageously demonstrated in Savannah just a few days later, they could take an awful wallop and survive."

"A destroyer sailor who could read the word, PHILADELPHIA, across a big gray box stern, as though he were taking a visual acuity test in some optometrist's parlor, might develop quite a fright that collision was imminent. Commander "Hap" Pearce decided to put his bow within a few feet of that cruiser's stern and go in with her. It was a good time for spelling practice on Edison's foc'sle. Many years later when I learned more about the characteristics of mines (an assignment as the U.S. Navy's Undersea Warfare Development officer), I mentally revisited Hap's decision and concluded it was a good one; some might reasonably disagree. At any rate, we went in with Philadelphia and got through the field without casualty. The field had been well planned and executed, but for the type of operation that ensued, the field gave us precious sea room just short of the three-fathom line. (Looking back, I figure a destroyer had a two-miles of sea room between going aground ashore and the inner edge of the minefield. For a cruiser, the fit was very, very tight.) So for the next six hours, Edison danced along this thin line."

"The situation ashore was so confused that no one seemed able to establish effective contact with their assigned Shore Fire Control Party. The cruisers outside the minefield were doing some direct interdiction fire (at longer ranges than they would have preferred for that type of fire). This was always a little risky because of the possibility of mistaking own forces for enemy forces. I would like to make it clear that the people at sea could always see the picture a good deal better than the Army ashore gave them credit for."

"We could see that other ships had not been so successful as Edison in getting through the mine field. I can remember HMS Abercrombie, that grand old name which was just recently (circa 1960) stricken from the British Naval Register, very low in the water from a mine explosion and no longer able to shoot. Other craft were similarly plagued. It is my recollection that we were the first or among the first to make contact with a Shore Fire Control Party. I believe we finally established contact with a party designated for USS Savannah. Either Savannah had been unable to contact this party or had passed the contact to us because of our better position with respect to the NLO. A word about this NLO. The term stands for Naval Liaison Officer. This man was assigned to the artillery ashore. He usually worked with an Army artillery spotter as a member of a Shore Fire Control Party (SFCP). An Army radio technician was assigned and also a poor arm-weary GI who did nothing but crank for power. These parties were unbelievably courageous and effective. In the fluid situation at Salerno on D-Day, this small party was often the advance group, deep in enemy held territory. (At Salerno, "deep" could be measured in feet or yards)"

"The Germans were now making a terrific counterattack on our precarious landing area. Some of the Tiger (Mark VI) tanks were actually moving southward along the beach to the beachhead. We (the Edison) were faced with counter battery fire from these tanks and other German gun emplacements throughout the remainder of this engagement. The flat-trajectoried 88-mm shell had a unique piercing sound as it passed between our Director and the #1 stack. We had been used to the fluttery sound of larger projectiles in arched trajectories. (Like our 5" 38s, most enemy artillery projectiles were subsonic. The 88, I later learned, had a 4,000 feet per second muzzle velocity, and when you heard the sound, the projectile was long gone. At Salerno ranges, the 88 shell was in a very flat trajectory, where a 'miss was as good as a mile', usually more. They had to hit you directly and hope you had enough metal to set off their fuze, which was essentially designed to be anti tank, armor piercing.)"

"We got right down to business with our newly adopted SFCP and went to work. From my own station in secondary AA on the after deck house, although we had a few air attacks the first afternoon, I was able to get quite a perspective on our participation in the engagement. The Skipper and the Gun Boss teamed up in a driving and dynamic display of destroyer gun power. The Exec. and Navigator teamed up in a most difficult job of high-speed navigation in restricted waters, while opening up fire lanes for the 5" guns. Some unseen bond between these two teams kept matters from getting completely out of hand. The Captain wanted to present an unpredictable target to enemy fire while maintaining our guns on firing bearings for long periods of time. I am sure the Exec. and Navigator did not actually have time to think about Rocks and Shoals (the vernacular name for Navy Regulations), as they kept us from straying back into the mine field to seaward or running aground on Salerno's shores. The engineers supplied flank emergency ahead and back in total disregard of acceleration curves."

"Since we were firing almost all of the time, and the water was full of spent cartridge cases-'brass'- it needs to be added that the firing cut-out cams would take Guns #1 and #2 out of action, or Guns #3 and #4, depending on how sharply we could turn in that mine safety zone and get going the other way. All the systems worked perfectly. Guns and engines and boilers are stress-tested to some per cent over normal, and the Edison worked that extra percent all the time in the no man's land of Salerno. Yes, we had to be re-bricked and re-gunned after Salerno, but the systems never failed under those punishing conditions."

"On some of the early targets, we had to fire rapid continuous (about 20 rounds per gun per minute) fire for one, two and in one grueling demonstration, for six minutes at a time. Although our *doctrine* told us this could be uneconomical of projectiles (rapid 'timed' fire was better) the 'spot' from the NLO was 'on' and the urgency in his voice conveyed to us a requirement for extreme performance. Later we went to continuous timed fire, more economical of projectiles and nearly as effective on a per unit time basis. The Army's Artillery General Officer ashore who was fighting this phase of his battle with our artillery, sent repeated messages of encouragement. Finally, in the waning hours of daylight, as we left the firing scene, he sent one of the most magnificent messages of appreciation to Rear Admiral Lyal Davidson that I have ever seen recorded. 'Thank God for the fire of the blue-belly Navy ships. Probably could not have stuck out Blue and Yellow beaches. Brave fellows these; tell them so. General Lange.' Later and without waste of language, he told vividly of German tanks piled up in rubble and how attack after attack of the German forces had been blunted, and finally turned back, and the beachhead made secure. Again, by mail we received from this expressive and appreciative source, photographs showing the terrific damage inflicted on twelve German tanks. They were piled up like scrap iron. Many of us were truly amazed at the localization of effective blast damage from concentrated 5" 38 HC fire."

"Those two destroyer shortage bugaboos may have been temporarily banished from mind, but inexorably we shot up our precious supply of ammunition and used up a significant measure of our limited supply of bunker fuel. Split plant, four boilers and those accelerations had taken a toll on our fuel. The projectile count by late afternoon (still 9 September) told its story. There were just a few high capacity projectiles left, all up in the handling rooms, directly under the guns served. We had expended about 1200 5" 38 HC shells. A few odd star shells were still available, some white phosphorus, and although my memory is rather dim on it, I believe we had a few armor piercing aboard. (We also carried and never used the VT-fuzed shells, sometimes referred to as 'influence fuzes.') We had started the day with extra HC projectiles and powder cartridges over and above our allowance. These had been lashed in the handling rooms. Such rat-packing was forbidden by Higher Authority and we would have had to reckon with this had we encountered rough weather. (In rough seas, we had experienced loose 5" projectiles from the #2 handling room falling through the hatch over the officer's bunkroom passageway, and sloshing into the wardroom.)"

"Though it was not fully apparent until dark, the guns on Edison were for the first time in my experience all white hot. They continued to glow on into the night, gradually subsiding to red, then dying out though still hot to the touch. The canvas tarp that covered Gun #3 to save topside weight had long since evaporated in flame. All the bloomers were completely destroyed. About mid-afternoon when we reported our ammunition state, we knew we were going to have to leave the firing area to make way for a ship that still had some punch in her. (It turned out to be the USS Trippe.) Edison was all shot out. (I used the term 'firing area' when I originally put down these thoughts without realizing that this was not a firing area in any operation plan. Admiral Davidson and our Skipper 'Hap' Pearce had carved out a firing area and this became by usage, the firing area.)"

"I can honestly say that a good many of us were just a little relieved at the opportunity to back off and light a cigarette. By late afternoon, the sweepers had marked the channels and we were somewhat easier going through the field on the way out than we had been on the way in. Darkness was beginning to set in as we were directed to assist in screening some of the attack transports which were still disgorging their human cargo."

"Unfortunately, it wasn't quite over yet. We departed the Salerno area, screening larger ships astern, on the next eve-

ning (10 September 1943), another hazy bright Italian moonlight night. The number of ghosts on our radarscope was almost beyond anything we had ever seen. And how rapidly
they moved! Edison's engineering force was again put to the
test as we attempted to pursue these phantoms and come to
grips with them. All of a sudden, we saw that characteristic
orange flash. I had seen it before with the USS Ingraham in
the North Atlantic. It was the mark of a ship whose magazines had exploded and was entirely different from the muffled poof near a transport, for example, when these were hit
below the water line. It turned out to be the USS Rowan, a
destroyer in our force, which had also gotten in her share of
shelling that day and was assigned to this first outbound convoy because needed more ammunition. (I learned later there
was a heavy loss of life. One fatality was Lt. (jg) Wiley
Mackie USN, a Naval Academy classmate of mine.) The
USS Bristol turned back to assist the stricken ship. All Bristol could do was pick up survivors, some badly injured, as
the Rowan was doomed. I do not know if the cause of the
Rowan's loss has ever been completely determined, but most
of us felt it probably had been either an E-boat torpedo attack
as evidenced by the radar phantoms, or a submarine lying in
wait. Or again, it may have been one of the moored mines
which had been cut loose, and drifted into the path of the
Rowan."

"Salerno's first phase, for Edison, ended the following
morning (September 11th) in Oran when we tied up. The destroyerman's view of an operation, while not claimed to be as
complete a view of the operation as a plans or staff man, is
certainly a first hand view. The destroyer man sees the little
fellow, and the big fellow, and he must work with them both.
I certainly do not recall that Edison ever had a period of time

in which the action was more intense, the enemy more tena-
cious, and the issue so starkly defined. The minefield certainly disrupted our timetable and increased our casualties.
The timetable in turn caused at least one U.S. infantry division not scheduled for Salerno to be diverted into the combat
area."

(Lieutenant Ed Meier of the Edison recorded his thoughts
of those events. His day by day account was usually recorded
within a few hours of the actual events he describes.)

"September 9. It is now 6:40 p.m. and I'm so dog-tired
that I can hardly stay awake, so this will be short and sweet.
At about 5:00 last night while only about 50 miles from the
Italian coast, we were told that an important radio announcement would be made at 6:15 by the Algiers and Rome
radios. And at 6:15 the inspiring news poured in that the
Italians had unconditionally surrendered to the Allies. We
were all so dumb-founded that for several seconds we sat
around starry-eyed with our mouths wide open. What effect
would this have on our assault force-would we move right
into Naples? None. We kept to our original plan and after an
air attack which lasted for over an hour we moved into our
assault positions. General Quarters sounded at sunset last
night (7:30) and we didn't secure until about 6:30 this morning. Then this morning about 10:00 there was another German air attack and from noon we were at Battle Stations firing on beach targets constantly for over 5 hours. We used all
except about 300 rounds of 5-inch ammunition. So when I
say I'm tired, I mean just that."

"The landings were all made successfully and I don't think
our losses have been at all heavy. As far as I know, no ship
has been sunk, although the Edison came within an ace of it

this afternoon thanks to the extreme accuracy of a shore battery. Those shells whistled by so close to us that if we hadn't
ducked they would have taken our heads off. There were
splashes all around us."

"The Army was very pleased with the close inshore fire
support given them by the Edison and the shore fire control
party continually complimented us. We fired on troops and
tank columns, road junctions, artillery emplacements, trucks
etc. and apparently our fire was excellent. In all we fired over
900 rounds of 5 inch ammunition. Boy - I'm tired - what a
day." (Edison had taken excess 5" ammunition aboard and
stowed it in the gun handling rooms. This accounts for some
of the difference between my shell count and Ed Meier's.)

"September 10. Regular as clockwork, the Germans were
over again last night. A sharp attack on the landing beaches
and supply dumps an hour after sunset and then their regular
4:00 milk run during which they attack ships in Salerno Bay.
With all the hundreds of ships out here they couldn't neglect
the Edison and after having duly lit us up with eerie flares,
which never seem to come down, a glide bomber came in
and whistled one in on our starboard quarter. It was too close
for comfort and all of us on the after deckhouse hit the deck
as if by instinct. The roar of an aircraft engine, the brilliant
light of flares piercing the darkness and lighting you up as a
singer on stage, the screeching whistle of the falling bombs
are the most terrifying combination that I can imagine. The
dull thud of the bomb hitting the water together with the
shock against the ship itself are most surely a source of comfort." (This is what Ed wrote. Probably, the "miss" was the
source of comfort.)

"Since we have expended over 2/3 of our ammunition, the
Edison has been relieved as fire support destroyer (by USS
Trippe) and is now patrolling outside the Bay of Salerno.

Last night a dispatch came in saying that today we were to shove off with a convoy of British ships for Oran, but as yet we are still patrolling. I surely hope we leave before darkness as we are all allergic to this place after dark. By the way, in those air attacks, several planes have already been shot down, one this morning was ablaze from stem to stern as she plummeted into the sea."

"September 11. The orders for our getting underway got fouled up and sure as shooting we got in on the regular air attack about 11:00 last night. Flares all over the place and the brightness of the moon led the German bombers in on their targets. One bomber apparently not being able to see us, however, got very close and being illuminated by his own flares, he would have been duck soup. But despite the fact that the director operator on the port 40's was right on the target and had his firing key closed, the pointer did not have his firing pedal down and consequently we didn't fire until he got well forward and out of range. Up forward, he released a torpedo, the wake of which was seen by people up forward, but it ran harmlessly away from us."

"About 2:00 this morning the convoy began to form up and we were finally given orders to proceed with them. Thank the Good Lord. General Quarters again about 2:30 however, due to a few flares being dropped, but by this time we were far enough out that the bombers missed us. At the same time word was received that enemy E-boats were in the vicinity and that the USS Rowan in searching for them had been torpedoed and probably blew up. The Bristol is searching for survivors now and has reported that she has already picked up the captain."

"We have lost quite a number of destroyers in the Sicilian and Italian campaigns. The Maddox and the Rowan have been sunk and the Roe, Swanson, Shubrick, Mayrant and Kendrick have been badly damaged."

"September 12. We have gotten down in the neighborhood of Sicily. Friendly fighters are overhead which naturally adds to our contentment. Hitler spoke last night trying to explain to his people that the Italian surrender had no military significance. Fighting has already been reported between German and Italian troops and the Germans have already succeeded in occupying the large northern Italian cities."

"September 13. (Ed Meier's account is at odds here with my data and with the Edison's Navy Department-written War Diary. On this date, I had us already in Oran. Ed kept notes day by day, and the War Diary of the Edison has many mistakes, so I would defer to Ed's chronicle concerning the date of our arrival in Oran after D-Day at Salerno.) Passed by Bizerte last night and although we are traveling very slowly due to the large amount of traffic in the channel, we will be in Oran possibly day after tomorrow. Speculation is running high that we will return to the States with this outfit."

"September 14. Arrived in Oran this morning and immediately fueled and took on ammunition. The transports which we brought in started to reload troops and since they are keeping us on a 1-hours notice, it looks as though they intend to shove us off again to Salerno. What a life.

September 15. They have now permitted us to go on a 4-hours notice and from the looks of things, we have an excellent chance of going back to the States."

"September 22. All hopes of going back to the States dissolved this morning when we were given sailing orders to escort the Brooklyn, who had just returned from a 4-week overhaul, to Bizerte. Oh well, c'est la vie, c'est la guerre. We had a nice stay in Oran and got rested up anyway. Got out to Ain El Turk for a swim a few days ago and we had a nice party out there, the feminine charm being lent to the occasion by nurses who are quartered out there. We had 4 quarts of Vermouth and had a nice time at the Club which is situated right on the beach. "

(I do not ever recall getting vermouth or champagne in these places. The drink of the day was called "eau de vie", a poor tasting liquid that did contain alcohol, thank heavens, because the Army assay of it also showed other liquid materials too vile to recall now. Another drink was beer, from bottles packed in sawdust, which the merchant skippers brought over and sold for outrageous prices. One brand I remember was Fort Pitt. At Malta, for Christmas of 1943, we got some good stuff and I will tell how we got it in a later section.)

"September 23. Got underway from Oran this morning en route to Bizerte and Palermo in company with the Brooklyn and USS Woolsey. We are making 25 knots and aren't sparing the horses, and are all wondering what kind of a deal they've got us in on now. The news broadcast this morning stated that the French, Italian and U.S. Ranger troops are in combat with the Germans on Corsica and a number of our officers seem to think that that is where we are going. At this rate of speed we should be off Bizerte early tomorrow morning."

"September 24. Arrived in Bizerte about 11:00 this morning and immediately proceeded to fuel. Conflicting orders and reports of future operations come in all day, but we're still here this evening and at last the picture has been clarified although still subject to change. The Brooklyn shoved off with the Plunkett tonight and the latest dope is that the Ludlow and Edison will escort a convoy to Palermo tomorrow."

(This completes this portion of Lieutenant Meier's day sequence in the period after the invasion of Sicily through the assault in Salerno Bay.)

My Father's Suitcase

In April, 1991 with wife Peggy I was looking into family genealogy. I found a suitcase my father gave me before his death. A news clip fluttered to the floor. I had not seen it before. Very likely it came from a Rochester (N.Y.) newspaper. He had cut it out some day in 1943. It bears an Associated Press date of October 17. News of this type traveled slowly in wartime. The Bristol is misspelled as Briston.

Illustration 28-A Faded World War II News Clip

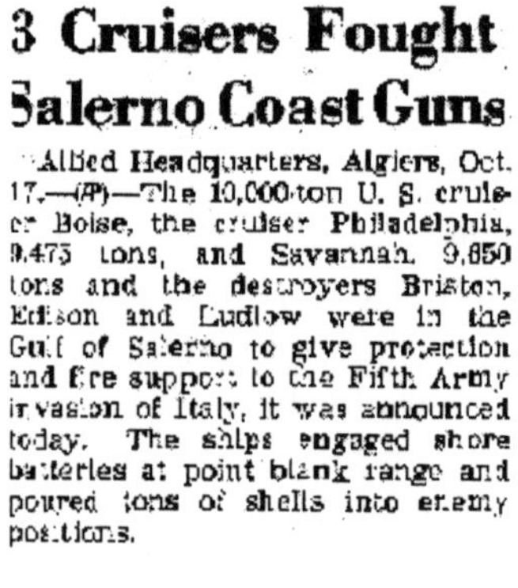

3 Cruisers Fought
Salerno Coast Guns

Allied Headquarters, Algiers, Oct. 17.—(P)—The 10,000-ton U. S. cruiser Boise, the cruiser Philadelphia, 9,475 tons, and Savannah, 9,650 tons and the destroyers Briston, Edison and Ludlow were in the Gulf of Salerno to give protection and fire support to the Fifth Army invasion of Italy, it was announced today. The ships engaged shore batteries at point blank range and poured tons of shells into enemy positions.

Seamanship, Navigation, Engineering, Gunnery

Once Edison decided to couple her fate with that of the USS Philadelphia and enter the minefield at Salerno, there were no ship formations to observe, no station keeping, and no ASW fishtailing. A sub in such shallow waters would have had to surface. Edison practiced no fuel economy plan. All boilers were on line. Nothing on Edison was going to be saved or held back this day. Looking back, it was Edison herself that was saved. Lady luck helped a crew that had been built on teamwork.

Don't run aground. Don't hit Philadelphia. Don't stray back into the minefield. One of the only two ships to make it inside the minefield by mid-morning to support the Southern Attack Force landings did not want to do to itself what the enemy was trying to accomplish, be put out of action.

Rarely, if ever, is a ship pressed to the limits of its performance in seamanship, navigation, engineering and gunnery all at once. I can recall long winter convoys where an escort ship navigator could have gone to bed at the exit port sea buoy and need to be waked only at the entry port sea buoy. The Convoy Commander's ship could handle navigation and all the escort needed to do was to keep formation. This is an outrageous example to make a point. Convoy work is probably the most redundant work in the world.

Edison was accelerating or slowing, making course reversals, dodging bombs or shells (mostly the latter), and straining eyeballs to see floaters as the drifting mines were called. The 5" main battery was in director automatic, pointed toward enemy beach armor at all times irrespective of the ship's course. This was direct fire! Hitler's surviving tanks finally turned around! Our Chief Fire Controlman, Jackson, had a clear view of this action in the rangefinder of his Mk 37 Director. Dick Hofer, our Gunnery Officer coordinated the four gun crews as they strained to keep up the rates of fire demanded. His frequent loading machine drills paid off. No gun missed a salvo unless the firing cutout cams prevented its firing.

Subsequent to D-Day at Salerno

The first day at Salerno was a maelstrom of air attacks, sea attacks, landings, and counterattacks. While Edison's principal contribution was made on D-Day, that day was by no means conclusive. In the subsequent days, the Germans organized a number of attacks that threatened the beachhead. For two days, the 13th and 14th of September 1943, plans were even made to re-embark troops already ashore with the Southern Attack force to plug holes in the center between the British Northern Force and the U.S. Southern Force. This did not have to be carried out but it is revealing of the tenuous hold we had on the beachhead. Unfortunately, General Montgomery's pursuit northward of the Panzers found the latter disengaging and linking up with the German defenders of Salerno and participating in German counterattacks on the beachhead. Montgomery's units arrived on the 16th of September after the survival of the beachhead was assured. The British 8th Army did participate in the subsequent capture of Naples on October 1, 1943. This took place about 10 days late in the Allied timetable.

The Rangers

Here, I need to post an insight on special troops the Edison escorted and helped get ashore in assault landings. This recollection comes from a soldier who fought as a Ranger in the Mediterranean campaign. Carl Lehmann was one of "Darby's Rangers." For U.S. military service, Carl first presented himself at a Navy Recruiting office in 1939. His attempt to enlist was aborted because the form he filled in called for the applicant to PRINT in all the spaces. Carl complied in all spaces except one, where he forgot and hand-wrote "white" instead of putting a W in the box for Race. When the Chief Petty Officer "threw my application papers back at me" for this oversight, Carl simply walked out. So, Carl characterizes his Navy enlistment attempt as that of a "surly" volunteer. Later, Carl became an Army Ranger.

Carl Lehmann joined the First Battalion, Rangers, in Ireland, and participated in the landings at North Africa, the campaign in Tunisia, the landings at Sicily/Licata, Salerno and Anzio. For the Licata beach landings that were supported by the USS Edison, Carl went ashore from the passenger boat, Princess Charlotte. During the campaign that began at the Anzio beachhead, the Germans took Carl prisoner at Cisterna. Carl is writing a book about the Rangers. The paragraphs in quotes below are taken from Carl Lehmann's words in e-mails of 1/10/98 and 1/12/98.

"I joined the First Battalion of Darby's Rangers in Ireland and made the landing in N. Africa and participated in the subsequent Tunisian campaign with them. Afterwards, the Third and Fourth Ranger Battalions and the reconstituted First formed in Tunisia and trained for Sicily. I went to the Third, commanded by the late Col. Herman Dammer, for the landing at Licata. The First and Fourth under Darby landed at Gela. After finishing up around Licata we moved around Agrigento and headed toward Porto Empodocle, having an easy time of it against poorly trained Italian troops. We were far ahead of the Third Division and had lost touch with communication to the rear. Field radios were not much in those days."

"My squad was doing a 'house to house' on the eastern edge of town, when, right before my eyes, a house nearer the beach dissolved in a cloud of dust. We then saw Philly's observation plane and the guys down on the docks spelled out 'US' and 'Yank' with barrels and boxes, causing the pilot to come down and land in the harbor. He flew the Colonel out to the ship, which supplied us with badly needed Navy chow. The Medic in our company, Bob Reed, had a brother on that ship and was allowed a visit."

"Philly also did great jobs at Gela and Salerno. Kraut tanks stood little chance against her guns. At Salerno, we also got great fire support from a British monitor, HMS Roberts-her sister ship, the Abercrombie hit a mine early and had to leave. I never saw the Roberts, but I can still hear the noisy travel of her 15-inch shells as they went through Chiunzi Pass above the coastal town of Maiori. She certainly, and the Navies generally, never received proper recognition of their importance at Salerno."

"One of the reasons for my writing the book about Darby's Rangers is to give credit where credit is due. One revisionist has gone into print bad-mouthing Darby and his men at Salerno. That person got it all wrong and I can prove he could not read a map or understand the terrain--doubt if he saw either. Moreover, memoirs of Generals and some of the historians seem to copy the same fallacies from one another. Scenes and sounds and smells and shocks of combat are best forgot by those there, and most are. That landing in Italy, the trek up the mountain, and much of the two weeks of furious activity remain indistinct blurs of excitement, terror and confusion, punctuated by a few vignettes clear and bright as yesterday's. The scream 'Amerikaner' with startled Kraut faces bobbing up, then down, flattening under my burst as I spun and flew instantly on winged feet. The Lieutenant pissing in his handkerchief and clapping it to his face at an idiot's shout, 'Gas!'. Looking DOWN at the tops of P-38s strafing a road, that vista revealed from Monte San Angelo above the Bay of Naples. Vesuvio. The road in the valley curving gently through Pagani, Nocera Inferiori and Cava to Vietri. Salerno, with Longfellow's 'sickle of white sand' around the Bay, laden with ships of war. Crawling slowly from foxhole to foxhole, a cheerful old Italian in ragged dress, greeting all with Mozzarella from a basketful of white balls, despite noisy 88s bursting about the Pass."

Samuel Eliot Morison's Volume IX, pages 298-314, of the History of United States Naval Operations in World War II, "Sicily-Salerno-Anzio", provides insights on action connected with the Salerno operation. The following paragraph on the USS Rowan's loss after its courageous performance during the assault landings is quoted:

"Assault shipping was supposed to be unloaded by the end of 10 September, and except for a few LSTs at the southern beaches, that was done........Rear Admiral (John) Hall in (USS) Samuel Chase sailed for Oran with 15 unloaded transports and assault freighters, escorted by ten destroyers, at 2215 September 10....Shortly after midnight, destroyer Rowan of the transport screen sighted a torpedo wake about 100 feet distant on the starboard bow....(There followed for Rowan, the description of a period filled with fast moving radar targets pursuit at 27 knots, and Rowan gunfire, followed by a return to the convoy, then another radar target astern. In bringing her guns to bear on this target, Rowan was struck by a torpedo according to her action report and Admiral Hall's report.) There was a tremendous explosion, probably in the after magazine, and she sank in 40 seconds. Bristol, detached from the transport screen, managed to rescue only 71 members of the crew. 202 officers and men went down with the ship. This sequence was also confirmed by a German E-boat division commander after the war who thought he had, in fact, sunk a 10,000 ton freighter."

In Theodore Roscoe's "United States Destroyer Operations in World War II", the author states that Rowan's skipper, Lieutenant Commander Ford survived the explosion and sinking, and that Ford credited a Torpedoman's Mate 2/c with setting depth charges on safe in the few seconds before the Rowan sank. Those who did survive can credit this man with inspiration and the cool head to act on it.

A radio-controlled bomb hit the SS Bushrod Washington on 14 September. The same fate befell the SS James Marshall on 15 September. Both ships were total losses.

Our intelligence data on the USS Edison in 1943 provided us with descriptions of two distinct Luftwaffe bomb systems, both guided all the way from a mother plane to impact. One was a rocket engine powered glide bomb, HS 293, which during the last part of its flight was right down on the water flying level until nosed down onto its target. We saw many attacks of this type, the favorite targets being the relatively slow-to-maneuver LSTs. Surface observers as well as controllers in the attacking plane could see the flare which the mother plane used to control the powered glider bomb, most often used in daylight attacks. The other, the FX 1400, was dropped from high altitude, and its ballistic trajectory could be altered through remote control of the tail vanes that stabilized the bomb. At night one could see the flare used to guide the tail vanes of the radio controlled ballistic bomb, but the bomb itself, used both day and night from high flying Dornier 217s, could only be seen in daylight in the last moments before impact.

On page 283 of his Volume IX, Samuel Eliot Morison's account refers to radio controlled glide bombs, which I feel consisted of one basic system with two variations. This was a glider bomb with rocket propulsion. One variation had a range of 8 miles and top speed of 570 mph and the other a range of 3 1/2 miles but with top speed of 660 mph. Trading range for speed could well have been a settable configuration of the same system prior to launch. This fits the description we had on board Edison for the HS 293 glide bomb. This system had a warhead of about 600 pounds. This system is not the same as the trajectory-alterable FX 1400 non-powered bomb that was shown in diagrams to us in 1943. Returning to Morison, on page 283, "Savannah was put out of action by one of these bombs." Savannah's bomb was the radio controlled ballistic bomb dropped from high altitude with trajectory alterable by radio control from the mother plane. It was not the rocket powered glide bomb but rather the far more deadly FX 1400 that hit Savannah's No. 3 turret, judging from the description below.

The USS Savannah is put out of action

(This next sequence begins about 0930 on 11 September and culminates about 15 minutes later. The paragraph is pieced together from the writings of Drake Davis, the son of a survivor of the bomb hit on the USS Savannah at Salerno.)

"She was lying to in her support area, awaiting calls for gunfire support, at 0930 September 11, when 12 Focke-Wulfe 190s (German fighter-bombers) were reported approaching from the north. The cruiser rang up 10 knots speed, which she increased to 15 knots after a heavy bomb had exploded close aboard Philadelphia, nearby. (Philadelphia sailors told us later that this near miss lifted the entire stern of the ship out of the water.) Ten minutes later, Savannah received a direct hit on No. 3 turret. The bomb which had been dropped from a Dornier-217 from 18,000 feet, detonated in the lower handling room. The blast wiped out the crew of the stricken turret and the No. 1 damage control crew in the central station, blew a large hole in the ship's bottom and opened a seam in her side."

(Drake Davis also refreshed my memory on the two distinct types of radio controlled bombs. Each gave its German mother planes a standoff bombing capability. Both of these bomb systems worked very well and we will visit them again in a later chapter. Drake characterized the Savannah bomb as a "Fritz-x" and has pictures of it. It first opened about a two foot hole in Savannah's #3 turret, penetrated 34 inches of steel to get into the #3 magazine, where it then detonated. When the USS Savannah finally made it into drydock in Malta, a 20-30 foot hole in her hull was exposed. The same weapon system was used in hitting a British cruiser. In this case, the bomb went all the way through the cruiser and detonated in the water under her keel! The DO-217 in Illustration-20 in this chapter is pictured carrying two of the Fritz-x, or FX-1400s ,as these were alternatively called.)

After many heroics, Savannah, for a time in a sinking condition without power, made it to Malta. Since the British, too, had a cruiser put out of action by a radio controlled bomb, two fresh cruisers were ordered into the Salerno action area in relief. One of the relief ships ordered up from Malta was the cruiser HMS Penelope, with whom Edison later would put in many hours of work. The U.S. cruisers Boise and Philadelphia used 70% of their ammo during the

9-15 September period. Ammo for the cruisers was so tight that the destroyer USS Gleaves was ordered to Malta to bring back some of Savannah's 6" ammunition. And before the beachhead had really been secured, not only had the U.S. 36th and 45th Divisions been fully committed, but also the 34th was to receive its baptism of fire. The 3rd Division was ordered up from its rest period in Sicily. Important elements of the 82nd airborne also helped turn the tide.

The U.S. employed counter measures ships at Salerno, notably the U.S. Destroyer Escorts, Herbert C. Jones and Frederick C. Davis. These were new and were "getting their feet wet" so to speak. I will go into some detail on what they managed to accomplish against radio-controlled weapons and other German air tactics, in Chapter Nine on Anzio.

From Morison, Volume IX, page 296, a statement is provided from the German Marshal Kesselring: "On 16 September, in order to evade the effective shelling from warships, I authorized a disengagement on the coastal front." Kesselring, though, had managed necessary withdrawals so effectively, and had shown such an intestinal willingness to dispute every inch of ground, that he was chosen by Hitler over Rommel stationed in the north of Italy to continue this dogged defense. Morison reasoned that had Rommel been under Kesselring's command during the Salerno beachhead battle, that Rommel's available divisions could have turned the tide in the German's favor and the Allies might have been thrown back into the sea. For their part, in late September 1943, the Allies missed many opportunities to interfere with the German evacuations of Sardinia and Corsica, where important German forces got out to help hold the Allies on a line north of Naples. Available French and Italian sea forces, under Allied direction, could have made those evacuations troublesome for the Germans.

Loss of the USS Buck

The U-boats were not finished with their favorite targets, United States destroyers. The USS Buck was patrolling at the north end of the Gulf of Salerno on 8 October. Pursuing an active radar contact, Buck was torpedoed by U-616 forward of her stack (she was a one-stacker). The Buck went down in about four minutes with loss of life exacerbated by depth charge explosions.

Buck's Executive Officer, and my personal friend, Lieutenant Commander G. S. Lambert, was among the large number of men lost. As Edison's Gunnery Officer, "Beppo" Lambert had been an active proponent of Edison's defined policy to leave depth charges on "safe" except during actual pursuit of a submarine contact. My belief, therefore, is that Buck's depth charge pattern was set when she began an attack run against an actual submarine contact. Obviously, Buck had neither the time nor surviving personnel or equipment to send an SOS. Waterlogged survivors welcomed three rafts dropped by an Army transport at mid morning on October 9. A Very pistol flare attracted the USS Gleaves late on the 9th. Only 94 out of 260 of the Buck's human complement had survived when the USS Plunkett and a British LCT arrived shortly after.

Jack Dacey provided the silhouette from which this next illustration was made. Jack Dacey's uncle, James J. Dacey Jr. was lost when the Buck went down.

Illustration 29-USS Buck in Profile

The following survivor tale comes from notes I made after a phone call on 12/28/97 with Helmuth Timm, MM1/c, a survivor of the sinking of the USS Buck.

"It was between 11 p.m. and midnight on 8 October when we were hit. I was in the after engine room. She sank fast. I barely had time to kick my shoes off and get in the water with my life jacket on. The magazines did not go off but a 600-pound depth charge off the rack at the stern did go off as the hull sank, and caused death or severe concussion to men in the water. I watched my Chief Petty Officer, P.U. Baker, sink below the waves. After being in the water a long time, I was picked up late the next night. I was taken to the hospital at Palermo and later to one in North Africa. I was in the hospital about three months. I had a severe concussion and double pneumonia. Dugan, our Chief Water Tender was in the hospital with me. Pete Kielar, MM1/c, another survivor, has been in touch with me. I believe our skipper, Lieutenant Commander Klein, who was lost in the sinking, received the Navy Cross for the sinking of that Italian submarine."

Mr. Timm recalled a Commander Durgin who was for a time the Squadron Commander of DesRon 13 during early Mediterranean duty but did not recall Captain Heffernan, who was ComDesRon 13 in the earlier North Atlantic convoys described in Chapter Four. It is quite likely that Commodore Heffernan's tour did not overlap Helmuth Timm's. E.

R. "Eddie" Durgin, not to be confused with his brother Calvin T. Durgin, who was skipper of the USS Ranger at Casablanca, was relieved as ComDesRon 13 by Commander Harry Sanders on September 15, 1943. By this date, the DesRon 13 flag was no longer on the USS Buck but was on the USS Woolsey, DD437.) I found Mr. Timm very alert during our phone conversation but he protested, as do all of us at "our age", that he had difficulty remembering names. Mr. Timm , age 82 when our conversation occurred in 1998, spoke from his son-in-law's home. His son-in-law is James Lingafelter, who assisted greatly in making this telephone call possible.

U-616 was a Type VIIC, built by Blohm & Voss, Hamburg, and commissioned 2 April, 1942. She made 9 war patrols, working first out of Danzig, then St. Nazaire and finally Toulon. Besides sinking the USS Buck, she damaged two other ships. She was herself sunk 17 May, 1944 in the Mediterranean east of Cartagena. Depth charges from USS Nields, Gleaves, Ellyson, Macomb, Hambleton, Rodman and Emmons, and bombs from 3 British Wellington aircraft put her down after a three-day action. U-616's entire crew of 53 men survived her sinking and were rescued.

Loss of the USS Bristol
On 13 October 1943, while the USS Bristol was escorting a Salerno-bound convoy off Algiers, she was torpedoed by U-371. This hit occurred near the forward stack (she was a two stacker) and the ship buckled in the middle. Bristol had only detected the torpedo noise on her listening gear for ten seconds before she was hit. Fortunately, a Torpedoman's Mate checked and made sure her depth charges were set on safe. Bristol had a little more time than Buck before she

made her plunge. Even with the keel broken, if a destroyer is not hit in a magazine, she has a few minutes to abandon ship, a procedure that Navy vessels rehearse. Of Bristol's complement of 293, 241 men were saved by two destroyers.

Edison had shared many sea and sea combat experiences with both Bristol and Buck. One of my recollections of Bristol was her outstanding record in giving aid to distressed ships. My classmate from the U.S. Naval Academy, Audley H. McCain served with distinction on the Bristol and survived the sinking.

U-371 was a Type VIIC, built by Howaldstwerke, Kiel, and commissioned 15 March 1941. She made patrols out of Kiel, Brest, Salamis and La Spezia/Toulon. Besides sinking the USS Bristol, she sank 13 ships for a total of 70,.000 tons and damaged 6 ships for a total of 30,500 tons. She was herself sunk on 4 May 1944 in the Mediterranean north of Constantine by depth charges from USS Pride, Joseph E. Campbell, the French Senegalais and the British HMS Blankney, Three of her crew were killed and 48 were rescued.

Allied Casualties at Salerno

For Salerno, Morison's figures showed the U.S. Navy with nearly 900 killed or missing and over 400 wounded. The U.S. Army lost over 2,000 killed or missing and had nearly 3,000 wounded. British Army losses were even heavier than the U.S. Army's casualties at Salerno. British Navy dead totaled 83, with 43 wounded.

Chapter Nine - Anzio; A Long Siege

Reproduced below are three dispatches. The first and second are a direct result of the Edison's gunfire on that first day at Salerno. These are part of what I referred to earlier in this story as Edison's fan mail.

Illustration 30-Dispatch from the USS Trippe

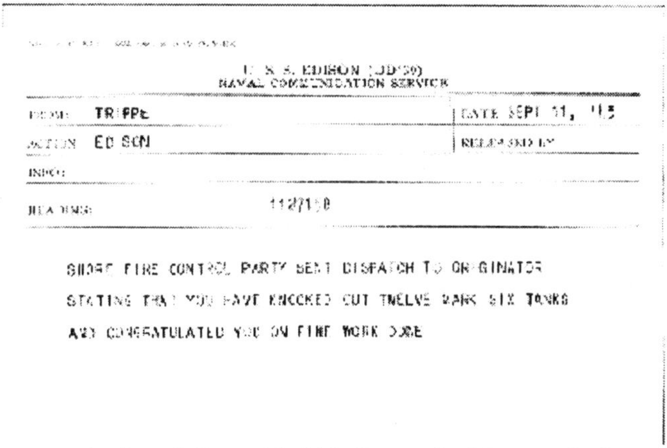

The message is dated Sept 11, '43. In capital letters below, I have typed out the body copy of the reproduction above. It was sent via the USS Trippe and was directed to the USS Edison.

SHORE FIRE CONTROL PARTY SENT DISPATCH TO ORIGINATOR STATING THAT YOU HAVE KNOCKED OUT TWELVE MARK SIX TANKS AND CONGRATULATED YOU ON THE FINE WORK DONE.

The following dispatch came to me in an e-mail from Ken Williams, who was a torpedoman on the USS Ludlow.

To D438, D439, D459

FOLLOWING RECEIVED FROM ARMY AAA THANK GOD FOR THE FIRE OF THE BLUE BELLY NAVY SHIPS AAA PROBABLY COULD NOT HAVE STUCK OUT BLUE AND YELLOW BEACHES AAA BRAVE FELLOW THESE TELL THEM SO-------- SIGNED GENERAL LANGE AAA WELL DONE BT

FROM CTG 81.5
TO EDISON, LUDLOW, BRISTOL, CRUISERS
UNDER MY COM.   SEPT 11 '43

This next dispatch passed through Radio Naples and was relayed by the U.S. S. Chicopee, a station ship in the U.S. Naval Communication Service network. The date was January 24, 1944, which places it in the Anzio assault phase. Since the reproduction may be hard to read, the body copy is typed below. Originator is the British Hospital Ship, Saint Andrew.

HAVE BEEN BOMBED THREE TIMES AND SHIP BADLY SHAKEN. HAVE NOW COMPLETED PICK- ING SURVIVORS FROM HOSPITAL SHIP SAINT DAVID WHICH HAS BEEN BOMBED AND SUNK. I AM PROCEEDING TO NAPLES.

Illustration 31-Dispatch from Hospital Ship

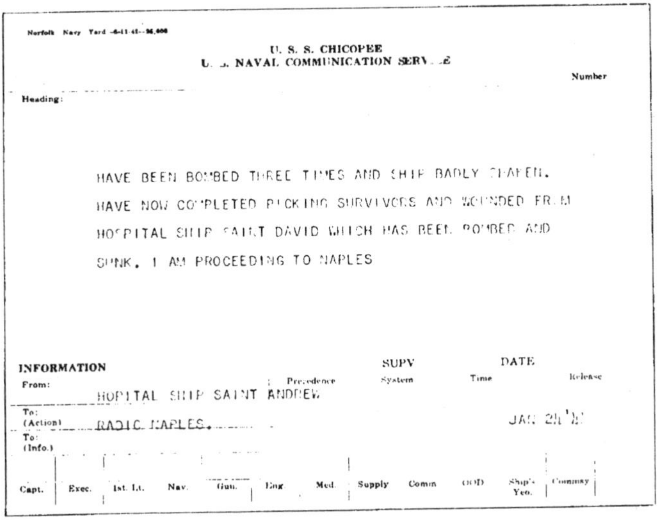

```
Norfolk  Navy Yard -6-11-42--96,000
                          U. S. S. CHICOPEE
                   U. S. NAVAL COMMUNICATION SERV..E
                                                              Number
 Heading:


        HAVE BEEN BOMBED THREE TIMES AND SHIP BADLY SHAKEN.
        HAVE NOW COMPLETED PICKING SURVIVORS AND WOUNDED FROM
        HOSPITAL SHIP SAINT DAVID WHICH HAS BEEN BOMBED AND
        SUNK. I AM PROCEEDING TO NAPLES


 INFORMATION                      SUPV        DATE
 From:                                        Time        Release
                                  System
         HOSPITAL SHIP SAINT ANDREW
 To:
 (Action)    RADIO NAPLES                         JAN 24 'N'
 To:
 (Info.)

 Capt.  Exec.  1st. Lt.  Nav.  Gun.  Eng.  Med.  Supply  Comm  (IOD)  Ship's  Commy
                                                                      Yeo.
```

One can see from Illustration 31 something of the barbarism of war. The bombing of clearly marked hospital ships, which I witnessed, could also have been an indication of oncoming desperation on the part of the German defenders of Europe. These hospital ships were lighted like Times Square and marked with huge red crosses horizontally and vertically.

Sardinia and Corsica

During September 1943, the islands of Sardinia and Corsica came into Allied hands. Again, despite 60 miles of open sea, the German High Command was able to plan and conduct an orderly evacuation first of Sardinia, and then of Corsica. The details are in some respect bizarre. French forces, both Navy and Army, were involved in retaking Corsica, the birthplace of Napoleon. But the rather extensive German garrisons and virtually all armor, transport and other military supply made it back to Italy as intact units. One Italian paratroop division, bent on fighting it out on the Nazi side, made it too. At the very end, the Allies bombed Leghorn (Livorno), one of the ports to which the Germans debarked, and caused some damage. Despite their preoccupation with the intense fighting at Salerno, the Allies had resources otherwise unengaged which could have made those evacuations more costly for Kesselring, who was the beneficiary of the result. One source that remained untapped was a still formidable Italian Navy. In retrospect, the loss of opportunity at the Straits of Messina and a short time later, Sardinia and Corsica, can be laid to leadership concentration on Salerno, and the prize it guarded, Naples. Also, France and Italy were being loosed from German control. Changes were occurring rapidly. The relationships needed for "futures" planning took time to develop in the all-new environment. Every high command structure should provide for a free thinking opportunity group, not wedded too strictly to the plan-at-hand.

An Aerial Torpedo; USS Beatty Is Lost

Mediterranean destroyers had faced bombs, submarine torpedoes and mines. Aerial torpedoes had been used against us but now one would draw blood. The Allies continued to bring in supplies and troops from the States for their growing Italian build-up through Salerno. But Naples had been the prize of the Salerno campaign. With the "scorched harbor" devastation by Kesselring's retreating troops gradually giving way to Allied readiness for use of port facilities in Naples, the really big convoys began to head for Naples. KMF-25A was a 23-transport "ship-train" escorted by Benson/Livermores from DesRons 15 and 16. Added to the protective force for this mixed British/American registry of troop and supply transports were three British destroyers and two Greek destroyers, plus the AA ship, HMS Colombo. The U.S. destroyer escorts Herbert C. Jones and Frederick C. Davis joined the transiting force after it entered the Mediterranean and headed east through the Tunisian War Channel. After KMF-25A passed Algiers and came up on Phillipeville, at a base speed of advance of 12 knots, the Luftwaffe descended out of the early evening darkness on November 6, 1943. Using poor visibility and coming from the eastern darkness into the western twilight, the sight advantage lay with the German pilots. Theirs was a mixed force of 9 bombers using glider bombs and 16 torpedo planes. Allied air coverage had been withdrawn before dark.

The USS Beatty was on the starboard flank, in position to catch the first pass of the attacking aircraft. The torpedo hit just after 1800 local time in her after engine-room on the starboard side, and broke the Beatty's keel. Below decks a valiant fight to save her was mounted while above decks, her guns boomed out in retaliation. The Germans had brought the right weapons and with unusual strength pressed home attack after attack, disabling the SS Santa Elena and the SS Aldegonde. Both later sank. Beatty's flooding finally broke her in two and she went down just five hours after being hit. Eleven sailors went down with her and one of the wounded died later. Beatty's gravesite is near that of the Bristol. Six German planes were downed. For this engagement, the Nazis had far the better of the tradeoff.

Destroyers alongside the jetty with steam up when departing merchantman is torpedoed

With her stateside dreams on hold, the Edison worked the Oran-Arzeu area during most of October 1943. A convoy of transports and merchant ships was convoyed safely from Oran to the Gulf of Pozzuoli, Italy from the 25th to the 28th of October. On the 29th, sailing alone, Edison stopped in Palermo for fuel and escorted the USS Brooklyn back to Naples. The 29th and 30th were spent in providing called fire for a shore fire control party on targets on beaches north of Naples. The Edison, in company with the USS Wainwright and the cruiser Brooklyn, went to Palermo on the 31st, where Edison fueled and took on ammunition. It should have been noted at the outset that destroyers took on fuel whenever a stop was made where fuel was available. It was a constant worry of the naval commanders and the destroyers themselves that the "cans" stay; "topped off." Edison then made passage with the Brooklyn to Bizerte. On November 5th, Edison screened Brooklyn on a trip to Malta arriving on the 6th. This was the Edison crew's first chance to see the damaged USS Savannah in drydock. It was a sobering sight. On the 9th, Edison and Brooklyn left for Palermo. After fueling, Edison left with a convoy for Oran. November 15, 1943 found Edison bound for Gibraltar and a rendezvous with other "Med" destroyers to take over the special escort duties of Atlantic destroyers. The mission was to continue the journey of the battleship USS Iowa on her important mission carrying President Roosevelt to Cairo. Iowa was under our protection during the western and central transit of the Mediterranean and our group turned the duty over to British ships for the eastern leg of the transit to Egypt. Edison was back in her homeport of Mers-el-Kebir on November 22.

A duty destroyer has more "conditions" than I can remember with certainty. Ed Meier referred to "4-hours" notice, a situation where you could risk a working party on the beach getting supplies. One hour's notice means all hands aboard, and "steam up" means you can cast off the lines and get underway. On December 16, for an original reason that I cannot recall, Edison, Trippe and Woolsey were all in this "steam-up" ready condition alongside the jetty at Mers-el-Kebir. About noon, word came that a submarine had attacked a small convoy that had departed from Oran. The location given was off Cape Falcon, Algeria. One merchantman was in sinking condition.

U-73 sailed from Toulon and a month's overhaul on her 15th mission of December 3, 1943. Her earlier Atlantic career had been crowned when she sank the British carrier HMS Eagle. U-73 was a 750-tonner, with four forward tubes, one tube aft, two twin 20mms and one quad 20mm topside for AA. Her skipper, Horst Deckert was 25 years old and had put the boat in commission as a midshipman. The 45-man crew plus four officers and a doctor were in their twenties. She stayed submerged during the day. Lacking a schnorkel she had to surface at night to recharge batteries. Recharging would occur in the four hours before midnight and she would surface again briefly just before dawn for fresh air. Just past noon on sunny December 16, her captain discovered a slow convoy, westbound with minimum escort.

A torpedo spread was fired and the SS John S. Copley of U.S. registry was hit. That convoy's escort group was so thin that none could be spared to run down a submarine contact, though they went to the aid of the Copley.

Oran was a busy port. An important troop convoy was making up for departure from Oran and one of the DesRon Seven screen destroyers. USS Niblack (DD424) was already out of the harbor. Niblack informed ComDesRon Seven, Captain Clay, in destroyer Plunkett that was about to join Niblack, of the torpedoed ship offshore. Niblack and destroyer Gleaves (DD423) were ordered by Clay to pursue contact of the presumed submarine.

For the identities of the destroyers in Captain Clay's DesRon Seven that participated in the effort to locate the submarine that torpedoed the SS Copley, I have relied on an article in a 1969 edition of U.S. Naval Institute Proceedings. The article was entitled "Night Fight Off Oran." It was written by Admiral Harry Sanders. Captain Sanders was ComDesRon 13 in December 1943. Richard Angelini, Historian of the USS Mayo, a reader of the Web edition of this story, e-mailed me 2/1/98 after reading the foregoing paragraph. He provides persuasive information that it was the USS Mayo and not the USS Gleaves that participated in the hold down effort on the enemy submarine. Angelini's information came from accounts of the attack on the SS Copley and accounts of subsequent actions taken by Niblack and Mayo. These accounts by sailors present on both the Mayo and the Niblack during the event appear in both Mayo and Niblack war diaries. According to Angelini, Mayo's presence is also corroborated in the book, Tin Cans and Other Ships. There appears to be a consensus that Benson and Gleaves of DesRon Seven joined the convoy after it was well out to sea. The Sanders' article written in 1969 may have relied on that Admiral's memory of what he learned from Captain Clay 25 years earlier. In the heat of the action, it is quite possible that the name of one ship in a squadron was substituted for another. I am disposed to stick with the eyewitnesses, namely sailors on the Niblack and Mayo. Sanders' DesRon 13 destroyers did not arrive on the scene until the hold down action was in progress.

With the sortie of a troop convoy under his command, Captain Clay had a major protection challenge of his own. Clay, therefore, got on the voice circuit to raise ComDesRon 13, to ask for his help. As DesRon 13 "Commodore", Sanders was using Woolsey, DD437, as his flagship. The first DesRon 13 flagship, the USS Buck, had been sunk off Naples. Sanders ordered Woolsey, Edison and Trippe under his command to get underway. They were moving in 45 minutes. Soon out past the jetty and into the Mediterranean, the three destroyers went by the wounded merchantman that was floating with good freeboard despite a large hole forward. (She was towed in that night.) Captain Sanders directed the suppression destroyers, Mayo and Niblack, to report back to their important convoy. ComDesRon 13 then deployed his three destroyers in a retiring search to obtain contact on the submarine. Edison on the left (west), Woolsey in the center and Trippe on the right (east), in a 90 degree line of bearing, were directed to pursue the search at 14 knots along an estimated retirement path of due north. Distance between search ships was 2400 yards.

This search began at 1730 local time; about 40 minutes later, base course was changed to east. At 1815, Woolsey, already with a record as a sub killer, obtained the first contact on her starboard quarter. Woolsey turned slowly through south, to west and then to northwest. Rudder and propeller noises needed to be minimized if the operator was to hold the contact on his pinging gear.

The sub skipper should know by now that he had been detected. Though confident that the contact was a sub, the Woolsey's sound operator then lost contact. Skipper (H.R. "Hank") Wier of Woolsey ordered a course reversal to the plotted position of the last contact, and the sonar operator regained faint but definite echoes. Woolsey dropped a full pattern (all six K-guns, each with 300 pound charges, and a number of 600 pounders, determined by the prescribed pattern, off the two stern roll-off racks). Edison and Trippe were directed to open up their range on Woolsey to 3500 yards.

With darkness upon the group, SG radar operators looked intensely at their screens. The group went north and then turned south southeast. Three-quarters of an hour of this ensued, and suddenly the Woolsey SG radar operator's eyes were riveted as his radar screen now showed four targets. The guest came from the deep! 1900 yards on Woolsey's port quarter, bearing about due north, was the newcomer. Woolsey's helmsman was given a full left rudder command, Woolsey's 5" guns that were bearing opened fire, and Woolsey illuminated with her 36inch searchlight. Tracers immediately came at Woolsey's light and two men were wounded. Edison picked up the radar contact at the same time as Woolsey and opened fire with the Woolsey. Trippe followed suit. Sanders could see that Woolsey was close to Trippe's line of fire and ordered Trippe to cease firing. Edison and Woolsey shells were hitting the sub and her deck personnel were jumping into the water. This was the U-73, which, mortally wounded, poked her bow high in the air and slid stern first back into the Mediterranean. The job took four hours.

Woolsey picked up four officers, including skipper Horst Deckert, and 15 enlisted men, while Edison and Trippe screened. After departure of Woolsey and Trippe for Oran, Edison searched for over two hours before she found 12 more men in the water. Let Joe Dwyer, then Edison's Assistant Engineering Officer, pick up the story in his memoir to me of April 1998.

"Darkness had settled over the Mediterranean Sea. From the depths of this darkness, sounds emanated that indicated there were survivors still in the water. Captain Pearce issued orders to Lieutenant Dwyer. 1) Search for survivors. 2) Do not allow survivors to communicate with each other."

"Since I knew little German, I solicited help from the crew. One crewmember suggested that saying, 'Haltz male!' would silence the survivors. With this indoctrination and our boat crew, the rescue mission began in the Edison's gig. Soon after shoving off from the Edison, sounds of a whistle like that of a sport's official, could be heard. Guided by whistle sounds, the rescue mission located and picked up 12 survivors of the sub. As they were brought aboard the gig, each was searched for weapons. One of the survivors had an arrangement tied to his legs that resembled a drag chute. It was approximately 30 inches in diameter with a cut-out of about six inches in the center. Apparently, it was designed to slow the rise of a human from the sub's depth for a crewmember using an underwater ejection device. When they were aboard the gig, they started to talk to each other. I then shouted, 'Haltz male!' and silence reigned. The gig returned to the USS Edison without incident, and the survivors were issued clean and dry clothing."

The gig brought in twelve men but we actually saved 11. The 12th, a warrant officer, could not be revived. Apparent cause was drowning. I was in charge of the survivors rescued by the Edison's gig. We took the survivors to the crew's quarters. Standing over them with guns drawn, we made them disrobe. We issued them survivor kits. These consisted of seersucker bathrobes and personal gear like combs, toothbrushes etc. The sub crew took to the combs immediately and crowded around a mirror to get their hair slicked down and presentable. I was flabbergasted at this, and with their obvious good spirits. Also, it seemed they had little interest at the time in where their crewmates were. I feel now that they pretty well knew who had been saved and who was lost. We had enough German language ability among us to find out that the officers had abandoned ship in the only boat the sub carried and the crew that were saved came topside and jumped immediately into the water. A search of their clothing showed that "school" had been held on the U-73 regularly. The survivors carried drawings in detail of every essential part of the sub. It was an old Type VIIB so probably we did not discover much that was new but the torpedo drawings, I knew, would hold interest for the intelligence types ashore when we turned them over for analysis.

What it was like to be on U-73 that night

Admiral Harry Sanders, who as ComDesRon 13 directed the U.S. destroyers in this action, published his 1943 interview with Horst Deckert, U-73's skipper, as part of the 1969 in the U.S. Naval Institute Proceedings. Here are excerpts from the USNI Proceedings article.

"Our exploding depth charges (from USS Woolsey) were the first warning that she (U-73) was being pursued.....from 1839 hours, when the Woolsey dropped her depth charges, until 1927 hours, when the U-73 surfaced,--an elapsed time of 48 minutes---Captain Deckert, his officers, and crew were struggling frantically to save their stricken vessel. The depth charges.....had exploded below the submarine, causing considerable damage. Seawater had poured in between the bow torpedo tubes, and a saltwater inlet valve for the diesel engine cooling system fractured, causing water to cascade into the engine room. The leaks could not be stopped nor could the incoming water be pumped out at a rate sufficient to maintain the trim. The U-73 had sunk to a depth between 525 and 755 feet." (I went out on a U.S. "Guppy" sub in the 1950s. She was built for "deep" diving, a pressure test depth of just 400 feet!)

"The U-73 was now in extremis. If she continued to sink, the tremendous ocean pressure would crush her hull like an eggshell. Captain Deckert exercised his last desperate option and, ordering all ballast tanks blown, he brought U-73 to the surface on one motor. Heavy machine guns were manned as fast as their crews could get up the hatch and the captain ordered full speed ahead on the main engines....Almost instantly, the U-73 found herself in the glare of powerful searchlights and in a rain of 5-inch shells. Her machine guns opened fire on the Woolsey's searchlight. In the eerie night duel, observers in the Edison counted three direct hits on the U-boat's hull. She was now filling with water and sinking fast by the stern. Captain Deckert ordered "abandon ship" just before the U-73 took her final dive, backwards, to her grave on the bottom of the Mediterranean."

".....After Captain Deckert had dried off and was given dry clothes, he was taken under guard to a stateroom. He was meticulously correct in his military bearing, rising and saluting smartly. 'Why', I asked, 'did you not fire your acoustic torpedoes at us?' 'Because', he said, 'the depth charge explosions warped the torpedo tube shutters and they could not be opened.' Deckert naively expressed his surprise that we had been able to 'see' his submarine as soon as she surfaced---in the black of night. His apparent honesty convinced us that German submarines were not getting timely intelligence on U.S. radar developments. We know from Hitler's own words that it took months for them to find out about our short wave aircraft radar."

'Short wave' in 1943 meant X-band, the wavelength used by SG radar technology. This was also built into our ASW patrol plane radar, in the APS-15 system that I used just after World War II in the Navy Privateer, PB4y-2. This radar was so precise that when land based radio approach facilities were inoperative in the Aleutians, many of our squadron planes made successful approaches even to "socked in" airfields with just the APS-15 operator guiding us to the runway.

"About midnight, the three destroyers tied up to the quay at Mers-el-Kebir. Admiral Davidson was there (his flag was now in USS Brooklyn), as was a strong Army guard. The Woolsey and the Edison debarked their prisoners. They were formed into two ranks and marched off. We, who were the victors, stared briefly at their departure, and then turned, somewhat wearily, to the matter of reports yet to be written and a war yet to be won."

Commodore Sanders had been a submarine skipper himself. Captain Wier of the Woolsey, commanded a ship which, in the course of the war, sank three U-boats. The two men cooperated brilliantly to put down the U-73. Deckert ran into a skilled team.

U-73 was a Type VIIB, built at Vegesacker Werft, Vegesack, and commissioned 30 September, 1940. She made war patrols out of Kiel, Kiel/St. Nazaire, and La Spezia. She sank 9 ships for a total of 65,000 tons, including HMS Eagle. The Eagle was sunk on 11 August 1942. U-73 damaged 3 ships for a total of 23,000 tons. U-73 was herself sunk 16 December 1943 near Oran by depth charges from the USS Woolsey and gunfire from Woolsey, Edison and Trippe. 16 of U-73's crew perished.

Malta; Second Visit by the Edison

My second Christmas aboard Edison stands in sharp contrast to my first in 1942, which had been in Port Arthur, Texas. On 21 December 1943, Edison and the USS Niblack, another DD of our class, left Oran screening Brooklyn on a trip to Malta, where we were in port in the Gran Harbor until 29 December 1943. All men aboard, including the engineering crew who often stayed below as a preference and had to be rousted out of their quarters got ashore more than once. The gondolas could get a little tipsy and their hanging lamps would sway when we got a little boisterous coming back to the ship, because we were often a little tipsy too. We visited the Palace of the Marquis and the Marchesa by invitation. We understood better why this little island had been able to resist the Nazi air onslaught so effectively. The people, who spoke at least five languages and had their origins in Africa and the Middle East as well as Europe, were fiercely independent. Malta was still a part of the British Empire in World War II. We were Britain's allies, and were welcomed in 1943 not just by the colonial rulers' native bureaucracy but by the people themselves. Most of us could not see beneath the surface and realize that Britain would be pushed out so soon after the War.

While there was destruction in Malta from the almost continuous Luftwaffe bombing, it was minimized because Malta's earth structure contains an enormous amount of a clay-like seams, which could be "carved" into building blocks, allowed to air out briefly, and used almost immediately to create new structures.

One of my few personal triumphs occurred during this visit in Malta. As noted earlier in this story, our senior officers had to bargain with merchant ship's officers returning to the States for fresh war cargo. The predominant transaction was for "spirits". Often, we paid up front and quite often that ship or that merchant officer did not return to the Mediterranean, or at least did not return to a place we could catch up with them and demand our "goods". The British Navy was "wet", with the crew getting rations of grog, a form of rum, and the officers obtaining mostly gin, but in some instances Scotch whiskey. At Gibraltar, a common social exchange was to visit the HMS Delhi or HMS Colombo for drinks, then have them over for dinner, when we were berthed alongside. So, one day in Malta in a rare moment of brilliance and initiative, I went around to a building that bore the entrance sign, NAAFI. It stood for Navy, Army and Air Forces Institute. I liked that "institute" designation, bringing to the establishment the dignity that all the British Islanders bring to themselves. In a visit to Ireland in the 1980s, I found little shops in every town, with the frequent appearance of a small sign of the establishment denoting the entrepreneur as a "turf accountant." NAAFI was a military victualling establishment. It was kind of a Supply Corps, but in a retail-like atmosphere rather than a warehouse. It reminded me of by-gone U.S. hardware stores with dark, somewhat oily looking, unpainted wood shelves and bins. With a smile in representing myself as being from the HMS Edison, the obviously well educated "clerk", knew full well from my uniform and accent that that could not be the case. I inquired about a ration of spirits. I was asked the number of officers assigned to the Edison. The ration would be apportioned based on complement. Then I was asked about preferences, and after some discussion, we settled on one bottle of Scotch and two bottles of gin for each officer. I duly signed my name and received the appropriate British tax stamps that I still have. The man who waited on me shook my hand as I left, and said quietly, "Reverse Lend Lease!"

I came back to the ship heavy-laden though not quite in the biblical sense. It was quite a catch for a junior officer who had negotiated for Edison far better than her senior officers had managed. I was, briefly, a star.

Early January 1944 Busywork

Niblack, Edison and Brooklyn left Malta for Palermo on 29 December, and at Palermo picked up a convoy to escort to Naples. Still in an escort role, Edison came back to Oran on 6 January. General Eisenhower began to disassemble his headquarters at Malta to concentrate on the cross channel invasion. British General Sir Henry Maitland Wilson was designated to take active command in the Mediterranean, with one key responsibility to push the German armies rapidly up the Italian peninsula. It was not to be. The U.S. Fifth Army bogged down at Monte Cassino north of Naples. On the Adriatic, the British Eighth Army was completely stalled by the Germans at the Sangro River. No one likes a stalemate. Allied operations now had uncontested air capability from Italy's major Foggia airbase.

Anzio; the Tip of the Sicily, Salerno Arrow

Most of the Allied leadership were disposed to keep the soft underbelly tense, but to refrain from more surgery. Not so the Prime Minister. Churchill wanted a landing at Anzio to break Kesselring's hold on northern Italy. As usual, he got what he wanted; as executed; however, Operation SHINGLE was the second of two plans created to land at Anzio.

General Alexander, who commanded the land forces attempting to uproot the Germans from the Gustav line above Naples, now commanded soldiers from many nations. The Fifth Army of General Clark and the British Eighth Army were still the anchors of the land position. Canadians and

New Zalanders had been involved from the beginning. Italian units and the colonials from many soon-to-emerge nations were right up on the firing line. French troops under General Juin fought with great courage in Italy. At sea it was almost as "all-worldly." French, Dutch, Polish and Greek warships were now fighting alongside the U.S. and British navies.

Amphibious Task Force 81, commanded by Rear Admiral F.J. Lowry, became the central unit of the American naval assault forces. Captain J. P. Clay as ComDesRon 7 in the USS Plunkett and Captain Harry Sanders, as ComDesRon 13 in the USS Woolsey brought elements of both of their destroyer squadrons. Available on D-day in addition to Woolsey and Plunkett were Wainwright, Trippe, Niblack, Gleaves, Edison, Ludlow and Mayo. In addition to assault day responsibilities, Captain Clay and some of his destroyers had the duty of getting the all important re-supply landing craft into Anzio. Specially equipped U.S. Destroyer Escorts Herbert C. Jones and Frederick C. Davis were involved right from D-Day as Anzio station ships. These two Destroyer Escorts, with advanced electronics counter measures equipment, participated in a technologically sophisticated sea mission. Later, they were spelled on station by the U.S. minesweeper Pioneer that had also taken aboard special equipment.

A level of command that existed for the larger landing operations at North Africa, Sicily and Salerno did not exist for the smaller Anzio operation. Rear Admiral Lowry had his flag in the USS Biscayne. There was no Admiral Hewitt at Anzio, with a responsibility to get the troops safely ashore, and then release fire support cruisers and destroyers under senior commanders to help them stay there. Lowry exercised both of these prior distinct levels of command.

I have attempted to note squadron and division identities for destroyers. Losses hit some destroyer divisions hard. Destroyers really never went into battle as squadrons or divisions. Team relationships of destroyers rarely persisted for groups of more than two or three ships. Anzio tested stamina as much as any other attribute. There were enough destroyers to get the job done but it took a lot of rotations and one-day rests to get the job done. Whatever destroyer was in the duty area when needed for gunfire support did that job and whatever destroyer was available to escort the re-supply forces did that job.

Destroyers Charles F. Hughes, Hilary P. Jones, Madison and Lansdale were scheduled to join the effort in February. This may not do justice their role. They may have been called in to replace exhausted ships and sailors when the Anzio operation became a very dangerous stalemate and the roadstead became became target practice for land based guns. But, that gets ahead of the story.

The Landing That Took 142 Days

The historical marker that Anzio was fated to become had first been thrashed out in November and December 1943 and the answer was that there would be no Anzio in the context of Allied World War II Mediterranean history. It was originally conceived as an Allied left hook to Kesselring's right flank, which faced Mark Clark's Fifth Army. It would be a fast, one division strength assault and penetration by the U.S. 3rd Infantry Division as part of Clark's forces. This force would effect a link up with Clark's main units advancing between Monte Cassino and the Tyrrhenean Coast. Frosinone, well past Cassino, would already be in safe hands to the rear of a probable link point, when the assault would be made from the coast. It was predicated on Fifth Army's ability to advance. It would leave the Germans facing strong and fluid movement whether they looked south or west. The

Rangers would lead the Anzio beach assault operation and it would begin December 20 when the Fifth Army expected to reach the vicinity of Frosinone.

In support of this strategy, Montgomery's Eighth Army began their push on the Adriatic side starting the 28th of November and Clark's forces moved forward on December 1. The Cairo Conference adjourned on December 7, and did not deal with the Anzio proposition, treating it as a theater decision even though it called for some temporary re-allocation of landing craft.

Neither Montgomery nor Clark made the progress that the original SHINGLE plan required and after some agonizing, the Anzio beach assault operation scheduled for about December 24, 1943, *was canceled* by the theater military commanders on December 22, 1943. Clark's main forces could not get by Cassino. Weather and the Sangro River had bogged Montgomery down. The Germans were defending and not giving ground.

SHINGLE Off, Then On Again

Enter British Prime Minister Winston Churchill to Tunis, Christmas Day 1943, on his way back from the Cairo Conference. With no CCS (Combined Chiefs of Staff) or JCS or Roosevelt to contend with, he called a conference and put a SHINGLE, not predicated on a Fifth Army success in getting to Frosinone, back into planning. This would be an operation to get *ashore and hold until General Clark's main forces arrived*. There was little deliberation on this plan. The Prime Minister wanted it, and had long championed the basic strategy to make the spine of Italy an arrow aimed at the heart of Germany. General Alexander did not want to oppose his Prime Minister. Ike was turning over his duties to Sir Henry Maitland Wilson and one British Admiral Sir John Cunningham was relieving his similarly named predecessor. Churchill's global partners had dispersed and were trying to get back home and digest what Cairo had decided. Churchill added one British infantry division to SHINGLE and obtained some LSTs that had been ticketed for England or Southeast Asia.

U.S. Major General Lucas would command the landed forces, consisting of the U.S. 3rd Infantry Division under Major General Truscott and the 1st British Infantry Division under Major General Penney. There would be three battalions of U.S. Rangers, two of British Commandos and one regiment of paratroops. One regiment of the U.S. 45th Infantry Division and two regiments of the U.S. 1st Armored Division would be in Naples on reserve. Rear Admiral Lowry had enough seaborne capacity (bottoms, tonnage) committed to give the landed forces 12 days of supply. Lucas' VI Corps had instructions to secure the beachhead and advance on the Alban Hills. No specific link up with the main body of the Fifth Army was targeted.

In mid-January 1944, the Fifth Army above Naples made another try to breach Kesselring's defenses, made some early progress, but on the day of the Anzio landings on January 22nd, Clark's forces yielded back to the Germans the Fifth Army's dearly won bridgehead over the Rapido River. This was not a very good precursor for an Anzio operation that was already going to be launched with fuzzy objectives.

Preparations and Assignments

Amphibious exercises were conducted in the Salerno-Naples area to ready Task Force 81 for a SHINGLE assault at Anzio. The operation itself was scheduled for January 22, 1944. The landing beaches laid out in the plans ran from a point below the Tiber Estuary on the Tyrrhenean Sea, south

317

to Nettuno, a resort town just over 30 miles south of Rome. The port of Anzio centered the targeted beaches. Success, it was hoped, meant outflanking the German forces at Cassino opening the way for the Allies to be over 50 miles behind the so-called Gustav line held by Kesselring's troops. The Allied thrust would put our troops but a few miles from Rome itself. Surely the Germans would have to fall back to a new line.

The British 1st Infantry Division would land to the north, supported by two British cruisers and a small destroyer force under Rear Admiral Mansfield, RN. Col. Darby's U.S. Rangers would land near Anzio, followed by the U.S. 3rd Infantry Division, which would land on beaches to the south of Anzio. These forces were supported by the U.S. cruiser Brooklyn and the British cruiser Penelope, supplemented by a contingent of DesRon Thirteen destroyers, Woolsey, with Mayo, Trippe, Ludlow and Edison. The follow-up supply landing craft would receive AA and ASW support from Captain Clay's DesRon Seven, with Clay's flag on Plunkett, plus Gleaves, Niblack, two British destroyers, two U.S. destroyer escorts, and two U.S. minecraft. A stout force of U.S. sweepers, AM and YMS type, would start work before H-Hour.

I will mention here an important change of command on D+3 where British Rear Admiral Mansfield became Commander Task Group 81.6, taking operational command of the overall support group. He replaced Captain Cary on the USS Brooklyn in this command function. The diversion of the British landing forces to the U.S. landing sector and beaches, on D+2, and the change in support group command left some loose ends, just when the Germans began to put into play their strengths against SHINGLE.

The Assault Begins

318

ANZIO; A LONG SIEGE

The assault at Anzio began at 0200 on January 22, 1944. By this date, Allied war commerce was moving in every direction in the Mediterranean. Assuming that the Germans could distinguish an assault convoy from a supply convoy, the Allied sea forces bound for Anzio took the usual misleading course from staging areas at Naples and Salerno (where a near disastrous rehearsal had taken place), toward Corsica, settling finally on the run to Cape D'Anzio. It began smoothly with little opposition. The rocket barrage in the British sector to the north began before their landing craft reached shallow water. U.S. Ranger assault troops went ashore at Cape D'Anzio's southern sector beaches. Before dawn the Allies had a solid beachhead. The probe troops were meeting little resistance. By early morning, sporadic defensive artillery fire began to "walk" toward our critical beach positions and the German Air Force made its appearance. Still, our troops were in Anzio not long after 8:00 a.m.

The Brits to the north faced mines, steep cliffs, surf and false beaches. By afternoon, it was decided to divert British sector follow up convoys and their troops and supplies through the U.S. sector to the south. With all forces now scheduled to go through the southern sector near Anzio, as an entry point, there developed two trains of thought regarding the warships supporting the assault. The first: With only one sector, was one of the support task groups superfluous? The second: With calls for fire so intermittent, should the cruisers stay in Naples until needed? Quite apart from Allied forces' need to re-think the entire support plan, the concentration of troop and supply replenishment through a single sector removed all ambiguity for the defenders on where to concentrate their fire.

I believe now that the primary offensive consideration in Allied ad hoc decisions was based on gunfire support, and

319

the primary defensive consideration was undersea, particularly submarine, defense. In reading over the material available, AA defense does not appear prominent in planning. As the beachhead deepened, a gap developed in the provisioning of gunfire support for this operation. For AA defense, there were no high performance naval aircraft, such as carriers might provide, for aircraft interdiction at Anzio. Carrier aircraft pilots are proficient in covering assault landings and seaborne supply operations. As our beachhead deepened, our light cruisers with 6-inch guns could not reach key targets. The Germans brought in long range guns that fired with impunity.

The seaborne force strength for Anzio was nothing like Salerno or Sicily. The on-station fire support contingent was relatively small. The cruiser concept practiced at Salerno was based on safely conducting assault forces, many in transports, to the beaches and then assigning the cruisers in teams with screening destroyers to help landed troops hold the beachhead and expand. For Anzio, an unending procession of landing craft to and from Naples and Salerno was the delivery scheme. As it evolved, only a kind of generalized cruiser force was made available. At times, cruisers went to Naples because they had nothing to do. At other times, cruisers tied up or anchored close-in at Anzio; one paid a dear price. Longer range naval guns, eight inch bore or larger, were critically needed at Anzio, and these were not available. What actually happened to the Anzio beachhead was not anticipated, so never planned for.

By the second day of the operation, the actual at-the-scene commanders of troop movements did some necessary improvising, against orders and to their credit. They determined to pre-load each truck to be embarked for Anzio so that these could be driven off the landing craft directly to their assignment. The Germans hit with force anyone waiting at dockside or in staging areas to be combat-loaded.

Early Destroyer Action

Although the frequency of German air attacks did not begin to pick up until the second day, the extended period in which the issue was in doubt was marked by a much higher frequency of pressed-home air attacks than had been experienced at Salerno and at Sicily.

Earliest mention of U.S. destroyer action at Anzio in the now-familiar role of fire-support goes to the USS Mayo, DD-422, commissioned right after the class namesake, Benson DD-421. Mayo was in action on the right flank of the beachhead on D-Day, the 22nd, and again on the 23rd and 24th of January. The following indented paragraphs in quotes were taken from an e-mail received from Orlando Angelini on 23 January 1998. (54 years had gone by)

"The Germans had moved up heavy guns to lambaste the Anzio beaches, and under this cover a Nazi force was trying to fight its way across the Mussolini Canal. Thanks to the USS Mayo, the Nazis were stopped on the tow-path of this waterway."

"The speed and accuracy of her (Mayo's) fire kept the Germans from counter-attacking across Canale Mussolini." The sentence above is a quote from Admiral Lowry. This quote also appears in Theodore Roscoe's United States Destroyer Operations in World War II.

"Mayo had been lending fire support at selected targets from January 22, 1944 until January 24, and at 2001 hours on the 24th, there was an explosion at the starboard side in the after engine room. The extent of the damage caused the after fire-room bulkhead to tear and flood the after fire-room, but all personnel from the after fire-room escaped with minor injuries. All hands in the after engine room perished. We were under an air attack during this period. At the time of the explosion, the Mayo was in a mine swept area. Not sure if it was a circling torpedo or a mine which caused the explosion. The Mayo dropped anchor to prevent us from floating into a heavy-laid mine field. The Mayo held together due to a riveted joint that was installed, that attached the aft section and the forward section together. Otherwise she would have broken in two."

"With six men killed, one missing and 25 wounded, the Mayo fought her battle-damage, and kept above water. At 2300 hours, the Mayo was taken in tow by a British tug, Prosperous, and towed to Naples in two days."

"I served aboard the Mayo from September 18, 1940 to decommissioning on March 18, 1946. At the time of the battle at Anzio, I was a Machinist Mate 2/c."

"s/s MMC Orlando A. Angelini"

After repairs, the Mayo made it to the Pacific for the Tokyo Bay surrender on September 2, 1945.

The U.S. destroyer Trippe was credited on January 23rd with helping Lucas' VI Corps stave off an attack by elements of crack German divisions seeking control of access roads to the Mussolini Canal. On the 25th Trippe provided counter fire for sweepers working in close to do cleanup work in the fire support areas and was relieved in that duty by Edison. YMS-30 (Yard Mine Sweeper with hull number 30) working on the shallow shore side of the area, struck one of the mines she was sweeping and her crew disappeared along with their little ship. It was a sobering experience for Edison's crew. Minesweeping is a perilous business. Later that day Edison, Ludlow and Gleaves provided strong fire support and the USS Brooklyn was called in to get at some more distant targets. The next day, mines again took a toll. The close-in sweepers were engaged in pulling people out of the water from a mined LST and a mined LCI. Under worsening weather only the LSTs that could get into the port were able to unload. Pontoon causeways would not work in those seas. One of the first Liberty ships in the Anzio supply chain stood off, and was all but hit by a glider bomb. Her crew was ordered to Abandon Ship but later her Armed Guard reboarded and manned her AA guns against air attacks.

The Luftwaffe made life miserable for all ships at Anzio. Although plans had been made on D-Day to divert forces scheduled for the British sector in the north down to the U.S. sector to the south, the forces already in motion toward the British sector landed in that sector and were supported by British cruisers and destroyers. The Luftwaffe pressed home strong attacks in this sector, with aerial torpedoes and rocket powered glider bombs. In a strong attack in the twilight of D+1 (the 23rd) one British destroyer was hit and eventually sunk by a torpedo. Another was disabled by a glider bomb and was towed to Naples.

One U.S. destroyer at Anzio mentioned in Theodore Roscoe's United States Destroyer Operations in World War II, is the USS Ludlow, DD-438, a squadron mate of the Edison. The Wehrmacht held a strong point at Littoria on the morning of the 26th. After 267 rounds from Ludlow's 5"38 guns, the feedback was "Nice going. No more Littoria". Later, on February 8, off Anzio, a large German artillery shell of a caliber likely more than five inches hit the Ludlow.

Ken Williams, a torpedoman aboard Ludlow that day, e-mailed the author in late 1997:

"My battle station was the torpedo director. As you well know, the torpedo director was mounted centerline on top of the pilothouse in the Benson-Gleaves class. Torpedomen are pretty useless when dueling with shore batteries. So, to earn our pay we would use the torpedo director to try and pick up muzzle flashes, give relative bearings of these flashes, and estimate their range. Coastal batteries were normally well concealed, using smokeless powder, and very difficult to spot. For 'protection', we had a canvas screen, about knee high.

"The Ludlow was working its way in to deliver close range fire support when we were hit. The projectile must have come from extreme range for it went vertically through the pilothouse through several decks and ended up in the scullery. Fortunately it did not explode."

"On its way through Ludlow's pilothouse, a fragment of the shell's rotating band (softer metal which is scored by the gun barrel's grooves and lands to make the shell rotate like a one-axis gyro, and therefore be stabilized) slashed Commander Creighton's (the skipper of the Ludlow's) leg, leaving him with a severe wound." (Theodore Roscoe's Naval Institute book, United States Destroyer Operations in World War II, credits Chief Gunner's Mate James D. Johnson of the Ludlow with heaving the hot projectile, already spilling a portion of its high explosive charge, over the side.)

With Lieutenant Cutler USNR now acting CO, the Ludlow went back to Naples: Here we pick up the thoughts of Ken Williams once more.

"An event that sticks out in my mind from this same time frame was when the USS Plunkett volunteered to re-ammo ship for us so we could get a night's rest. The Plunkett had taken a bomb hit on its after deckhouse and was in Naples for emergency repairs. They were going Stateside; we had to be back at the Anzio beachhead in time for the morning air raid. They gave us the opportunity to get some sleep."

"Was seventy-six as of yesterday (written in an e-mail in late 1997). Consequently, must have just turned twenty-one for Operation Torch. Joined the Navy Dec. 31, 1940 on a six-year enlistment and put the Ludlow in commission March 5, 1941 as a lowly Apprentice Seaman. Captain Lyle Wiley Creighton was the best skipper that I had ever served under. He was tough but fair. He would advance competent people in rate, but refuse to transfer them. We had a high priced crew when the Capt. was wounded at Anzio. When we came back to the States, the crew was practically all cleared out to new construction. I went to the USS Zellars, DD-777."

Captain Creighton recovered and was back in action at Southern France in August of 1944, though not with Ludlow.

Progress
Naval losses were mounting, especially in the British sector, but by the morning of the 25th, the Allies had a

"beachhead" almost seven miles deep along a front of about 14 miles.

The following is from Theodore Roscoe's U.S. Naval Institute account. "In action at Anzio, she (the USS Edison, Commander H.A. Pearce) fired 1854 rounds of 5-inch 38 ammunition at 21 separate targets. With 101 rounds fired on January 29, she turned a parade of Nazi trucks and armored vehicles into a roadside junk pile." From exuberant shore fire-control parties, Edison received one congratulatory message after another. Here are some verbatim extracts.

FIRE EFFECTIVE VERY VERY GOOD BRASSED OFF A BUNCH OF KRAUTS

MANY ENEMY TROOPS KILLED BY YOUR FIRE GOOD WORK

PILOT SAID YOUR FIRE WAS VERY EFFECTIVE YOU WERE HITTING RIGHT ON THE ARTILLERY PIECES YOU WERE FIRING AT

EFFECT OF FIRE MACHINE-GUN EMPLACEMENT IN BUILDING TOTALLY DESTROYED

YOUR LAST TARGET WAS A TOWER BEING USED AS AN OBSERVATION POST YOU DEMOLISHED IT COMPLETELY

These are good words, and we will have more of them. But, the Anzio beachhead as a breakout wedge to Rome or wherever, soon became fully sealed off as Kesselring moved his German defenders rapidly and skillfully. In the very early going, however, our troops ashore made some good progress.

How Early Anzio Operations Were Supplied

A close analogy to Anzio in more recent 'cold war' times would be the Berlin airlift. To keep Berlin alive, during a period in which the Russians sealed off all the agreed upon surface supply entry points to that city, U.S. transport planes brought in all life support. They even airlifted coal.

For Anzio re-supply, Captain Clay had 39 British LSTs, 20 LCI(L)s, and 6 LCTs. That is a lot of transport. But, by D+1 we had over 40,000 soldiers ashore. They needed weapons, ammunition, and food. On the evening of the 24th, with Allied command changes in the immediate offing, this first major follow up convoy arrived off Anzio and was pummeled by 15 fighter bombers, then 40 more, then 50 after dark in a continuous raid. A 500-pound bomb scored a grievous hit on the U.S. destroyer Plunkett, with heavy loss of life and crippling of one engine. She made it back to port. The action occurred just before the underwater explosion on the USS Mayo described earlier. In the same raid, while fully lighted in accordance with International Law, a British hospital ship was hit and sunk. By the first of February, more than 100 LST off-loadings had been accomplished at the port alone, using the speed-up scheme of the pre-loaded trucks.

Command of Sea Forces

The command structure for naval gunfire support became as fluid as the action on the ground ashore. The British thought it was foolhardy to keep cruisers on station without firing missions if they could be based in Naples and make it quickly back to Anzio when needed. Rear Admiral Mansfield RN, in HMS Orion, became gunfire support commander on the 23rd, and decided to send HMS Penelope back to Naples. But Penelope had been paired with the USS Brooklyn with fire support duties for the U.S. assault sector to the south. U.S. Rear Admiral Lowry, the overall naval commander for SHINGLE and counterpart to U.S. Major General Lucas as overall commander of the ground troops, immediately questioned whose authority was being invoked on sending one of the cruisers assigned to him, the Penelope, back to Naples.

There may have been a bit of "face" involved in what then transpired. The actual "signal" to withdraw Penelope was rescinded. Nevertheless, HMS Penelope, HMS Orion with Rear Admiral Mansfield, and HMS Spartan, all left the area. On the beginning of the third day of the assault at Anzio, the heavy duty fire support ship remaining there was the USS Brooklyn, and her skipper, Captain R.W. Cary (yes, he the skipper survivor on Savannah at Salerno) again became the gunfire support commander for Anzio. But, as it turned out, just for a day. The U.S. destroyers remained and two surviving British destroyers still in the northern support area remained available.

The following day, D+3, the 25th of January 1944, Rear Admiral Mansfield returned on HMS Orion and resumed duty as gunfire support commander. The weather on the 24th had turned rough and windy. The British Peter Force to the north completed its rerouting plan to the southern sector and came under Rear Admiral Lowry's command. Rear Admiral Troubridge RN who had commanded the Peter Force landing operations to the north was now out of a job and returned to Naples. We are not finished yet with these naval command shifts.

One point is not mentioned with enough emphasis in the sources we have reviewed for insights on the Anzio beachhead. While seaborne gunfire support at Anzio was never quite as pivotal as it was in those first days at Salerno, it became crucial. When the Germans squeezed the Allied perimeter back to within our ships' gun range, the Navy again became the Army's artillery. To this shore bombardment mission, I can attest, was added a heightened effort on Anti Aircraft defense, both for self-preservation and for ongoing supply operations for the beachhead. The German air force became a four-month visitor, calling several times every day.

Lowry's Dilemma

It was a term I never heard until the ill-fated U.S. Somalia effort of the 1990s, but Rear Admiral Lowry at Anzio experienced an early version of "mission creep". He faced an unremitting overhead challenge from the Luftwaffe. His forces had to contend with submarines and mines. He needed longer-range guns to support advancing troops. He asked for guns that could reach beyond the six-inch gun barrels of his cruisers. He was told that no such firepower was available. The U.S. had heavy cruisers and battleships in the Atlantic being readied for the Normandy invasion. So did the British. I have never seen an explanation of why these were not available for Anzio. Perhaps Anzio had become an orphan in the command structure.

Fairly rapidly, the VI Corps outran its naval artillery yet began experiencing incoming artillery of very large caliber. Units of the U.S. 3rd Infantry Division reached the ridge before Cisterna on the 26th but the Germans now had portions of 10 divisions in the field heading for Anzio. By the 28th, the VI Corps positions were such that our naval gunfire support range could only help on the flanks. Edison provided gunfire to the right flank twice on the 28th. The whole effort was like a wind-up clock running down. The weather entered a period of low cloud cover, rain and lashing winds. Close in air support for our forces left much to be desired. The British 1st Infantry Division made it to, but could not take Campeleone. The U.S. 3rd Infantry got close to Cisterna. These locations define the geography, where, about the 28th of January 1944, the Alban Hills, and the severance of road and railway between Campeleone and Cisterna as objectives, became grist for military debate. Recriminations about Generals Lucas, Clark and Alexander appear in analytical discussions of the times. Our soldiers fought valiantly. So did the naval crews at sea. It is my hindsight judgment that failure of the Allied force commanders to coordinate their Italian main front efforts with their flanking effort at Anzio doomed the latter to stalemate. The assault phase at Anzio had been successful. The rapid turnover of Allied command functions may have meant that failure was at no one's door. Kesselring, in effect, used his troops twice, once to stop Clark and then to seal off the Anzio perimeter.

From hope for a quick victory, the situation turned to a dogged effort to hold the beachhead. The Allies quickly committed two more U.S. divisions, the 45th Infantry Division and the 1st Armored, as it became apparent that we might have trouble defending what we had gained while having to abandon the Alban Hills as an objective. German defense forces also contained General Clark's Fifth Army. Kesselring simply reshaped the Gustav line to wall off the Anzio assault forces, tying enough of them down so that he no longer had to worry about any Allied end runs. German long-range artillery was brought in and the anchored Liberty ships that replaced the landing craft in the supply train came under fire. I can still see in my mind's eye those Liberty ships being abandoned when shelling of the harbor became too intense. Our naval forces had no answer for German long-range artillery. The Germans did not have to rely on accuracy. Anzio was a small town with a small harbor and all the

Germans had to do was to lob the shells into a zone. They'd hit something.

Loss of HMS Spartan and SS Samuel Huntington

On the 29th of January, HMS Spartan, a beautiful British cruiser, went down right off the mole at Anzio. Anchored, she was easy prey for a guided bomb hit which tore open vital compartments. Shortly after Spartan capsized, the Liberty ship Samuel Huntington was hit. These attacks took place just after sunset one evening as Edison crewmen looked on in horror. We were close to the Spartan when she was hit. Before I die, I would like to find out what mission required a naval warship like Spartan to be dead in the water, anchored or tied up or both, during a period when the Luftwaffe controlled the airspace. I can understand losing a ship underway which has had some chance to evade. I can understand a cargo ship being stationary while having to unload. The Huntington later was pulled out a short distance by a tug that gamely fought Huntington's fires. The Liberty was loaded with ammo and gasoline and had to be abandoned. She blew up and sank early the next morning.

Technology on Demand

Back on the U.S. home front, the scientific community of the United States, sometimes in cooperation with the British, turned out endless improvements in radar and in countermeasures. This went on in addition to complete weapon systems development, including aircraft systems and an effort we never knew about, the A-bomb.

Without going into detail, our Navy warships used "deperming" and "degaussing" to protect them from magnetic influence mines. A magnetic mine lies on the bottom and is set off when a steel-hulled ship passes over it. To my knowledge, neither the Germans nor the Italians used such mines in waters that the Edison traversed. We regularly faced the anchored "contact" mines set off when a ship ruptured an electro-chemical "horn" that protruded from the mine case. Nevertheless, Edison would go occasionally go into an East Coast deperming station to have the bulk of its magnetic signature neutralized. At sea, we would "swing the ship" through the entire circle of the magnetic compass and every fifteen degrees would re-set the current through our permanently installed degaussing coils. These were copper coils installed to offset the induced magnetism of the earth's magnetic field. At the same time we would correct the deviation table for our magnetic compass.

The National Defense Research Committee (NDRC), set up in 1940 and headed by noted scientist Vannevar Bush, provided our country an effective fast reaction capability. When the German or Japanese war machines seemed to score big with some new weapons, the NDRC would devise and then provide a countermeasure. Call it Applied Engineering. Their first task was to define the problem. This was a critical prerequisite, as occasionally our seaborne forces' first reaction to an encounter resulted in a faulty or incomplete assessment. The German acoustic torpedo was terrifying to any ship with rotating propellers. After a couple of ineffective tries, the scientists and engineers in NDRC came up with the very simple and effective FXR which when properly streamed and towed, emitted frequencies to decoy the torpedo. This was described earlier in this story. For their part, the British, whose gun stabilization was based on spirit levels (I could not believe this until I saw it) invested more effort in tactics development. They developed the "creeping attack", where two ASW vessels would conduct a joint operation to send a sub to the bottom. One surface unit "pinged" and its "silent" partner was vectored over the contact and dropped the depth charge pattern. Again, very effective.

At Anzio, the German radio-controlled ballistic bombs and the radio-controlled glider bombs were entering their prime period of use. German pilots practiced at Salerno and got in some telling blows. Admiral Lowry's action report stated that 70 red alerts in the first ten days at Anzio warning of imminent Luftwaffe attack resulted in 30 pressed-home attacks. The most effective Luftwaffe tactic was the heavier type raid at evening twilight, when dive-bombers, torpedo bombers and radio control "mother" plane bombers were used in combination. The Japanese had taught the Navy in the Pacific that a dive bomber pilot who intends to press his attack all the way home can only be stopped with a river of AA steel. The Luftwaffe pilots for the most part did not have that kind of dedication, but conventional bombing still proved successful against us and also helped to set our defending ships up for torpedo attacks and radio-controlled bomb attacks.

That radio frequency (RF) link used to control the German stand-off weapons was the focus of U.S. countermeasures' scientists and engineers effort; they operated on a very compressed time scale. I developed a fuller appreciation for this in an assignment after the war. In 1951, I was assigned as Project Officer for VX-2, an experimental squadron that flew F6F drone aircraft controlled from F8F fighter "chase" planes. The RF "carrier" frequency was the key to success or failure. When handing control over to ground control for landing the drone, we practiced a strict, "my carrier is off" protocol so that ground control could then declare "my carrier is on". Having two carrier frequencies on at once would almost always cause the drone to go out of control. So, at Anzio, *ten years before my drone experience*, our specially equipped destroyer escorts were outfitted to jam the carrier frequency link. The Luftwaffe mother plane would lose control and their missile would go astray. Another job performed with great effectiveness by the Herbert C. Jones or the Frederick C. Davis, whichever DE was on station at the time, (and one was always there during the Anzio effort) was to listen in on the German pilot's voice radio frequencies. The voice intercepts enabled the "duty" DE to tell us when the German pilots were taxiing, when airborne, and when they had arrived over the assault area, because surprisingly they jabbered all the time. Very few red alerts at Anzio came without some early warning from our countermeasure ships. Anzio would have been much worse had we not had two specially equipped destroyer escorts on our side.

Unbeknownst to me, we actually had *three* vessels qualified for such duty at Anzio. In a letter dated 7 September 1998, Ron Wright, who was a Quartermaster First Class aboard the minesweeper USS Pioneer, informed me that Pioneer was part of that rotation. She too had been outfitted with the electronic counter-measures gear. Ron excerpted directly from Pioneer's War Diary with these quotes:

"3-11-44 1015 relieved USS H.C. Jones as 'Jig Ship' and 'Harbor Master'....3-11-44- to 3-19-44 patrolled at 5 knots in the anchorage at Anzio and controlled daily arrivals and departing ships. 3-19-44 relieved by the Jones."

High Point, Low Point

By the 29th of January 1944, using the beaches and the port, the Allies had landed almost 70,000 men from 200 LST-trips and seven Liberty ships. We had over 500 guns and over 200 tanks in the beachhead. The Rangers moved in the darkness of 29-30 January to Cisterna across an open plain. This was coordinated with advances by units of the U.S. 3rd Infantry Division toward a vital highway and railroad track. The USS Edison participated in its last major Anzio shoot, getting off 336 rounds of 5" ammunition on the flanks, and earning the dispatch, "VERY EFFECTIVE. MANY ENEMY TROOPS KILLED BY YOUR FIRE. GOOD WORK." The British 1st Division moved toward the crossroad at Campeleone.

The Germans reacted in much greater force than our intelligence foresaw. At Cisterna, two Ranger battalions were surrounded and forced to surrender. The U.S. 3rd Division was forced back, the British 1st Division took heavy losses and an attempt by the newly arrived (in full strength) U.S. 1st Armored Division's tanks to swing around the front toward Rome became bogged down in soft, wet earth. Cisterna had been the high point, and it became the point where the Allies began to give up dearly won ground. The Germans would go on the offensive just a few days later.

Command Changes

Rear Admiral Lowry in Biscayne departed on 1 February and on 2 February, control of the SHINGLE ship area off Anzio, passed to Rear Admiral Morse, RN. Lowry was left with the duty of preparing support convoys for Anzio. 1 February marked a milestone on the Edison. Lt. Stanley Craw, USNR, relieved Edison's Executive Officer, the upbeat and capable Lt. James Abner Boyd USN. I served many watches and during many actions with both of these fine officers. I never saw "Jake" Boyd again and he has gone to his rest, but I will never forget his gracious treatment of every shipmate. Craw was the first of an increasing flood of distinguished reservists to attain the high post of XO of a DD in World

War II. He continued his naval career as CO of several fine destroyers after World War II. I have had brief phone calls with him and he wrote me during the effort to compose the web edition of this story.

I am not sure if the Cisterna setback prompted it, but General Wilson, SACMED, declared 1 February as the end of the "first phase of the winter campaign." We certainly had not succeeded in the original objective to get to Rome. Possibly, the General made his declaration of completion of a phase as a morale builder. On 2 February, Rear Admiral Mansfield RN became more or less the permanent commander of escort, supply and naval gunfire support. A system of relieving naval gunfire ships with slightly rested ships from Naples set in. The Edison made many trips going and coming, with some very high-speed trips to the beachhead when our troops ashore seemed threatened.

Several of these trips were made in company with the British cruiser, HMS Penelope, which became as much a friend to us as the USS Philadelphia had been earlier. This was never just a milk run. Air attack was always just moments away, but again it was the deadly sub that hurt the most. Sometimes there were gunfire support missions on targets the Germans controlled *between* Naples and Anzio. I can recall that gunfire support on these occasions was usually directed at indirect fire coordinates described as "road junctions." We were not with Penelope when she was torpedoed and sunk on 18 February 1944 by a U-boat on the Naples-Anzio run between Ponza and Cape Circe. The Germans still owned this bit of shoreline and their lookouts could help reconnoiter for their subs.

We speculated later about whether Penelope had a destroyer or two escorting her, and also about whether our presence might have made a difference. U.S. commanders were religious about screening cruisers with good ASW tin cans, but sometimes the British would go off by themselves.

Penelope had an illustrious war record. As part of British force K in 1941 and 1942, consisting of two light cruisers and two destroyers, Penelope had a key role in denying the Axis freedom of action along the sea route from Italy to North Africa.

The next Illustration is from a photo slide of Penelope.

Illustration 32-The British Cruiser Penelope

Torpedoman Ken Williams served on the USS Ludlow. He has contributed to this story in a number of places. The following paragraphs in quotes are taken from Ken Williams' e-mail to the author dated 1/31/98.

"Your speaking kindly of the HMS Penelope brought forth many warm thoughts of her. She was known as HMS Pepperpot of Malta. Whenever I saw her, she invariably had holes from bomb or shell fragments in her stacks and gun-tubs. There was always a rivalry between us and the Brits; but there was admiration, too.

"From the haze of 50+ years, I recall the HMS Spartan when she went down. She got hit in the sunset air raid and was burning badly. The Brits stayed aboard and continued to fight the fire until a high level bomber laid a stick of bombs on the brightly illuminated target. Whenever we got the word, Red Shingle, we went to battle stations. But it wasn't till the Brits sounded their sirens that we really paid attention."

"The Germans were massing just north of the Tiber River and we wanted to bring in some cruisers to break up this concentration. The Ludlow was assigned to protect five minesweepers that were to sweep a channel for the cruisers. Minesweepers sweep at five knots, barely underway, so they make a good target. We battled all the way up to the end of the channel and battled back to the Anzio beachhead. We then got the orders we did not want to hear. "Go back up, the channel has to be wider." The second time, coming back down, we were getting no return fire but the Sweeps were still whaling away with their 3" guns. Our Capt asked, What is your target? The Sweeps replied, We ain't got no target. It just makes us feel better."

The Germans Attack

On the fifth of February 1944, with a hundred tanks and nearly four hundred artillery pieces, about half of the guns

338

over 105mm, General Eberhard von Mackensen started pounding the 3rd Infantry Division in their positions before Cisterna. At this same time, another battle for Monte Cassino on the Fifth Army front above Rome was also heating up. At Anzio, the Germans had been pouring shells over 170mm in a steady pounding of the roadstead. (The Edison and her sister destroyers had five-inch guns and our cruisers were equipped with six-inch guns. Six-inch shells are just under 155mm. Anzio was one of the few assault locations in World War II where the U.S. was outgunned.)

After softening up Allied positions at Anzio on February 16, General Mackensen launched an all-out attack to drive the Allies back to the sea. With six Divisions, he drove back to within seven miles of Anzio itself. That was his high point. With the 1st Armored and the 45th Infantry Divisions leading the waves, General Lucas' VI Corps counterattacked. Naval gunfire was back within range. The flying weather cleared and Allied aircraft entered the fray in force.

By the 22nd of February 1944, General Lucas' VI Corps had repulsed the attack. The General then lost his job. Major General Lucian Truscott, his deputy, replaced him. General Clark took this action in response to pressure from General Alexander, and probably from Prime Minister Churchill, who had had some uncomplimentary things to say about Major General Lucas. On 29 February, the Germans tried one more attack, and failed, losing many soldiers killed and taken prisoner. The Anzio front stalemated until the Allies breached the Gustav line in May 1944. When that occurred, the Germans began to retreat once again in Italy. The main European action scene then shifted to Normandy and Western Europe.

Overhaul, Ships and Personnel Both in Need of
During the latter phase of the long Anzio stalemate, the
Edison finally made it back to the States for overhaul at
Bayonne, New Jersey. I disclosed earlier the embarrassing
incident of the flooding of one of our ammo magazines during the Bayonne phase of the overhaul. Another interesting
sidelight of almost every overhaul was the constant use of
cutting torches to take out a watertight door and then welding
the door back in again. Two such doors must have swapped
places three times while I was aboard. One was a "dogged"
door and one was a "Quick Opening Door" where the securing dogs were controlled by a wheel on the door. With
changes in officer personnel, I can only surmise that one officer felt it would be best to have the quick opener in one
bulkhead and the individually dogged door in another. Then,
the next shift of personnel would reverse the decision.

I can only conjecture the amount of asbestos we swallowed when the jackhammers would be right over our bunk
all night. Still, that pounding was better than enemy shells.

Edison needed a couple of side trips into the Brooklyn
Navy Yard to replace her 5" guns and re-brick her boilers.
The crew got some rest. Some of us got married.

Here are three reminders of the days of the Italian campaign of World War II.

The first of these Illustrations is an already faded 1984
Associated Press photo printed in the Springfield (MA) Union newspaper on the occasion of the 40th anniversary of the
creation of a U.S. cemetery at Anzio.

Illustration 33-The U.S. Cemetery at Anzio

Italian children lay flowers on the graves of U.S. soldiers killed in the fighting following the Anzio invasion 40 years ago

Italy honors dead at Anzio

SR 1/22/84

ANZIO, Italy (UPI) — Italy marked the 40th anniversary of the World War II Allied landings on the beaches of Anzio with ceremonies Saturday at cemeteries where almost 38,000 American, British and German soldiers are buried.

Undersecretary of Defense Bartolo Ciccardini represented the Italian government at the ceremonies, attended by military attaches from the U.S. and British embassies, local mayors and hundreds of citizens.

Buses and cars took the crowd to the three cemeteries, the British at Anzio, the American at nearby Nettuno, and the German site at Pomezia, a few miles inland from the broad beaches where the Allies landed on Jan. 22, 1944.

An Italian military detachment provided honors, and children placed flowers on the graves. About 7,000 U.S., 4,000 British and 16,000 German soldiers are buried there.

The Anzio landings were designed to achieve the quick liberation of Rome.

The next Illustration shows a U.S. Ranger smoking in the foreground. Vesuvius (in Italian, Vesuvio) is smoking in the background.

Note the Ranger flash on the left shoulder, the cut down leggings, and the light pack. Both facilitated speed-marching, at twice the infantry pace. The light pack also helped as you stepped off the landing craft when it was stuck on the second or third sandbar. You weren't so likely to go straight to the bottom. Another identifying feature is a Fairborne-Sykes fighting knife and scabbard tied to the right leg.

341

Illustration 34-Ranger Carl Lehmann Lights Up

The Illustration that follows is Vesuvius taken from the USS Edison, anchored in the Bay of Naples. One day in 1944 Vesuvius left a layer of ash on Edison's main deck.

Illustration 35-Vesuvius with Plume

Chapter Ten - Southern France

Destroyers; Two Main Types Fought World War II

If the Fletcher class U.S. destroyers won the war in the Pacific, the Benson/Livermore class won the war in the Atlantic/Mediterranean. I realize that the premise is an exaggeration, but I offer it to emphasize that destroyers played a major role in World War II. In the Atlantic they helped the Allies survive the early onslaught of the U-boat. In both oceans, and in the Mediterranean, destroyers helped the troops get ashore. In the Pacific, destroyers performed the dangerous picket duty against Japanese kamikaze aircraft.

The action portion of this Chapter for the Edison covers the landings in Southern France on August 15, 1944. We will come to that event in our story after covering Edison's progress during the late winter, spring and summer of 1944. In summary, Edison left the Mediterranean for New York in late February 1944, after finishing her chores at Anzio. Edison skipped, or was skipped by, the Normandy Invasion of June 1944. I will relate, however, a curious role that Edison and the other Mediterranean destroyers and cruisers played relative to the cross channel invasion from England to France.

As we approach the final chapters of this story of a Benson/Livermore class destroyer in World War II, there will be more anecdotes. I have a number that I have wanted to put in earlier but I felt that the thread of the story should first be established.

Not long after the story of this Chapter was completed, I left the Edison. I have done some research to help complete Edison's story for the period I was not aboard. But, my words will not speak with the force that being aboard provides. I want to leave the modern reader of these lines with a sense of what the cadres of enlistees and reservists and draftees coming into service just before or at the outset of World War II were like.

World War II: The Birth of Multiculturalism?

The Naval Academy types joined their units, for war service, with some training and some education for a lifetime career in that service. I have made it known at various points in the story that the U.S. Naval Academy and its graduates were the victims of technology lag. I felt it especially in ordnance, electronics and steam engineering. Notwithstanding, the USNA education gave us some insight on what we were supposed to know. Reserve Officer Joe Dwyer, who later became Edison's Engineering Officer, was the Chief Chemist in a comb factory when he reported aboard Edison as an Ensign. After the War, Joe was responsible for the success of a company that specialized in the manufacture of homogenizing equipment. Jim Hughes was another reserve officer whom I first knew as an Ensign on the USS Edison. Jim Hughes is today, early 1998, a "sitting" Administrative Law judge for the State of California. Seaman Abraham "Abe" Simon, who found reading and writing the English language a challenge, came to the Edison as the owner of a successful junk and salvage company. I am sure that Abe used to cringe when he helped sweep thousands of spent five-inch brass cartridge cases over the side.

There is no doubt that the Navy denied opportunity to black men during the period of my service on the USS Edison. Those aboard Edison performed outstanding service in their rating assignments but they had little or no choice in what those assignments were. I am indebted to Chief Radioman Albert T. Waters of the USS Edison for sending me his comprehensive muster list of those who served aboard the Edison. I referred to that list for the spelling of the names of Franklin L. Williams, Leonard W. Williams and Julius Zeigler, young black men who served aboard Edison during my tour of duty. These men never flinched during the ship's hundreds of calls to battle stations. These men looked forward to a better country to return to.

Northerners or Southerners, Polish or Irish or Filipino, we were all aboard a U.S. warship with a common focus. Graduate degrees, college degrees, high school diplomas and equivalency certificates, were among our credentials. Men with trade school backgrounds and job skills in welding or carpentry were mixed in with office clerks and bureaucrats

Officer or enlisted, aboard the Edison I never heard anyone make anything of the different paths to service taken by reservists, draftees, and regulars. We were all men of the Edison, proud of our service in her, and proud of our service with each other. Every man aboard valued his heritage and each one of us listened with fascination when another one of us would reveal a bit of his past. This is still going on, as I found out when the e-mail feedback came in from the publication of this story on the World Wide Web. Here is another excerpt from Electrician Warren Blake's recollections from the war years.

"I remember Henry Reilly, Ed Stolarz, Harry Halligan, Robert Morris, Gerry Randall, Larry Whetstine, and Joe Zock. Larry Whetstine went home with me one weekend, to Hamden, Connecticut. I can't recall where the ship (the Edison) was at the time. Probably either Portland or Boston. Larry was a pretty tall guy, and when my mother saw him she said, 'My gosh son, you are as big as Big Stoop.' Big Stoop was a cartoon character of that era. I believe he was in the comic strip, "Terry and the Pirates." It was probably about fifteen years ago that I read in one of Jean Whetstine's Edison Newsletters that someone inquired where Larry got the nickname, 'Stoop', so I wrote to Jean to tell her that my mother was the culprit!"

"Early on, in North Atlantic convoy duty the reality of death came close to me. The Awatea incident brought home to me the uncertainty of life when I lost two very good friends in Ingraham, DD444, and later in the war, others on Buck and Benson, and I don't know how many others. Most not yet twenty years old, me being just 18 when Ingraham went down. This was one of several convoys in which the rescue vessel HMS Toward served with us. Many years later (in 1980), I met the skipper of Toward, and we've been close friends ever since. He was born on the Isle of Skye and is a bagpiper, we having met when we both became members of a Scottish cultural society. He was living in Belfast Maine when we met, and is now living in Pennsylvania. Peter Mac-Pherson by name, he is a real gentleman."

"I don't recall just how many convoy crossings we made, interspersed with dockside alterations in Boston (one being when our liquid cooled 50 cal. machine guns were replaced with 20mm Oerlikons) and one fairly long yard availability in Brooklyn, where we went into drydock. I spent my first night in the engine spaces on 'cold iron watch'. Boy, oh boy! Was it ever cold! Life became more bearable when we made trips down south on special assignment. Up the Mississippi to New Orleans, where the First Lieutenant had the ship washed down topside with 'fresh water', which made the ship look like a Hershey bar, when it dried! Connection to city water when we got dockside, cured that. Up the Sabine River to Port Arthur, Texas, where the country is so flat that ships on the river looked like they were high and dry, on land. I think that this trip was made sometime after the invasion of North Africa, at Casablanca."

"Casablanca, and dodging shells from ship and shore battery, and torpedoes from subs. That was a hectic week. Armistice Day 1942? Hah! We were still fighting in one area or another since the first attack on the 8th of November. One evening, right after chow, I was standing on the main deck hungering for a pipe full of tobacco that was denied me, for we were refueling from a tanker and the 'smoking lamp' was out. All of a sudden, all hell broke loose, and three large transports in close proximity were torpedoed. Mooring lines and fuel lines to the tanker were severed, and we got underway, pronto and spent quite a while trying to track down the sub, or subs. This was getting too close for comfort!"

"Escorting ships back to the states and back to Casablanca. On the first trip back to Casablanca after the invasion, I was ashore on liberty with two other Edison men, when I was pinched for the first time by Shore Patrol. We had just come out of a bar, and I noticed a SP Officer and two ratings across the street (a very crowded street) at a distance of about 50 feet. We hadn't gone but about the same distance parallel with them, when I was tapped on the shoulder and asked why I hadn't saluted the officer. This one took me by surprise, because at that distance, and with all the civilians and service personnel in between, it never entered my mind. Well we wound up on report by this officer and were taken back to Edison, which was outboard of Texas and two other cans. As soon as we were underway for the states again, with leaves coming up, Cap'n. Headden held mast and surprised me by asking me if I thought 4 hours as 'Capt. of the head' was appropriate punishment! It seems that several skippers were tired of this particular shore patrol officer harassing their men on liberty, but had to account for the arrests by the SP and make a report of punishment. Anyway, I didn't mind polishing troughs and such too much, as I knew I was getting leave in New York. I think that it was after this trip to New York, that we convoyed a tanker to Port Arthur. Somewhere in this time span, we made one trip into the Med and tied up in Oran. I had only been in the Med once during the war, so it had to be on Edison. It seems to me that it was after this trip that we went to Brooklyn for yard period. This was in the spring of '43, and when we came out of the yard, we tied up at Bush Terminal in Brooklyn, I suppose for supplies."

"I was out on the starboard yard-arm (I can think of a lot of other places I'd rather have been) replacing bulbs in the yard-arm blinker lights when Morris, EM2/c yelled up that I'd been transferred (I sure wished that I had a parachute!). A call had come for Edison to supply an EM2/c for a new Fletcher class DD, whose crew was at Long Beach, N.Y. By the time I had gotten down to the deck, orders for W. Blake, EM2/c had been drawn up and I had 30 minutes to pack my bag. I was given an advance in rating to EM2/c to facilitate transfer (Morris was an experienced movie operator and knew how to dicker with other ships and stations, to get the best movies, and the Exec didn't want to lose him!)."

I will summarize the rest of Warren Blake's e-mail contribution to this story. After his service on Edison, he served on the Fletcher class DD, USS Kidd, then on the battleship Wisconsin, then on DD890, the destroyer Meredith, all before becoming a civilian in late 1946. These ships all served in the war in the Pacific. After four years as a postwar civilian, Warren received a surprise "invitation" from the Navy to return to active duty, the Navy being short in its artificer branch. Instead of going to Korea in his specialty, as an electrician, (the artificer shortage mentioned in his recall to active duty) Warren was sent to DD864, the destroyer H.J. Ellison, as master-at-arms with European duty. This gave Warren an opportunity to visit the grave of his brother who died of wounds received in World War II and was buried in England. Another brother was flying B-25s over Rabaul and Bougainville when Warren was in that area on the USS Kidd. Warren's second separation came on December 20, 1951 at Norfolk VA. He then again resumed his civilian career as a fireman in Hamden, Connecticut. I believe that Warrren Blake's subsequent experience in the war in the Pacific in World War II to be typical of an experienced rating detached from an Atlantic destroyer. Returning to Europe in a subsequent, surprise re-enlistment, was not typical. But, in the Navy, any transfer in duty assignment always brought surprises.

Westbound in Ballast

We have some time to account for after leaving the Mediterranean for rest and overhaul, reaching the States in March 1944. Edison left Palermo on the 14th of February 1944, Algiers on the 18th, and Oran on the 21st, bound for Casablanca. Our orders were to await the arrival of convoy GUS-31. We made a rendezvous with this convoy on 26 February 1944 and got underway for New York. An Edison log entry of March 4, 1944 states that the Liberty ship SS Amelia Earhart joined our New York bound convoy that day. The Edison was the "top dog" in this convoy, and in fact the only "dog", as destroyers are sometimes called, in the convoy. The rest of the escorts were Destroyer Escorts. Our skipper, Lieutenant Commander Hepburn A. Pearce was the Convoy Commodore.

Things had certainly changed in the Atlantic. A convoy of this size with a destroyer and nine destroyer escorts was a revelation to those of us who had been baptized on the North Atlantic runs of 1941-1942. Then it was a scarce allotment of U.S. destroyers with a U.S. or Canadian Coast Guard cutter or Canadian corvette added from time to time.

That February-March 1944 convoy assignment was a long trip with over 100 Liberty ships, in ballast, making a rough Atlantic sea crossing. Each day began with a "body count" of the Liberty ships. We would cross through the convoy from flank to flank, reading the convoyed ship's name off its stern. TBS employed very high frequency (for that era) voice communication. It was still restricted to warships. The methods for communicating with merchant ships were based on such limited options as the 500-kilocycle distress frequency. It took several passes through the nine or ten convoy columns, first one way and then back, then over again etc., to accomplish the daily check-off. It was an exercise in seamanship, because the prevailing wind and sea relative to the zig or the zag in zigzagging convoys effected your transit differently each time. Some Liberty ships with engineering or exceptional ballast problems would be lagging and our transit through the convoy would contain a dimple to accommodate the straggling column. Our Captain let me keep the conn for this on the mornings that I had the 0800-1200 watch and I appreciated his confidence in me. On the 16th of March, the convoy arrived off the East Coast and dispersed into units destined for different ports.

Edison's March 1944 log also shows that we made Gravesend Bay at New York for off loading ammo on 18 March. For that period, the log also shows that Lieutenant Richard "Dick" Hofer, Annapolis Class of 1942, was detached from the USS Edison on 20 March, 1942, to proceed to NAS Dallas for flight training. Dick Hofer's departure meant that I had become the Edison's Gunnery Officer. There was no ceremony. Lambert, Boyd and Hofer had been Edison's Gunnery Officers. These men had set a high standard of performance.

I was to see Dick Hofer just once more, at the Sanford Florida, Naval Air Station in 1951 or 1952. The meeting was pure chance. I had piloted an F6'F aircraft to Sanford and while on the tarmac, encountered Dick walking to his plane, a JRF Grumman Goose. Dick was killed shortly after that last meeting, while flying that JRF on an instrument approach into Albuquerque, NM. Word was that they hit a mountain peak.

Leave and Recreation

As evidence of U.S. progress in the War, Edison personnel were permitted "leave" when we got to the yard at Bayonne, NJ, just after the middle of March 1944. Most leaves were of the three-day variety, but some were longer. Three days would let you get to the Northeast Corridor, Pennsylvania Rail Road, with stops in Newark, New Brunswick, Trenton, North Philadelphia Station, Broad Street and 30th Street Stations in Philadelphia, Wilmington, Baltimore and Washington, D.C. Many GIs on one day liberties would sleep (try it, sometime) in the coach cars on this line just to take a girlfriend out for an evening, and be back at the ship the next morning. Taxi drivers in New York knew well where Sand Street was in Brooklyn, the home of the Brooklyn Navy Yard. My first sight of the new battleship, USS Iowa, was when the Edison and she were in adjacent dry docks at the Brooklyn Navy Yard. A destroyer looked like a tugboat in that setting. In fact, destroyers could be nested two abreast, and three deep in the dock and not go past the stern of the Iowa. Another favorite docking station was the 35th Street Pier on the East River. I have examined one of the early Edison photos reproduced earlier in this story and Edison appears to have just gotten underway from 35th Street.

There is no poll of the number of us who got married during the March/April 1944 New York/New Jersey yard availability. Lieutenant Craw and I acted as best man for each other on successive days, his marriage taking place in a church in New Jersey and mine in St. Patrick's Cathedral in Manhattan. Joe and Gert Dwyer got married up in Massachusetts. I would guess 20 marriages, officers and crew, at least. (If anyone wants to find out why the "boomers" were so concentrated, these are the facts.) I had three days leave. My wife, Peggy, "picked the day" we got married. It turned out to be April 1, 1944, April Fools Day, in a Leap Year. (I've kidded you a lot about the wedding date you picked, Peggy, but it is quite clear we took the only date that was available.) We were married by a Monsignor, who later became the Bishop in residence at the Cathedral. His name was Flannelly. That wedding ceremony, (no flowers or music-it was Lent, the Saturday before Palm Sunday in the Catholic Church) was our high point in the Church, until we made it to our 50th a few years ago. My New York State Uncles, Vincent and Donald Dailey, helped us get a marriage license on short notice, helped us arrange a wedding ceremony on a Saturday afternoon at 6 p.m. during a light snow storm, and arranged a reception and dinner at the Biltmore Hotel in New York City. "Helped us" is an understatement because I do not recall doing any of it. Finally, they engaged our wedding suite at the Barclay, a lovely hotel in Manhattan near the Grand Central Station, and the General Manager sent flowers to the room. It was the first time I did not have to bid my date good night at the Lobby elevator. Most of our meals the next three days were at the King of the Sea restaurant on Third Avenue. It was all seafood, but I liked their Nesselrode pie.

An East River Event

In the early dusk of one inclement day, Edison came into New York harbor, with dock space assigned at 35th Street on the East River. Entering New York was always an event because it meant some of us would get ashore. It was always somewhat tense, though, because the skipper and the navigator would have one of us deck officers in training to conn the ship. There is a turn necessary around Governor's Island to stay in the channel. The navigator or the quartermaster used "ranges", a pair of marks on Manhattan skyline structures, one behind the other, as targets to line up on the pelorus. These navigation aids (more properly, piloting aids) enabled a ship to more precisely define where to make its course change. A strong current was running this foul evening and the conning officer and then the skipper gave way sooner than usual to a port pilot, who came over to us in a small boat from the Pilot Boat near the Ambrose Lightship. The pilot confidently conned the ship up the East River and with signals, beckoned to two Moran tugs to make fast to us with lines, one on the bow and one on the stern. In the slip right next to where we were headed was a beautiful white seagoing yacht, one of many that the military commandeered at the outset of World War II. This yacht had a beautiful clipper bow, with an engraved figurine of a proud lady at the top of her prow. She was tied up with bow toward the river.

The pilot got us headed into our dock. I had never seen such a rapid upstream current. The two tugs were to hold us off the dock against the current, and gradually let us come down on the dockspace. The tugs were pulling hard to offset the movement of the East River. With about 200 feet of space to the dock, the line from the forward tug snapped. Our bow began to set down on the dock at high speed; we were headed for a concussion beyond any help the bumpers draped over the starboard side could give. It was an emergency, and the pilot looked helplessly at Captain Pearce. Pearce did not hesitate. I had never seen this happen before! "I'll take it pilot.", he said, and in the same breath gave orders with the annunciator, ALL ENGINES BACK, EMERGENCY! He ordered the tug at the stern to get clear and out of the way. Edison's available horsepower, probably 30,000 at that point, took hold. Just before smashing her bow into the dock, Edison pulled clear, backing into the East River at high speed. Right into the path of a tug with five coal barges in tow! No need to expect anything from that assemblage except that they would plow straight into us. ALL ENGINES EMERGENCY AHEAD! By now, the engineers below would be sweating. "How did the Germans get a sub into the East River?", some of them might be asking. PORT ENGINE BACK TWO THIRDS! We had to twist and parallel the river heading outbound, move forward out of the way of a train of coal barges, and somehow snake between that river traffic and the shore. I was on the after deckhouse. Our stern cut an arc toward the next pier. That white clipper bow and her tranquil lady passed directly overhead, just. We made it.

"Hap" Pearce was truly a seaman, first class. After things got under control and the pilot reestablished contact with tugs, the Captain, showing no particular emotion, calmly asked the pilot if he was ready to take us back to 35th Street.

He was and he did. I am sure that the pilot appreciated the Captain's gesture of confidence in him. I also realized that the pilot was now aware that he was in the presence of a real ship handler who knew how to use the power of his ship when that power was needed. The engineering gang of the Edison deserved a big hand too. I am giving it somewhat tardily, but with feeling, on behalf of all of us topside "witnesses."

That Leave Came to an End Too Soon

Next, Edison was off to Casco Bay, Maine. Edison with its single whaleboat, anchored out. It was cold and foggy. The chill got through to the bone. When I went aboard, Edison had two motor whaleboats. These were skippered by a coxswain or bos'ns mate. Their engineers were Motor Machinist's Mates, MoMM, a rating different from the Machinist Mate who operated Edison's steam turbine plant. One difference was recognition that a diesel engine powered the whaleboat. Soon after I came aboard, one whaleboat was removed. When we still had two, one was the Captain's Gig and the other was for the crew. With some skippers, not ours, the other was for all the officers and crew except the skipper. Some skippers never shared their Gig. Gigs are fitted a little fancy, with sort of curtain-type tassels draped under the overhang. But, when there was just one boat for the entire ship, the fancies kind of went away. There was a flag flown when the whaleboat was used as a Gig and removed if the Captain was not aboard.

These boats were very seaworthy in the hands of a good crew. I can recall at Hampton Roads (Norfolk Naval Operating Base anchorage) one very rough morning coming back from liberty and the petty officer in charge at the boat landing ordered that no boats leave the landing until the sea calmed. Captain Pearce, knowing Edison had to get under-way by 8:00 a.m., ordered the coxswain of the Edison's Gig to get underway and take us back to the Edison. We made it.

Casco Bay seemed dark and dreary all the time. Anchored out with Edison and other destroyers was the USS Denebola flying the flag of ComDesLant (Commander, Destroyers Atlantic Fleet). In peacetime, a station-ship such as the Denebola that did not actually go any place, and would help out with "services" to destroyers. In wartime it was every ship for itself. One nice extra service would have been the loan of liberty boats; not that Portland, Maine was the most desirable liberty town on the East Coast of the USA. But, you could drink there.

Leaning is Different from Rolling

All destroyer sailors have stood on the deck of a rolling ship. Edison rolled as high as 57 degrees when I was aboard. Still, the effect of standing on the deck of a ship not under-way, but listed over at 20 degrees, just hanging there, is an experience that really scared me. It happened one night in Casco Bay, during a non-underway emergency that took place in the middle of another emergency. We were to get underway the next day, the 20th of April 1944 in convoy, with orders, many of us divined, that would take us to Nor-mandy and the cross channel invasion. (Yes, now I had enough time aboard to begin to speculate on "where next?" We had no actual knowledge then that the cross channel would be at Normandy.) Since it was the last night in the States, and since we had worked very hard to be ready to go with such schemes as CSMP (which I will come back to), we pushed the limit on the number of people allowed liberty. The whaleboat was crowded on each trip and it was in con-stant transit. I was OOD that night and Joe Dwyer had the engineering duty. The Captain went ashore early and the Executive Officer went ashore late. The Captain came back aboard somewhat the worse for wear. No movie scriptwriter could have dreamed up the next few hours.

Joe Dwyer was still learning to be Engineering Officer, and I had never quite experienced the responsibility for the whole ship, a kind of "Full Monty" responsibility. Just about dusk, Joe reported that we had sprung a leak in a fresh water tank. Now, destroyers treat fresh water like liquid gold. It is a necessity for the engineering plant. The evaporators that make fresh water work off the almost-spent steam. The scuttlebutts (drinking fountains) are fed "almost" fresh water that is not good enough for the boilers and turbines. Human showering is mostly a saltwater affair with a failed invention called salt-water soap. The Edison could not depart for battle on the morrow with a leak in a fresh water tank. I sent a signal to the USS Denebola for help on dealing with the problem. The immediate response signal, summarized, offered no help. "Fix it yourself!" Amplified, in context, "Doesn't the Edison know that the entire Fleet in this Bay sorties tomorrow for momentous operations in Europe?"

Joe told me his men figured they could get the hole up out of the water if we listed the ship about 20 degrees. Irrespective of whether we got help or not, we would have to get the hole up out of the water. There was no prospect of a drydock. Portland did not even have one. So, at Joe's direction, his men, skilled and to all appearances confident, started pumping oil and water to the port side. Gradually, Edison heeled over, and inch by inch, our welders now hanging on a scaffold, reported the impending "arrival" of the suspect hole. After four hours of anxious step by step pumping, the hole emerged above the waterline. It was about amidships on the starboard side. Everything loose on deck had to be secured.

Just as Joe's men were preparing their torches to weld a hastily fabricated patch over the hole, a boat approached from the flagship, the USS Denebola. A weary Commander (three gold stripes on the sleeve) came up (or over) the ladder we put down, and took in this scene with great puzzlement, while he moved ever so carefully about our slanted deck. "I want to see your Captain. I have Secret sailing orders for him to sign for!" Whew! The Captain is ill, too ill to see you, was my response. "Well then, I want to see your Executive Officer." Sorry sir, he is ashore. "What on earth is going on here? Tomorrow you sail. No Captain! No Exec! And this crazy operation going on when I cannot even stand up on the main deck." Well sir, we asked for your help but you turned us down. We are doing our best. "OK. I'll be back at 0200. Make sure you are straightened out and I can get the CO or the XO to sign for Secret sailing orders. These orders are the most important you will ever get." Yes Sir, we will do our best.

Sure enough, he came back at 0200 the next morning. Now, though the Captain had come back aboard, he was really in no condition to see anyone. The XO had until 0600 to return. I did not think a junior officer could persuade gold-braid-on-the-cap to come back once more at 0600. Joe's men now had the patch on and wanted to test the compartment by putting some air pressure on it before we pumped fluids back and righted the ship. Good evening, Commander. Watch your step sir. We are still tilted over. "I want to see the Captain or the Executive Officer." Sorry sir, the Executive Officer is not aboard and the Captain is too ill to see you. (I thought the man was going to go bonkers. Joe, standing at my side, was just as scared as I was.) "What in heaven's kind of ship is this, anyway? Leaving in a few hours, still listing like crazy, no senior officers available!" Sir, if I could make a suggestion. You have had a long night visiting all these destroyers. If you would let me have the sealed package, I will take it in to the Captain's stateroom and get him to sign and bring you back the signature just as fast as I can. "Never supposed to do anything like this, but the Fleet has to sail, and I want to make extra sure this one sails with it. OK. No more funny business, please."

So, I took the package into the skipper's stateroom off the starboard passageway. He was in deep sleep in his bunk that was on an inner bulkhead. I put the orders into his open safe, and signed his name, and brought the receipt back to the Commander. Here you are, Sir. Have a pleasant morning. He never spoke as he got back into his launch and disappeared into the Casco fog. Joe told me the test was OK, and he started the pumping operation in reverse. At about 0630, still over about 15 degrees, the bell from the skipper's stateroom rang. I ran from the quarterdeck and presented myself at his side. "Why in hell can't I get up out of this bunk?" Sorry sir, we are still heeled over and you are in kind of a V-shaped slot there until we get level again. Please read these orders. It apparently tells where we are going and when.

TO DO and DONE

Oh yes, the Current Ships Maintenance Project (CSMP). By April of 1944, Jim Hughes had become the First Lieutenant. At our previous type ("type", meaning destroyer) inspection, probably in or around Norfolk, maybe a half year earlier, the DesLant "destroyer type" people had given us a poor mark because our CSMP file was not up to date. During the April 1944 Casco Bay stay, the destroyer type officers on the Denebola told us to be ready to stand inspection while we were anchored there. The inspection was held and we got good marks. (This was before the fresh water tank episode.)

We were especially lauded because our CSMP file was up to date. Jim Hughes had discovered the discrepancy report in which we had received the bad mark during the previous inspection. He found it just a day or so before this Casco Bay inspection. Jim had his shipfitters construct two shiny, aluminum boxes with beautifully fitted, hinged, covers. Both were labeled CSMP in large letters. Both obviously were built to hold 8 x 10 1/2inch U.S. government letter-sized documents. One box was labeled TO DO. The other box was labeled DONE. The Edison "done" fine. After the inspection party departed, I looked inside the two covered boxes. There was no document inside either box. I do not believe there ever was.

An Eastbound Show of Force
On 20 April, 1944 Edison's two week stay in Casco Bay ended as she headed back into the Atlantic with an all-warship force. Many of the ships had been in Casco Bay with us but other cruisers and destroyers rendezvoused offshore from other ports. This was my first time at sea without cargo ships, and we did not even have a fleet tanker with us to fuel the destroyers. (Cruisers fueled us when there were no tankers.) On this day, too, though I did not realize it until reading Theodore Roscoe's book on Destroyer Operations in World War II, the USS Lansdale took a torpedo while guarding a Mediterranean convoy. She was another Benson/Livermore sunk by aerial torpedo.

The speed of advance of our all-warship convoy, much faster than the fastest merchant convoy, took us to the Azores in just a little over five days. The destroyers fueled there and this force was underway again.

We were not going to England or the British Isles to await the cross channel invasion. We were going back to the

Mediterranean, only this time instead of slinking through the Straits of Gibraltar in the dead of night, we were going through at high noon, and hoped the German spotters in Algeciras, Spain, *would surely see us*, and count us! It was the conjecture around the ship that the Allied High Command wanted the Germans to think that the next major thrust would come from the south of Europe. And for all most of us really knew, maybe it would. The sealed orders I had signed for revealed our next mission, but I was not among those on the Edison who had a "need to know" even though I was now about the fifth senior officer of our 23 aboard. I had begun as the junior officer in the 10-officer complement Edison had when I joined the ship. Irrespective of the predictions about our next action assignment, a magnificent fleet of 25-30 U.S. cruisers and destroyers sailed through the Straits of Gibraltar at noon Greenwich time on 29 April and arrived in Oran on 1 May 1944.

Edison left Mers-el-Kebir the next day to assist in the escort of convoy UGS-39. From 8 May to 13 August, Edison served in various AA and ASW assignments for ships transiting Italian waters. There was a brief time out for gunnery exercises 11-14 July 1944. On 13 August, 1944 Edison left Palermo, Sicily for her assignment in DRAGOON, scheduled for August 15, 1944. During this period, we lost more Benson/Livermore destroyers participating in the Normandy Invasion.

USS Corry

In the spring of 1942, before I graduated from the U.S. Naval Academy, our modest berthing and anchorage facility at Annapolis was visited by the USS Corry. She was the first Benson/Livermore class destroyer I had ever seen. From our Annapolis seawall we could speculate about some of the events of her time trials. One unmistakable sight occurred when Corry's two screws, each driven by 25,000 Shaft Horsepower, were given All Ahead Flank Emergency. (From my memory, this signal was "All Ahead Flank" on the annunciators, sounded twice in succession to indicate "Emergency".) Corry's stern settled down like a fast speedboat, which she was, and her bow seemed to hydroplane. I did not know until later that she was making over 37 knots but I was impressed with the sight. I also learned later that the shallow Chesapeake did not allow the absolute top speed to be achieved. It was about that time that the Naval Academy's annual First Class Midshipman auction was held for assignments after graduation, and as I related at the outset of this story, I put in for Destroyers, Atlantic Fleet. I now feel that perhaps, subconsciously, the Corry visit to USNA influenced my decision.

The USS Corry was lost during one of ANVIL's (Normandy Invasion's) first D-Day close fire support missions at Utah Beach. She struck a mine that broke her keel. Normandy is not chronicled in this story because Edison was not there. But, I did want to note Corry's loss and also the losses of the destroyers USS Meredith and the USS Glennon before the assault phase of the great cross channel invasion came to an end. In a later Mediterranean action, we lost the Destroyer Escort Frederick C. Davis. She had served brilliantly at Anzio with the U.S. Destroyer Escort Herbert C. Jones and the USS Pioneer.

She Left Her Anchor in Napoli

Edison managed a few liberties in Naples. We took what might be considered an extra liberty our first time in that beautiful harbor. We had been reminded to look at the charts before anchoring there. Naples was a deep-water anchorage.

The bottom would usually be about 40 fathoms down. This depth was much greater than our anchorages in other world harbors. Jim Hughes, our First Lieutenant, ordered his deck gang to transfer some chain from the port anchor chain to the starboard anchor chain to accommodate the extra depth. In most anchoring situations, the anchor detail could order the chain snubbed at 15 fathoms and be assured the anchor was already on the bottom. Not so at Napoli. Human habits are hard to break. On our first trip in, the charts for our assigned anchor position showed about 42 fathoms of water. The navigator (Stan Craw) told the skipper (Hap Pearce) that Edison had arrived over the assigned anchor position coordinates. The skipper used the bull horn to tell the First Lieutenant (Jim Hughes) on the focs'le,"NOW!" Jim said, "Let Go", and the chain sped up out of the chain locker with the anchor as the driving force. The specially marked fifteen-fathom "shot" ran by and Jim, out of habit, ordered the capstan operator to snub the chain just as the fifteen-fathom shot hit the water.

"Report the chain," ordered the Captain. "Up and down, no strain", reported the foc'sle. "Back down ten turns," ordered the skipper, and then asked again, "Report the chain." "Up and down, no strain," reported Jim from the anchor detail. "Where are we, navigator?" asked the skipper. "About a quarter mile from our anchor position." responded Stan Craw. "Jim, bring up that anchor," spoke the Captain. Orders were given to the capstan motor operator and the chain slowly came up out of the water. Sure enough, the fifteen-fathom shot came out of the Bay of Naples, neatly split in half. So then the Captain looked, and we all looked, for the anchor buoy which would mark the anchor position on the bottom. "Jim, how much line did you have on the anchor buoy?" "Fifteen fathoms, Captain." So, there in Napoli Bay is

a nice anchor, which at one time could be found if you snor-
keled to 25 fathoms and found the anchor buoy. I assume the
anchor buoy and its line have disintegrated over the past fifty
years. Jim has taken a lot of kidding about the "up and down,
no strain" event, which the rest of us relished as a sanity
break from the serious business of shooting, and being shot
at.

DRAGOON

Beginning at Christmas, 1943, right on through the Italian
campaign in 1944, Prime Minister Churchill used every argument and worked every channel of communication possible to persuade Roosevelt and Eisenhower that the route
through northern Italy was the best choice for beating the
Nazis. He wanted the southern France strategy abandoned.
He won some converts, but General Eisenhower was never
convinced. President Roosevelt sided with his Generals. After the landings, with the outstanding success of the main
thrust from the Normandy beaches, coupled with the slower
pace of the Cherbourg prong of the assault, the Allied commanders became even more fully convinced that logistics
alone demanded ports in the south of France. At its peak,
even given the amazing job in clearing devastated Cherbourg
to make her a seaport once again, that port could not handle
the tonnage of a Marseilles. The decision to throw the weight
of Patton's Army eastward and leave Brittany to die on the
vine, meant that Brittany ports were out of the question to
make up the logistics deficiency that several successful Allied armies now required. On 8 July 1944, General Sir Henry
Maitland Wilson, Eisenhower's successor for all Mediterranean operations, put in motion the plan to invade the south of
France.

SOUTHERN FRANCE

The veteran 3rd, 36th and 45th U.S. infantry divisions were readied for the assault phase. They would become the nucleus of a new U.S. 7th Army under Lieutenant General Alexander Patch. For the assault phase, these would be commanded by Lieutenant General Lucian Truscott and be called the VI Corps. Two French divisions, also withdrawn from Italy, would become the French II Corps which would be supplemented by a French tank and motorized infantry brigade. To minimize language difficulties during first assault hours, the French troops would come in a major follow up landing, close behind the assault forces. It would still be Admiral Hewitt's job to get these forces successfully ashore. Under Hewitt, Rear Admiral Frank Lowry would handle the west flank, toward Marseilles, with the U.S. 3rd Division to go ashore. Rear Admiral Bertram Rodgers, USN, would command the landings of the U.S. 45th Division in Baie de Bougnon in the center pointed toward St. Tropez. Rear Admiral Don Moon, USN would be in charge on the right flank, with the U.S. 36th Division, whose own right flank would reach toward Cannes. We had worked with Lowry before at Anzio, Rodgers had come from the Pacific, and Moon had commanded tough landings at Utah Beach in Normandy. Each had the primary responsibility to get one U.S. assault division, with added units, successfully ashore. Rear Admiral Lyal Davidson would again command naval gunfire support. Recalling the German targets "beyond ship's gunnery range", a problem the cruisers and destroyers at Anzio could not handle, Admiral Hewitt asked Admiral King for heavier-gunned warships to augment Hewitt's Eighth Fleet.

Five battleships were made available, Nevada, Texas, Arkansas, all old U.S. Battleships (BBs), along with HMS Ramillies and the French BB, Lorraine, which we had seen in North African ports. I never laid eyes on these heavies during

DRAGOON. Heavy U.S. cruisers Augusta and Tuscaloosa were added. Light cruiser Quincy was added to Brooklyn and Philadelphia, helping to make up for the absence of the damaged Savannah. It would be Edison's assignment to work this assault with Tuscaloosa and Rear Admiral Morton Deyo. Seven British and two American escort carriers would provide air cover and air support. There would be a major pre-dawn paratroop landing, followed by a softening bombardment from the sea and then an 0800 local time daylight troop landing. Admiral Davidson and a member of his staff had gone to Normandy to examine German shore defense fortifications. The planners expected to face some heavy guns in the assault phase of DRAGOON but knew they would not find the heavy guns and fortifications in the depth experienced at Normandy. On the fifth of August, laden with combat fatigue from Normandy, Admiral Moon took his own life and was replaced by Rear Admiral Spencer Lewis, USN.

For those who recall code names, the name Overlord, the long planned invasion operation across the English Channel, moved into its actual assault phase with the name, Neptune. Anvil had been the long-term planner's name for the Southern France invasion during its preparation, but the assault phase became known as Dragoon.

Edison's officers and men often speculated, during the four invasion operations preceding Southern France, about success and the prospects for the end of the War. But no one aboard Edison during the extensive preparation for DRAGOON, had the remotest idea then that the final sustained period of dramatic enemy action in Edison's commissioned life span was at hand.

The Chain of Command

The senior officers are more tuned to the chain of command while the junior officers and crew complement are less aware of command structure, though we generally had an idea who the next-up boss was. A destroyer and its skipper going into action are part of a chain of command. It is spelled out on paper before the operation takes place. Then, in the fast pace of action that follows, the chain of command can change by the minute, with no paperwork whatsoever! The plan adjusts to the realities, to what the enemy does, and to what our forces have accomplished or failed to accomplish.

It had been Edison's good fortune, whether escorting to the place of assault, defending against air attack or surface attack or sub-surface dangers, or while under the direction of a shore fire control party, to generally re-attach to Admiral Lyal Davidson's command often enough to feel at home with him. This feeling of attachment persisted just as strongly as our bond with a destroyer division or destroyer squadron commander. During DRAGOON, Admiral Davidson moved his flag to the USS Augusta, another ship well known and trusted by us.

These treasured connections were not operative for Edison during the Southern France assault. Davidson and Augusta were kept busy on the west flank of the operation while Edison was either directly under Admiral Deyo on Tuscaloosa, or working for an SFCP, both of which were on the eastern flank of operations. We preferred the SFCP assignments. A bond with Tuscaloosa and her flag officer never jelled for the Edison. This coolness came as the result of different approaches to the exercise of command. I was aware of a subtle change at the time, but could not have articulated my thoughts then. Reviewing my recollections for

JOINING THE WAR AT SEA

this story, the differences I then only sensed have become clearer.

"I am going in!" was Admiral Davidson's electric announcement from USS Philadelphia as he confronted the yet-to-be-swept minefield at Salerno.

"Go in and draw their fire and we will back you up." were the words from Tuscaloosa at Cannes almost a year later.

If I had any other point to make in the distinctions between the quoted phrases above, I would make it. Rear Admiral Deyo's needs expressed to us were appropriate for the challenges faced by for the "Camel" support force, as our force during DRAGOON was code-named. Destroyers screened, destroyers protected, destroyers put themselves between main opposing larger warship armadas, and they always "drew fire." All warships are expendable, destroyers just a little more so than cruisers. In the next chapter, we will examine one such expendable intervention episode in which our Pacific destroyer and destroyer escort counterparts participated. The situation developed in a major Pacific battle in which destroyers and destroyer escorts performed the role of physically intervening between an overpowering line of Japanese battleships and a group of sitting duck U.S. escort carriers. Those escorts were there to do much more than draw fire, but they did that too.

It is clearer to me now than it was in 1943 and 1944 that the situation Deyo faced in the Gulf of Cannes was entirely different from the situation Davidson confronted in the Bay of Salerno.

Notwithstanding, I can just never forget how Rear Admiral Davidson in the USS Philadelphia saw his role and Philadelphia's role so aggressively in that furious first day at

Salerno. It could have been disaster for the Admiral and his flagship. Philadelphia, too, lived just as charmed a life as the Edison.

Rear Admiral Deyo proved to be more of a communicator than Rear Admiral Davidson. Deyo publicly and unstintingly commended the ships under his command. Examples will be forthcoming.

Other Bonds Held Fast

Our old friends Woolsey and Ludlow would be with us in the Camel Force, along with U.S. destroyers Parker, Kendrick, Mackenzie, Mclanahan, Nields, Ordronaux, Boyle and Champlin. Champlin was commanded by my company officer at the U.S. Naval Academy, Lieutenant Commander F.E. Fleck. In addition to the U.S. heavy cruiser Tuscaloosa, we had the U.S. cruisers Brooklyn and Marblehead, the battleship Arkansas, the HMS Argonaut, and the French cruisers Duguay-Trouin and Emile Bertin. The latter was one of the most graceful looking warships I have ever seen. Together, these warships were defined as the Bombardment Group for Task Force 87, Camel Force. The flagship for Rear Admiral Lewis was the attack transport, USS Bayfield.

Seeing Marblehead, the cruiser he'd helped save from near annihilation by the Japanese in a very early Pacific engagement, must have made Captain Pearce a proud man. For some reason, historian Samuel Eliot Morison labeled Marblehead a light cruiser in Volume XI of his History of United States Naval Operations in World War II. She had an eight-inch main battery and that was the standard that differentiated a "heavy" cruiser from the six-inch gun "light" cruisers. But, Marblehead was quite old, witness her sponson guns, so Morison may have downgraded her a bit.

A U.S. Navy recognition photo slide from World War II is the original for the next Illustration, France's Emile Bertin.

Illustration 36-French Cruiser, Emile Bertin

Drake Davis, historian of the USS Savannah, provided the next illustration, a photo of the light cruiser Brooklyn. Edison spent considerable time with the 15-gun cruisers, Brooklyn, Philadelphia and Savannah in 1942, 43 and 44.

Illustration 37-USS Brooklyn

Illustration 38-Liberty Ship in North African Port

In the distant center of IIllustration 38 is a Liberty ship, the mainstay of the U.S. cargo fleet in World War II. About 2700 were built on EC-2 hulls. My friend Bill Rowan sailed on hull No. 78 as a cadet. He characterized the propulsion as "three cylinder, up and down jobs." Toward the end of the war, U.S. shipyards began turning out Victory ships, a cargo hull that replaced the Liberty. The Victory ships had cleaner lines and geared turbine propulsion.

The "E" in the EC-2 Liberty ship hull designation stands for Emergency. The U.S. Maritime Commission was established in the 1930s and embarked on a building program to rebuild the U. S. merchant fleet, then at its lowest ebb. A series of hulls, C-1, C-2 and C-3 was programmed, with the C-2 hulls of nice faired lines scheduled to get geared turbine propulsion. This ambitious program was in progress when the war clouds erupted in Europe. The British, desperate for shipping, persuaded the U.S. Maritime Commission to authorize a speedup in construction. One of the necessary byproducts of this decision was to coarsen the hull lines of the C-2 and to go to steam reciprocating engines, with water tube boilers that were oil fired. Fastest availability was the British objective. Credit the United States authorities for heeding Britain's pleas. New yards and new ships sprung into being in 1941, before Pearl Harbor. One decision did not come until late 1941. An "armed" merchant vessel was anathema to the citizens of the United States. One more amendment to the Neutrality Law on 13 November 1941 finally removed this impediment and these ships would henceforth be armed. The United States was still not at war when President Roosevelt declared, "Each new ship strikes a blow at the menace to the nation and for the liberty of the free peoples of the world. We propose that these ships (the Liberty ships) shall sail the seas as intended, and to the best of our ability shall protect them from torpedoes, bombs or shells." And so went forth a huge fleet of 7100 ton, 11 knot cargo ships. To the best of our ability, we did protect them, but torpedoes, bombs, and shells took their toll. So did mines, which the President did not mention in his summary of dangers.

Liberty ships were converted to an incredible number of uses. They met an incredible variety of ultimate fates. While enemy ordnance took a big toll, groundings, collisions, founderings and other natural disasters helped cheat the postwar shipbreakers. Shortly after the war, one Liberty was lost in foul weather carrying 4500 caskets to Europe to bring back the bodies of U.S. servicemen buried there. Possibly contributing to the large number of "operational" losses was the absence of important equipment. Liberty ships went to sea without radio direction finders, without fire detection systems, without emergency diesel generators and without lifeboat radios. Another provisioning shortage resulted in shortening their anchor chains from 300 fathoms to 240, and then to 210 divided 135 on one anchor and 75 on the other. Many Liberties went to sea with just one anchor. They had no gyrocompass though space was provisioned for one. L.A. Sawyer and W. H. Mitchell compiled the story of "The Liberty Ships." This book was published by Lloyd's of London Press Ltd. More than just vital statistics, this book contains hundreds of fascinating sea stories that brought home to me how little I really knew of the role of the Liberty ships in World War II. I have mentioned in these pages a few Liberty ships by name that the Edison encountered in World War II. Each one is covered in that book.

The Operation Begins

In planning for Dragoon, our leadership was able to apply lessons learned from our four earlier assault operations beginning with Casablanca. Admiral Hewitt, and others who joined him in a special pleading that had been ignored in earlier invasions, succeeded in getting a powerful pre-landing bombardment, and an 0800 daylight assault landing time. The sea bombardment took its place in a sequence of orchestrated air bombing operations begun as early as April 1944. These airborne operations were gradually stepped up in intensity and covered the shoreline from west of Marseilles all the way to Genoa, Italy. Despite the broad extent of the air bombers target shoreline, and the judicious employment of "equal bomb" treatment to all sectors along that shoreline, the Germans were able to correctly anticipate that the Rhone River delta and the Rhone valley would be our main thrust. And with the nearly 900 major vessels underway, "in their own bottoms" as some put it, carrying nearly 1500 craft, not in their own bottoms, Allied timing was no puzzle to the

Germans. The German forces were just now spread too thin to do too much about it. They had too many fronts to defend. They were where Marshal Stalin wanted them.

Prime Minister Winston Churchill's vision of postwar Europe proved quite accurate. That vision surely influenced his interest in having our forces penetrate Europe from the south. But the U.S. vision of defeating Germany first, and as fast as possible, meant that our main forces were disposed in the west, and not in some Adriatic-Aegean front where the Allies could become involved in countries closer to Josef Stalin's objectives. Eisenhower's armies were primed to shorten the War in Europe and shorten it they did. The Allies were not primed to become involved in central European politics. Destroyer folks did not muse about these matters. It would have been distracting and non-productive. If these thoughts are distracting to this story, I plead guilty. This author is in a bit of a discovery process himself, *as the connection between theater events in World War II becomes clearer to him.* I am on a journey of my own here, not so much to recall what I did know (some of which was in error) but to recall what I did not know.

Here is an August 14, 1944, CINCMED dispatch, re-addressed by CTG 87.7 (Camel Bombardment Group) to Edison and all ships in this command:
-QNL- -A- 7Y3 141745 7YY3 -A- CINCMED BT
TUSCALOOSA AND CAMEL FORCE GENERAL WILSON AND ADMIRAL CUNNINGHAM WISH YOU GOOD LUCK, YOUR ENTERPRISE WILL MAKE HISTORY AND WILL GIVE A FATAL BLOW TO THE ENEMY.

The time of receipt (TOR) of this message was August 14, 1944 at 1645, a quarter to five p.m. local time. Rear Admiral Deyo forwarded the dispatch to us.

Five thousand paratroops, from 396 transport planes that departed from airfields near Rome, made the first landings in darkness. Pathfinder planes, night fighters, and airborne radar jamming aircraft preceded them. The Allied aircraft took a path from the northern point of Corsica to the French coast, along which they were guided by three beacon ships located along the shoreline well clear of our approaching sea forces. The air-drops, both of the chutists and the gliders, were targeted around Le Muy and were completed without serious opposition by shortly after 0500 on the fifteenth of August. This group had Le Muy in hand by afternoon, had seized a German corps command quarters, had taken several hundred prisoners, and were linked up with the 45th division which had landed over the beaches, all before the end of D-day. Every one of the 396 planes got safely back to base.

The second landings, still in the darkness, involved 3,000 U.S., British, Canadian and French commandos with a special mission on the western flank of the landings. Prior to the deployment of this Sitka Force, smaller groups landed on the group of offshore islands, capturing prisoners and discovering that some of the heavy fortifications were in fact wooden dummy guns. Others were real and Augusta had to pound away with her main battery. One had sufficient encasements to call for the 15-inch shells from the HMS Ramillies. Landings on the coast itself at Cap Negre began about 0200 on the 15th of August. One objective was to cut the defender's communications and access between Toulon and our assault beaches to the east. With some more help from Augusta and HMS Dido, these landings accomplished their mission and linked up with U.S. 3rd Division units shortly after noon on D-day.

Edison's Fifth D-day Begins

First, of course, the sweeps. Their day began at 0515, with the objective to clear boat lanes for the three main attack forces. Drone boats to clear explosive underwater obstacles were then employed. The use of this technique still presented problems but worked better here than during the pre-invasion training exercises in Italy. With first light appearing, waves of Allied land based bombers began their drops just before 0600. This continued until about 0730, overlapping the sea bombardment commenced by HMS Ajax. Scout planes from the U.S. light cruisers Philadelphia, Brooklyn and Quincy were catapulted into the air when the low mist that obscured targets dissipated.

The Alpha Force, embarking the U.S. 3rd Infantry Division, would land in the Baie de Pampelone. This was the westernmost of our main forces, except for the Sitka Force that had been clearing the islands off Cap Negre. Sitka troops were then to get astride the coast road to Toulon to prevent the enemy from moving forces toward our landing beaches. Delta Force, with the 45th Division would land in the center, on the eastern promontory of the Golfe de St. Tropez. The Camel Force, with the 36th Division, would land at Beach Red in the Golfe de Frejus and at Beach Green to the east on Cap Drammont. This Division's primary responsibility was to get moving along the road up the Rhone Valley toward Vichy and Lyon, and lead the charge to the linkup with Eisenhower's armies moving east from their successful Normandy invasion beaches. The 36th also presented a right flank, toward Cannes, Nice, Monaco and eventually toward Genoa. We had no picture at my level of the overall strategy.

On the job training informed me that our sea forces were to protect this right flank, to assist in advances of our troops into Cannes and Nice, and to help erect a holding wall to keep the main northbound 7th Army free of flank attacks and harassing artillery from the eastern flank. This part settled in on us something like Anzio, although the weather was better and we were now supporting a winning hand rather than a bogged down force.

Edison took up her fire support station just before 0400 on the 15th of August, 1944. At 0746, we were fired on by a shore battery and at 0800 returned fire. At 1605, our War Diary states that we fired on and destroyed a pillbox. We were under air attack just after dusk at 2110. We could see a DO-217 making a pass over the staging area. We fired at it but did not hit it. It wasn't the Director crew's fault. By mistake, I had left a 5mil deflection spot in the computer from the previous shore firing mission.

Beach Red presented a plethora of obstacles, mines, heavy weapons, and well protected defenders. Several minesweepers were sunk and the sweeper force did not get the first phase of the sweep accomplished. Our forces were therefore impeded in getting personnel ashore to deal with underwater demolition responsibilities. The landing craft were coming in on schedule so the decision was made to move the Beach Red stream of boats to Beach Green, which had been heavily defended, but which had yielded. The destroyer Ordronaux took up landing craft re-direction tasks here and did a marvelous job under tight circumstances. Beach Red was still badly needed. Every beach was needed for the logistics challenge, so the 36th Division resolved to take Beach Red from the rear and they did. But it was the 19th of August before the Golfe de Frejus was cleared of most of the defender's death traps. Other units of the 36th proceeded east to the west shore of the Golfe de Napoule. The city of Cannes was across the Gulf, on the Gulf's eastern shore.

All in all, the Alpha and the Delta forces met all of their D-day objectives and then some. Camel Force was held up momentarily by their Beach Red impasse. But by the end of the 16th, all major units of the 3rd, 36th and 45th Divisions were ashore with full supplies. St. Raphael fell on the morning of the 16th. Strong forces began to move westward toward Toulon and Marseilles. We still had to get two follow up French Divisions ashore to go with General de Lattre's French II Corps, to which had been entrusted the vital mission of taking Toulon and Marseilles. The supply chain that Eisenhower counted on was stretched out in already-loaded bottoms all the way back to the east coast of the United States. Marseilles was a critically important port. Moving men and materiel across beaches would never work for the million man thrusts needed to defeat Hitler.

A Touch of Class

I want to take a few lines here to relate something about the man we knew as Admiral Hewitt. It comes from Morison's Volume XI, The Invasion of France and Germany. Admiral Hewitt went ashore on the morning of the 16th of August, 1944, with James Forrestal, U.S. Secretary of the Navy, General Patch, commanding the 7th Army, and Admiral Lemonnier of the French Navy. In two jeeps, this party drove into St. Raphael. The townspeople peered out of windows and doors with curiosity. Admiral Hewitt stood up in his jeep, and pointed at the officer's cap of Admiral Lemonnier, a cap that was conspicuously French. With that, the townspeople formed an immediate crowd, and spontaneously broke out in song, The Marseillaise. That event tells a lot about Admiral Hewitt.

We Move East

It was toward the Golfe de Napoule that Edison's main attention was drawn after D-day. A heavy battery on an island just offshore presented danger to the flank of the 36th Division. Edison would be involved in dealing with it. The character of the shore and the land behind it changed dramatically as one moved eastward toward Cannes.

This visual splendor of red stone sand and blue Mediterranean was not lost on me. Salerno's shoreline had been just as beautiful in its way, but at Southern France I was the Gunnery Officer and could see so much more through the Director's optics than with our 7x50 binoculars. Chief Fire Controlman Jackson and I jabbered all the time either by yelling or through the sound powered phones, as we would discover one land feature after another. I particularly recall the rail yards on the north side of the Gulf and the spur line that reached west from there, right to one of our Camel Force landing beaches. We took out our share of boxcars and locomotives until our troops had secured the area.

Where Are Those Batteries Firing From?

That is surely what Rear Admiral Deyo wanted to know. I can tell you how we helped him find out. This came as we were directed to draw enemy fire, and received assurance that we would be backed up by the Tuscaloosa. On one trip into the Golfe de Napoule (we referred to it as the Gulf of Cannes then) on an assigned mission, our skipper pointed our ship straight in. For example, let us say that our heading was North or 000 degrees true. From where we suspected the major battery harassing our troops was located, our target angle, to them, would be 045. In other words, they were broad on our starboard bow. Sure enough, *we drew their fire.*

As the splashes drew closer, and we could see from the height of the splash plumes that these were big shells, the Captain went from 10 knots ahead, to 5 knots astern, by giving appropriate commands to the engine room. Hap Pearce was giving the German fire control people credit for good ranging, and for getting a fire control solution to our forward speed at something between 5 and 10 knots. Sure enough, the next salvo of splashes was way out ahead of us. They had .been fooled. They had not thought to put "minus 5 knots" into their solution. This trick will only work once in a given situation so at other times we used speed ahead, course changes, and smoke. While we were directed to draw their fire, we *were not directed to get hit*. It was clear from his comments to bridge personnel that our skipper was not at all keen about such tactics.

More Dispatches

Military teletypewriters printed in all CAPS. The military message form, the "daddy" of our telegram and our e-mails, is not highly embellished. Some dispatches used AR, to mean Acknowledge Receipt, a feature still missing in most of our e-mail systems in 1998. Some messages reveal a BT, to denote the start of the *content* of the transmission. Most used X, in lieu of periods, or orally, as "stops". All dispatches came with a date/time group. The first two numerals are the day of the month; the last four are the time of day in military jargon. An alphabetic suffix is sometimes used to reveal the time zone. The ones below with the suffix B, are in the second time zone east of Greenwich, or two hours forward of (later than) Greenwich Mean Time. That time zone was local time for Southern France. Like e-mail, when the sender is under some pressure, spelling suffers. Not to worry, the meaning was usually clear. Realism benefits from scanning these into the page but the faded carbons leave something to be desired. So, here, I will re-key them and I promise to indicate with parentheses where I alter them.

The first one, reproduced on an early page in this chapter, was a general "pump up the troops" message from the high command. The first line showed that the entire chain of command, four levels, joined together in the message. British General Wilson was CINCMED.

This next dispatch is an early situation report for DRA-GOON.

152230B SITUATION REPORT 152000B
OBSTICALS AND ARTILLERY FIRE ON SHORE NAVY DID NOT LAND 142 INF ON BEACH 264A AS PLANNED X 142 INF WAS LATER LANDED OVER BEACH 264B X AT 152000B 142 AND 143 INF WERE TO ATTACK FROM A LINE OF DEPARTURE U-566372--584346, 142 INF ATTACKING FREJUS AND 143 INF ATTACKING THROUGH ST RAPHEL AND BEACH 264A TO ARGENS RIVER TO CONTACT 45 INF DIV X 141 INF ADVANCED NORTH FROM BEACH 265A, LEADING ELEMENTS REACHED APPROXIMATELY S 295600 X 180 INF ADVANCED NORTH NORTHWEST AGAINST SLIGHT OPPOSITION, LEADING ELEMENTS REACHING U 460290, U 490315 AND U 5530 X 157 INF ADVANCED WEST AND SOUTHWEST, LEADING ELEMENTS REACHING U 440177, U455215 AND U 465255 X 179 INF LANDED AND ASSEMBLED VICIN-ITY U487226 X ELEMENTS OF 117 CAVALRY RE-CONNAISSANCE SQUADRON REACHED U 415242 AND U 450280 X SEVEN INF OF THREE INF DIV CON-TACTED FRENCH COMMANDO FORCE ALONG WEST

ROAD AT U365308 X 30 INF REACHED AREA U 3913---
(u 3916) X 2 BT 15 INF ATTACKING ST TROPEX AT
END OF PERIOD X NO CONTACT BETWEEN DIVI-
SIONS OF FRECN COMMANDOS LANDED SUCCESS-
FULLY AT CAP NEGRE AT 150230B X DESTROYED
BATTERY AND BLOCKED COASTAL ROAD TO THAT
AREA X ONE COUNTERATTACK REPULSED X PASS
TO CONTROL OF 6 CORPS AT 150800B X COMBAT
COMMAND SUDRE OF FRENCH ARMORED DIV AR-
RIVED IN ASSULT AREA PERPARED TO LAND OVER
45 DIV BEACHES PRIOR TO MIDNIGHT, 15 AUGUST X
ADVANCE INLAND PROCEEDED VERY SATISFA-
CORILY DURING THE AFTERNOON FROM BEACHES
WHICH WERE ASSULTED DURING MORNING X

That dispatch could well have been the earliest situation
reports for DRAGOON. It is good news because it fit the
plan very well, even showing that our forces were ahead of
the plan schedule. Every staff officer to any ranking officer
would rush this kind of news into his boss, and would hope
that the "good" part of the good news, would in some way
rub off on the messenger.

The next message is from COM WNTF, Commander
Western Naval Task Force, Admiral Hewitt.

170820B
SUCCESSFUL COMPLETION OF INITIAL PHASE OF
DRAGOON HAS BEEN MADE POSSIBLE BY EXCEL-
LENT PRELIMINARY TRAINING AND MATERIAL
PREPARATION AND BY EXCELLENT PERFORMANCE
OF DUTY IN ACTUAL OPERATION BY ALL CON-

CERNED. WELL DONE TO ALL. WE MUST NOW MAKE EVERY EFFORT TO LAND FOLLOW UP TROOPS AND SUPPLIES WITH MAXIMUM RAPIDITY AND SUPPORT ADVANCE.

It was good to hear from the man who has led you since the beginning of the Mediterranean operations and to learn from him that a "phase" had been successfully completed. I doubt if there was a hard and fast time line in the plan. I think that the leadership made these decisions ad hoc. The "initial phase" at Anzio took much longer than anticipated; it ended on the note of settling down for the long haul since we did not push the Germans out. At Southern France, the defenders were pushed out of there quickly and Hewitt sounded the note that our Allied forces' momentum requires the supply train to function on all cylinders. I must admit that during the combat period itself I really did not comprehend the big picture. While our forces at sea made some mistakes along the way and I could see those, I should have been giving greater credit to our leadership for the vision they had about how to win the war.

This next message came from Rear Admiral Deyo. He is passing along to us what our "customer", the 36th Division Commanding General, thought about our work.

-P- -A- 7W4 171413B 7WW4 GR 72 BT
GENERAL DAHLQUIST INFORMS ME THAT FROM HIS OWN OBSERVATIONS AND REPORTS FROM HIS COMMAND THE FIRE SUPPORT OF THIS GROUP WAS MOST EFFECTIVE AND WELL EXECUTED X GERMAN PRISONERS UNIFORMLY EXPRESSED ADMIRATION OF THE NAVAL GUN FIRE X I WAS PARTICULARLY PLEASED WITH THE INITIATIVE EFFI-

CIENCY AND BOLDNESS OF THE ORDRONAUX (a destroyer) IN PROTECTING THE BOAT WAVES DURING THE DELAYED LANDING X YOU HAVE ALL PERFORMED YOUR TASKS SKILFULLY AND THOROUGHLY X WELL DONE AND BEST LUCK BT - TOR: 1315

TOR stood for Time of Receipt. We still had tasks to perform, but nothing compared with the tasks of the 3rd, 36th and 45th Infantry Divisions of the U.S. Army as they became swallowed up in the landmass of Europe. They were not likely to see or hear or experience naval gunfire again in their lifetimes. Some of those lifetimes were short. The dispatch also contains "GR 72", which stands for Group 72, the word count. Military communication was often interrupted and incomplete so the word count helped the addressees to figure out if they had received the entire message. This is a redundancy, like the parity count in today's computer communications. Those readers who worked in some aspect of communications in war time can again see much in today's communication customs that owe a lot to practices developed in military communications. These practices go back well before World War II.

The final message is in two parts, one from SAC, the Supreme Allied Commander, General Eisenhower, either at his HQ in England or occasionally at the front with his Generals. One can sense in this exchange that Ike knew he would not be in touch with his Admirals like he had been over the past two years.

COMMANDER IN CHIEF HAS RECEIVED THE FOLLOWING MESSAGE FROM THE SUPREME ALLIED COMMANDER BEGINS AWILL YOU PLEASE CONVEY

TO ALL RANKS OF THE ALLIED NAVIES UNDER YOUR COMMAND MY CONGRATULATIONS AND THANKS FOR THE MASTERLY MANNER IN WHICH THE INVASION FORCES HAVE BEEN MARSHALED TRANSPORTED LANDED SUPPORTED AND SUPPLIED SINCE THE INCEPTION OF THE OPERATIONS IN SOUTHERN FRANCE THE REMARKABLE SUCCESS OF THE OPERATION COULD NOT HAVE BEEN ACHIEVED WITHOUT HAVING ALL BEEN DISPLAYED IN SUCH MARKED DEGREE. 251600 AUGUST. THE FOLLOWING REPLY HAS BEEN MADE TO THE SUPREME ALLIED NAVIES UNDER MY COMMAND. ALL OFFICERS AND MEN CONCERNED IN THE OPERATION OFF SOUTHERN FRANCE WILL BE HONORED BY YOUR PRAISE. THEY ARE PROUD OF THE PART THEY HAVE PLAYED IN CONTRIBUTING TO THE SUCCESS OF THE OPERATION UNDER YOUR SUPREME COMMAND WHICH HAS (led) TO THE 7TH ARMY GREAT VICTORY.

The Right Flank

There was still work to be done. I will reproduce a few words from the Edison's War Diary.

"The period from 17 August through 22 August was spent in giving close fire support to the post assault phase of Operation Anvil. Edison fired on an enemy observation post on 17 August and the SFCP reported 'fire very accurate.' On 18 August she fired on anti-aircraft batteries and an enemy pillbox with direct hits reported. The grand climax came on 21 August when she trained her guns toward enemy occupied buildings. Sixty rounds of 5-inch ammunition were fired into the buildings and a very elated SCFP reported, 'Direct hits, very good shooting.' "

"Again on 22 August Edison moved in to fire on an enemy strong point. Results for this bombardment were not observed due to a radio casualty. Later she was called on to destroy a concentration of enemy trucks. So effective was her fire that after 48 rounds, the shore party reported, "Mission successful, no vehicles left. Good shooting.' Two enemy gun emplacements also took the brunt of Edison's guns later in the day."

It was on the 22nd of August that Frank Barber, the gun captain of Gun #2, was hit by shrapnel from an enemy shell that landed up forward near the ship, and whose plume contained not just water but some "hard" stuff.

The period from 22 August to 22 September was extremely busy for the USS Edison. Cannes fell on the 24th of August and Nice on the 30th. All of the French coastline eastward from the landing beaches belonged to the Allies by 9 September. Edison was on fire station at all times except for a very short liberty time at St. Tropez. I can recall sitting in the Edison's Division Commander's cabin, my stateroom as long as we had no brass aboard, doing a little praying. I prayed "The Memorare" for those who know the prayer. It was, and is, my favorite prayer. I did not sleep much, but hung around the bridge even when I was not OOD. The calls for gunfire kept coming in, and the bridge crew would provide me early clues that I should be ready to get back up into the Director for General Quarters. Edison had tried Condition II's "watch and watch", keeping two guns manned, instead of the single ready gun during Condition III's "watch in three". World War II will never be replicated but if it were, as CO, I would never use "watch and watch". Helmsmen, and others including this author, simply slumped over onto the deck in a dead sleep. The human body just cannot manage it, so my wish was always to go to GQ and if necessary, eat cold rations there. At General Quarters, the ship is ready for anything; the watertight integrity is at its best, and the full crew is at the ready, whereas all other "conditions" involve a compromise.

Let me emphasize that this period was by no means a one-destroyer show. Twelve or more destroyers under Rear Admiral Deyo worked these same waters. Each ship experienced success, and each encountered some bizarre happening. One published report that 80 fire missions had been undertaken has to have been a major, and for military public relations, out-of-keeping, understatement. Some destroyers could count nearly 80 firing missions by themselves.

The Final Days for Edison's Primary Mission

We had guns. We had torpedoes. We had depth charges. While I was aboard, Edison never fired a torpedo in anger. We dropped hundreds of depth charges. We fired thousands of 5inch shells and used up three sets of gun barrels. A look at the Edison or any other destroyer of her class, a look at how space was allotted above decks and below for ordnance, and a look at the war records, all of those looks make the case that the designers got it right. Edison's primary mission involved her firepower. My last month aboard found me totally immersed in that mission. I was also the beneficiary of the selflessness of Edison's crew and their care of her equipment. From Lambert through Boyd and Hofer, Edison had the right leadership for her primary gunfire mission. Edison's Chief Petty Officers were outstanding and they worked to indoctrinate and inspire a crew second to none. That crew executed, in every way called upon. If the ship's gun power and its use validated the designers and the shipboard ordnance personnel, Edison had the supporting cast and propulsion systems that never failed to get her to the scene of action, on time, and ready. And also, out of trouble, when it came our way. We were lucky, too.

We fired during the night of the 23rd of August on a railroad gun and other gun emplacements. The SFCP could not ascertain the final damage because of darkness. On the 25th of August, in the Bay of Anges three miles southwest of Nice, Edison fired on a gun emplacement that was giving our troops a going over. After 60 rounds, we got the message, "Very good shooting. Several direct hits," from our SFCP. Edison fired again on the 26th on enemy troop concentrations with no confirmation of effect. Our most likely targets were now being found to the east of Monaco into Italy.

The 31st of August found Edison at the Southern end of Cape Martin firing on a gun emplacement. "Very good shooting." was the verdict. Later that day, another gun emplacement was pounded but ended in a "cease fire" when fire obscured the result. We were taking very little counter battery fire now, and there was very little enemy air activity. Because the water was deep, mines were much less of a problem. We had a couple of days of excitement defending against one-man human-guided torpedoes. One of our destroyers captured a German operator. This prisoner conveniently revealed where a second such weapon/operator was maneuvering and he too was captured and his weapon was sunk.

On 1 September 1944, Edison went back to the scene of the earlier gun emplacement where the results had been in doubt and after 55 rounds, the shore spotters reported, "Mission successful." We had three more targets that day. For the first of these, fire again obscured the results. For the second, the result was, "Target completely destroyed." This was an enemy gun in a house, and took 36 rounds.

Edison was very busy on 2 September 1944. The first mission involved a dual purpose defense gun (likely, an 88mm gun) and earned us a, "Mission successful." after 48 rounds. It took more rounds and more time for the next target but the SFCP gave us a "cease fire" and then "There is no more activity there." German mortar platoons were dealt with next and the effort deemed successful after 60 rounds. Late in the afternoon we went back to GQ at 1832. We expended 120 rounds to help our advancing troops take out a fort with the result, "pretty well destroyed." Edison also made enemy use of a highway a bit hazardous and ceased firing when our shore spotters told us, "That is good for now, will call later if we need you."

On 8 September, Edison was pulled out of the firing line and according the record, moored alongside the USS Denebola in the Gulf of St. Tropez. I do not recall this respite and was a little surprised when I did the research and discovered that the Denebola was over here with us. She is the support ship whose "embrace" we had left in April in Casco Bay, and a ship I had consigned forever to Casco Bay. I am sure that we used the three days for upkeep and then it was back to firing station on the 14th of September, 1944. I am almost sure there was no liberty ashore during this period, but we caught up on our sleep, and most likely had to "air bedding", always a way to keep us occupied when we had "nothing else to do." Our departure from St. Tropez was also the occasion for praise from ComCruDiv Eight, Rear Admiral Deyo, on USS Tuscaloosa. "The Edison, in the execution of fire support missions, both day and night, displayed an aggressive spirit. Her effective fire caused much damage to the enemy.

Her intrepidity under fire of hostile shore batteries was of the highest order." Although Hap Pearce still got a little hot under the collar when Rear Admiral Deyo's name came up, the latter must have observed the little backing down maneuver in the Golfe de Napoule when Pearce fooled that battery off Cannes. That is the only way I can interpret the phrase, "intrepidity under fire."

Back on station on the 14th, our first target was a self-propelled gun and 50 vehicles. After 72 rounds, the SFCP message was, "Mission accomplished. Very good shooting, all targets destroyed including self-propelled gun." The day's remaining two targets were exceptions to our diet of land targets. One was an enemy merchant ship with another, unidentified object, in the water near that ship. Both took several hits from Edison's guns. The merchantman was left settling in the water and the other target sank before it could be identified. Writing almost 54 years later, the possibility that this was a human torpedo with its mother ship occurs to me. On the 15th, we took a bridge south of Cape Mortola under fire. This bridge was important because it could support German armor being brought in to harass our landing force. We used 28 rounds, and in effect damaged the approaches to the bridge so that the bridge itself was temporarily "out of service." A convoy of trucks was then disabled as a consequence of making the road they were on impassable.

On the 16th the Edison was at work five separate times. A gun emplacement, a supply warehouse, a storage tank, a troop concentration with trucks and support personnel absorbed 91 rounds. The storage tank took 14 rounds by itself but smoke obscured results. The heavy concentration of troops and trucks, all near the gun emplacement, brought this evaluation, "Tore hell out of battery. Every round counted. Men and trucks are dispersed." This had taken another 89 rounds. The 17th was a similar day. There were five targets. Threats from enemy coastal guns, troops, and trucks were eliminated and a bridge was reduced.

Liberty at St. Tropez

We were sent back to St. Tropez, this time for liberty ashore. While anchored off a now peaceful St. Tropez, I was among those permitted to go on liberty. I went with the Captain and a couple of others to a villa owned by an American and commandeered by some military unit as an "entertainment club." There was a pool and we swam. They had wine and we drank. I drank too much, much too much. I realized I needed to get back to the ship so I left on foot to go to the landing we were using. I took a short cut, I was told later, through fields that had not been swept for land mines. The luck of the inebriated, I assume, got me to the dock. I was noisy aboard the whaleboat (gig) and insisted on sitting on the engine cover, a no-no. The Executive Officer had come from some other duty and was also aboard and properly objected to my "condition." When I got back on Edison, I was informed by the OOD that the Executive Officer had confined me to my quarters and relieved me of my duties. This disciplinary action occurred, according to my 1985 inspection of the Edison's log at the National Archives on Pennsylvania Avenue in Washington D.C., on the 20-24 watch on 20 September, 1944. The next entry of interest to me during that National Archives visit 40 years after the incident, appeared in the 08-12 log of 21 September, 1944. I discovered that Dailey was returned to duty in view of "present operating conditions", and the Edison was underway at 1546 on the 21st to relieve the USS Ludlow on firing station.

It was good for me that we were busy again, firing on the 22nd. Remorse is better handled with some distracting "activity." And heaven knows if I would have been sent back to duty had it not been for the need to go back to the firing area. I saw Captain Pearce a couple of times in later years, and Stanley Craw once, and neither seemed to have had my inappropriate episode on their minds. Mostly, I was ashamed and shame is with oneself.

The first targets on the 22nd of September 1944 were a storage dump containing gasoline and equipment, enemy artillery emplacements, troops and a mortar platoon. A bridge and a rail terminal were also fired on. Flames at or near the storage dump gave us an indication of success there. One last target deserves special mention.

My Last Go at Gunnery; an "Interested" Spectator

On 22 September 1944, the day after being released from my deserved confinement to quarters, we were working up the coast well east of Cannes, past the Italian Riviera toward a place in Italy called Ventimiglia. This trip began had begun on a stunning Riviera day and the first "shoots" had been rather routine. (See earlier paragraphs.) We had been told that there was an active 88mm battery at Ventimiglia. I never found out what that place was twenty miles from, and would wish later that it had been twenty miles from us. The Edison and the Woolsey were told to find the battery, and "take it out." Finding enemy artillery emplaced and camouflaged ashore is not an assignment for destroyers. The only way to do it without a SFCP or air spotting, and we had neither, was Admiral Deyo's Southern France D-day prescription to "draw their fire." So we worked our way east and gradually closed the shore to five or six thousand yards. Suddenly, we were in the fight of our lives. A four gun, 88mm, radar-controlled battery opened up on us and *their ranging salvo was right on*. That battery could fire as fast as we could. He knew where we were, obviously, and we had little idea where he was. No flashes and no smoke were visible ashore. Yes, we fired, but like the sweepers that the Ludlow guarded at Anzio, we could only shoot at where fire "might" be coming from. Unlike Ludlow's sweepers at Anzio on their final pass, these Germans were firing rapidly, and accurately, at us.

Like cornered animals, Woolsey and Edison twisted and turned and built to top speed of over thirty knots on two boilers. Our only strategy was to open the range, but we had to change target angle constantly and hope the accuracy of the German radar in ranging was not matched by a rapid calculating fire control system. To mask our target angles, both destroyers immediately made smoke from the chemical generators first, and then with their power plants too. I estimate that we were within easy range of a four-gun 88mm battery for fifteen agonizing minutes. We finally abandoned shooting at them, knowing that the shoreline itself was now out of our range, in addition to not being sure where they were.

Salvo after salvo landed right alongside Edison and Woolsey. It helped that there were two of us. Two targets to track, both behind smoke and both changing course at high speed, prevented the shore battery from picking us off one at a time. My final assessment is that the German MPI-Mean Point of Impact- was too tight. Four shells missed over and then four shells would miss short. The Germans were not getting a straddle with a single salvo. We escaped, with prayers, and a sheepish feeling of having accomplished nothing worth talking about or recording. I am almost embarrassed to present it here.

On the 24th of September at 2202, Edison rendezvoused with USS Philadelphia and sailed for Marseilles, arriving on the 25th. It was my only visit to that great port, now in our hands, and I did not get ashore. On the evening of the 25th, we left with the Philly to go to St. Tropez, leaving on the 26th for Oran, where Edison moored alongside the SS Yankee Arrow at Mers el Kebir on 28 September, 1944. We would move over alongside the Vulcan the next day.

The Story of the Yankee Arrow

In the Web edition of this tale, the beginning and the end of mention of the Yankee Arrow was the line in the paragraph above. On May 26, 1998 I finished the final words of the Web edition and had posted the closing Chapter Twelve on the website. That same day, I received an e-mail from Seward Buckley. He wrote that his father-in-law served in the Armed Guard on the Yankee Arrow. One question Seward posed was the casualty count on the Yankee Arrow and another was that ship's final disposition.

Memories come back a bit at a time. When Edison arrived off Oran on 28, September 1944, twenty-seven months in the war zone were coming to an end for me. We came alongside the Yankee Arrow in the gathering darkness of that late September day. I had only the slightest recall of that last visit to Mers-el-Kebir when Seward Buckley's e-mail arrived. A glimmer of a thought then came down to me through the years that all was not right that evening on the Yankee Arrow. I must have been too wrapped up in my impending trip to the USA to inquire further. Usually, my native curiosity would have led to some questions on my part.

We had arrived off Oran with the USS Philadelphia. Philly was an imposing U.S. cruiser. Her berth had been picked out before arrival. She had an Admiral aboard. Destroyers were berthed wherever there was room and occasionally had to lie to while berthing decisions were being made. My original impression of that last Mediterranean port entry was that we were temporarily to tie up alongside the

Yankee Arrow and the next day we would be moved to our own berth when the morning traffic departed.

In failing to be more aware that something was amiss with the Yankee Arrow I even failed to note that she was a tanker. Whenever possible, the first priority of a port director or harbormaster in receiving a wartime destroyer was to get her fueled. I am sure now that my concerns about a temporary moor were selfish. I possibly thought of having to change berths as a potential interference with my own departure from Edison. It is almost a certainty that we went alongside Yankee Arrow that evening to take fuel aboard from her.

What was there about the Yankee Arrow that would have more fully engaged my attention had I not been so self-absorbed? An important source for maritime historians looking into World War II is "A Careless Word.....A Needless Sinking", by Captain Arthur R. Moore. The name of the book does not do it justice. The name, indeed the cover itself, was taken from Poster #24 published for the U.S. Office of War Information. I could not find a single instance in the book for which that warning was applicable. Moore's book stands as a carefully researched compendium of U.S. flag merchant ship losses in World War II. With that book as a reference, I determined (in 1998) that the Yankee Arrow was one of a family of "Yankee...." tankers built for Socony Vacuum Oil Co. at Camden NJ in 1921. She displaced 8046 Gross Tons, was 441 feet long, with a beam of 57 feet and a draft of 37 feet. Socony stood for Standard Oil Co. of New York, part of the Rockefellers' Standard Oil empire. When the U.S. government forced Standard Oil to break up, Socony Vacuum became Mobil, Standard Oil of NJ became Esso, then Exxon, and so on. Her picture shows Yankee Arrow to have a tanker's long silhouette, with the relatively high stack aft characteristic of World War I construction and a low bridge structure forward.

Still using Captain Moore's data, Yankee Arrow began her last departure from the U.S. in convoy UGS-9, leaving May 2, 1943. Her skipper was John Belgonen. Ship's company included 42 merchant mariners and 25 in the Naval Armed Guard detachment.

One member of that detachment was David Lloyd Fluharty Sr., Seward Buckley's father-in-law. David enlisted in late 1942 (like so many, his draft notice came in the mail a day or so after his enlistment) and sailed aboard the Yankee Arrow as a deck rating in her Armed Guard. Before the war ended, David had become a Boatswain's Mate 1/c ready to take the exam for Chief Boatswain's Mate. He recalls that the Yankee Arrow with UGS-9 took the southern route, and arrived in Algiers in June 19, 1943. The convoy's 8-9 knot pace and the ocean steaming distance of her long southern sea transit accounted for the five weeks at sea. Possibly because Yankee Arrow sported a 4"50 cal. gun on her stern, a 3"50 forward and numerous 20mm guns, she was assigned a sailing station at the center rear of the convoy and carried the U.S. Navy's Convoy Commodore. The southern route might encounter subs, the Mediterranean portion of the passage was exposed to enemy aircraft and the U.S. was still short of destroyers. Destroyer escorts were just coming available. This was 1943.

Yankee Arrow shifted ports from Algiers to Oran in late June or July 1943. Mediterranean shipping lanes were buzzing with activity as Tunisia fell and the landings on Sicily began. At 0700 on the morning of August 3, 1943, en-route in convoy from Oran to Sicily with her precious fuel cargo, Yankee Arrow hit a mine. Allied sweeps were already on 24-hour duty in the Tunisian War Channel but mines remained and floaters were an ever-present threat. Fire immediately enveloped the tanker forward and rapidly spread back to the midships area. David Fluharty recalls that he had just gotten into a hammock under a gun turret when the blast dumped him out onto the deck but did not severely injure him. Survivors forward had to jump into the water because of the heat and flame, while survivors aft began to fight the fire and give aid to the burned and to those who had jumped. Fluharty recalls cutting rafts loose for the men overboard. Captain Moore's book states that the British destroyer HMS Cleveland (L-46) and the Polish destroyer Krakowiak, (L-115) stood by. Doctors aboard the destroyers gave first aid to men picked out of the water who had been doused with burning oil. The Yankee Arrow got her fire under control in half an hour made it to landfall off Bizerte by late morning under her own power. Channel entry to Lake Bizerte was considerably delayed. A sunken ship blocked the passage. This obstacle was being worked on and had to be dismasted and moved to provide clearance under the tanker's keel. While waiting some days to use the channel, David Fluharty recalls that the Yankee Arrow had to refuel one of Italy's surrendered destroyers. It seems that Italy had capitulated while Yankee Arrow was in her precarious wait for approval to use the channel into Lake Bizerte. He recalls that Yankee Arrow's crew felt that refueling an Italian warship so soon after hitting an enemy mine was "hard to take."

Five members of the merchant crew lost their lives, along with two men in the Armed Guard. The ship's Purser, Ray E. Jett, died at 1530. Two men taken to Malta and one man taken to Bizerte died of their wounds. Edward Pesibry, an AB, was never accounted for. The other casualties were Wiper John Findlay, Ordinary Seaman Jesus Guerra and

Utilityman Willard R. Johnson. Captain Moore's book did not list the names of the Armed Guardsmen who were lost.

The Yankee Arrow served as station fueling ship in Bizerte until her cargo was gone. She was then put in drydock in Bizerte. The most urgent emergency work was done and she was declared fit to proceed to Oran. At Oran, with its more substantial repair facility, the Yankee Arrow again went into drydock. David Fluharty recalls extensive examination and discussion about repairs. The assessment that the damage had come from a mine was confirmed. The final decision was that Yankee Arrow would not sail again. On December 9, 1943, after necessary repairs, she was made a fueling station ship in Mers-el-Kebir and in January 1944 custody was turned over to the French. Her U.S. merchant crewmen were sent back to the States. David Fluharty did not wait that long for reassignment. He was first ordered aboard the Booker T. Washington, a Liberty ship. In a letter dated 18 June, 1998, David wrote, that to his knowledge the Booker T. was the only ship at the time with a black skipper. While at anchorage with other ships staging for the Anzio invasion, the Booker T. Washington was severely damaged in a bad storm. Apparently some ships dragged their anchors and swung into others, causing damage to all. After temporary repairs, the Booker T. Washington returned to the U.S. David Fluharty was then ordered to the Amphibious Force and went on to further service in the Pacific until war's end.

New Duties Beckon

My shipboard duties were completed 30 September 1944. I had had orders to naval flight training for some time. I was awaiting a relief (stipulated as a necessary requirement for my detachment by our Captain) in the person of an officer from a South Pacific minesweeper, who, of course, never came. To the consternation of the Captain, I was then detached "without relief" in a modification of my original orders. John Perry, a Naval Academy graduate from the Class of 1944, was detached with me. He also had orders to flight training. We were directed to wait in Oran, Algiers for an Army Air Force (MATS-Military Air Transport Service) C-47 to take us to Port Lyautey in Morocco. Then, as it turned out, we would leave on an Army Air Force C-54 for Patuxent River Naval Air Station, Maryland, via landings in the Azores and Newfoundland. The flight crew came from American Export Airline's early international operations. These men had received commissions in the U.S. armed forces.

Edison left Oran on 1 October, 1944, and resumed escort duties along with some training exercises. She made port stops in Gibraltar, Oran, Toulon, Marseilles, Naples, Horte in the Azores, and New York where she arrived with a convoy on 17 January for an extended yard overhaul. On 16 February, while backing out of her slip at Earle, New Jersey, the SS Benedick struck Edison. No personnel were injured, but Edison sustained a bad gash and required immediate and extensive yard repairs. These took until 7 March 1945 when she again went to Earle for ammo and resumed her place in active service. On the 17th of May 1945, Lieutenant Commander W. J. Caspari, USN relieved Commander H. A. Pearce as CO, USS Edison. Stanley Craw had left earlier. In an amazing coincidence, Pearce and Craw were reunited as CO and XO respectively of the destroyer USS Sarsfield in their next duty. (Lieutenant Commander Sarsfield had been the skipper of the Maddox, lost in the Gela landings at Sicily. He did not survive the bombing by a Nazi plane.)

In two closing chapters, I will cover a few more details of the Edison's career from the beginning of 1945 until her decommissioning in 1946. For the remainder of Edison's sea journeys I will be relying on official records and the memories of other officers and men.

At Ventimiglia, Italy, on September 22, 1944, both Dailey and Edison had fired their last round in anger in World War II. Until writing this story, that fact had completely eluded me. It still seems amazing in retrospect. The war had another year to go. War's end seemed a distant prospect in September 1944, too distant for me to ever contemplate in calendar terms. Thousands upon thousands would still die. God bless them all.

Chapter Eleven - Germany Capitulates

Form a Task Force, Execute a Mission, Disperse

Gather, operate, disperse. That sequence described our lives. There was little time to reflect on what happened to the assault troops that we had helped get ashore. Where now, after the landing, were Army divisions like the 3rd Infantry, the 36th Infantry, the 45th Infantry, the First Armored, and units of Darby's Rangers? Their peril extended long after our primary missions were accomplished. Their sacrifices brought us victory in the titanic land war in Europe. This distancing from the realities of our most recent soldier-partners occurred even with our own sister warships. We were with them for times and then separated for times.

DesRon 13, as a squadron of destroyers, had faded into history by the middle of 1944. DesDiv 25, one of the two original DesRon 13 divisions, consisting of the Ludlow, Woolsey and Edison with the addition at times of Benson, Mayo, or Madison, worked together occasionally, but war stirred the pot constantly. The original destroyer relationships of 1942 gave way by 1944 to newly constructed and intact, squadrons of destroyers and destroyer escorts. The destroyer escorts were now the backbone of ASW. Many of the surviving early World War II Benson/Livermore destroyers came to be identified as those specialized in the close in, "shoot 'em up" missions. Some of those early destroyers were still present in ASW screens, but were there now primarily to enhance a convoy's anti-aircraft defense capability. Such was the duty the destroyer USS Lansdale was executing when she was sunk in April, 1944.

An Allied defeat at Salerno would have been a major setback. Indeed, as I learned later, there had been high level discussion during its early phase of abandoning the hard won southern beachhead and lightering those troops off to link up with the British who had the northern sector responsibility. That would have been an enormously complicated maneuver, totally unplanned with respect to availability of assault craft and support ships. Morale would have taken a terrific jolt. Had the German High Command been willing to pull down its troops in northern Italy to join Kesselring in the Naples/Salerno area, they might have hurled us back at Salerno. That did not happen. The U.S. forces, instead of pulling back, brought in all the reserves available from Sicily and with their naval gunfire ships as artillery, beat the Germans back and won the day. Anzio worked out to be a long and soldier-wise, costly, effort. It was costly at sea, too. Our effort to advance north of Naples, with its ill-defined objectives, stalled out. At the Anzio beachhead, as at Salerno, the Germans attempted a major counter thrust but the Allies, in both cases, were prepared to make sure that it failed. Finally, at Southern France, those of us in the assault business could begin to see that the Allies now had the makings of victory in their grasp.

No Specific Turning Point, But Clues Were There

In those days, I certainly did not develop any sense of a specific turning point for the war in Europe. Each of us stayed focused on the day's challenges. Salerno taught those of us in the assault business that our teamwork with the Army had blossomed into a formidable amphibious warfare capability. I sensed the changes in strategy along the way but I could not have articulated them. The success of the landings in Southern France, with our 7th Army advancing north to link up with the Normandy invasion forces, demonstrated that the Allies were up to more than a general tightening of the screws on Hitler in Europe. The Allies were now ready to carve up some of his armies

The picture at sea in the Atlantic and Mediterranean was improving too. Again I doubt if those involved in that still very dangerous convoy work were aware of a turning point. Later in this Chapter, this story will take another look at what was happening at sea. We will re-visit the challenges met by convoys, spanning six months in time, for the transits in the western Mediterranean required to bring supplies to Italy, Southern France, Egypt, India and Russia. Those consulting just the specific reports covering the actions of those convoys, who had not been told how it all came out might infer that the issue of the European seawar was as much in doubt in the Fall of 1944 as in the Fall of 1943.

This was actually not the case at all. Within the times framed by convoys KMF-25A and UGS-38, the situation changed dramatically. Convoys were loading in England and in east coast ports of the U.S. for their ultimate destinations. Intermediate stopping points were no longer needed for contingency purposes. Reflecting those new realities, in a change of escort strategy, convoys in 1944 would now keep their screens and naval command structure intact from port of origination to port of destination.

Let me reemphasize that World War II destroyer-men rarely discoursed at any length about the overall course of the war. For just one reason, they were too busy.

The Allied High Command: 1942 to War's End

For the core of this story, I was a very junior officer. I accepted the naval leadership structure without question. I have commented on some glitches along the way. I now have the benefit of an examination, after 55 years, of the U.S. military leadership and the structure that President Franklin Roosevelt put in place in the immediate aftermath of Pearl Harbor. I can now better see how this group of U.S. leaders lent their talents and energies to the creation of what became known as the Allied High Command.

For the most part, the Allied commands did not permit themselves to get into thinking ruts. When the leadership perceived that our side had gained an advantage, they were quick to exploit that advantage. Though not viewable from the deck of a destroyer, there was a "big picture", and our military leaders lost little time in exploiting the advantages gained. Historians have accorded U.S. World War II leaders deserved recognition as heroes. From my own re-examination of the destroyer war in the Atlantic and Mediterranean areas, I have developed other appreciations for those wartime leaders. For the most part, they listened to each other. The majority of them were very smart. They knew what they could count on from the "rank and file" and they pushed it hard. At the outset of this story, it never entered my mind that I would be presenting such views. The story itself convinced me.

Coming back to the Edison and the destroyer perspective, by 1944 I could see that assault landings had become a specialty for some destroyers. Convoy work had become a specialty for destroyer escorts, with U.S. destroyers and British cruisers supplementing convoy screens for Anti Aircraft defense upon entering the Mediterranean. At Gibraltar, or at Alboran Island, just inside the western Mediterranean, these AA supplement ships would be added to the eastbound convoys. The Allied High Command now had the luxury of putting past experience to work, rather than plugging any available ship into emergency service to fill slots.

In Chapter Twelve, I will take another page or two from the annals of our sister destroyers in the Pacific War. The Edison was to go to the Pacific before her World War II duties were over. An unlikely communications event on the Edison in 1944 brought me then to a brief side-glance at that Pacific War.

FCTF-Pacific

One evening when the Edison was anchored in the Bay of Naples, and I was the OOD in port, the Captain came back from liberty. He had had a few. Liquor, or wine, whatever, the stuff loosened him up. He was normally a very quiet, introspective man. He was also very intelligent. I have not researched his class standing at the Naval Academy, but he had that kind of native intelligence that does not always translate into high class standing. His mind was constantly at work. And during World War II, his mind was always at work on how to beat the enemy.

This particular evening, the skipper came into the wardroom. That was unusual. His normal place to be was either in his stateroom in port, or in his emergency stateroom on the bridge or the bridge itself when underway. A destroyer skipper in World War II got very, very little sleep.

There was no activity in the wardroom that evening. It was after dinner and few officers were aboard. Lieutenant Commander Hepburn A. Pearce sat down on the transom. Called "transoms", these were wide divans along the skin of the ship. There was one on each side of the wardroom under the now plugged-up portholes. (Quite distinct from the transom found across the top of a door, there is a nautical tradition for the word "transom" as used here.) These were divans, long enough to sleep on (often officers in transit had to sleep on them), which were made of some synthetic, leather-like material. It was like the Naugahyde automobile replacement seat covering used after the war. These materials were all supposed to be flameproof. Just as I was about to go back to the quarterdeck, the Captain said, "Frank, is the Communications Officer aboard?" I knew that he was aboard, and that the man he wanted was Lieutenant Chancy Torrance. (Mother, I hated it when you called me France, but I forgave you when I discovered that Chancy was a name option that you did not pick.) Chauncey Torrance was one of the most engaging men I have ever met. I knew him a little extra because I was one of the four officers aboard who knew the emergency code setting of the Electric Coding Machine-ECM, before that acronym was usurped by Electronic Counter Measures. I called for Chauncey to come to the wardroom. He probably never forgave me. He was about to be introduced to a kind of "sweat" exercise.

"Chauncey, I want to send a Secret dispatch to the Commander Fast Carrier Task Forces-Pacific." said the Captain. Chauncey looked like he had been struck by lightning, but give him a lot of credit, he kept his cool. The skipper was always doodling his ideas on those little communications pads, and he had been working on this one, as Chauncey and I realized when he told us, "Go over this to see that I have not made any grammar errors or left anything out." Now, both Chauncey and I knew that the Captain was part of a destroyer chain of command in Naples, Italy, and that there were a dozen or more "higher authorities" between the Edison and an Admiral in the Pacific. We also knew that this dispatch would have to go to Radio Annapolis and then to Radio San Diego and out across the Pacific. And we also knew that if you were not an addressee you were not supposed to "break", i.e. decode, messages not intended for you. And we also knew that that protocol was constantly breached and that surely some high command along the way, puzzled, would break that message. And that then we would all be in some federal prison. When we read what he wanted to send, we knew we had to talk him out of it. Here is my best recollection of the dispatch.

"To: COMMANDER FAST CARRIER TASK FORCES PACIFIC (we found out later it was Admiral Marc Mitscher)
From: COMMANDING OFFICER, USS EDISON
Subject: NIGHT ATTACK TACTICS ON JAPANESE FLEET

"Launch black cat squadron (these were night flying lagoon-based PBY seaplane aircraft) to get in behind Japanese Fleet at night. Direct these planes to drop flares behind Japanese warships. Launch dive-bombers and torpedo bombers from your carriers before dawn, timed to get Japanese Fleet silhouetted in front of flares dropped by black cat planes. Deliver attack and recover carrier aircraft after dawn."

/s/ H.A. Pearce, Commanding Officer, USS Edison"

With courage, Chauncey spoke first. "Captain, I know you have given a lot of thought to this. I know that your earlier experience being attacked by the Japanese aircraft in the South Pacific has made you think a lot about what we could do to counter attack. This is entirely logical and there are no errors that I can see. It gives us a weapon we would not normally have because our carriers do not operate planes at night. But please Captain, protocol would suggest that you might go to our Division Commander and see if he has an idea as to how to get this idea put into play."

"Thanks Chauncey, but the idea will be squashed if we do it that way." the Captain responded. "Send it out." I was an onlooker. I had no ideas about how we could even slow this one down. We actually spent more than minutes, probably an hour to try to keep the Skipper from getting, at the very least, a reprimand. Chauncey took the dispatch and Chauncey sent it out.

Two weeks later Chauncey Torrance brought me a copy of a Speedmail. It was addressed to the CO USS Edison and signed by Admiral Mitscher. Speedmail was a sealed envelope containing official mail that was physically moved by the fastest available, secure, aircraft courier service. It said, in effect, "Thank you for your suggestion. It is incorporated into our battle plans and will be considered for use at the first opportunity that circumstances permit. I am always happy to receive suggestions from the commanders of destroyers under my command."

Zowie! That little dispatch had gotten all the way to the Admiral in the Pacific, who first treated it with the respect its originality required, and then did not even look up to see if the Edison was a part of his Force. Mitscher's instinctive thought was to thank the originator. And despite my fears and Chauncey's foreboding, for once the protocol was observed and no one along the way decoded ("broke" was the vernacular word) the message.

I can recall an event where an officer of the Edison and I, and events where some of the petty officer watch standers and I, were partners in some challenge like the one above. Most of these were little pieces of ordinary life. When the Captain wanted to "vent" a little on the TBS about the Admiral's "draw their fire" strategy, Lt. (jg) Marvin Tanner down in our new CIC right under the pilot house would find something that interrupted the TBS transmitter. A few collaborative events were life threatening, thankfully very few.

Chasing a loose 600-pound depth charge on the main deck aft was one where a torpedoman and I gave up finally when the solid green water almost put both of us over the side. Let it roll around and hope that the safety train keeps it unarmed. In Chapter Ten, I covered an assignment that Joe Dwyer and I carried out together in Casco Bay. Joe, now 82 (in 1998) favored me with a story of an event that occurred after I left the Edison. I will get to Joe Dwyer's story near the end of this chapter

Convoys Transit the Mediterranean

KMF-25A

As Hitler's Mediterranean sea bases were overrun in 1943 and early 1944, the number of his subs in the Mediterranean declined. Goering's air force endeavored to fill the breach in interdicting Allied shipping in the Mediterranean. KMF-25A, originating in the United Kingdom with cargo in 26 ships for Palermo and Naples transited into the eastbound Tunisian War Channel of the Mediterranean on 6 November, 1943. The escort force of eight U.S. destroyers was under U.S. command, both force and command a rarity for this routing of a United Kingdom-originating convoy. HMS Colombo, an AA cruiser, plus three British Hunt class destroyers and two Greek destroyer escorts supplemented the U.S. destroyer screen. At sunset, all escorts went to battle stations as Allied fighters returned to their bases. Just after sunset, U.S. destroyer Laub's radar picked up a number of aircraft to the north. Laub was the assigned radar picket ship out ahead of the convoy and similar dispositions found U.S. destroyers Beatty and Tillman on the starboard and port quarters, respectively. All destroyers made smoke. From about 1800 to 1830, Luftwaffe glide bomb and torpedo attacks were pressed home. The U.S. destroyer Beatty was hit by a torpedo in the after engine room about 1815. With her keel broken, Beatty sank about 2300. Once the escort screen had been punctured, two transports were torpedoed. These were the SS Santa Elena, of U.S. registry and the Dutch merchantman, the Marnix van St. Aldegonde. Edison had convoyed the latter ship many times. The U.S. screen commander directed five of his screen destroyers plus transports Monterey and Ruyz (Dutch registry) to assist in rescue operations. Four more U.S. destroyers were ordered out of Algiers and tugs were ordered out of Philippeville to assist in the rescue operations. Santa Elena sank in the outer harbor of Philippeville and the Aldegonde grounded on the way in. Over 6,000 men were rescued. Loss of life was greatly minimized by effective rescue efforts.

KMF-26

The personnel rescue success of Convoy KMF-25A was not repeated with Convoy KMF-26, which sustained grievous human loss on 26 November 1943. Again, German air delivered the damaging weapons. A coordinated attack by planes carrying glide bombs, and others carrying torpedoes, was made. These attacks usually took up an entire hour. This almost casual approach on the part of the Luftwaffe was probably because Allied fighter cover was usually withdrawn at sunset. The attack on KMF-26 began about 1640, well before the 1730 sunset. The USS Pioneer's action report states that two friendly fighters were covering on station and more came in as the attack proceeded. KMF-26 received shadowing aircraft warnings from Mediterranean shore-based stations but received no warning of actual aircraft attack. For my first insights on this attack, I am indebted to Drake Davis, Webmaster of the USS Savannah. His research diligence uncovered reports from the British Naval Historical Branch, the U.S. National Archives and Records Administration, the U.S. Army, and CinClantFlt regarding the sinking of the troopship SS Rohna. Drake provided copies of much of his archive from which I drew material related to KMF-26. According to a 5 May 1944 report of the Casualty Branch of the U.S. Army's Adjutant General's Office, the attack began about 1700 hours and originated on the port quarter of the convoy that was on course 100 degrees True. At its inception therefore, sun or horizon favored neither attacker nor defender.

The Henschel Hs 293 glide bomb was now a preferred Luftwaffe weapon against convoys at sunset and approaching darkness. Within our convoys, radio link jamming equipment was now available. It was new (late 1943) and not yet completely installed so we did not have much experience in using it. With escorts absorbed in dodging torpedoes from one section of German aircraft, other German aircraft could deliver radio-controlled glide bombs with a much better chance of hitting major convoy targets. From the glide bomb carrying aircraft, a target would be selected. That plane, acting as "mother" plane would descend to about 4,000 feet on a course parallel to the target. Just forward of the target's beam, the rocket-powered missile would be released. Initially, it would be controlled to fly parallel to the mother plane while radio-link flight controls were checked out. Then the missile would be turned toward the target and nosed over to get down to an approach altitude near the water in level flight. At the chosen point the missile would be nosed into the target. This final phase could be accompanied by any last minute course correction needed. Merchant ships and LSTs were favorite targets, since they were capable of putting up the least flak and were incapable of last minute maneuvers to avoid being hit.

411

As it left Gibraltar behind, KMF-26 proceeded with 17 ships in five columns screened by ten escorts. Destination was Port Said, Egypt. In company with four other ships, the SS Rohna sailed from Oran on 25 November 1943 and joined the convoy at 1530 on the 25th. She became the second ship in the port column and her 2nd officer, J.E. Wills, in his report to the Admiralty, stated that the convoy was then in 6 columns and totaled 24 ships. Rohna, out of India but with Canadian Registry, had 2,000 U.S. troops aboard, with their equipment, and a crew of 218. The minesweeper, USS Pioneer, AM105, also joined the convoy off Oran, Algiers on the 25th. Six escorts were British and four were U.S. In addition to Pioneer, the USS Portent, the U.S. Destroyer Escorts Herbert C. Davis and the Frederick C. Jones were in the escort. For the afternoon of the 26th, 2nd Officer Wills' reported good visibility with the sea made up in a long swell.

The following paragraph appears in the "Remarks" section of the USS Pioneer's report to CincLant:

"No messages were received prior to or during the attack regarding enemy planes or convoy action. We received no information on joining convoy, as to who was the senior escort. We had no radio code call assigned."

A report by 2nd Officer Wills of the Rohna:

"No warnings of enemy aircraft were received. I came off the bridge at 1620 on the 26th of November (1943) and went to my cabin for tea. About ten minutes later I thought I heard gunfire. I had just arrived on the bridge when I saw a splash in the water about 100 feet from the stern of the anti-aircraft cruiser HMS Coventry. The Coventry was at this time ahead of the centre of the convoy, off our starboard bow. (This was likely the HMS Colombo. There is no mention of Coventry in official KMF-26 action reports. The identity of the U.S.

escorts present, and their location, is consistent in the various action reports. The British Naval Historical Branch report of 30 November 1943 by the British Senior Officer present and the Pioneer action reports do not agree as to the British ships present. The British report also speaks of three Do-217s in the early part of the raid before the Heinkel 177s arrived.).........The extra 2nd Officer ran to sound the alarm bells, and everyone went to action stations. (Rohna carried one 4"gun, one 12 pounder, six Oerlikons, two Hotchkiss, and two Twin Lewis) For the next forty minutes there were enemy aircraft constantly in sight...They kept out of range and appeared to be attacking the escorts....I saw several glider bombs released. At this time I did not know anything about these glider bombs, to me they appeared to be British fighters attacking the bombers and being shot down."

The convoy did not alter course or reduce speed. The enemy planes continued skirting the convoy, making direct attacks on the escorts, and I learned later that a torpedo attack was made on the convoy; their intention was to cripple the escorts before attacking the merchant ships. Shortly after 1700 several other enemy aircraft appeared, and at one time I saw four in formation off the port quarter. At 1725, I observed two bombers approaching from the port quarter, flying at approximately 3,000 feet. One attacked the ship ahead, the other, when he was abeam of us, swerved towards us and launched a bomb from about 2 points before the beam. At this time we were 15 miles from Djidjelli, North Africa, steering 100 degrees true at 12 knots."

"When first released the bomb appeared to be a little below and to the starboard of the plane, it then closed the plane, shot downwards, swerving to the right of the plane and a red glow appeared in its nose. When it was half way I realized that it was a glider bomb; I gave orders for the port Oerlikon to fire, but I do not think any hits were scored. The bomb struck the ship in the engine room on the port side, just above the water line. No. 4 bulkhead collapsed, and the Radio Officer who was on the boat deck at the time said that a lot of debris, soldier's kits, tin hats etc. were thrown into the air. (The bomb struck a troop compartment. The consensus was that not less than 300 men were either killed outright then or injured beyond helping themselves.) The vessel listed slightly to starboard, the shell plates about 6 feet above the water level on both the port and starboard sides were blown upward and outward. I went to the boat deck and released the bolly bands from the boats....The Master decided that nothing could be done and ordered 'Abandon Ship'. (Since all electrical power had been lost, this order was not broadcast throughout the ship.)"

One of the post-action reports states that the plane controlling these glide bombs would stay well out of 20mm and 40mm fire ranges. One report recommended using the small caliber weapons to fire at the bomb itself.

The rest of the Rohna story is pure disaster. 1,015 of the 2,000 troops in passage were lost. Discipline was lost. The following is a paragraph that Charles Finch, a U.S. Army survivor of the disaster, wrote in his story, "Death! An Instant Away".

"Screams of pain and fright are coming from everywhere in the total darkness, but soon with help the bunks are lifted from the several trapped men and we check for injuries. The choking dust and smoke is beginning to clear away and we see a faint light coming from the open door that leads out into the open deck as we are helped to our feet. (Finch's body had taken shrapnel that remained embedded and proved painful but not life threatening.) Three of the men seem to be dead and two others are battered and bruised but safe for the moment at least. The back of my shirt is soaked with blood but as yet there is no pain. When I see all the wood splinters lying on the floor I realized that I must have been scratched as I flew along the floor. I am elated that I am one of the lucky ones."

"Then I saw Joe. He and I had volunteered to help with the deck gun and he had been picked. There he was with one arm gone, part of the left side of his face missing and blood all over the place. He saw me and stuck out his hand and said, 'help me', in sort of a high pitched voice not unlike a small child. But there was nothing I could do. He died right there before me. I was in shock!"

The story of attempts to launch boats is full of equipment failures, crew failure and troop panic. Charles Finch reports the boat launching equipment was all rusted and the boats impossible to lower. Sometimes, in desperation, one or both falls of some lifeboats were slashed and the boats either dove into the water or hung uselessly. According to Finch, sometimes these lifeboats plunged vertically into the water with men clinging to the boat or the fall, and in other cases a falling lifeboat would hit men who were already struggling for life in the water. The sea swell compounded the difficulty. There had been 22 boats. One was successfully launched with ship's crew aboard and pulled away. Six boats were rendered useless by the bomb. The 2nd Officer reported that most of the 101 rafts were thrown overboard or released. Reports also indicate that floating hatch covers were adopted as rafts by some in the water.

Last to leave the Rohna were the Master, Chief Officer, 2nd and 3rd Officers and four American soldiers. This party went over the side about one half-hour after the main group, upon hearing a rending sound and feeling the stern settle rapidly. Rohna sank about one hour after being hit.

HMS Atherstone and USS Pioneer stayed behind to take survivors aboard. HMS Atherstone's report notes that the SS Clan Campbell also remained behind to pick up survivors, and that the Rohna burned so furiously that Atherstone laid a smoke screen in case follow up bombers came to finish them off. The tug Mindful came out from Bougie to assist. Clan Campbell's freeboard was so high that it was difficult to get ropes to survivors and have them hang on long enough to come aboard. Clan Campbell, Pioneer and Atherstone landed 819 survivors at Philippeville. Rescue efforts of Mindful, HMS Holcombe and an unidentified tug brought the total U.S. Army survivors to 966. Four of seven American Red Cross workers were saved. Sixteen men were alive when picked out of the water but died before reaching a port. The bodies of 3 officers and 77 enlisted men were picked out of the water or washed ashore. Rohna's crew casualties were also heavy. Darkness, the swell, the use of the belt type pneumatic life jackets, the cold water, a strong set of the current and inexperience in water survival spelled death for all but the strongest as the night wore on. Many who had made it to a rescue vessel expired from wave action that dashed them against the side of a vessel ill equipped for life saving. The last known survivor was picked out of the water about 0700 on the 27th of November.

The U.S. minesweeper Pioneer and HMS Atherstone were the heroes in this disaster at sea. Pioneer alone picked up 606 survivors and Atherstone, while also recovering survivors, coolly defended the rescuers from further attack. One report stated that Atherstone dodged five of the glider bombs during the early part of the attack and observed enemy torpedo planes attempting to mop up at the close of the Luftwaffe phase of the event. Pioneer estimated that 40-50 glider bombs had been released during the full fury of the attack and identified one flight of attacking planes as being Heinkel 177s. Pioneer's official report in the "Remarks" section states that the attack began at 1640 and puts the base course of the zig-zagging convoy at 123 degrees True. Pioneer's War Diary states that the Rohna was hit at 1715. Rohna personnel have it closer to 1730. The setting sun was on the starboard quarter. Pioneer reported four near misses and shrapnel wounds to three men. The following Illustration is page one of Enclosure A to the CinClant 7Cl-42 report submitted by the USS Pioneer.

Illustration 39-From Action Report, USS Pioneer

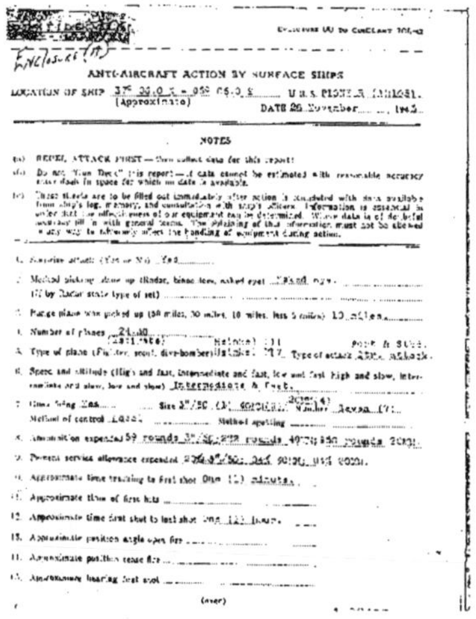

UGS-37

The convoy commander, CTF 65, was Captain W. R. Headden. He had been my first skipper on the USS Edison. For this passage, the escorts were designated as Task Force 65. In the ship-train, there were 60 merchantmen and six LSTs. There were eight U.S. destroyer escorts and Headden's flagship, the U.S. Destroyer Escort Stanton, was one of them. Five U.S. destroyers, British AA cruiser HMS Delhi (which I had been aboard once at Gibraltar), and three British rescue tugs completed the strong escort contingent. This was a Norfolk, Virginia to Bizerte assignment for Task Force 65. Its entry into the Mediterranean was well publicized by German reconnaissance aircraft and by coast watchers in Spain.

With a clear sky and a calm sea, the Luftwaffe struck the convoy in the evening of April 11, 1944 off Cape Benegut, Algeria. In 12 columns, making just over 7 knots, the convoy was fairly tight in spacing, as passage into the Tunisian War Channel would demand. The Destroyer Escorts were on the perimeter, three to port and three to starboard, with Holder and Forster ahead, at 3,000 yards. The U.S. destroyer Lansdale carrying radio link jamming equipment was on the port side. Anti Aircraft cruiser Delhi was on the port quarter between the escorts and the convoy. The destroyer contingent, less Lansdale, was astern, with the descending moon.

An enemy aircraft was reported overhead just before 2300. It was joined by up to ten more by 2315. The white pathfinder flare appeared ahead just minutes later. With that marker, flares began to dot the port flank. Escorts, on command, made smoke beginning at 2330. A beehive of planes had arrived in the immediate vicinity by 2335 as flares now completely illuminated the entire force. Stanton's guns spoke at that point and the Ju-88s and Do-217s commenced a well-coordinated attack. Destroyer Escort Holder took a torpedo shortly thereafter. Lansdale detected radio glide bomb control signals at about midnight. Stanton was straddled by a stick of bombs shortly thereafter. The last flare went out about a half-hour after midnight. The Task Force had done its job and no convoy ship was damaged. But, this trip generated other fireworks related to escort vessel tactics. Holder lost 16 men at torpedo impact and transferred 12 wounded men to Destroyer Escort Forster. Without any propulsion of her own, Holder was towed by HMS Mindful to Algiers. Fleet tug Choctaw got her back to the states where her condition was deemed too poor for any repair attempt.

Captain Headden later criticized the USS Lansdale for putting up skimpy AA fire. Admiral Hewitt defended Lansdale, stating that she used the AA doctrine her Mediterranean experience taught her. Hewitt then criticized Headden for ordering smoke 15 minutes later than he could have and for using it in the wrong sectors. With respect to sector use, Hewitt opined that the aircraft were on instruments and did not need the horizon that Headden's smoke obscured. From my later aviator experience, my own view is that any horizon is most helpful to an attacking aircraft. Probably both Headden's criticism of Lansdale and Hewitt's second criticism of Headden came a little too readily and were not useful. The questions raised would have better been handled in a discussion. Unfortunately, the pace of World War II did not permit much discussion at the operating level.

UGS-38

The F in these convoy designations meant Fast, and the S meant Slow. To a destroyer sailor, the F meant Slow, and the S meant Slower. UGS-38 approached Cape Benegut, eastbound, just two weeks after UGS-37. There were 11 U.S. Destroyer Escorts. The flag was in Coast Guard Cutter Taney. H.J. Wuensch, United States Coast Guard commanded the Taney. Captain W.H. Duvall USN was CTF 66, escort and convoy commander. In the convoy were 85 merchant vessels, the U.S. Coast Guard cutter Duane and two Navy fleet oilers. Destroyer Lansdale was again an AA supplement ship, along with H.N.M.S. Heemskerck. There were two British minesweepers and one British tug.

Heemskerck, an AA cruiser from the Netherlands, joined at Gibraltar and was stationed with Lansdale on the port side of the convoy. U.S. minesweepers Sustain and Speed, along with Lansdale had the glide bomb radio link jamming gear. Minesweeper Speed was ahead of the convoy and Sustain was on the beam to starboard. The convoy approached Cape Benegut on April 20, 1944.

Captain Duvall had promulgated his gunnery doctrine. According to Theodore Roscoe's "United States Destroyer Operations in World War II", sometime just before the Mediterranean transit of this convoy, Duvall stated: "Doctrine this area directs escorts to fire machine guns only at seen targets at night and only when satisfied own ship's position is known to plane. At longer ranges, main-battery controlled fire only will be used." The first phrase is certainly a reiteration of Admiral Hewitt's concept and is the direct result of experience in the Mediterranean. The extra caveat, "only when satisfied own ship's position is known to plane", would mean refraining from shooting at a bomber or glider bomb when they clearly had a bead on another ship in your force. The phrase certainly appeals to self-preservation but Edison never received such instructions and I am glad she did not.

Again, despite all the convoy search radar, the Luftwaffe got in on the convoy without early warning. The attack took place just three miles off Cape Benegut. In three waves of about 10 planes each, using the coast for radar cover, the attack on UGS-38 came about 25 minutes after sunset on 20 April, 1944. The first waves of enemy aircraft were torpedo bombers. Captain Duvall noted in his action report the complete absence of fighter protection.

The attack came from the east, almost directly from the waters the convoy was about to transit. The attackers came in low, with no flare announcements, using low lying shore as a shrouding background and moonlight to the west as an horizon to outline their targets. Destroyer Escort Lowe spotted five attackers just after 2100. Torpedoes from several leading Ju-88s were dropped and SS Paul Hamilton was hit with deadly effect. SS Samite was also hit. The second wave of aircraft split, some taking the starboard and some the port. Torpedoes hit the SS Stephen T. Austin and SS Royal Star. The next wave went at the port side of the convoy. Although Lansdale was credited with effective AA fire, a torpedo struck her. The Royal Star and the Paul Hamilton went to the bottom. After a fight to save her, the USS Lansdale also sank. We will come back to the fight to save Lansdale.

In his commentary Admiral Hewitt felt that even with surprise, smoke should have been used. My only interpretation is that Admiral Hewitt had come around to agreeing with Captain Headden that denial of any horizon to enemy aircraft was important. This attack succeeded because horizon and radar advantage went to a Luftwaffe that could choose its attack sector. Any possibility of silhouette was denied to the AA gunners of the escorts who faced a dark coastal background now completely devoid of light. In his report after the attack, Hewitt asked for more firepower and for more effective use of firepower from Destroyer Escorts. But, these were ASW ships in a compromised environment where the Luftwaffe still had an offensive sting. What Hewitt really needed for these convoy transits was more destroyers.

The airborne torpedo entered Lansdale's forward fire room and broke her keel. With all power lost, Lansdale could do little but let the sea have its way. Her CO ordered the crew to abandon ship about 2130. She broke up and sank shortly thereafter. 235 men survived the initial blast and were picked up by U.S. Destroyer Escorts Menges and Newell. Forty-seven men were not recovered.

Mare Nostrum: The Mediterranean Is Whose Sea?

It was never Mussolini's, despite the appeal of the Latin expression. It was, before the U.S. arrived, a bloody tug of war between the British and the Germans. After the fall of Tunisia to the British and the steady increase of U.S. North African land forces in the period from November 1942 to May of 1943, the British lifeline to Suez was firmly reestablished. When Sicily and all Italy from Naples south had fallen to the Allies, both the British and the U.S. had major new commitments in land forces that needed supplies.

The Mediterranean convoys told stories of heroism, of U-boat attacks, of difficulties in rescue at sea, and of the Luftwaffe challenge to control of the sea. It is not apparent from our reprise of the convoy actions above, that, by August of 1944, both the U-boat and Luftwaffe had short future prospects in the Mediterranean Sea. The facts, though, are indisputable. Shortly after the capture of Marseilles and Toulon in September 1944, Allied convoys entered the Mediterranean from the Atlantic and then the individual merchant ships dispersed, moving unescorted and independently to destination ports. If I had been told on September 30, 1944, the day of my departure from the Edison at Oran, that such a state of affairs was at hand, I would have reacted in disbelief. Nothing I had witnessed would have prepared me for such a change in the tides of war.

Visualize the Mediterranean as a giant saucepan lying on its side. The lid is the rim of Southern Europe where it meets the sea. The bottom sits on the shelf of North Africa. The Allies had scoured this saucepan clean, from top to bottom. It became theirs. It had been taken at great sacrifice. At the very end, the pan cleaned up suddenly. The last blows struck at our convoys by the Luftwaffe were as severe as the first. The enemy just left. They were no more. It had taken from November 1942 to October 1944 to drive them out.

Over Two Years since Edison's Last Visit

Lieutenant Joseph Justin Dwyer, Engineering Officer of the USS Edison in 1945, a friend and shipmate from 1942-44, and a friend over the intervening years, supplied this next vignette in Edison' life. This occurred in the period after my detachment from the Edison. Here is Joe Dwyer's tale of a 1945 Edison assignment:

"In early April 1945, the USS Edison was assigned to escort a convoy of ships headed for the United Kingdom. Enroute to England, difficulty with the sonar equipment developed, and finally the sonar system failed completely. Although the Edison then had a reduced capacity to provide ASW protection, she continued in the screen for the duration of the passage."

"It was during this passage, on April 12, 1945, that Edison's crew received word of the death of President Roosevelt. (Everyone put down a mile marker in their own lives wherever they were when Roosevelt died. The author was on a Missouri Pacific Railroad coach car en-route from Ottumwa,

Iowa to Norfolk, Virginia when the coach car's loudspeaker told us this momentous news.) The question we on the Edison asked was: 'Who is Harry Truman?' It gradually dawned on us that Mr. Truman's political star rose during the early 1940s, while the western allies were preoccupied with fighting the war."

"As the convoy approached England, the Edison was diverted to escort a convoy ship to Le Havre, France. After assuring this ship's safe passage into Le Havre, the Edison proceeded to Southampton, England, and was put into drydock for sound gear repairs. This drydocking revealed that down near the ship's keel, the entire sound dome and its contents, had sheared away. While the ship was in drydock, some crewmembers accepted an invitation to play golf at a local course, a pleasant diversion. After temporary repairs around the sonar dome structure, the Edison assumed a position in the screen of a convoy headed for New York. The ship arrived safely in New York in late April or early May. About one week after this return to the States, the joyous announcement of V-E Day was made on May 8, 1945."

An examination of records relevant to Edison's war history reveals that this visit to Southampton, England in April of 1945, was Edison's first visit to the British Isles since the fall of 1942. The invasion at Casablanca in November of 1942 had begun Edison's period of Mediterranean service. That service was to last over two years. Some of those perilous hours had seemed long, but reflections 55 years later make Edison's entire commissioned life seem like a moment to me now.

GrossAdmiral Doenitz agreed to unconditional surrender terms on May 7, 1945. German General Jodl and U.S. General Walter Bedell Smith signed the papers at Rheims (sometimes, Reims) in northeastern France on May 7, shortly before three in the morning. It was still May 6 in the U.S. The Russians signed on May 8, 1945 the day now recognized as V-E Day. There was no glamorous Versailles, no fancy railroad car. World War II was still in progress. By mid-June 1945, Admiral Stark was able to report that not one U.S. Navy operating ship or landing craft was left in European waters. A massive flow to the Pacific was in progress. Except for new cadres of military government personnel, the U.S. naval names left in Europe were Admiral Stark and Admiral Ghormley. The rest, sailors and airmen particularly, left like ships in the night. Massive numbers of Army-men and their war supplies departed almost as fast.

Sobering Numbers

If the British, who took staggering losses in all classes of its naval warships, had not been there first, there would have been nothing to fight for in the Mediterranean when we arrived off North African shores in November 1942.

I have used the term, Benson/Livermore, to define a class of early U.S. World War II destroyers. I include the almost identically equipped single stackers like the Roe and the Buck, the Rowan, the Rhind and the Mayrant. The U.S. Navy committed these kindred classes of its new, early World War II destroyers, to the conflict in the Atlantic Ocean and the Mediterranean Sea. With commitment comes sacrifice. Out of 19 U.S. destroyers lost in the Atlantic/Mediterranean theater, 13 were from these classes, and five were World War I holdovers. One destroyer, the Warrington, built between the wars, was lost in a hurricane. Not one of the combat casualties was lost in vain. Each was participating in operations that would make the enemy pay a price. All went down with honor intact. These were busy ships. They were used in ASW escort of merchant convoys, in convoy Anti Aircraft screens, in escort of larger warships and in shore bombardment. At Anzio, these ships were the harbor defense ships. These were truly multi-purpose ships, and multi-talented too. In every assignment they succeeded in their missions.

Torpedoes were the prime killers, followed by mines and then bombs. The undersea explosions usually broke a destroyer's keel. Some, like the Kearny, the Hambleton and the Mayo, survived. Cheating the deep was the result of fast work by their crews, prompt help from assisting ships and favoring seas.

The U.S. Navy gave up its larger warships reluctantly. The only major U.S. cruiser casualty that occurred on "our watch" was the USS Savannah and she survived to make it into Malta. Cruisers, note well the company you kept.

Merchantmen took heavy punishment. In the larger context of the Atlantic and the Mediterranean, to German and Italian subs alone, the Allies had lost over 2800 merchant ships adding up to nearly 15,000,000 tons of shipping and cargo.

By the third week in May 1945, the Allies in the Atlantic theaters sailed no more convoys. Ships proceeding independently were told to re-light their navigation lights. On the Midshipman Cruise of 1940, the Atlantic Squadron (three battleships) used blue lights for passageway illumination. Not long after, red light replaced blue light because red gave off less white light. All of my Atlantic sailing experience had occurred under "Darken Ship" conditions.

For Sea Combatants, Any Pause Was Welcome

Though they left Europe in a hurry, Atlantic and Mediterranean-based ships would take some time getting to the Pacific War. The trip back across a less-threatening Atlantic Ocean would provide some moments of relaxation.

"Goober Peas", with apologies to a Civil War songwriter-

Sittin' on my tin can, it's a summer day,
Chattin' with my messmates, passin' time a-way
Lyin' in the shadow, underneath the breeze,
Goodness how delicious, eatin' goober peas.

Peas, peas, peas, peas, eating goober peas.
Goodness how delicious, eating goober peas.

When a cruiser passes, the sailors have a vow,
To cry out at their loudest, "Hey Mister get a scow",
But another pleasure, enchantinger than these,
Is wearin' out your molars, eating goober peas.

Peas, peas, peas, peas, eating goober peas.
Goodness how delicious, eating goober peas.

I think my song has lasted, almost long enough;
The subject's interesting, but rhymes are mighty rough.
I wish this war was over, when, free from rags and fleas,
We'd kiss our wives and sweethearts and gobble goober peas.

Peas, peas, peas, peas, eating goober peas.
Goodness how delicious, eating goober pcas.
Goodness how delicious, eating goober peas.

I changed just seven words to convert this song from a soldier's to a sailor's ditty.

Change of Command

While Edison was on keel blocks in drydock #4 at the Brooklyn Navy Yard, Lieutenant Commander W. J. Caspari USN relieved Lieutenant Commander Hepburn A. Pearce USN as Commanding Officer, USS Edison. The day was 17 May 1945 and the time was 1400. Caspari became Edison's fourth and final skipper. Edison was being readied to join the tide of men and materials to swell the ranks of those fighting the Japanese in the Pacific.

Chapter Twelve - Passage to the Pacific, and to History

A casualty statistic. In World War II, the U.S. killed-in-action (KIA) count numbered about 300,000. Of these, the U.S. Navy lost 20,000 and the U.S. Marines 25,000.

Death is such a final matter. The statistics of death came home to me more than once in the reading that I did to refresh myself on these events of over 50 years ago. The battle stories always used the qualifiers, "about" or "approximately" or "light" or "heavy" in their recounting of killed-in-action figures. In another case, the phrase "six dead and one missing" remains in my mind. If I were to go back now and make a conscientious search of my own phrases in this story, I am certain to discover that I repeated some of those approximations of casualty figures.

The dead were dead. The missing, in the context of most sea disasters, were certainly dead. There were no "approximately" dead sailors. The soldier who was killed in an action in which we took "light casualties" represented an irrevocable loss to his loved ones. Whether they numbered nine hundred and one, or just one, each time I was confronted by death in World War II, it made me sad. The German Warrant Officer of U-73 whom we could not revive in 1943 is a part of my memory. When a man or woman dies (while not always shown as combat casualties, women who died serving in World War II, many of them nurses, deserved to be considered combat casualties) that person is entitled to be identified and counted as precisely as our knowledge permits. In war, that has not always happened.

429

At World War I's Verdun in France nearly one million soldiers died. Verdun's caves are tombs for thousands of Unknown Soldiers from both sides. These men have no specific cross or star to mark their loss. Beginning with the Korean Conflict, and reaching a crescendo in the aftermath of Vietnam, the citizens of the U.S. began to demand more accountability in behalf of the individual who lost his or her life. I can understand that concern better now that I have told this story.

Edison did lose a young sailor named Foley. He was a striker in the fire control gang. While on liberty, Foley fell off a cliff in Oran on 20 July 1944. He was killed instantly. As his department head, I was the officer in charge of the burial platoon and the honors firing squad. I had to find a military Burial Manual and read it hurriedly because I had no prior experience, thank God. I borrowed a sword. We wore blues with leggings. We were a little ragged in marching behind the coffin, and none of the three rifle volleys actually sounded quite like a single shot. But, it was a dignified, somber, service. Seaman Foley, I have always wondered if your family had you brought back from that cemetery in Oran. We did our best. I have never forgotten your enthusiasm to learn.

In some compilations, a significant number of wartime deaths are so-called "operational", meaning not due to enemy action. We need to be reminded that *the preparation for war* is dangerous. The life given is just as courageously lost irrespective of the statistical segment it occurs in.

There is a possibility that the finality of the naval death is one reason why some chose to be wartime sailors. The vacant faces we saw on the U.S. combat soldiers in the North African "rest" camps foretold a life that none would want. A poem by Wilfred Owen, the famed World War I poet provides one look at what lay ahead for many men.

430

Disabled

Now he will spend a few years in Institutes.
And do what things the rules consider wise,
And take whatever pity they may dole.

Tonight he noticed how the women's eyes
Passed from him to the strong men that were whole.

How cold and late it is! Why don't they come
And put him into bed? Why don't they come?

A sinking is sudden death for a ship as well as for many in the ship's company. Ships die in other ways too. Stanley Craw, my last Executive Officer on the Edison, who went on to command several U.S. destroyers after the war, visited the mothballed USS Edison in Charleston, SC. He told me that it was eerie. His telling words were, "None of the people who were supposed to be there were there." From that visit to a haunting relic in a river of decommissioned ships, waiting for their turn in the scrap yard, springs the thought that there is a positive meaning for the warrior hulls left on the bottom of the sea. Those sea graves are perpetual memorials.

Ludlow, Woolsey and Edison, of the original DesRon 13's nine destroyers, survived the war. Both Woolsey and Ludlow, the latter twice, took serious shell hits and fatalities. Edison alone went unscathed except for Frank Barber, the gun captain of Edison's Gun 2. Frank received the Purple Heart for a flesh wound from a near miss during a shelling we took during the Southern France operation in August of 1944.

Soldiers, sailors and airmen breathe life into their units. Bomber crews are an example, be they ten men in a Liberator or two men in a dive-bomber. Army Divisions or Battalions or Platoons take on lives of their own. In Darby's Rangers, they came Battalion-sized. The story that forced its way back into my consciousness after 55 years was this memoir of a U.S. destroyer and its crew.

A destroyer crew forms a mutual protection society. These past chapters have shown how this worked so well for destroyers in combat roles. Cruisers also received deserved attention in this narrative. I have not done justice to the brave minesweepers in this story. Names for fleet minesweepers like Auk, Osprey, Raven and Pioneer remain in my memory. Their smaller wooden hulled brethren, known usually only by hull numbers, were also expendable, and frequently expended. Carriers and battleships have been mentioned though the venue of the Edison and her sister destroyers rarely included them.

Our Captains, including "Hap" Pearce, who turned in the longest stint as skipper of the Edison, were men of active minds who were forced to try new ideas when protocol was lacking, either because a Standard Operating Procedure, SOP, did not exist or did not work. Captain Murdaugh pioneered the outreach search for U-boats shadowing a convoy on the surface, and success led to new escort-of-convoy tactics. Captain Headden put tremendous emphasis on lookout training, not always popular in cold, driving precipitation when effective radar had already been installed on the Edison. But lookouts could see underneath the scan of the radar beam, and at night would report a ship hull-down over the horizon, sometimes moments before the radar "confirmed" such a target.

Captain Pearce was constantly absorbed by the challenge of survivors in the water where depth charge explosions led to life-ending concussion. With shipfitters, and carpenters, and electricians, he tried a number of home-built propelled raft schemes. Though Edison never perfected a workable solution, the motive that so absorbed him in these efforts never left our thoughts. Edison's watch standers learned to set and unset depth charge patterns in seconds. This piece of my story comes to an end with a persisting question. After examining many World War II records, I never discovered any wartime Navy order to leave depth charges set on "safe" until alerted to an enemy submarine.

With mechanically expert teams augmented by advice from radar operators and fire controlmen, Captain Pearce successfully deployed an Edison-built radar-reflecting target to be anchored as a fire control aiming offset. (He had some deployment help from accomplices in landing craft.) These "targets" were effective along coasts where the gradients were so shallow that tides alone could make the charts in error enough to throw off our shore gunfire support effort. Edison usually required just one "ranging" salvo in shore bombardment before going to rapid fire.

Though I did not serve aboard with Edison's last skipper, Lieutenant Commander Caspari, I knew him and liked him when he was a First Class Midshipman and I was a plebe at the Naval Academy. I am sure that he worked to maintain and enhance Edison's performance, and that he was concerned with the well being of her crew.

Edison's leadership would have meant nothing without the Edison bluejackets. Insights reported in this story from seamen who served aboard other destroyers have confirmed that their officer-crew relationships developed with the same crucial mutual respect and support that developed on the USS Edison.

A destroyer is an instrument of death in its mission to sustain the life of the country it fights for. Well-manned, and with some luck, a destroyer is an instrument of life for the men who crew her. The life jackets most of us wore were a daily part of another paradox. Human habits, combined with government issue, made life at sea in wartime even riskier than it needed to be. The pneumatic belt type life jacket was worn by everyone as a more comfortable choice than the kapok jackets that came up behind the neck. The British officer survivors of the Rohna uniformly extolled the virtues of the U.S. belt type pneumatic life jacket issued to their Army passengers, despite the fact that non-swimmers drowned in the hundreds when the midsection remained out of water as the wearer became exhausted. There was another paradox with this jacket. It did not take many weeks of wear before the belt type jacket would crease so sharply that small holes became visible along the folded edges. The two carbon dioxide cylinders would discharge quickly into the jacket and just as quickly out the holes. Useless! I would estimate that a third of our men at any one time had no life belt protection whatsoever. Between issues of new jackets, I put in my time as one of those who blithely overlooked this anomaly.

In the matter of life and death, timing takes many dimensions. Forty-eight of my Naval Academy classmates were killed in action in World War II. That represents just under 10% of our graduating class lost between June 19, 1942 and August 1945. Just thirty of our class perished in Navy operations during the next 15 years after World War II, a period that included the Korean conflict. The number of World War II KIA from the Naval Academy classes of 1940 and 1941 was proportionately higher than the number lost from my class. Those two classes supplied the Junior Officer cadre for the battleships lined up and sunk at Pearl Harbor. Comparable statistics would be apparent for Naval Reserve officer classes, and Naval Training Station boot camp classes. Servicemen were transferred from ships that survived, only to be lost on ships that were sunk. Other servicemen transferred from ships that were eventually sunk, but made it to ships that survived. Some men were survivors of two sinkings; some survived one sinking but not the next.

The Edison was in mined waters, but a mine was not in her critical space at the moment of Edison's passing. In like manner, the enemy torpedo was there but the Edison had not quite gotten there yet. The bomb struck water that the Edison had just passed through. Salvoes of shells groped for the Edison without quite finding her. As the USS Savannah demonstrated at Salerno, a superbly led and trained crew can help a ship survive the effect of near catastrophic damage and even revive the ship's vital systems. That was cheating the odds. The destroyer Mayo demonstrated similar survival instincts. Aside from the practice of always keeping your ship underway, "dodging the bullet", mostly meant that it wasn't marked for you.

I have written about the success of the Allied High Command in pursuing victory in Europe. Victory in the Pacific against Japan involved sacrifices by the Dutch, the Australians, the New Zealanders, the Chinese, Solomon Islands' natives and Philippine men and women. Even in a quick assessment of manpower and logistics, however, one can quickly see that there was no Allied Command effort in the Pacific involving the magnitude of the inter-nation coordination required with Britain, Russia, Canada, India and later the Free French in the struggle to defeat Hitler. This does not mean that a decision by King and Marshall for the Pacific theater came any easier than a decision they made in the battle to defeat Hitler.

The same two U.S. military leaders, wearing their Allied "hats", who helped make V-E day a reality, General Marshall and Admiral King, were concurrently the architects of Pacific War resource allocations and command choices. The delegate operational commanders in the Pacific were Admiral Nimitz and General MacArthur. While dealing with the rationing of forces and the rationalization of objectives in the Atlantic War, Marshall and King had to keep hopes and initiatives alive in the Pacific. Even the U.S. Presidency had a "change of command" when Vice President Harry Truman was sworn in as President of the United States to replace the fallen Roosevelt. Truman, Roosevelt and Churchill had "rank" on Marshall and King, but to their great credit listened to both. In the Pacific, though Marshall and King in turn had the advantage of "rank" over MacArthur and Nimitz, the role assumed by Marshall and King was not exercised by rank. It is a tribute to Admiral King and General Marshall that they kept a winning focus in two very different and very complex war theaters while directly engaging the persons of two Presidents and a Prime Minister in one effort, and two war heroes in the other.

The relationship between General Marshall and Admiral King in the conduct of World War II is worthy of study by historians. Author Richard Frank, in his book "Guadalcanal", provides some early insights on the relationship. As our nation moved beyond isolationism, King and Marshall moved our military toward its new responsibilities.

PASSAGE TO THE PACIFIC AND TO HISTORY

A Real Event, An Imaginary Conversation

Lieutenant Commander W. J. Caspari relieved "Hap" Pearce as Edison's skipper during a May 1945 sound gear overhaul in the Brooklyn Navy Yard. It is now 27 June, 1945. The USS Edison has just entered the Panama Canal on her way to the Pacific. The war in Europe was over in May but the war in the Pacific rages on.

An Edison plank owner and a young bluejacket, the latter underway in a Navy warship for the first time, have been passing some time reading a newsmagazine about a Pacific sea battle that took place in the Fall of 1944 while Edison had been concluding her duties in the Mediterranean. What follows is my excerpt from published eyewitness accounts of one phase of the engagement. The account I reference was written by Rear Admiral C.A.F. Sprague and Lieutenant Philip H. Gustafson and appeared in "The United States Navy in World War II", published by William Morrow. It was edited and compiled by S. E. Smith. The Sprague/Gustafson episode in the compilation was titled, "They Had Us on the Ropes."

The day is October 25, 1944. The time is 0600 local time. The umbrella name for the action is the Battle for Leyte Gulf. Our troop transports and their men and supplies were in the second week and most critical phase of getting assault forces ashore. Leyte was the first step in reclaiming the Philippines from the Japanese. Those islands had been home waters for the Japanese Fleet since early 1942, a period of over two and one half years.

Three powerful Japanese fleet forces undertook a coordinated thrust in an attempt to undo all that Nimitz and MacArthur and our Pacific ground, sea and air forces had accomplished beginning at Guadalcanal in August of 1942.

437

In their boldest foray, the Central Force of the three Japanese fleets swept around the north end of Samar Island on a southerly course at high-speed bent on completely disrupting U.S. landings in progress in Leyte Gulf. A carrier based ASW patrol pilot reported to Rear Admiral C.A.F. Sprague's flagship, "Enemy surface force of 4 battleships, 7 cruisers and 11 destroyers sighted 20 miles northwest of your task group and closing in on you at 30 knots." Somewhat irritated that the young Ensign was mistakenly reporting a main component of Admiral "Bull" Halsey's U.S. Third Fleet, Sprague called for the pilot to re-check his identification of this fleet. Sprague turned his thoughts back momentarily to the day's first worry, his mission to support, with carrier air strikes, our troops consolidating the Leyte beachhead.

The young pilot's next report was, "Ships have pagoda masts." After this electrifying report, the Ensign then made a dive bomb attack on a Japanese cruiser, striking close to it with his two depth charges.

Sprague knew immediately that a never-before event in naval history was about to occur. Thin walled U.S. CVEs ("jeep" carriers created by converting merchant ship hulls to small aircraft carriers) were about to be annihilated by what turned out to be one of the most heavily gunned surface fleets of all time. Sprague's force, even as it turned abruptly eastward at 0650, away from the Philippine islands and away from the Japanese, could make at best 20 knots. The Japanese at 30 knots would close fast. Here are the force strengths. Rear Admiral C.A.F. Sprague's unit was part of Admiral Kinkaid's 7th Fleet, with the mission to cover the Leyte Gulf landings. Known as Taffy 3, this Sprague's force (another Admiral Sprague commanded another group in Kinkaid's fleet) consisted of 6 escort carriers, 4 destroyers and 3 destroyer escorts. Japan's Admiral Kurita had four new battleships (he began with five, but the Mushashi had been sunk by our planes and submarines the day before), 7 cruisers, and 11 destroyers. The Japanese force's "pagoda" masts began poking up on the Sprague force's horizon at about 20,000 yards. Visual contact!

Although many of his carrier planes were over Leyte Gulf supporting the landings, at 0656 Sprague ordered all of his planes that were still available to launch a torpedo or bombing strike on Kurita's Central Force. Fortunately, for launching its remaining planes, Taffy 3's course change to the east was into the wind. At 0657, Sprague ordered his vulnerable carriers to make smoke from their stacks and to augment it with chemical smoke from tanks normally carried by their aircraft. All escorts were directed to cover the rear of the retreating carriers and make all smoke possible.

Rear Admiral Felix Stump with the next light carrier group to the south launched bomb and torpedo strikes, as did units from Rear Admiral Thomas Sprague's force, 70 miles to the south. Proceeding east had another benefit for Taffy 3, a Pacific squall. Carrier-launched Avengers and Wildcats, operating singly or at best in pairs, and scrambling to get airborne and into the action, began to draw a wall of Japanese flak, but a U.S. Air Group Commander quickly scored a hit on the battleship Nagato. With salvoes from the Japanese now reaching high intensity around Taffy 3's escort carriers, the U.S. force darted into the squall at 0713. The shelling abated and there was a moment to think. Mainly, what was the best course to prolong the action and extract the most damage before all U.S. ships were sunk?

Sprague turned southeast and then south. Sprague's objective was to draw this Japanese Force away from Leyte Gulf, its real target, and hopefully draw them into range of U.S. carrier aircraft forces that could punish them, irrespective of

Taffy 3's losses. Although his track resembled the right half of a circle, and he was sure that the Japanese would shorten the distance by using the diagonal, Sprague wanted to get between the Japanese and the assault landing areas. He ordered his destroyers and destroyer escorts, now between him and the Japanese Center Force, to make a torpedo attack as a delaying barrier.

The next Illustration is the picture that confronted Taffy 3's escorts as they formed for the torpedo attack. It is reproduced here from a photo on page 359 of "The U.S. NAVY An Illustrated History", by Nathan Miller, as it appeared in the Bonanza Books Edition of the volume originally published by American Heritage in 1977. I could not find a credit for the photo.

Illustration 40-Admiral Kurita's Battle Line

Even though the Japanese, for unexplained reasons, had followed Sprague's carrier units around the half circle and did not take the shortcut, when the carriers emerged from the squall heading south, the range to the Japanese began to close dramatically. 20,000 yards was very soon down to 15,000 yards, at which range it became peashooting time for the large bore guns on Kurita's battleships. Taffy 3's destroyer torpedo attack turned them away for a brief period and one torpedo found a Japanese battleship. The U.S. escort ships survived that first run. The carrier USS St. Lo, using its one aft facing five-inch gun, scored three hits on a Japanese cruiser running ahead, which had closed the range to 1400 yards! That same gun on the CVE USS Kalinin Bay and the one on the CVE USS White Plains scored hits. On the latter, Admiral Sprague's account notes that a battery officer sang out, "Just hold on a little longer boys; we're sucking them into 40-mm range." Although a humorous observation, it was also the only time anyone who reported on this battle noted what a triumph Sprague had achieved by drawing the Japanese into the tail chase. Some accounts noted the enormous advantage in the number of gun barrels that lay with the Japanese. From the same enumeration of the Japanese 16-inch, 8-inch and 6-inch gun barrels, one can calculate an even more overwhelming *weight-of-shell* advantage that the Japanese could deliver. Each U.S. CVE had the one five incher, which fired aft. Though still terribly disadvantaged in firepower, the odds dramatically improved for Sprague when the Japanese could only fire their forward guns while Sprague kept every one of his out-manned force's guns, though of smaller caliber, able to shoot.

With the Japanese battleships holding the center stage astern, the Japanese finally split their cruisers and destroyers into two forces, one on each quarter of Sprague's force, now

JOINING THE WAR AT SEA

giving the Japanese three arcs of fire. The U.S. carriers were in a rough circle, their escorts in a larger arc around the rear, and every ship in the U. S. force was maneuvering violently to shake off the intense Japanese shelling. All the CVEs were now taking a pounding. Flagship USS Fanshaw Bay was hit 6 times. USS Kalinin Bay took 16 hits. USS Gambier Bay was hit and lost one engine reducing her speed to 14 knots. At 2,000 yards range to the nearest Japanese warships, in a rain of 8-inch shells, Gambier Bay finally was holed so many times that she sank. The situation was now desperate. Sprague ordered the escorts to run directly between the Japanese once again for smoke laying. U.S. destroyers Hoel and Johnson, and the U.S. destroyer escort Roberts, were fatally hit during this maneuver and dropped back out of sight. Planes from the other escort carrier groups used every torpedo and every bomb and then in final acts of desperation used every bullet in strafing attacks on the Japanese ships. Except for the Gambier Bay that had sunk, all of Sprague's remaining five carriers could still make full speed. At 0925, the Japanese main body, still centered on their battleships, and still at an inexplicable 10,000 yards, made a wasteful torpedo attack. With those torpedoes running out their courses harmlessly, some being strafed and exploded by our aircraft, the Japanese then just as unexpectedly retired. They could actually have rammed and sunk Taffy 3's five remaining carriers.

Commander Amos Hathaway, skipper of the U.S. destroyer Heermann tells in "The United States Navy in World War II", what it was like to execute the final stage of the escort intervention commands that Admiral Sprague ordered to save his carrier force. At the rear of the formation when the Heermann broke out of one of the smoke palls, Hathaway could see that he was directly astern of one of his own carriers, and saw a Tone class 8 inch Japanese cruiser pummeling that carrier. The Heermann first had to get the Japanese cruiser on a bearing different from the carrier so Heermann could open fire and be sure that only the Japanese warship was in Heermann's line of fire. 12,000 yards is ideal range for the 5" 38 battery, and a U.S. destroyer is still a pesky target at that range for an 8-inch battery. Notwithstanding, a red 8 inch splash was 1,000 yards short of the Heermann, and the red splashes were walked closer in 100 yard steps until the Heermann took a damaging but not fatal hit. Somehow, reported Hathaway, the Japanese did not realize that they had found the range. The following salvo was an "over" and destroyer Heermann was not hit again. Twelve minutes later, the Japanese Center Force turned back toward San Bernardino Strait leaving one of their own blazing cruisers behind.

At 2130, safely back into San Bernardino Strait from whence they had come, the Japanese Center Force retired. Adding up all the engagements that made up the Battle for Leyte Gulf, tonnage sunk greatly favored the U.S. side. Most U.S. destroyers had used up all their torpedoes. Sprague's Taffy 3 escort force lost two destroyers and a destroyer escort. Taffy 3 had lost one carrier, but they had prevented the powerful Japanese Center Force from executing their primary mission to stop the U.S. re-occupation of the Philippines.

Destroyers had made a difference. So much so, that the destroyer radar picket ship in the Pacific became the first target for a new, the Kamikaze aircraft. Kamikaze translates to "Divine Wind." A force of Japanese aviators had been carefully selected and briefly trained to dive their bomb-laden aircraft right into U.S. warships. The day of Admiral C.A.F. Sprague's story, October 25, 1944, also marked the first intensive use of the Kamikaze forces that the Japanese air strategists had been planning for several months.

Early Kamikaze success kept more than one U.S. student pilot in the Navy flight program. In the autumn of 1944, the U.S. Navy Primary Flight Training Command embarked on a period of forced attrition. These accelerated "washouts were the result of an excess number of pilots in training. With the advent of the Kamikaze, the high rate of washouts in the Navy's aviator program tapered off immediately. Some U.S. Navy student pilots with so-so flight marks, surely marked for a "Down" in C-stage acrobatic flight checks, took new hope. I know. I was one of them.

So, what did the experienced Edison plank owner tell the new recruit in this imagined conversation after both read about U.S. destroyers and destroyer escorts in the Battle for Leyte Gulf? I have always felt that some medal should be given for the tension, the nail biting, and the dire forebodings that precede battle. Once in the battle, you are fighting for your life and really do not have time to think about danger. Perhaps it occurred to the veteran to tell the recruit that the Edison was just one gun short of being a Fletcher class "flush deck" destroyer and could actually move faster than her slightly bigger brother. Edison never lacked for rate of fire. Edison never lacked accuracy. Edison never lacked speed. The Edison had led a charmed life. Perhaps the veteran then engaged the recruit in an upbeat conversation. Edison was on her way to a new environment. She could stand on her own.

Perhaps only those of us who had served aboard a Mediterranean destroyer and been detached to other assignments would fail to have been upbeat for the recruit. For we might have reflected, that shorn of squadron or division mates, or even a convoy to keep her occupied, Edison' passage across the Pacific found her for the first time a loner.

Final Sailing Days

Most of June 1945 found Edison involved in training exercises operating out of Guantanamo Bay, Cuba, often in company with the USS Eberle. Edison left Cuba for the Panama Canal on 25 June 1945 and went through the Canal on 27 June 1945. More repairs were attended to in San Diego beginning on 6 July. On 27 July, 1945, Edison sailed for Pearl Harbor. She arrived there on 2 August and engaged in Pacific Fleet training exercises. The USS Edison sailed for Saipan on 1 September 1945. World War II had concluded with V-J Day on August 15, 1945. Edison seamen rescued a man overboard from the USS Dawson at 2103 on 12 September 1945. He had been in the water over two hours and Edison's superb lookout tradition worked again in spotting him.

The end of World War II in the Pacific provided more symbolism for a Navy man than the victory in Europe with the destruction of Hitler's armed might. Most of us have a memory of the Marines on Mt. Suribachi at Iwo Jima because of the famous photograph. This memory has been revived by the controversy over whether the original or a staged picture actually made it into print. The sailor kissing the girl in Times Square on V-J Day is memorable. For me, no other symbolism matches the Japanese signing the surrender papers on the USS Missouri in Tokyo Bay on September 2, 1945. I have reprinted one view of it in the Illustration that follows. I have actually taken only the right hand portion of the full scene. That scene is a picture credited to the U.S. Army and it appears in" The American Heritage Picture History of World War II" by C. L. Sulzberger, edited by David G. McCullough, copyright 1966. The copy I have is in the Bonanza Books Edition, copyrighted in 1966 by American Heritage Publishing Co. Inc. (A new edition has been announced.) I can almost talk myself into believing that the lone destroyer in the background of this signing ceremony is a Benson/Livermore destroyer.

Illustration 41-Surrender on the Missouri

In Europe they had signed earlier armistices in railroad cars. The city of Versailles was a symbol both of European victory and defeat. I do not know who would have been in the U.S. Navy's official representation party had there been a formal surrender of Hitler's forces in Europe. One of our top generals in Europe noted that it was instead a "battlefield surrender." In any event, the Benson/Livermore "delegate" would have been far down on any official list of guests.

Those in the U.S. Navy will have to take their symbolism from the surrender of the Japanese in Tokyo Bay. There, the U.S. Navy was well represented, and the scene, the quarterdeck of the U.S. battleship Missouri, will do just fine for Navy men. I have seen many photos of the surrender, but none better than the one pictured

Edison arrived in Saipan on 13 September 1945. After high winds caused her anchor to drag on 13 September, Edison took on supplies and ammunition (either out of habit or to get it shipped back to the U.S.) in Tanapag Harbor on the 14th, sailing for Sasebo, Japan on the 16th. She arrived there on 22 September 1945. Edison made the Far Eastern ports of Nagasaki, Japan, Nagoya, Japan, Matsuyama, Japan and Mindanao in the Philippine Islands. On 3 November, 1945 Edison departed Nagoya for Adak, Alaska. En route she served as North Pacific weather station before entering Adak harbor in December 1945. On 2 January 1946, the USS Edison departed Adak for the Canal Zone, transiting the Canal for the Atlantic on 11 January 1946.

The Edison dropped anchor next at Charleston, South Carolina and was placed out of commission there on 18 May, 1946. Woolsey, Edison and Ericcson were later removed from Charleston to berths in the Philadelphia Navy Yard. In 1965 all were sold to scrap dealers. The Ludlow came out of mothballs and after a stint as plane guard for carriers training new aviators at Pensacola, was sold to the Greek Navy. She too, was later scrapped in Greece. So in very brief mentions we learn of the final exit of Benson/Livermore WW II destroyers with hull numbers 437, 438, 439 and 440 from U.S. naval history, expendable from the beginning to the end of their glorious careers. Lipsett of New Jersey paid $87,000 in 1965 for Edison for her scrap value.

Final Contacts with a Seaman First Class

I saw my former Edison skipper "Hap" Pearce three times after our service together on the Edison. He went to work for Arthur D. Little on the Concord Turnpike outside of Boston after he retired from the Navy. We had lunch together at a restaurant on Route 128 near the Massachusetts Turnpike and again at a Howard Johnson's restaurant near Arthur D. Little on the circle that terminates the eastern end of Route 2 in Massachusetts. Our final time together came when he, Joe Dwyer and myself met at a Catholic church in Weymouth Massachusetts for the second marriage of John Robert Signore, an Edison Machinist Mate, whose first wife had passed away. The Signores gave a nice reception after the wedding and the three wardroom refugees, with our wives, sat together at one of the tables the Signores set up for us.

Cries in the Night

In June of 1948, I was ordered to the U.S. Naval Postgraduate School in Annapolis, Maryland. My family went into Navy Housing, which is not the same as Navy Quarters. Still available in Annapolis, three years after World War II ended, were row upon row of huts called, "The Homoja Village." Those corrugated, stifling, almost windowless half-cylinder shaped huts became home to two families. Our family moved into one of these dwellings with two small children. After making a fast trip with labor pains to the Naval Hospital on the Severn River at the Naval Academy, and after being ordered by the Chief Nurse there when she arrived "not to have that baby until the Doctor gets here", my wife Peggy brought an infant babe back to our steamy summer cubicle; that made us five in all.

Navy wives, officer or enlisted, quickly form a number of informal mutual aid groups. How to get to the Commissary. How to get to the Infirmary. How to get to the Ship's Store or PX. How to get to a movie and who will baby-sit. Children's birthdays were frequent and well remembered. The wives needed those children's birthday parties too.

Other less visible relationships developed among wives of servicemen. Of trust. Of support. Adjacent cubicles were right next to each other. A thin wall separated you from the other end of the hut you lived in. Babies crying were understood, accepted by all, and not even commented upon. But male adults screaming in the night? Somehow these women could quietly say, "Joe woke up screaming last night." Discreet conversations brought forth advice on what the screams meant and how to help Joe, or Tom or Dick. With their intuition, these women knew that Navy medicine was not the way to go. These women learned that time and understanding were the answers.

Makeover for the Surly Draftee

I saw a letter to the Editor of the Wall Street Journal in its edition of January 9, 1998. The Letters Editor hit just the right theme in the headline for the letter that the Journal reprinted. The editor's headline was "WW II Vets Fought for Their Special Ladies." I'll reprint part of the letter. Stephen Ambrose's book, "Citizen Soldiers. How They Fought - and Won" had just been published. John Lehman, a former Secretary of the Navy, had reviewed it for the Journal's edition of December 22, 1997. Bud Markel, President of the 484th Bomb Group Association, of the 49th Bombardment Wing,

15th Air Force, wrote to the Journal from Redondo Beach, California.

"John Lehman's review of the book struck a warm note with this humble Army Air Force engineer-gunner. Mr. Ambrose says in the introduction to his book that the World War II citizen soldier, whether enlisted or drafted, fought not for cause or for patriotism, but for the safety of his buddies and the pride of his unit."

"I would like to add something else - the strong identification with our war vehicles. As a World War II veteran tells his war stories, inevitably his ship, tank or aircraft is mentioned. In effect, our vehicles represented all of the people in our lives. That is the reason these vehicles were humanized. One could observe mechanics and air-crew members pat the side of their aircraft and talk to it. A gunner might mutter under his breath, 'old girl, don't forget your promise to bring us home today.'"

This story's Prologue expressed my dismay at a feature article that had appeared in the Wall Street Journal in early 1997. In that article, the author quoted some senior brass in the volunteer Army as pleased that they did not have to deal with "surly draftees." It leaves me in a better frame of mind as this story concludes to see that the Wall Street Journal, in its coverage of the Stephen Ambrose book, has introduced its 1998 readers to author Ambrose's more balanced view of citizen soldiers.

Appendix

These are the people who encouraged me via e-mail, telephone and letter to persevere in writing the story. Much of their encouragement took the form of their added insights to these events. Their recollections helped fill in the spaces. It occurs to me now that filling in the spaces is what this story is all about.

-mail

Name, association with story, <u>e-mail address</u>
Orlando Angelini, Crewmember USS Mayo, <u>Aange12317@msn.com</u>
Richard Angelini, Historian USS Mayo, <u>angelr@gte.net</u>
Warren Blake, Crewmember USS Edison, <u>wblake@mint.net</u>
Steve Booth, Reader interested in WW II, <u>sbooth@execpc.com</u>
Robert W. Burns, Nephew of Red Cross Nurse Margaret Somerville,
    Rescued from SS Vigrid sinking, <u>rwbejk@albanyonline.net</u>
Jonathan Cook-Fisher, grandson of Commander Cook,
    Supply Officer of USS Electra, <u>SDPrtHead@aol.com</u>
Jack Dacey, nephew of James J. Dacey,
    Crewmember USS Buck, <u>jdacey6108@aol.com</u>
Susan Reilly Devore, daughter of Henry Reilly,
    Crewmember USS Edison, <u>Doverdevo@aol.com</u>
Charles Finch, Survivor HMT Rohna, <u>CfinchRail@aol.com</u>
Ira J. Gardner, son of Ira L. Gardner,
    Crewmember USS Philadelphia, <u>i.gardner@worldnet.att.net</u>
David Hughes, son of Herbert Hughes, Royal Marine from New Zealand,
    Survivor of HMS Spartan at Anzio, <u>david.hughes@ait.ac.nz</u>
Bob Javins, Crewmember USS Ludlow, <u>javinsludlow@olg.com</u>
Tim Koerber, son of H. George Koerber,
    Crewmember USS Edison, <u>Tkoerber@aol.com</u>

Dean Lambert, brother of G.S. 'Beppo' Lambert, Crewmember on
    USS Edison, lost on USS Buck, alambert@cp-tel.net
Carl H. Lehmann, Soldier in Darby's Rangers, carlhl@ix.netcom.com
Pete Mogor, son of Alex Mogor
    Crewmember USS Edison, pthomas@snip.net
John Christopher Russell, son of William Harry Russell,
    Crewmember USS Edison, jcrus@erols.com
Dave Shonerd, classmate of author USNA '43, dshonerd@webtv.net
Tanya M. Sommers, granddaughter of Frank Barber,
    Crewmember USS Edison, ZBWB80A@prodigy.com
Rick Sotis, son of Jack Sotis,
    Crewmember USS Edison, SotiHunter@aol.com
Bob Swanson, son of Harold Swanson,
    Crewmember USS Augusta, ship@internet-esq.com
Tom Taylor, son of William F. Taylor,
    Crewmember USS Edison, ttaylor088@aol.com
Stewart Valcour, son of John Henry Valcour, soldier in transport on
    SS Awatea, valcour@nbnet.nb.ca
Theodore A. Waters, son of Albert T. Waters,
    Crewmember USS Edison, twaters@sunnews.infi.net
Ken Williams, Crewmember USS Ludlow, torp@ibm.net
Ron Wright, Crewmember USS Pioneer, USSPioneer@aol.com

Mail

Stanley Craw, crewmember USS Edison, 67 Maple Drive, Spring Lake
Heights, NJ 07762
Joseph Dwyer, crewmember USS Edison, 45 Christopher Drive 121,
Methuen, MA 01844
Jim Hughes, crewmember USS Edison, 1050 Whitebook Drive, La
Habra, CA 90631
Edward Meier, crewmember USS Edison, 10 Dolphin Drive, Vero
Beach, FL 32960
Helmuth Timm, survivor USS Buck

Jean Whetstine, Editor Edison Newsletter, 10635 Byron Road, Byron, MI 48418; Jean's husband, Larry Whetstine, Crewmember USS Edison

John Weld, staff Rear Admiral Richmond Kelly Turner ComPhibSoPac, P.O. Box 76, Yarmouth Port, MA 02675

URLs

USS Savannah, http://www.concentric.net/~drake725

USS Augusta, http://www.internet-esq.com/USSAugusta/index.htm

Destroyerman's List, http:// www.inetworld.net/txo/ddlist.htm

USS Dyess, http://www.extremezone.com/~pomeroy/dyess/

USS Mayo, http://home1.gte.net/angelr/mayo5.html

Darby's Rangers, http://208.227.204.96/../index.htm

U-boats, http://uboat.europe.is/boats

Morris Rosenthal, http://www.daileyint.com

Dailey International Publishers, http://www.daileyint.com

North African Scenes

Illustration 42-Hangars&Chambres&Ships

Illustration 43-Self Protection

Illustration 44-Mother and Child

Illustration 45-Veiled Ladies